DICKENS ON FRANCE

DICKENS ON FRANCE

Edited by John Edmondson

Interlink Books

An imprint of Interlink Publishing Group, Inc.
Northampton, Massachusetts

First American edition published in 2007 by

INTERLINK BOOKS
An imprint of Interlink Publishing Group, Inc.
46 Crosby Street
Northampton, Massachusetts 01060
www.interlinkbooks.com

Introductions and notes © John Edmondson, 2007

Library of Congress Cataloging-in-Publication Data
Dickens on France : fiction, journalism, and travel / edited by John Edmondson.
    p. cm.
Includes bibliographical references and index.
ISBN 978-1-56656-688-9 (pbk.)
1. Dickens, Charles, 1812–1870—Travel—France. 2. France—Literary collections.
3. France—Description and travel. 4. Dickens, Charles, 1812–1870—Appreciation—
France. 5. Novelists, English—19th century—Biography. I. Edmondson, John, 1950–
PR4592.F73D53 2007
823'.8—dc22

                                2007006601

Cover images: Detail from "France in Departments", drawn and engraved by John Archer, published in The National Encyclopedia Atlas, 1868. Caricature of Dickens crossing the Channel by André Gill, used as the cover illustration for the 14 June 1868 issue of L'Éclipse, reproduced by courtesy of the Charles Dickens Museum, London. Train image: courtesy Millbrook House. Author photo © Photocraft (Hampstead) Ltd.

Printed and bound in Canada

CONTENTS

Introduction *vii*
Acknowledgments *xix*
Note on the texts *xx*
List of illustrations *xxiii*
Glossary of titles *xxv*

one   LONDON TO PARIS BY TRAIN *1*
            "A Flight" *5*

two   CROSSING THE CHANNEL TO CALAIS *17*
            "The Calais Night Mail" *23*
            Extract from *Little Dorrit* *33*

three   ON THE ROAD: THROUGH FRANCE TO SWITZERLAND *37*
            "Travelling Abroad" *40*

four   HOLIDAYS IN BOULOGNE *55*
            "Our French Watering-Place" *60*

five   GOING NORTH: COUNTRY WAYS, TRAVELLING PLAYERS,
                FUN AT THE FAIR *77*
            "In the French-Flemish Country" *81*

six   AN AWAKENING IN A SLEEPY TOWN *95*
            "His Boots" (from *Somebody's Luggage*) *99*

seven   A FLÂNEUR IN PARIS: CITY LIFE (AND DEATH) *121*
            Extract from *Pictures from Italy* *130*
            "Railway Dreaming" *131*
            Extract from "New Year's Day" *141*
            "Some Recollections of Mortality" *146*

eight   GOING SOUTH: LYON, THE RHÔNE, AND AVIGNON *159*
            Extract from *Pictures from Italy* *162*

nine   FROM TRAVELOGUE TO FICTION   *173*
Travelling through France:
    Extract from *Pictures from Italy*   *179*
    Extract from *Dombey and Son*   *181*
Marseille:
    Extract from *Pictures from Italy*   *191*
    Extract from *Little Dorrit*   *194*
Sens and Chalon-sur-Saône:
    Extract from *Pictures from Italy*   *196*
    Extract from *Mrs Lirriper's Legacy*   *201*
    Extract from *Little Dorrit*   *221*

ten   THE FRENCH REVOLUTION   *225*
"Judicial Special Pleading"   *230*
Extracts from *A Tale of Two Cities*:
    Quartier Saint Antoine   *235*
    The Aristocracy   *239*
    The Storming of the Bastille   *250*
    The Terror   *258*
    The Guillotine   *260*

eleven   SLAUGHTERHOUSES, RAILWAY CATERING, AND OTHER
        FRENCH LESSONS   *267*
    "A Monument of French Folly"   *275*
    "The Boy at Mugby" (from *Mugby Junction*)   *289*
    "Insularities"   *300*

twelve   LANGUAGE SKILLS AND THE ENGLISH   *309*
    Extract from *Nicholas Nickleby*   *314*
    Extract from *Our Mutual Friend*   *320*

Notes   *329*
Bibliography   *407*
Index   *415*

INTRODUCTION

"Charles Dickens, Français naturalisé, et Citoyen de Paris." This is how Dickens signed a letter from Paris to his friend John Forster in 1847, during his first long stay in the city (*Life*, 5, Chapter 7). A couple of weeks later, he wrote to another friend that he had become "an accomplished Frenchman" (*Pilgrim*, 5, p 11). Light-hearted pleasantries though these were, they are nonetheless indicative of an early affection for France and an instinctive affinity with French life and culture. As the pieces in this collection demonstrate, this was an attraction that would persist and deepen as Dickens became increasingly familiar with the country and its people. It is no surprise to learn from his son Henry Fielding Dickens that such joking allusions to his own "Frenchness" became characteristic:

> He had a very strong love of his country, though he himself used to say, laughingly, that his sympathies were so much with the French that he ought to have been born a Frenchman. (*Memories of My Father*, 1928, p 28.)

We know from the published correspondence that Dickens visited France at least twenty times during his life. On six of those occasions he took up residence there for an extended period – in Boulogne for three to four months in 1853, 1854, and 1856 and in Paris for two to three months in 1846–47 and 1862 and six months in 1855–56. He first crossed the Channel in 1837, when he was 25, on a short trip to northern France and Belgium, but did not go back to the Continent until 1844, when he travelled through France on his way to Italy (and saw Paris for the first time). He returned for his first long stay in Paris in 1846 and then did not, as far as is known, revisit the country until 1850. The large majority of Dickens's visits were therefore made in the 1850s and 1860s, the period of Napoléon III and the Second Empire.

The nature of Dickens's relationship with France and the reasons for his attraction to it are explored in the chapter introductions and articulated by Dickens himself in the various articles, stories, and extracts presented in this collection. As for many people who feel in some sense "at home" in another country, many of the qualities that led Dickens to be so "very fond of France" (*Pilgrim*, 10, p 445) were those that he found lacking or inadequately represented in his own country. Thus he was immediately impressed by the cultural vibrancy of Paris. Shortly after his 1846–47 residence there he wrote to Émile de la Rue about the profound impression the city had made on him, stating that the

> ... general appreciation of, and respect for, Art, in its broadest and most universal sense, in Paris, is one of the finest national signs I know. They are 'specially intelligent people... (*Pilgrim*, 5, p 42.)

In later years, the Parisians' cultural enthusiasm and perceptiveness were in evidence at his public readings – his friend the American publisher James T. Fields remembered his pleasure at their quick understanding:

> He liked to talk about the audiences that came to hear him read, and he gave the palm to the Parisian one, saying it was the quickest to catch his meaning. Although he said there many always present in his room in Paris who did not fully understand English, yet the French eye is so quick to detect expression that it never failed instantly to understand what he meant by a look or an act. (*Yesterdays with Authors*, 1872, cited in Collins, 1981, p 315.)

Cultural sophistication tends to encourage open-mindedness and Dickens was struck too by what he saw as a respect for individuality and a tolerance of the unusual among the French, and the Parisians in particular, which contrasted sharply with a prevailing intolerance of the unconventional in his home country. Many of the expatriate British and American writers and artists who flocked to Paris in the 1920s and 1930s would have known exactly what he meant. "It is not what France gave you but what it did not take away from you that was important," as Gertrude Stein put it ("An American and France," 1936). In "Insularities" Dickens provides a sartorial illustration:

> On the continent of Europe, generally, people dress according to their personal convenience and inclinations. In that capital which is supposed to set the fashion in affairs of dress, there is an especial independence in this regard. If a man in Paris has an idiosyncrasy on the subject of any article of attire between his hat and his boots, he gratifies it without the least idea that it can be anybody's affair but his; nor does anybody else make it his affair. If, indeed, there be anything obviously convenient or tasteful in the peculiarity, then it soon ceases to be a peculiarity, and is adopted by others. If not, it is let alone. In the meantime, the commonest man in the streets does not consider it at all essential to his character as a true Frenchman, that he should howl, stare, jeer, or otherwise make himself offensive to the author of the innovation.

Plus ça change…. Almost a hundred years later, another English writer made the same point in similar terms:

> One thing I love about the French is that … if they see anything unusual they accept it politely and don't guffaw. Not a single pedestrian who has passed me during my morning exercises has even turned his head. They see a man in a white sweater and golf bags bending and stretching and they say to themselves, 'Ah, a man in a white sweater and golf bags bending and stretching. No doubt he has excellent motives, and in any case it has nothing to do with me.' (P.G. Wodehouse, letter of 27 November 1945, in Donaldson, 1990, p 103.)

As well as this general respect for the independence of others, Dickens frequently stresses the comparatively courteous behavior he encounters all over France in everyday social interaction. He returns to this aspect of France many times, highlighting its impact on the quality of life, on the way people relate to each other and on the standards and efficiency of systems and services. The perception informs his café musings in "Railway Dreaming," for example, which he develops into a discussion of the social advantages of the Parisian café against the disadvantages of the British equivalent:

Forth ... comes a pleasant waiter, scrupulously clean, brisk, attentive, honest: a man to be very obliging to me, but expecting me to be obliging in return, and whom I cannot bully – which is no deprivation to me, as I don't at all want to do it. He brings me, at my request, my cup of coffee and cigar, and, of his own motion, a small decanter of brandy and a liqueur-glass. He gives me a light, and leaves me to my enjoyment. The place from which the shop-front has been taken makes a gay proscenium; as I sit and smoke, the street becomes a stage, with an endless procession of lively actors crossing and re-crossing. ... The gas begins to spring up in the street; and my brisk waiter lighting our gas, enshrines me, like an idol, in a sparkling temple. A family group come in: father and mother and little child. Two short-throated old ladies come in, who will pocket their spare sugar, and out of whom I foresee that the establishment will get as little profit as possible. Workman in his common frock comes in; orders his small bottle of beer, and lights his pipe. We are all amused, sitting seeing the traffic in the street, and the traffic in the street is in its turn amused by seeing us. It is surely better for me, and for the family group, and for the two old ladies, and for the workman, to have thus much of community with the city life of all degrees, than to be getting bilious in hideous black-holes, and turning cross and suspicious in solitary places! I may never say a word to any of these people in my life, nor they to me; but we are all interchanging enjoyment frankly and openly – not fencing ourselves off and boxing ourselves up. We are forming a habit of mutual consideration and allowance; and this institution of the café (for all my entertainment and pleasure in which, I pay tenpence), is a part of the civilised system that requires the giant to fall into his own place in a crowd, and will not allow him to take the dwarf's; and which renders the commonest person as certain of retaining his or her commonest seat in any public assembly, as the marquis is of holding his stall at the Opera through the evening.

This little case study of café culture, with its examples of courtesy and tolerance, social leveling, and the desire to engage with life, represents much that Dickens admired about France. It also exemplifies what he saw as the readiness and ability of the French people to make much of little, both in their domestic lives and in their public entertainment – a readiness and ability, in other words, to make the most of life. He writes of Lucie Manette,

> Although the Doctor's daughter had known nothing of the country of her birth, she appeared to have innately derived from it that ability to make much of little means, which is one of its most useful and agreeable characteristics. (*A Tale of Two Cities*, Book 2, Chapter 6.)

This again is a theme to which he frequently returns – in, for example, "Our French Watering-Place," "In the French-Flemish Country," and *Mrs Lirriper's Legacy*. Mrs Lirriper characteristically provides a useful summary:

> ... I had formed quite a high opinion of the French nation and had noticed them to be much more homely and domestic in their families and far more simple and amiable in their lives than I had ever been led to expect, and it did strike me between ourselves that in one particular they might be imitated to advantage by another nation which I will not mention, and that is in the courage with which they take their little enjoyments on little means with little things and don't let solemn big-wigs stare them out of countenance or speechify them dull...

The French, then, knew how to have a good time and that useful ability provided another reason for Dickens's attraction to France: it was fun. "There are public amusements in our French watering-place," he says of Boulogne, "or it would not be French." His affectionate accounts of such events as provincial fairs and fêtes, market days in small towns, and theatrical performances by travelling players convey his admiration of the general exuberance, the – it is impossible to avoid the cliché – *joie de vivre* that characterizes them. Paris, a city changing before his eyes as Haussmann remodelled it, sparkled and glittered with increasing brilliance: "No Englishman knows what gaslight is," wrote Dickens in the 1863 article "The Boiled Beef of New England," "until he sees the Rue de Rivoli and the Palais Royal after dark." For Mrs Lirriper in *Mrs Lirriper's Legacy*, everyone in Paris seemed "to play at everything in this world,"

> And as to the sparkling lights my dear after dark, glittering high up and low down and on before and on behind and all round, and the crowd of theatres and the crowd of people and the crowd of all sorts, it's pure enchantment. (*Mrs Lirriper's Legacy*.)

When he arrives in Paris at the end of a "A Flight," Dickens's excitement is just as palpable as Mrs Lirriper's:

> The crowds in the street, the lights in the shops and balconies, the elegance, variety, and beauty of their decorations, the number of theatres, the brilliant cafés with their windows thrown up high and their vivacious groups at little tables on the pavement, the light and glitter of the houses turned as it were inside out, soon convince that it is no dream; that I am in Paris, howsoever I got here.

It would be misleading, however, to suggest that Dickens took out a pair of rose-tinted spectacles every time he set foot in France. His early impressions of Paris were not all favorable, and even when he grew to love it he was not oblivious to its darker side (see the introduction to "A Flâneur in Paris"). His portrait of Lyon in *Pictures from Italy* could hardly be described as complimentary and he considered Marseille, again in *Pictures from Italy*, "a dirty and disagreeable place." And in many of his articles on France, he balances his praise of certain French characteristics and practices with criticism of others that strike him as undesirable – the treatment of calves in "A Monument of French Folly," the Morgue in "Railway Dreaming," the "bad smells" and "decaying refuse" in his love-letter to Boulogne "Our French Watering-Place," and so on. As he puts it in "Railway Dreaming,"

> There were many things among the Mooninians [Parisians] that might be changed for the better, and there were many things that they might learn from us.

Nevertheless, his praise of France and the French far outweighs his criticisms and there is little doubt as to where he thought most of the learning needed to be done. As Dickens became increasingly disenchanted with the state of his own nation, the comparison of the two countries served to heighten his discontent. Writing to Forster about his admiration of the "fearlessness," "bold drawing," "dashing conception," and the "passion and action" of the French art on display at the Exposition Universelle of 1855, he bemoans the quality of the British paintings exhibited, in which "mere form and convention-alities usurp..., as in English government and social relations, the place of living force and truth":

> There is a horrid respectability about most of the best of them –
> a little, finite, systematic routine in them, strangely expressive
> to me of the state of England itself. (*Life*, 7, Chapter 5.)

This "horrid respectability" and its associated narrow-mindedness are famously portrayed to memorable and damning effect in the character of Podsnap in *Our Mutual Friend*, but readers will find many other illustrations of them in this collection. They are displayed in one way or another, for example, in the behavior of the English travellers "Monied Interest" and the "Demented Traveller" in "A

Flight," the "compatriot" in "The Calais Night Mail" and "Some Recollections of Mortality," and the British arrivals in Boulogne typified by "Johnson" in "Our French Watering-Place."

Aside from serving as effective satirical critiques of certain British weaknesses, these (still recognizable) travelling types also highlight Dickens's fascination with the experience of travel, from which they derive. When he crosses the Channel by steamer, or travels through France by train or coach, it is the sensation and experience of the journey that engage him as he constantly reflects on his own psychology as a traveller and on the behavior of his fellow passengers. As he wanders about the streets of Paris, his real interest is not in the sights but in the nature of the people and the spirit of the place. Sightseeing is rarely more than a tedious obligation:

> ... there were the cathedrals that I got out to see, as under some cruel bondage, in no wise desiring to see them... ("Travelling Abroad.")

It is precisely his preoccupations with what lies beneath the surface of the places and people he encounters, and with his own psychology and situation as traveller and outsider, that give Dickens's travel-related writing on France depth and longevity, rendering it of much more than just historical interest for the contemporary reader. These preoccupations also, as the chapter "From Travelogue to Fiction" demonstrates, provided him with the perceptions and understanding that he was able to apply to such strong effect in fictional contexts. The extended and virtuoso description of Carker's flight from Dijon in *Dombey and Son*, for example, draws on Dickens's imaginative analysis of his own experience of a long coach journey from Boulogne to Chalon-sur-Saône and on his understanding that every journey is psychological as well as physical, with every sight and sound filtered through the individual consciousness of the traveller and colored according to his or her state of mind.

Apart from the pieces included in this collection, and granting the obvious exception of *A Tale of Two Cities*, of which only extracts are reproduced here, France and the French make few other substantial appearances in Dickens's fiction. The final scenes of "The Story of Richard Doubledick" in *The Seven Poor Travellers*, the 1854 Christmas Number of *Household Words*, take place in Avignon and Aix. The opening section of the 1855 Christmas Number, *The Holly-Tree Inn*, includes a brief but colorful description of the inns of France. In *Little Dorrit*, Book 2, Chapter 18, there is a short account of Mr Dorrit's trip from Calais to Marseille via Paris, where he visits a "famous jeweller's." In *David Copperfield*, Chapter 40, Mr Peggotty tells of his travels through France in search of Little Emily. In *Bleak House*, Chapter 12, we have a glimpse of Sir Leicester and Lady Dedlock in Paris as they leave the city and travel back to the coast on their homeward journey.

In *Bleak House* too is Hortense, that famously sinister and volatile French maid:

> My Lady's maid is a Frenchwoman of two-and-thirty, from somewhere in the southern country about Avignon and Marseilles – a large-eyed brown woman with black hair; who would be handsome but for a certain feline mouth, and general uncomfortable tightness of face, rendering the jaws too eager, and the skull too prominent. (*Bleak House*, Chapter 12.)

The specific geographical origin of Hortense is significant. As she herself explains to Esther in Chapter 23, "Mademoiselle, I come from the South country, where we are quick, and where we like and dislike very strong." Dickens seems to have identified spontaneity as a characteristic of the French in general: in his 1869 essay "On Mr Fechter's Acting," he refers to their "suddenness and impressibility" in contrast to the "slowly demonstrative Anglo-Saxon way." However, he associates the more extreme manifestations of those qualities with the south of France and specifically with the Mediterranean heat and exoticism of Marseille. In *Little Dorrit*, the malevolent Rigaud (aka Blandois and Lagnier), although Belgian-born and a self-styled "citizen of the world," makes his first appearance in a prison cell in Marseille, where he also has a home, and seems to carry with him something of the angry heat of that city, so memorably evoked in the novel's opening chapter, wherever he goes. Even the sympathetic

Monsieur Gabelle in *A Tale of Two Cities* has a vengeful streak, thanks to his southern origins: finding his house besieged by a revolutionary mob, Gabelle

> ...withdrew himself to his house-top behind his stack of chimneys: this time resolved, if his door was broken in (he was a small Southern man of retaliative temperament), to pitch himself head foremost over the parapet, and crush a man or two below. (Book 2, Chapter 23.)

Apart from French scenes and characters, there are other ways in which Dickens's experiences of France and the French feed into his fiction. It is not difficult, for example, to identify the inspiration for Wemmick's whimsical garden in *Great Expectations* (Chapter 25), with its grand design on a comically small scale, as the "Property" of Monsieur Beaucourt-Mutuel (Dickens's Boulogne landlord) – see the descriptions in "Our French Watering-Place" and in a long letter to John Forster of June 1853 (*Life*, 7, Chapter 4). In the same novel, Orlick's room at Satis House is described as "not unlike the kind of place usually assigned to a gate-porter in Paris" (Chapter 29). In *Our Mutual Friend*, litter-strewn London is contrasted with Paris, where the *chiffonniers* scour the streets for rags, paper, and other scraps. A wind in the London streets circulates that "mysterious paper currency," but

> In Paris, where nothing is wasted, costly and luxurious city though it be, but where wonderful human ants creep out of holes and pick up every scrap, there is no such thing. There, it blows nothing but dust. There, sharp eyes and sharp stomachs reap even the east wind, and get something out of it. (*Our Mutual Friend*, Book 1, Chapter 12.)

And towards the end of *Our Mutual Friend*, a little country fair is in progress on the evening of Bradley Headstone's attack on Eugene Wrayburn (Book 4, Chapter 6). Surely, as Dickens described the poor amusements of this humble festivity, with its "despairing gingerbread" and its "heap of nuts, long, long exiled from Barcelona," he was contrasting it in his mind with the far more joyous equivalents he had witnessed across the Channel – such as the fair featured in "In the French-Flemish Country," with its "ravishing perfumery and sweetmeats."

Dickens also uses a character's attitude towards France to highlight or reveal something about his or her state of mind. For example, the failure of Lady Dedlock in *Bleak House* and Edith Dombey in *Dombey and Son* to find relief from their boredom even in Paris speaks to the depth of their world weariness (*Dombey and Son*, Chapter 35; *Bleak House*, Chapter 12). Similarly Mr Dombey, the coldest and dullest of men in his obsession with his business and his sense of his own importance, finds Paris in turn "cold" and "dull" (*Dombey and Son*, Chapter 35); as he has nothing within him that can respond to the city, Paris becomes simply the sad reflection of his own character. Again in *Dombey and Son*, the comically small-minded footman Towlinson has a tendency to rail against the French, "for this young man has a general impression that every foreigner is a Frenchman, and must be by the laws of nature" (Chapter 35). And in *Our Mutual Friend* the very nasty Silas Wegg comments disparagingly that "the Frenchman was never yet born as I should wish to match" (Book 1, Chapter 7), thus appropriately dissociating himself in his mean-spiritedness from the nation that Dickens elsewhere describes as "teeming with gentle people" ("Our French Watering-Place").

One other aspect of Dickens's interest in France that feeds into his fiction (and also into his journalism) is his substantial knowledge of the French language, a knowledge he applies in a stylistic technique that has produced mixed reactions among his readers. This is his tendency to introduce French syntax and literal English equivalents of French words and expressions into the direct speech of his French characters. For example,

'Eh well!' said Madame Defarge, raising her eyebrows with a cool business air. 'It is necessary to register him. How do they call that man?' (*A Tale of Two Cities*, Book 2, Chapter 16.)

Although some may find the deliberately awkward English

distracting, for others the technique provides an effective way of reminding the reader that the characters are "in reality" speaking a foreign language and of enabling anyone with a reading knowledge of French to understand precisely what they are saying in their native tongue. It also, since language reflects culture, serves to highlight cultural differences – sometimes pointedly, as in the case of the greater formality and politeness in the language of everyday conversation in France (see the interchanges in "A Monument of French Folly," for instance). The technique, no doubt, stems from Dickens's own pleasure in the language, which he appears to have mastered to a high level (see the chapter on "Language Skills and the English").

As these introductory remarks suggest, the relationship between writer and place is intricate and multifaceted. In bringing together a wide range of Dickens's writings on France – extracts from the novels, shorter fiction, travel narrative, and journalism – this collection demonstrates the many ways in which his responses to the country and its people provided inspiration for his work, enriched his understanding and enhanced or influenced his ideas. With this design in mind, the selections are arranged thematically rather than chronologically. A brief introduction to each chapter provides background, context, and commentary. The annotation at the end of the volume deepens the background and broadens the context with historical, political, social, cultural, literary, topographical, biographical, and other information. And at the heart of the book, of course, are the selections themselves – these compelling and disparate stories, fact and fiction, each distinct and with its own clear purpose, but all joined together by the common thread of their creator's enduring and productive affection for France.

ACKNOWLEDGMENTS

I have the very good fortune to live just a short tube ride away from three great research libraries. I am especially grateful for the resources and to the staff of the wonderful London Library in St James's Square, where much of the research for this book was done. The helpfulness and efficiency of the staff at the British Library in St Pancras, with its excellent facilities, and at the Newspaper Library in Colindale are also gratefully acknowledged.

Thanks to the existence of "Gallica" (http://gallica.bnf.fr), the ambitious online project of La Bibliothèque nationale de France which allows electronic access to an ever-widening range of books and documents, I was able to locate and consult rare French texts in the time it takes to make a few keystrokes.

I acknowledge with many thanks the helpfulness of the Service des Archives Municipales of the Mairie de Boulogne-sur-Mer, which replied promptly and fully to my detailed questions on points of local history.

I cannot list here the numerous useful and fascinating websites I visited in pursuit of all kinds of minute detail and it would be unfair to single out a few. I therefore simply acknowledge the extraordinary resource of the Internet and the dedication of the many academics and enthusiasts who create and maintain informative and valuable sites on all manner of specialist subjects. Although most information on the Internet cannot safely be regarded as authoritative and has to be verified elsewhere, with the help of the now astonishing powers of Google I found many leads and clues on such sites – and in some cases they opened doors that I suspect would otherwise have remained firmly closed.

I am grateful to Jim Ferguson of Signal Books for courteously putting up with missed deadlines and for his valuable editorial suggestions.

Finally, I thank the following friends, some of whom provided me with nuggets of information and all of whom listened with patience: Martine Bretéché, Brian Dutton, Martin Garrett, Audrey Martin, Regis Maubrey, Susan Thompson, and Stephen Wanhill.

A NOTE ON THE TEXTS

The primary sources for the various works by Dickens in this volume are listed below. Where indicated, reference has been made to other editions and occasional minor amendments to spelling and punctuation in those texts have been incorporated where they eradicate minor inconsistencies or inaccuracies in the primary source. All the editions used as primary textual sources were published in Dickens's lifetime and with his approval. The Gadshill edition, often used here for secondary reference, was published by Chapman and Hall in 1897–99 and described as "printed from the Edition that was carefully corrected by the author in 1867 and 1868," but it incorporates some minor corrections and sub-editorial changes of its own. For articles first published in *Household Words* and *All the Year Round* that were subsequently included in the *Reprinted Pieces* and *Uncommercial Traveller* collections, the texts are based on those that appeared in the collections. For the texts as they originally appeared in the periodicals (variations are minor), the authoritative four-volume edition of Dickens's journalism edited by Michael Slater is highly recommended.

Other editorial interventions are minor. Dickens's use in some of the pieces of "-or" instead of "-our" endings (for example, color/colour) has been standardized to the British "-our" (Dickens himself did not feel strongly about this issue – see his letter to Miss Coutts of 11 July 1856, *Pilgrim*, 8, pp 160–161). The full point has been omitted in the contractions "Mr" and "Mrs". The en dash replaces the original em dash when it is used for punctuation and the em dash is retained where its function is that of an ellipsis or to indicate interrupted speech. Many common words have been modernized (for example, the hyphen has been removed from "to-morrow," "to-day" and "to-night"), while less common words (for example, "pine-apple," "summer-time") have been left as Dicken's wrote them. Occasional obvious typographical errors in the original texts have been silently corrected.

Selections in order of appearance:

"A Flight." Primary: Library Edition, Vol 8, comprising Vol 2 of the *Old Curiosity Shop* and *Reprinted Pieces*, Chapman and Hall, London, 1858. Secondary: Gadshill Edition, Vol 34, comprising *Reprinted Pieces*, "The Lamplighter," "To Be Read at Dusk," and "Sunday Under Three Heads," Chapman and Hall, London, 1899.

"The Calais Night Mail." Primary: Charles Dickens Edition, *The Uncommercial Traveller*, Chapman and Hall, London, 1868. Secondary: Gadshill Edition, Vol 29, *The Uncommercial Traveller*, Chapman and Hall, London, 1898.

Little Dorrit extracts. Primary: Bradbury and Evans, London, 1857. No differences were noted between the text of the selected extracts in this edition and that in the definitive Clarendon edition of 1979 (edited by Harvey Peter Sucksmith, Oxford University Press, 1979).

"Travelling Abroad." Primary: *The Uncommercial Traveller*, Chapman and Hall, London, 1861. Secondary: Gadshill Edition, Vol 29, *The Uncommercial Traveller*, Chapman and Hall, London, 1898.

"Our French Watering-Place." As for "A Flight," above.

"In the French-Flemish Country." As for "The Calais Night Mail," above.

"His Boots." Primary: *All the Year Round*, Christmas Number, 4 December 1862. Secondary: Gadshill Edition, Vol 31, *Christmas Stories Vol 1*, Chapman and Hall, London, 1898.

Pictures from Italy extracts. Primary: Bradbury and Evans, London, 1846. Secondary: Gadshill Edition, Vol 28, *American Notes and Pictures from Italy*, Chapman and Hall, London, 1898.

"Railway Dreaming." *Household Words*, 10 May 1856.

"New Year's Day" extract. *Household Words*, 1 January 1859.

"Some Recollections of Mortality." As for "The Calais Night Mail," above.

Mrs Lirriper's Legacy extracts. Primary: *All the Year Round*, Christmas Number, 1 December 1864. Secondary: Gadshill Edition, Vol 32, *Christmas Stories, Vol 2*, Chapman and Hall, London, 1898.

Dombey and Son extract. Primary: Bradbury and Evans, London, 1848. Secondary: Library Edition, Chapman and Hall, London, 1868.

"Judicial Special Pleading." *The Examiner*, 23 December 1848, p 1.

A Tale of Two Cities extracts. Primary: *All the Year Round*, 14 May 1859 ("The Wine-Shop"); 25 June 1859 ("Monsieur the Marquis in Town"); 27 August 1859 ("Echoing Footsteps"); 1 October 1859 ("Calm in Storm"); 26 November 1859 ("The Footsteps Die Out For Ever"). Secondary: Gadshill Edition, Vol 21, Chapman and Hall, London, 1898.

"A Monument of French Folly." As for "A Flight," above.

"The Boy at Mugby." Primary: *All the Year Round*, Christmas Number, 10 December 1866. Secondary: Gadshill Edition, Vol 32, *Christmas Stories, Vol 2*, Chapman and Hall, London, 1898.

"Insularities." *Household Words*, 19 January 1856.

Nicholas Nickleby extract. Primary: Chapman and Hall, London, 1839. Secondary: Cheap Edition, Chapman and Hall, London, 1848.

Our Mutual Friend extract. Primary: Chapman and Hall, London, 1865. Secondary: Gadshill Edition, Vol 23, Chapman and Hall, London, 1898.

LIST OF ILLUSTRATIONS

Page 4. "Paris: Place Vendôme" by Isidore-Laurent Deroy, from the series *France en Miniature*, *c* 1845.

Page 22. "Calais: entrée du port" by Isidore-Laurent Deroy, from the series *France en Miniature*, *c* 1845.

Page 33. "Souvenir de Calais: embarcadère du chemin de fer, quai de Marée, vue prise de la Citadelle" by Charles Rivière, *c* 1860.

Page 39. "Leaving the Morgue," illustration by G.J. Pinwell of a scene in "Travelling Abroad" for the Charles Dickens Edition of *The Uncommercial Traveller*, 1868. Engraved by the Dalziel Brothers.

Page 59. "Boulogne: vue de l'Établissement des Bains" by Isidore-Laurent Deroy, from the series *France en Miniature*, *c* 1845.

Page 61. "Passengers landing at Boulogne from the Folkestone boat," unsigned illustration from *Harper's Weekly*, 2 October 1858.

Page 65. "Street in the Fisherman's Quarter, Boulogne," unsigned illustration from *Harper's Weekly*, 2 October 1858.

Page 80. "Intérieur d'une chaumière dans le département du Nord: la leçon de lecture" by P. de Katow, engraved by Henri Linton, from *Le Monde Illustré*, 1866.

Page 98. Illustration by Charles Green of a scene from "His Boots" for the Second Illustrated Library Edition of the *Christmas Stories*, 1876. Engraved by the Dalziel Brothers.

Page 129. "Rue de Rivoli" by Michel Charles Fichot, engraved by Alexandre Collette, *c* 1855.

Page 140. "Porte et Boulêvard St Denis, vus du Boulevard Bonne

Nouvelle" by Philippe Benoist and A. Bayot, published in 1858 in the series *Paris dans sa Splendeur*, 1857–60 (three-volume edition, 1861).

Page 145. "Franconi's Olympic Circus, Champs Élysées, Paris" by Eugène Lami, engraved by C. Mottram, illustration for *L'Été à Paris*, 1843.

Page 161. "Lyon, vue de la Côte de Fourvières," engraving by Le Petit, *c* 1850.

Page 178. "La cathédrale de Sens," engraving of 1866 from a drawing by H. Clerget.

Page 229. "Arrestation de Mr de Launay, Gouverneur de la Bastille, le 14 Juillet 1789," engraved by Pierre Gabriel Berthault after a drawing by Jean Louis Prieur, from the series *Tableaux Historiques de la Révolution Française*.

Page 274. "Marché de Poissy, le jour du concours pour le choix des boeufs gras, le 24 février" by Edmond Morin, engraved by Henri Linton, from the journal *L'Illustration*, 1859.

Page 313. "Nicholas engaged as Tutor in a private family," illustration by Phiz (Hablot Knight Browne) for chapter 16 of *Nicholas Nickleby*, 1838–39.

GLOSSARY OF TITLES

This short glossary provides background information on several titles frequently mentioned in the text or referred to without further explanation.

All the Year Round. Weekly journal published and edited by Dickens from 1859 until his death in 1870 (when his son Charley took over the editorship).

Daily News. Paper launched on 21 January 1846, with Dickens as editor. He resigned on 9 February, handing over to John Forster who remained in the post only until October. Dickens contributed various pieces to the paper during his editorship and for a brief period after his resignation, including "Travelling Letters," which would provide the basis for the first few chapters of *Pictures from Italy*.

Household Words. The predecessor to *All the Year Round*. Weekly journal edited by Dickens and published in association with Bradbury and Evans from 1850 to 1859.

The Examiner. Radical weekly paper founded in 1808 by John and Leigh Hunt. John Forster held various positions on the paper and was its editor from 1847 to 1855. Dickens contributed a number of articles in the 1830s and 1840s.

The Letters of Charles Dickens, British Academy Pilgrim Edition. The most recent and the definitive edition of Dickens's correspondence, extensively annotated and widely praised for its outstanding scholarship. Published in twelve volumes between 1965 and 2002. Supplements continue to appear in *The Dickensian* as new letters come to light and are authenticated. Referred to throughout as *Pilgrim*.

The Life of Charles Dickens. The extensive and important biography by Dickens's close friend John Forster. First published in three volumes in 1872–74, Forster subsequently revised it into two volumes and twelve "books" for the 1876 edition. All references to Forster's biography are to this latter edition, using the shortened title *Life* and citing book and chapter number.

Reprinted Pieces. Collection of 31 of the many stories and articles that Dickens contributed to *Household Words* (one, "A Plated Article," was written collaboratively with W. H. Wills – see Lohrli, 1973, p 93). Dickens selected the pieces himself and decided on their order of appearance (see letter to Henry Bradbury of 3 July 1858, *Pilgrim*, 8, p 594). *Reprinted Pieces* was first published in 1858, and seems to have come into being to flesh out Volume 8 of the Library Edition of his works, in which it appears after the second volume of *The Old Curiosity Shop*.

The Uncommercial Traveller. Volume edition of the occasional "Uncommercial Traveller" papers that Dickens contributed to *All the Year Round*. The first edition, 1861, comprised the first series of papers, published in the magazine during 1860. The 1865 edition added the second series, published during 1863. The posthumous 1874 edition added a further series of articles published in *All the Year Round* in 1868–69 under the heading "New Uncommercial Samples."

chapter one

LONDON TO PARIS BY TRAIN

("A FLIGHT")

"A Flight" is a high-energy impressionistic account of a train–boat–train journey from London to Paris. It appeared in *Household Words* on 30 August 1851 and was included in *Reprinted Pieces*, 1858. The article was inspired by a new 11-hour express service, which had been introduced on 1 May 1851. A South Eastern Railway Company announcement in *The Times* on 29 April explained how it was done:

> LONDON TO PARIS IN 11 HOURS – SEA PASSAGE TWO HOURS ONLY. Important Special Express Service, via Dover and Calais, and Folkestone and Boulogne, alternately – on and after the 1st May, a SPECIAL EXPRESS TRAIN, first and second class, will leave the South Eastern Railway Terminus, London-bridge, every morning, reaching Paris in the evening; changing the hours of departure from London so as to suit the tide and prevent all delay.

Subsequent daily advertisements gave the departure times of these "tidal" trains for the following few days. The irregularity of the schedule enabled close coordination with the departure and arrival of the steam ships and achieved a saving of around one-and-a-half hours over the previous daytime journey. (The tidal express service was even faster than the night mail, which left at 8:30 p.m. and arrived in Paris at 9 a.m.)

Impressive though this latest reduction in travel time may have been, it pales into insignificance by comparison with what had been achieved over the past few years. The transport revolution was in progress. During the 1840s railway expansion had proceeded at breathtaking speed – some 6,000 miles of railway were opened in Britain between 1840 and 1850. Dickens's first trip to Paris in 1844, on his way to Italy, was by coach. In the early 1840s the coach journey from London to Dover alone took around ten hours, and in "A Flight" Dickens remembers the "two-and-twenty hours of long long day and night journey" on the other side of the Channel. Writing from Paris in February 1847, he was able to tell a friend about the imminent opening of the railway between Amiens and Abbeville (*Pilgrim*, 5, p 28), which left only the section from Boulogne to Abbeville to be completed. The London–Paris journey time, excluding stoppages, was now about 18 hours, of which six were spent travelling by coach from Boulogne to Abbeville station to catch the train for Paris (*A Hand-Book for Travellers in France*, 1847). By the end of 1847 the line had been extended to Neufchâtel and the short remaining section to Boulogne opened in 1848. The railway from Calais to Paris was completed in the same year. When Dickens next went to Paris in June 1850, he was amazed at the change. "The twelve hours' journey here is astounding," he wrote to his friend John Forster, "marvellously done, except in respect of the means of refreshment, which are absolutely none." (*Life*, 6, Chapter 6.) Judging from the food and drink enjoyed by the passengers in "A Flight," the catering seems to have improved by the time the article was written.

On that 1850 trip, Dickens took the Dover–Calais night mail, leaving on the evening of 22 June and arriving at "a quarter before 9" on the 23rd (letters to Miss Coutts, 22 June 1850 and to Catherine Dickens, 23 June 1850, *Pilgrim*, 6, pp 115–116). He next travelled to Paris on 10 February 1851, again by the night mail (letter to Miss Coutts, 10 February 1851, *Pilgrim*, 6, p 285). It seems that these two trips provided the personal experience on which he drew for "A

Flight" – Dickens did not travel on the new 11-hour service before writing the article. For up-to-date details of the tidal express, he worked from notes taken by his Sub Editor, W.H. Wills, on a short trip to Paris at the end of July 1851. Dickens mentions the "Paris-trip notes" in a letter to Wills of 10 August 1851 (*Pilgrim*, 6, p 457) and chases him for them on 13 August:

> I am now going at once to do the 'Flight to France.' I think I shall call it merely 'A Flight' – which will be a good name for a fanciful paper. Let me have your notes by return. Don't fail. (*Pilgrim*, 6, p 459.)

Wills travelled to Paris on 28 July. According to the South Eastern Railway Company's advertisement in *The Times* of 26 July 1851, the tidal express train on the 28th left London at 7:20 a.m. and took the Folkestone–Boulogne route (the route taken in "A Flight").

Thus "A Flight" is a composite piece, with its factual base in Wills's journalistic notes of a very recent trip and Dickens's recollections of his previous two journeys to Paris. From this foundation, Dickens constructs a driving narrative to mirror the new speed and ease of travel. As he marks out the route by stages and places, he weaves into his narrative a rich variety of impressions, fancies, and opinions. He muses on his fellow passengers (fantasizing about the most attractive woman in the carriage, satirizing the English passengers). He reflects on the psychology of travel (the happy dependence of the traveller, his isolation from the outside world caught in glimpses as the train speeds through it, the relative shifts in confidence as people get further away from and closer to their own country). He remembers past journeys. And, at last, he experiences the sheer delight of arriving so conveniently in Paris and of walking in its streets on the evening of the very same day he left London.

Place Vêndome, Paris, c 1845

A FLIGHT

When Don Diego de—I forget his name – the inventor of the last new Flying Machines, price so many francs for ladies, so many more for gentlemen – when Don Diego, by permission of Deputy Chaff Wax[1] and his noble band, shall have taken out a Patent for the Queen's dominions, and shall have opened a commodious Warehouse in an airy situation; and when all persons of any gentility will keep at least a pair of wings, and be seen skimming about in every direction; I shall take a flight to Paris (as I soar round the world) in a cheap and independent manner. At present, my reliance is on the South Eastern Railway Company, in whose Express Train here I sit, at eight of the clock on a very hot morning, under the roof of the Terminus at London Bridge,[2] in danger of being "forced" like a cucumber or a melon, or a pine-apple. And talking of pine-apples, I suppose there never were so many pine-apples in a Train as there appear to be in this Train.

Whew! The hot-house air is faint with pine-apples. Every French citizen or citizeness is carrying pine-apples home.[3] The compact little Enchantress in the corner of my carriage (French actress, to whom I yielded up my heart under the auspices of that brave child, "MEAT-CHELL," at the St James's Theatre[4] the night before last) has a pine-apple in her lap. Compact Enchantress's friend, confidante, mother, mystery, Heaven knows what, has two pine-apples in her lap, and a bundle of them under the seat. Tobacco-smoky Frenchman in Algerine[5] wrapper, with peaked hood behind, who might be Abd-el-Kader[6] dyed rifle-green, and who seems to be dressed entirely in dirt and braid, carries pine-apples in a covered basket. Tall, grave, melancholy Frenchman, with black Vandyke beard,[7] and hair close-cropped, with expansive chest to waistcoat, and compressive waist to coat: saturnine as to his pantaloons, calm as to his feminine boots, precious as to his jewellery, smooth and white as to his linen: dark-eyed, high-foreheaded, hawk-nosed – got up, one thinks, like Lucifer or Mephistopheles, or Zamiel,[8] transformed into a highly genteel Parisian – has the green end of a pine-apple sticking out of his neat valise.

Whew! If I were to be kept here long, under this forcing-frame, I wonder what would become of me – whether I should be forced into a giant, or should sprout or blow into some other phenomenon! Compact Enchantress is not ruffled by the heat – she is always composed, always compact. O look at her little ribbons, frills, and edges, at her shawl, at her gloves, at her hair, at her bracelets, at her bonnet, at everything about her! How is it accomplished? What does she do to be so neat? How is it that every trifle she wears belongs to her, and cannot choose but be a part of her? And even Mystery, look at *her!* A model. Mystery is not young, not pretty, though still of an average candle-light passability; but she does such miracles in her own behalf that, one of these days, when she dies, they'll be amazed to find an old woman in her bed, distantly like her. She was an actress once, I shouldn't wonder, and had a Mystery attendant on herself. Perhaps, Compact Enchantress will live to be a Mystery, and to wait with a shawl at the side scenes, and to sit opposite to Mademoiselle in railway carriages, and smile and talk subserviently, as Mystery does now. That's hard to believe!

Two Englishmen, and now our carriage is full. First Englishman, in the monied interest – flushed, highly respectable – Stock Exchange, perhaps – City,[9] certainly. Faculties of second Englishman entirely absorbed in hurry. Plunges into the carriage, blind. Calls out of window concerning his luggage, deaf. Suffocates himself under pillows of great coats, for no reason, and in a demented manner. Will receive no assurance from any porter whatsoever. Is stout and hot, and wipes his head, and makes himself hotter by breathing so hard. Is totally incredulous respecting assurance of Collected Guard that "there's no hurry." No hurry! And a flight to Paris in eleven hours!

It is all one to me in this drowsy corner, hurry or no hurry. Until Don Diego shall send home my wings, my flight is with the South Eastern Company. I can fly with the South Eastern, more lazily, at all events, than in the upper air. I have but to sit here thinking as idly as I please, and be whisked away. I am not accountable to anybody for the idleness of my thoughts in such an idle summer flight; my flight is provided for by the South Eastern, and is no business of mine.

The bell! With all my heart. It does not require *me* to do so much as even to flap my wings. Something snorts for me, something shrieks for me, something proclaims to everything else that it had better keep out of my way, – and away I go.

Ah! The fresh air is pleasant after the forcing-frame, though it does blow over these interminable streets, and scatter the smoke of this vast wilderness of chimneys. Here we are – no, I mean there we were, for it has darted far into the rear – in Bermondsey where the tanners live.[10] Flash! The distant shipping in the Thames is gone. Whirr! The little streets of new brick and red tile, with here and there a flagstaff growing like a tall weed out of the scarlet beans, and, everywhere, plenty of open sewer and ditch for the promotion of the public health, have been fired off in a volley. Whizz! Dustheaps, market-gardens, and waste grounds. Rattle! New Cross Station. Shock! There we were at Croydon. Bur-r-r-r! The tunnel.

I wonder why it is that when I shut my eyes in a tunnel I begin to feel as if I were going at an Express pace the other way. I am clearly going back to London, now. Compact Enchantress must have forgotten something, and reversed the engine. No! After long darkness, pale fitful streaks of light appear. I am still flying on for Folkestone. The streaks grow stronger – become continuous – become the ghost of day – become the living day – became I mean –

the tunnel is miles and miles away, and here I fly through sunlight, all among the harvest and the Kentish hops.

There is a dreamy pleasure in this flying. I wonder where it was, and when it was, that we exploded, blew into space somehow, a Parliamentary Train,[11] with a crowd of heads and faces looking at us out of cages, and some hats waving. Monied Interest says it was at Reigate Station. Expounds to Mystery how Reigate Station is so many miles from London, which Mystery again develops to Compact Enchantress. There might be neither a Reigate nor a London for me, as I fly away among the Kentish hops and harvest. What do *I* care!

Bang! We have let another Station off, and fly away regardless. Everything is flying. The hop-gardens turn gracefully towards me, presenting regular avenues of hops in rapid flight, then whirl away. So do the pools and rushes, haystacks, sheep, clover in full bloom delicious to the sight and smell, corn-sheaves, cherry-orchards, apple-orchards, reapers, gleaners, hedges, gates, fields that taper off into little angular corners, cottages, gardens, now and then a church. Bang, bang! A double-barrelled Station! Now a wood, now a bridge, now a landscape, now a cutting, now a—Bang! a single-barrelled Station – there was a cricket match somewhere with two white tents, and then four flying cows, then turnips – now the wires of the electric telegraph are all alive, and spin, and blurr their edges, and go up and down, and make the intervals between each other most irregular: contracting and expanding in the strangest manner. Now we slacken. With a screwing, and a grinding, and a smell of water thrown on ashes, now we stop!

Demented Traveller, who has been for two or three minutes watchful, clutches his great coats, plunges at the door, rattles it, cries "Hi!" eager to embark on board of impossible packets, far inland. Collected Guard appears. "Are you for Tunbridge, sir?" "Tunbridge? No. Paris." "Plenty of time, sir. No hurry. Five minutes here, sir, for refreshment." I am so blest (anticipating Zamiel, by half a second) as to procure a glass of water for Compact Enchantress.

Who would suppose we had been flying at such a rate, and shall take wing again directly? Refreshment-room full, platform full, porter with watering-pot deliberately cooling a hot wheel, another porter with equal deliberation helping the rest of the wheels bountifully to ice cream. Monied Interest and I re-entering the carriage first, and being there alone, he intimates to me that the French are "no go" as a Nation. I ask why? He says, that Reign of Terror of theirs was quite enough. I venture to inquire whether he remembers anything that preceded said Reign of Terror? He says not particularly. "Because," I remark, "the harvest that is reaped, has sometimes been sown." [12] Monied Interest repeats, as quite enough for him, that the French are revolutionary, "—and always at it."

Bell. Compact Enchantress, helped in by Zamiel (whom the stars confound!), gives us her charming little side-box look, and smites me to the core. Mystery eating sponge-cake. Pine-apple atmosphere faintly tinged with suspicions of sherry. Demented Traveller flits past the carriage, looking for it. Is blind with agitation, and can't see it. Seems singled out by Destiny to be the only unhappy creature in the flight, who has any cause to hurry himself. Is nearly left behind. Is seized by Collected Guard after the Train is in motion, and bundled in. Still, has lingering suspicions that there must be a boat in the neighbourhood, and *will* look wildly out of window for it.

Flight resumed. Corn-sheaves, hop-gardens, reapers, gleaners, apple-orchards, cherry-orchards, Stations single and double-barrelled, Ashford. Compact Enchantress (constantly talking to Mystery, in an exquisite manner) gives a little scream; a sound that seems to come from high up in her precious little head; from behind her bright little eyebrows. "Great Heaven, my pine-apple! My Angel! It is lost!" Mystery is desolated. A search made. It is not lost. Zamiel finds it. I curse him (flying) in the Persian manner. May his face be turned upside down, and jackasses sit upon his uncle's grave![13]

Now fresher air, now glimpses of unenclosed Down-land with flapping crows flying over it whom we soon outfly, now the Sea, now Folkestone at a quarter after ten. "Tickets ready, gentlemen!" Demented dashes at the door. "For Paris, sir? No hurry."

Not the least. We are dropped slowly down to the Port, and sidle to and fro (the whole Train) before the insensible Royal George Hotel, for some ten minutes.[14] The Royal George takes no more heed of us than its namesake under water at Spithead, or under earth at Windsor, does.[15] The Royal George's dog lies winking and blinking at us, without taking the trouble to sit up; and the Royal George's "wedding party" at the open window (who seem, I must say, rather tired of bliss) don't bestow a solitary glance upon us, flying thus to Paris in eleven hours. The first gentleman in Folkestone is evidently used up, on this subject.

Meanwhile, Demented chafes. Conceives that every man's hand is against him, and exerting itself to prevent his getting to Paris. Refuses consolation. Rattles door. Sees smoke on the horizon, and "knows" it's the boat gone without him. Monied Interest resentfully explains that *he* is going to Paris too. Demented signifies that if Monied Interest chooses to be left behind, *he* don't.

"Refreshments in the Waiting-Room, ladies and gentlemen. No hurry, ladies and gentlemen. No hurry, ladies and gentlemen, for Paris. No hurry whatever!"

Twenty minutes' pause, by Folkestone clock, for looking at Enchantress while she eats a sandwich, and at Mystery while she eats of everything there that is eatable, from pork-pie, sausage, jam, and gooseberries, to lumps of sugar. All this time, there is a very waterfall of luggage, with a spray of dust, tumbling slantwise from the pier into the steamboat. All this time, Demented (who has no business with it) watches it with starting eyes, fiercely requiring to be shown *his* luggage. When it at last concludes the cataract, he rushes hotly to refresh – is shouted after, pursued, jostled, brought back, pitched into the departing steamer upside down, and caught by mariners disgracefully.

A lovely harvest day, a cloudless sky, a tranquil sea. The piston-rods of the engines so regularly coming up from below, to look (as well they may) at the bright weather, and so regularly almost knocking their iron heads against the cross beam of the skylight, and never doing it! Another Parisian actress is on board, attended by another Mystery. Compact Enchantress greets her sister artist – Oh, the Compact One's pretty teeth! – and Mystery greets Mystery. *My* Mystery soon ceases to be conversational – is taken poorly, in a word, having lunched too miscellaneously – and goes below. The remaining Mystery then smiles upon the sister artists (who, I am afraid, wouldn't greatly mind stabbing each other), and is upon the whole ravished.

And now I find that all the French people on board begin to grow, and all the English people to shrink. The French are nearing home, and shaking off a disadvantage, whereas we are shaking it on. Zamiel is the same man, and Abd-el-Kader is the same man, but each seems to come into possession of an indescribable confidence that departs from us – from Monied Interest, for instance, and from me. Just what they gain, we lose. Certain British "Gents" about the steersman, intellectually nurtured at home on parody of everything and truth of nothing, become subdued, and in a manner forlorn; and when the steersman tells them (not unexultingly) how he has "been upon this station now eight year, and never see the old town of Bullum yet," one of them, with an imbecile reliance on a reed, asks him what he considers to be the best hotel in Paris?

Now, I tread upon French ground, and am greeted by the three charming words, Liberty, Equality, Fraternity, painted up (in letters a little too thin for their height) on the Custom-House wall – also by the sight of large cocked hats, without which demonstrative head-gear nothing of a public nature can be done upon this soil. All the rabid Hotel population of Boulogne howl and shriek outside a distant barrier, frantic to get at us. Demented, by some unlucky means peculiar to himself, is delivered over to their fury, and is presently seen struggling in a whirlpool of Touters[16] – is somehow understood to be going to Paris – is, with infinite noise, rescued by two cocked hats, and brought into Custom-House bondage with the rest of us.

Here, I resign the active duties of life to an eager being, of preternatural sharpness, with a shelving forehead and a shabby snuff-coloured coat, who (from the wharf) brought me down with his eye before the boat came into port. He darts upon my luggage, on the floor where all the luggage is strewn like a wreck at the bottom of the great deep; gets it proclaimed and weighed as the property of "Monsieur a traveller unknown;" pays certain francs for it, to a certain functionary behind a Pigeon Hole, like a pay-box at a Theatre (the arrangements in general are on a wholesale scale, half military and half theatrical); and I suppose I shall find it when I come to Paris – he says I shall. I know nothing about it, except that I pay him his small fee, and pocket the ticket he gives me, and sit upon a counter, involved in the general distraction.

Railway station. "Lunch or dinner, ladies and gentlemen. Plenty of time for Paris. Plenty of time!" Large hall, long counter, long strips of dining-table, bottles of wine, plates of meat, roast chickens, little loaves of bread, basins of soup, little caraffes of brandy, cakes, and fruit. Comfortably restored from these resources, I begin to fly again.

I saw Zamiel (before I took wing) presented to the Compact Enchantress and Sister Artist, by an officer in uniform, with a waist like a wasp's, and pantaloons like two balloons. They all got into the next carriage together, accompanied by the two Mysteries. They laughed. I am alone in the carriage (for I don't consider Demented anybody) and alone in the world.

Fields, windmills, low grounds, pollard-trees, windmills, fields, fortifications,[17] Abbeville, soldiering and drumming. I wonder where England is, and when I was there last – about two years ago, I should say. Flying in and out among these trenches and batteries, skimming the clattering drawbridges, looking down into the stagnant ditches, I become a prisoner of state, escaping. I am confined with a comrade in a fortress. Our room is in an upper story. We have tried to get up the chimney, but there's an iron-grating across it, imbedded in the masonry. After months of labour, we have worked the grating loose with the poker, and can lift it up. We have also made a hook, and twisted our rugs and blankets into ropes. Our plan is, to go up the chimney, hook our ropes to the top, descend hand over hand upon the roof of the guard-house far below, shake the hook loose, watch the opportunity of the sentinel's pacing away, hook again, drop into the ditch, swim across it, creep into the shelter of the wood. The time is come – a wild and stormy night. We are up the chimney, we are on the guard-house roof, we are swimming in the murky ditch, when, lo! "Qui v'là?" a bugle, the alarm, a crash! What is it? Death? No, Amiens.

More fortifications, more soldiering and drumming, more basins of soup, more little loaves of bread, more bottles of wine, more caraffes of brandy, more time for refreshment. Everything good, and everything ready. Bright, unsubstantial-looking, scenic sort of station. People waiting. Houses, uniforms, beards, moustaches, some sabots, plenty of neat women, and a few old-visaged children. Unless it be a delusion born of my giddy flight, the grown-up people and the children seem to change places in France. In general, the boys and girls are little old men and women, and the men and women lively boys and girls.

Bugle, shriek, flight resumed. Monied Interest has come into my carriage. Says the manner of refreshing is "not bad," but considers it French. Admits great dexterity and politeness in the attendants. Thinks a decimal currency may have something to do with their despatch in settling accounts, and don't know but what it's sensible and convenient. Adds, however, as a general protest, that they're a revolutionary people – and always at it.

Ramparts, canals, cathedral, river, soldiering and drumming, open country, river, earthenware manufactures, Creil. Again ten minutes. Not even Demented in a hurry. Station, a drawing-room with a verandah: like a planter's house. Monied Interest considers it a band-box, and not made to last. Little round tables in it, at one of which the Sister Artists and attendant Mysteries are established with Wasp and Zamiel, as if they were going to stay a week.

Anon, with no more trouble than before, I am flying again, and lazily wondering as I fly. What has the South Eastern done with all the horrible little villages we used to pass through, in the *Diligence*?[18] What have they done with all the summer dust, with all the winter mud, with all the dreary avenues of little trees, with all the ramshackle postyards, with all the beggars (who used to turn out at night with bits of lighted candle, to look in at the coach windows), with all the long-tailed horses who were always biting one another, with all the big postilions in jack-boots – with all the mouldy cafés that we used to stop at, where a long mildewed tablecloth, set forth with jovial bottles of vinegar and oil, and with a Siamese arrangement of pepper and salt, was never wanting? Where are the grass-grown little towns, the wonderful little market-places all unconscious of markets, the shops that nobody kept, the streets that nobody trod, the churches that nobody went to, the bells that nobody rang, the tumble-down old buildings plastered with many-coloured bills that nobody read? Where are the two-and-twenty weary hours of long long day and night journey, sure to be either insupportably hot or insupportably cold? Where are the pains in my bones, where are the fidgets in my legs, where is the Frenchman with the nightcap who never *would* have the little coupé-window down, and who always fell upon me when he went to sleep, and always slept all night snoring onions?

A voice breaks in with "Paris! Here we are!"

I have overflown myself, perhaps, but I can't believe it. I feel as if I were enchanted or bewitched. It is barely eight o'clock yet – it is nothing like half-past – when I have had my luggage examined at that briskest of Custom-Houses attached to the station,[19] and am rattling over the pavement in a Hackney cabriolet.[20]

Surely, not the pavement of Paris? Yes, I think it is, too. I don't know any other place where there are all these high houses, all these haggard-looking wine shops, all these billiard tables, all these stocking-makers with flat red or yellow legs of wood for signboard, all these fuel shops with stacks of billets painted outside, and real billets sawing in the gutter, all these dirty corners of streets, all these cabinet pictures over dark doorways representing discreet matrons nursing babies. And yet this morning – I'll think of it in a warm bath.

Very like a small room that I remember in the Chinese Baths upon the Boulevard,[21] certainly; and, though I see it through the steam, I think that I might swear to that peculiar hot-linen basket, like a large wicker hour-glass. When can it have been that I left home? When was it that I paid "through to Paris" at London Bridge, and discharged myself of all responsibility, except the preservation of a voucher ruled into three divisions, of which the first was snipped off at Folkestone, the second aboard the boat, and the third taken at my journey's end? It seems to have been ages ago. Calculation is useless. I will go out for a walk.

The crowds in the streets, the lights in the shops and balconies, the elegance, variety, and beauty of their decorations, the number of

the theatres, the brilliant cafés with their windows thrown up high
and their vivacious groups at little tables on the pavement, the light
and glitter of the houses turned as it were inside out, soon convince
that it is no dream; that I am in Paris, howsoever I got here. I stroll
down to the sparkling Palais Royal, up the Rue de Rivoli, to the Place
Vendôme. As I glance into a print-shop window, Monied Interest, my
late travelling companion, comes upon me, laughing with the highest
relish of disdain. "Here's a people!" he says, pointing to Napoleon in
the window and Napoleon on the column.[22] "Only one idea all over
Paris! A monomania!" Humph! I THINK I have seen Napoleon's
match? There WAS a statue, when I came away, at Hyde Park Corner
and another in the City,[23] and a print or two in the shops.

I walk up to the Barrière de l'Etoile,[24] sufficiently dazed by my
flight to have a pleasant doubt of the reality of everything about me;
of the lively crowd, the overhanging trees, the performing dogs, the
hobby-horses, the beautiful perspectives of shining lamps: the
hundred and one inclosures, where the singing is, in gleaming
orchestras of azure and gold, and where a star-eyed Houri[25] comes
round with a box for voluntary offerings. So, I pass to my hotel,
enchanted; sup, enchanted; go to bed, enchanted; pushing back this
morning (if it really were this morning) into the remoteness of time,
blessing the South Eastern Company for realising the Arabian Nights
in these prose days, murmuring, as I wing my idle flight into the land
of dreams, "No hurry, ladies and gentlemen, going to Paris in eleven
hours. It is so well done, that there really is no hurry!"

chapter two

CROSSING THE CHANNEL
TO CALAIS

("THE CALAIS NIGHT MAIL"; EXTRACT FROM
LITTLE DORRIT)

"The Calais Night Mail" was published in *All the Year Round* on 2 May 1863. It was the first in the second series of "occasional papers" that Dickens wrote for the journal in the guise of the Uncommercial Traveller, a persona he had created in 1860 (the first series was published between January and October of that year). These articles all appeared under the heading "The Uncommercial Traveller" and were not given individual titles, like "The Calais Night Mail," until they were collected in volume form as *The Uncommercial Traveller* in 1861 and, including the second series, 1865. Dickens resurrected the persona once more for a series of individually titled articles tagged "New Uncommercial Samples," which began in *All the Year Round* on 5 December 1868 (these were collected posthumously in the 1874 edition of *The Uncommercial Traveller*).

The Uncommercial Traveller himself is introduced in the 28 January 1860 issue of *All the Year Round* in a short preamble to the first article in the series. As his name suggests, this narrator is the opposite of the commercial or business traveller – he travels anonymously, without material motive or influence:

> No landlord is my friend and brother, no chambermaid loves
> me, no boots admires and envies me. No beef or tongue or ham
> is expressly cooked for me... When I go upon my journeys, I
> am not usually rated at a low figure in the bill; when I come
> home from my journeys, I never get any commission.

Bestowed with the inevitable "otherness" of any traveller, he is positioned as a contemplative observer, speaking directly and personally to the reader about his opinions, his impressions, his experiences and his own past.

The coining of the name "Uncommercial Traveller" may owe something to Sterne's *A Sentimental Journey*, with its comic list of travelling types ("Sentimental Traveller," "Inquisitive Traveller," "Vain Traveller," etc) and its similarly idiosyncratic narrator. According to Forster, the name "expressed a personal liking" for the functions and management of the charitable Commercial Travellers' Schools, which Dickens supported (*Life*, 8, Chapter 5). Perhaps more obviously, however, it seems to have been chosen in satirical opposition to the increasing emphasis on commercial and economic interests in social and political affairs. The Traveller is resolutely engaged on the side of humanity and the imagination:

> I am both a town traveller and a country traveller, and am
> always on the road. Figuratively speaking, I travel for the great
> house of Human Interest Brothers, and have rather a large
> connexion in the fancy goods way. Literally speaking, I am
> always wandering here and there ... seeing many little things,
> and some great things, which, because they interest me, I
> think may interest others.

For readers who wish to pursue further the ideas and influences behind Dickens's creation of the Uncommercial Traveller persona, the fourth volume of *Dickens' Journalism* (Slater and Drew, 2000, pp xv–xiv) and *Dickens the Journalist* (Drew, 2003, pp 152–154) provide useful insights.

In "The Calais Night Mail," this "humble representative of the uncommercial interest" undergoes a stormy passage from Dover to

Calais on his way to Paris (the journey continues in "Some Recollections of Mortality," also included in this volume). At the beginning of the article, Dickens recalls his painful first crossing of the Channel, when he had arrived in Calais "a mere bilious torso, with a mislaid headache somewhere in its stomach." That journey was in July 1837. On his arrival in Calais on 2 July he wrote to Forster that he had been "very sick" and nervously anticipated a similar experience on the way back: "I shall see you, please God, directly we return – at least, so soon as my sea-sickness shall have disappeared" (*Pilgrim*, 1, pp 280–281).

By the time he wrote "The Calais Night Mail," however, Dickens had made the crossing many times and had grown much more accustomed to the heaving and rolling of the cross-Channel steamers. In this article, with its playful stream-of-consciousness passages, we find the narrator a seasoned traveller, adopting a comically familiar strategy for avoiding the dreaded sickness: he forces himself to run through the verses of a popular ballad in an effort to keep his mind off his immediate situation – but reality persists in making its presence felt.

Dickens's description of the misery of a rough Channel crossing would have been all too familiar to many of his contemporary readers. The sea passage took about two hours and in the 1850s and 1860s the steam packets were still relatively small and light. All but the most hardy of travellers had reason to dread a rough crossing. Writing in 1894 in *Our Railways*, John Pendleton commented,

> The passengers whose good or evil fortune it was to cross to Calais thirty years back in the little boat *Ondine* no doubt have a vivid recollection of the boisterous sea and the wave-splashed deck – and their intense longing to die. (Pendleton, 1894, 1, p 455.)

Murray's *Handbook for Travellers in France*, 1864, warned:

> Excellent fast steamboats cross the Channel between France and England; still they are often crowded to inconvenience,

and in rough weather passengers are liable to be wetted by the rain or spray. The passengers, especially ladies, should therefore take with them a small change of raiment in a hand bag...

And a very disgruntled Horace Greeley, crossing the Channel back in 1851, wondered why the boats were not more like those in his native America and evoked a scene very like that in "The Calais Night Mail":

> We came on quite rapidly to Dover ... but there lost about an hour in the transfer of our baggage to the steamboat, which was one of those long, black, narrow scow contrivances, about equal to a buttonwood 'dug-out,' which England appears to delight in. They would not be tolerated as ferry-boats on any of our Western rivers ... In this wretched concern, which was too insignificant to be slow, we went cobbling and wriggling across the Channel (27 miles) in something less than two hours, often one gunwale nearly under water and the other ten or twelve feet above it, with no room under deck for half our passengers, and the spray frequently dashing over those above it, three-fourths of the whole number deadly sick (this individual of course included), when with a decent boat the passage might be regularly made, in spite of such a smartish breeze as we encountered, in comparative comfort. (*Glances at Europe*, 1851, p 14.)

After his rough crossing in "The Calais Night Mail," the Uncommercial Traveller does at least have the good fortune to enter Calais at high tide:

> For we have not to land tonight among those slimy timbers – covered with green hair as if it were the mermaids' favourite combing-place – where one crawls to the surface of the jetty like a stranded shrimp, but we go steaming up the harbour to the Railway Station Quay.

In *Little Dorrit* (1855–57), Arthur Clennam has no such luck. He arrives at low tide:

> After slipping among oozy piles and planks, stumbling up wet steps and encountering many salt difficulties, the passengers entered on their comfortless peregrination along the pier.

And, seen through Clennam's eyes, the "slimy timbers" offer no mermaid fantasies:

> The long rows of gaunt black piles, slimy and wet and weather-worn, with funeral garlands of sea-weed twisted about them by the late tide, might have represented an unsightly marine cemetery.

Calais was not among the most favored of towns. According to Murray's *Handbook for Travellers in France*, 1864, "after an hour or so it becomes tiresome, and a traveller will do well to quit it as soon as he has cleared his baggage from the custom-house…" But travellers' perceptions of their journeys and the places they visit are determined by their states of mind. For the troubled and tired Arthur Clennam, everything in Calais is dull and deadening, and a little sinister. For the Uncommercial Traveller, relieved to be on dry land again and happy to be continuing his journey, the bustle and confusion around the harbor seem to greet him like old friends and the town, for all its lack of glamour, is a welcome sight because it marks not only the end of the watery part of his journey but also his arrival in France.

Calais pier and harbour entrance, c 1845

THE CALAIS NIGHT MAIL

It is an unsettled question with me whether I shall leave Calais something handsome in my will, or whether I shall leave it my malediction. I hate it so much, and yet I am always so very glad to see it, that I am in a state of constant indecision on this subject.

When I first made acquaintance with Calais, it was as a maundering young wretch in a clammy perspiration and dripping saline particles, who was conscious of no extremities but the one great extremity, sea-sickness – who was a mere bilious torso, with a mislaid headache somewhere in its stomach – who had been put into a horrible swing in Dover Harbour, and had tumbled giddily out of it on the French coast, or the Isle of Man, or anywhere. Times have changed, and now I enter Calais self-reliant and rational. I know where it is beforehand, I keep a look out for it, I recognise its landmarks when I see any of them, I am acquainted with its ways, and I know – and I can bear – its worst behaviour.

Malignant Calais! Low-lying alligator, evading the eyesight and discouraging hope! Dodging flat streak, now on this bow, now on that, now anywhere, now everywhere, now nowhere! In vain Cape Grinez,[1] coming frankly forth into the sea, exhorts the failing to be stout of heart and stomach: sneaking Calais, prone behind its bar,[2] invites emetically to despair. Even when it can no longer quite conceal itself in its muddy dock, it has an evil way of falling off, has Calais, which is more hopeless than its invisibility. The pier is all but on the bowsprit, and you think you are there – roll, roar, wash! – Calais has retired miles inland, and Dover has burst out to look for it. It has a last dip and a slide in its character, has Calais, to be especially commended to the infernal gods. Thrice accursed be that garrison-town,[3] when it dives under the boat's keel, and comes up a league or two to the right, with the packet shivering and spluttering and staring about for it!

Not but what I have my animosities towards Dover. I particularly detest Dover for the self-complacency with which it goes to bed. It always goes to bed (when I am going to Calais) with a more brilliant display of lamp and candle than any other town. Mr and Mrs Birmingham, host and hostess of the Lord Warden Hotel,[4] are my much esteemed friends, but they are too conceited about the comforts of that establishment when the Night Mail is starting. I know it is a good house to stay at, and I don't want the fact insisted upon in all its warm bright windows at such an hour. I know the Warden is a stationary edifice that never rolls or pitches, and I object to its big outline seeming to insist upon that circumstance, and, as it were, to come over me with it, when I am reeling on the deck of the boat. Beshrew the Warden likewise, for obstructing that corner, and making the wind so angry as it rushes round. Shall I not know that it blows quite soon enough, without the officious Warden's interference?

As I wait here on board the night packet, for the South Eastern Train to come down with the Mail,[5] Dover appears to me to be illuminated for some intensely aggravating festivity in my personal dishonour. All its noises smack of taunting praises of the land, and dispraises of the gloomy sea, and of me for going on it. The drums upon the heights[6] have gone to bed, or I know they would rattle taunts against me for having my unsteady footing on this slippery deck. The many gas eyes of the Marine Parade twinkle in an offensive manner, as if with derision. The distant dogs of Dover bark at me in my mis-shapen wrappers, as if I were Richard the Third.[7]

A screech, a bell, and two red eyes come gliding down the Admiralty Pier[8] with a smoothness of motion rendered more smooth by the heaving of the boat. The sea makes noises against the pier, as if several hippopotami were lapping at it, and were prevented by circumstances over which they had no control from drinking peaceably. We, the boat, become violently agitated – rumble, hum, scream, roar, and establish an immense family washing-day at each paddle-box. Bright patches break out in the train as the doors of the post-office vans are opened, and instantly stooping figures with sacks upon their backs begin to be beheld among the piles, descending as it would seem in ghostly procession to Davy Jones's Locker. The passengers come on board; a few shadowy Frenchmen, with hatboxes shaped like the stoppers of gigantic case-bottles; a few shadowy Germans in immense fur coats and boots; a few shadowy Englishmen prepared for the worst and pretending not to expect it. I cannot disguise from my uncommercial mind[9] the miserable fact that we are a body of outcasts; that the attendants on us are as scant in number as may serve to get rid of us with the least possible delay; that there are no night-loungers interested in us; that the unwilling lamps shiver and shudder at us; that the sole object is to commit us to the deep[10] and abandon us. Lo, the two red eyes glaring in increasing distance, and then the very train itself has gone to bed before we are off!

What is the moral support derived by some sea-going amateurs from an umbrella? Why do certain voyagers across the Channel always put up that article, and hold it up with a grim and fierce tenacity? A fellow-creature near me – whom I only know to *be* a fellow-creature because of his umbrella: without which he might be a dark bit of cliff, pier, or bulkhead – clutches that instrument with a desperate grasp, that will not relax until he lands at Calais. Is there any analogy, in certain constitutions, between keeping an umbrella up, and keeping the spirits up? A hawser thrown on board with a flop replies, "Stand by!" "Stand by, below!" "Half a turn ahead!" "Half a turn ahead!" "Half speed!" "Half speed!" "Port!" "Port!" "Steady!" "Steady!" "Go on!" "Go on!"

A stout wooden wedge driven in at my right temple and out at my left, a floating deposit of lukewarm oil in my throat, and a compression of the bridge of my nose in a blunt pair of pincers, – these are the personal sensations by which I know we are off, and by which I shall continue to know it until I am on the soil of France. My symptoms have scarcely established themselves comfortably, when two or three skating shadows that have been trying to walk or stand, get flung together, and other two or three shadows in tarpaulin slide with them into corners and cover them up. Then the South Foreland lights[11] begin to hiccup at us in a way that bodes no good.

It is about this period that my detestation of Calais knows no bounds. Inwardly I resolve afresh that I never will forgive that hated town. I have done so before, many times, but that is past. Let me register a vow. Implacable animosity to Calais everm— that was an awkward sea, and the funnel seems of my opinion, for it gives a complaining roar.

The wind blows stiffly from the Nor'-East, the sea runs high, we ship a deal of water, the night is dark and cold, and the shapeless passengers lie about in melancholy bundles, as if they were sorted out for the laundress; but for my own uncommercial part I cannot pretend that I am much inconvenienced by any of these things. A general howling whistling flopping gurgling and scooping, I am aware of, and a general knocking about of Nature; but the impressions I receive are very vague. In a sweet faint temper, something like the smell of damaged oranges, I think I should feel languidly benevolent if I had time. I have not time, because I am under a curious compulsion to occupy myself with the Irish melodies. "Rich and rare were the gems she wore,"[12] is the particular melody to which I find myself devoted. I sing it to myself in the most charming manner and with the greatest expression. Now and then, I raise my head (I am sitting on the hardest of wet seats, in the most uncomfortable of wet attitudes, but I don't mind it,) and notice that I am a whirling shuttlecock between a fiery battledore of a lighthouse on the French coast and a fiery battledore of a lighthouse on the English coast; but I don't notice it particularly, except to feel envenomed in my hatred of Calais. Then I go on again, "Rich and rare were the ge-ems she-e-e-e wore, And a bright gold ring on her wa-and she bo-ore, But O her beauty was fa-a-a-a-r beyond" – I am particularly proud of my execution here, when I become aware of another awkward shock from the sea, and another protest from the funnel, and a fellow-creature at the paddle-box more audibly indisposed than I think he need be – "Her sparkling gems, or snow-white wand, But O her beauty was fa-a-a-a-r beyond" – another awkward one here, and the fellow-creature with the umbrella down and picked up – "Her spa-a-rkling ge-ems, or her Port! port! steady! steady! snow-white fellow-creature at the paddle-box very selfishly audible, bump roar wash white wand."

As my execution of the Irish melodies partakes of my imperfect perceptions of what is going on around me, so what is going on around me becomes something else than what it is. The stokers open the furnace doors below, to feed the fires, and I am again on the box of the old Exeter Telegraph fast coach,[13] and that is the light of the for ever extinguished coach-lamps, and the gleam on the hatches and paddle-boxes is *their* gleam on cottages and haystacks, and the monotonous noise of the engines is the steady jingle of the splendid team. Anon, the intermittent funnel roar of protest at every violent roll, becomes the regular blast of a high pressure engine, and I recognise the exceedingly explosive steamer in which I ascended the Mississippi when the American civil war was not, and when only its causes were.[14] A fragment of mast on which the light of a lantern falls, an end of rope, and a jerking block or so, become suggestive of Franconi's Circus[15] at Paris where I shall be this very night mayhap (for it must be morning now), and they dance to the self-same time and tune as the trained steed, Black Raven. What may be the speciality of these waves as they come rushing on, I cannot desert the pressing demands made upon me by the gems she wore, to inquire, but they are charged with something about Robinson Crusoe, and I think it was in Yarmouth Roads that he first went a seafaring and was near foundering (what a terrific sound that word had for me when I was a boy!) in his first gale of wind.[16] Still, through all this, I must ask her (who *was* she I wonder!) for the fiftieth time, and without ever stopping, Does she not fear to stray, So lone and lovely through this bleak way, And are Erin's sons so good or so cold, As not to be tempted by more fellow-creatures at the paddle-box or gold? Sir Knight I feel not the least alarm, No son of Erin will offer me harm, For though they love fellow-creature with umbrella down again and golden store, Sir Knight they what a tremendous one love honour and virtue more: For though they love Stewards with a bull's-eye[17] bright, they'll trouble you for your ticket, sir – rough passage tonight!

I freely admit it to be a miserable piece of human weakness and inconsistency, but I no sooner become conscious of those last words from the steward than I begin to soften towards Calais. Whereas I have been vindictively wishing that those Calais burghers[18] who came out of their town by a short cut into the History of England, with those fatal ropes round their necks by which they have since been towed into so many cartoons, had all been hanged on the spot, I now begin to regard them as highly respectable and virtuous tradesmen. Looking about me, I see the light of Cape Grinez well astern of the boat on the davits to leeward, and the light of Calais Harbour undeniably at its old tricks, but still ahead and shining. Sentiments of forgiveness of Calais, not to say of attachment to Calais, begin to expand my bosom. I have weak notions that I will stay there a day or two on my way back. A faded and recumbent stranger pausing in a profound reverie over the rim of a basin, asks me what kind of place Calais is? I tell him (Heaven forgive me!) a very agreeable place indeed – rather hilly than otherwise.

So strangely goes the time, and on the whole so quickly – though still I seem to have been on board a week – that I am bumped rolled gurgled washed and pitched into Calais Harbour before her maiden smile has finally lighted her through the Green Isle, When blest for ever is she who relied, On entering Calais at the top of the tide. For we have not to land tonight down among those slimy timbers – covered with green hair as if it were the mermaids' favourite combing-place – where one crawls to the surface of the jetty like a stranded shrimp, but we go steaming up the harbour to the Railway Station Quay.[19] And as we go, the sea washes in and out among piles and planks, with dead heavy beats and in quite a furious manner (whereof we are proud), and the lamps shake in the wind, and the bells of Calais striking One seem to send their vibrations struggling against troubled air, as we have come struggling against troubled water. And now, in the sudden relief and wiping of faces, everybody on board seems to have had a prodigious double-tooth out, and to be this very instant free of the Dentist's hands. And now we all know for the first time how wet and cold we are, and how salt we are; and now I love Calais with my heart of hearts!

"Hôtel Dessin!" (but in this case it is not a vocal cry; it is but a bright lustre in the eyes of the cheery representative of that best of inns.)[20] "Hôtel Meurice!" "Hôtel de France!" "Hôtel de Calais!" "The Royal Hôtel, Sir, Angaishe ouse!" "You going to Parry, Sir?" "Your baggage, registair froo, Sir?" Bless ye, my Touters, bless ye, my commissionaires, bless ye, my hungry-eyed mysteries in caps of a military form, who are always here, day or night, fair weather or foul, seeking inscrutable jobs which I never see you get! Bless ye, my Custom House officers in green and grey; permit me to grasp the welcome hands that descend into my travelling-bag, one on each side, and meet at the bottom to give my change of linen a peculiar shake up, as if it were a measure of chaff or grain! I have nothing to declare,

Monsieur le Douanier, except that when I cease to breathe, Calais will be found written on my heart.[21] No article liable to local duty have I with me, Monsieur l'Officier de l'Octroi,[22] unless the overflowing of a breast devoted to your charming town should be in that wise chargeable. Ah! see at the gangway by the twinkling lantern, my dearest brother and friend, he once of the Passport Office, he who collects the names! May he be for ever changeless in his buttoned black surtout, with his notebook in his hand, and his tall black hat, surmounting his round smiling patient face! Let us embrace, my dearest brother. I am yours à tout jamais – for the whole of ever.

Calais up and doing at the railway station, and Calais down and dreaming in its bed; Calais with something of "an ancient and fish-like smell"[23] about it, and Calais blown and sea-washed pure; Calais represented at the Buffet by savoury roast fowls, hot coffee, cognac, and Bordeaux; and Calais represented everywhere by flitting persons with a monomania for changing money – though I never shall be able to understand in my present state of existence how they live by it, but I suppose I should, if I understood the currency question – Calais *en gros*, and Calais *en détail*, forgive one who has deeply wronged you. – I was not fully aware of it on the other side, but I meant Dover.

Ding, ding! To the carriages, gentlemen the travellers. Ascend then, gentlemen the travellers, for Hazebroucke, Lille, Douai, Bruxelles, Arras, Amiens, and Paris! I, humble representative of the uncommercial interest, ascend with the rest. The train is light tonight, and I share my compartment with but two fellow-travellers; one, a compatriot in an obsolete cravat, who thinks it a quite unaccountable thing that they don't keep "London time" on a French railway, and who is made angry by my modestly suggesting the possibility of Paris time being more in their way; the other, a young priest, with a very small bird in a very small cage, who feeds the small bird with a quill, and then puts him up in the network above his head, where he advances twittering, to his front wires, and seems to address me in an electioneering manner. The compatriot (who crossed in the boat, and whom I judge to be some person of distinction, as he was shut up, like a stately species of rabbit, in a private hutch on deck) and the young priest (who joined us at Calais) are soon asleep, and then the bird and I have it all to ourselves.

A stormy night still; a night that sweeps the wires of the electric telegraph with a wild and fitful hand; a night so very stormy, with the added storm of the train-progress through it, that when the Guard comes clambering round to mark the tickets while we are at full speed (a really horrible performance in an express train, though he holds on to the open window by his elbows in the most deliberate manner), he stands in such a whirlwind that I grip him fast by the collar, and feel it next to manslaughter to let him go. Still, when he is gone, the small small bird remains at his front wires feebly twittering to me – twittering and twittering, until, leaning back in my place and looking at him in drowsy fascination, I find that he seems to jog my memory as we rush along.

Uncommercial travels (thus the small small bird) have lain in their idle thriftless way through all this range of swamp and dyke, as through many other odd places; and about here, as you very well know, are the queer old stone farm-houses approached by drawbridges, and the windmills that you get at by boats.[24] Here, are the lands where the women hoe and dig, paddling canoe-wise from field to field, and here are the cabarets[25] and other peasant-houses where the stone dove-cotes in the littered yards are as strong as warders' towers in old castles. Here, are the long monotonous miles of canal, with the great Dutch-built barges garishly painted, and the towing girls, sometimes harnessed by the forehead, sometimes by the girdle and the shoulders, not a pleasant sight to see. Scattered through this country are mighty works of VAUBAN,[26] whom you know about, and regiments of such corporals as you heard of once upon a time, and many a blue-eyed Bebelle.[27] Through these flat districts, in the shining summer days, walk those long grotesque files of young novices in enormous shovel hats, whom you remember blackening the ground checkered by the avenues of leafy trees. And now that Hazebroucke slumbers certain kilometres ahead, recall the summer evening when your dusty feet strolling up from the station tended hap-hazard to a Fair there,[28] where the oldest inhabitants were circling round and round a barrel-organ on hobby-horses, with the greatest gravity, and where the principal show in the Fair was a Religious Richardson's[29] – literally, on its own announcement in great letters, THEATRE RELIGIEUX. In which improving Temple, the dramatic representation was of "all the interesting events in the life of our Lord, from the Manger to the Tomb;" the principal female character, without any reservation or exception, being at the moment of your arrival, engaged in trimming the external Moderators[30] (as it was growing dusk), while the next principal female character took the money, and the Young Saint John disported himself upside down on the platform.

Looking up at this point to confirm the small small bird in every particular he has mentioned, I find he has ceased to twitter, and has put his head under his wing. Therefore, in my different way I follow the good example.[31]

The quai de Marée at Calais (the "Railway Station Quay"), with the railway
terminus on the right, c 1860

EXTRACT FROM LITTLE DORRIT

(CLENNAM IN CALAIS)

*Narrative context: Arthur Clennam has crossed to Calais to visit Miss
Wade in search of information as to the whereabouts of the criminal
Rigaud. Rigaud has stolen papers that incriminate Mrs Clennam
(Clennam's supposed mother) and confirm Little Dorrit's right to an
inheritance. The extract is from Book 2, Chapter 20.*

The passengers were landing from the packet on the pier at Calais. A
low-lying place and a low-spirited place Calais was, with the tide

ebbing out towards low water-mark. There had been no more water on the bar[1] than had sufficed to float the packet in; and now the bar itself, with a shallow break of sea over it, looked like a lazy marine monster just risen to the surface, whose form was indistinctly shown as it lay asleep. The meagre lighthouse all in white, haunting the sea-board as if it were the ghost of an edifice that had once had colour and rotundity, dripped melancholy tears after its late buffeting by the waves. The long rows of gaunt black piles, slimy and wet and weather-worn, with funeral garlands of sea-weed twisted about them by the late tide, might have represented an unsightly marine cemetery. Every wave-dashed, storm-beaten object, was so low and so little, under the broad grey sky, in the noise of the wind and sea, and before the curling lines of surf, making at it ferociously, that the wonder was there was any Calais left, and that its low gates and low wall and low roofs and low ditches and low sand-hills and low ramparts and flat streets, had not yielded long ago to the undermining and besieging sea, like the fortifications children make on the sea-shore.

After slipping among oozy piles and planks, stumbling up wet steps and encountering many salt difficulties, the passengers entered on their comfortless peregrination along the pier;[2] where all the French vagabonds and English outlaws in the town (half the population) attended to prevent their recovery from bewilderment.[3] After being minutely inspected by all the English, and claimed and reclaimed and counter-claimed as prizes by all the French, in a hand-to-hand scuffle three quarters of a mile long, they were at last free to enter the streets, and to make off in their various directions, hotly pursued.

Clennam, harassed by more anxieties than one, was among this devoted band. Having rescued the most defenceless of his compatriots from situations of great extremity, he now went his way alone; or as nearly alone as he could be, with a native gentleman in a suit of grease and a cap of the same material, giving chase at a distance of some fifty yards, and continually calling after him "Hi! Ice-say! You! Seer! Ice-say! Nice Oatel!"

Even this hospitable person, however, was left behind at last, and Clennam pursued his way, unmolested. There was a tranquil air in the town after the turbulence of the Channel and the beach, and its dulness in that comparison was agreeable. He met new groups of his countrymen, who had all a straggling air of having at one time over-blown themselves, like certain uncomfortable kinds of flowers, and of being, now, mere weeds.[4] They had all an air, too, of lounging out a limited round, day after day, which strongly reminded him of the Marshalsea.[5] But, taking no further note of them than was sufficient to give birth to the reflection, he sought out a certain street and number, which he kept in his mind.

"So Pancks said," he murmured to himself, as he stopped before a dull house answering to the address. "I suppose his information to be correct and his discovery, among Mr Casby's loose papers, indisputable; but, without it, I should hardly have supposed this to be a likely place."

A dead sort of house, with a dead wall over the way and a dead gateway at the side, where a pendant bell-handle produced two dead tinkles, and a knocker produced a dead flat surface-tapping, that seemed not to have depth enough in it to penetrate even the cracked door. However, the door jarred open on a dead sort of spring; and he closed it behind him as he entered a dull yard, soon brought to a close at the back by another dead wall, where an attempt had been made to train some creeping shrubs, which were dead; and to make a little fountain in a grotto, which was dry; and to decorate that with a little statue, which was gone.

The entry to the house was on the left, and it was garnished, as the outer gateway was, with two printed bills in French and English, announcing Furnished Apartments to let, with immediate possession. A strong cheerful peasant woman, all stocking, petticoat, white cap, and ear-ring, stood here in a dark doorway, and said with a pleasant show of teeth, "Ice-say! Seer! Who?"

chapter three

ON THE ROAD: THROUGH FRANCE TO SWITZERLAND

("TRAVELLING ABROAD")

"Travelling Abroad" was published in *All the Year Round* on 7 April 1860 as part of the first series of "Uncommercial Traveller" papers (see p 17). Written in the age of the train, it looks back to the days of the coach, with Dickens remembering his early travels on the Continent. He draws in particular, but not exclusively, on his journey through France to Italy in 1844 (part of which is described in *Pictures from Italy*), his journey to and travels in Switzerland in 1846 (he and his family stayed there for six months), and a three-month residence in Paris in the winter of 1846–47.

The narrative is geographically sequential, pulling together disparate incidents, memories, impressions, fancies, and reflections as the "travelling chariot" of the Uncommercial Traveller takes him on a flight of the imagination from London to Dover, along the country roads of northern France to Paris and then on through France to Strasbourg and finally to the mountains of Switzerland. In the course of this journey of the mind, Dickens evokes memories of his own childhood, of his trusted courier Louis Roche, of travelling for hours along dusty French roads and stopping at country inns, of wanderings in Paris (including his frequent visits to the Morgue), of a rainy night in Strasbourg and of the villages and dramatic scenery of the Swiss mountains. Perhaps most of all, however, "Travelling Abroad" is about the nature of travel itself and the sensation of travelling. The article is both a product and an expression of "that delicious traveller's-trance which knows no cares, no yesterdays, no tomorrows, nothing but the passing objects and the passing scents and sounds."

Dickens clearly drew his inspiration for "Travelling Abroad" from Laurence Sterne's *A Sentimental Journey through France and Italy*. There are echoes of Sterne in the tone and style of this personal, whimsical, and episodic piece. The incident that gives the narrative its framework recalls the "Preface in the Desobligeant" chapter of Sterne's novel. In *A Sentimental Journey* the narrator, looking for a carriage to buy or hire in a Calais coach-yard, steps into one to try it out and proceeds to reflect at length on the nature of travel and travellers. In "Travelling Abroad" the Uncommercial Traveller, looking for a coach to buy in a London warehouse, steps into one and immediately embarks on his fanciful journey. Like *A Sentimental Journey*, "Travelling Abroad" starts abruptly as if in mid-narration ("I got into the carriage"). And like the "Preface in the Desobligeant," it stops with a jolt as the narrator is brought back to reality by a banal intrusion.

Dickens leaving the Morgue (illustration by G.J. Pinwell)

TRAVELLING ABROAD

I got into the travelling chariot[1] – it was of German make, roomy, heavy, and unvarnished – I got into the travelling chariot, pulled up the steps after me, shut myself in with a smart bang of the door, and gave the word "Go on!"

Immediately, all that W. and S.W. division of London began to slide away at a pace so lively, that I was over the river, and past the Old Kent-road, and out on Blackheath, and even ascending Shooter's Hill, before I had had time to look about me in the carriage, like a collected traveller.[2]

I had two ample Imperials[3] on the roof, other fitted storage for luggage in front, and other up behind; I had a net for books overhead, great pockets to all the windows, a leathern pouch or two hung up for odds and ends, and a reading-lamp fixed in the back of the chariot, in case I should be benighted. I was amply provided in all respects, and had no idea where I was going (which was delightful), except that I was going abroad.

So smooth was the old high road, and so fresh were the horses, and so fast went I, that it was midway between Gravesend and Rochester, and the widening river was bearing the ships, white-sailed or black-smoked, out to sea, when I noticed by the wayside a very queer small boy.

"Halloa!" said I, to the very queer small boy, "where do you live?"

"At Chatham," says he.

"What do you do there?" says I.

"I go to school," says he.

I took him up in a moment, and we went on. Presently, the very queer small boy says, "This is Gadshill we are coming to, where Falstaff went out to rob those travellers, and ran away."[4]

"You know something about Falstaff, eh?" said I.

"All about him," said the very queer small boy. "I am old (I am nine), and I read all sorts of books. But *do* let us stop at the top of the hill, and look at the house there, if you please!"

"You admire that house?" said I.

"Bless you, sir," said the very queer small boy, "when I was not more than half as old as nine, it used to be a treat for me to be brought to look at it. And now, I am nine, I come by myself to look at it. And ever since I can recollect, my father, seeing me so fond of it, has often said to me, 'If you were to be very persevering and were to work hard, you might some day come to live in it.' Though that's impossible!" said the very queer small boy, drawing a low breath, and now staring at the house out of window with all his might.

I was rather amazed to be told this by the very queer small boy; for that house happens to be *my* house, and I have reason to believe that what he said was true.[5]

Well! I made no halt there, and I soon dropped the very queer small boy and went on. Over the road where the old Romans used to march,[6] over the road where the old Canterbury pilgrims used to go, over the road where the travelling trains of the old imperious priests and princes used to jingle on horseback between the continent and this Island through the mud and water, over the road where Shakespeare hummed to himself, "Blow, blow, thou winter wind,"[7] as he sat in the saddle at the gate of the inn noticing the carriers;[8] all among the cherry orchards, apple orchards, corn-fields, and hop-gardens; so went I, by Canterbury to Dover. There, the sea was tumbling in, with deep sounds, after dark, and the revolving French light on Cape Grinez[9] was seen regularly bursting out and becoming obscured, as if the head of a gigantic light-keeper in an anxious state of mind were interposed every half minute, to look how it was burning.

Early in the morning I was on the deck of the steam-packet, and we were aiming at the bar[10] in the usual intolerable manner, and the bar was aiming at us in the usual intolerable manner, and the bar got by far the best of it, and we got by far the worst – all in the usual intolerable manner.

But, when I was clear of the Custom House on the other side, and when I began to make the dust fly on the thirsty French roads, and when the twigsome trees by the wayside (which, I suppose, never will grow leafy, for they never did) guarded here and there a dusty soldier, or field labourer, baking on a heap of broken stones, sound asleep in a fiction of shade, I began to recover my travelling spirits. Coming upon the breaker of the broken stones, in a hard, hot, shining hat, on which the sun played at a distance as on a burning-glass, I felt that now, indeed, I was in the dear old France of my affections. I should have known it, without the well-remembered bottle of rough ordinary wine, the cold roast fowl, the loaf, and the pinch of salt, on which I lunched with unspeakable satisfaction, from one of the stuffed pockets of the chariot.

I must have fallen asleep after lunch, for when a bright face looked in at the window, I started, and said:

"Good God, Louis,[11] I dreamed you were dead!"

My cheerful servant laughed, and answered:

"Me? Not at all, sir."

"How glad I am to wake! What are we doing, Louis?"

"We go to take relay of the horses. Will you walk up the hill?"

"Certainly."

Welcome the old French hill, with the old French lunatic (not in the most distant degree related to Sterne's Maria[12]) living in a thatched dog-kennel half way up, and flying out with his crutch and his big head and extended nightcap, to be beforehand with the old men and women exhibiting crippled children, and with the children exhibiting old men and women, ugly and blind, who always seemed by resurrectionary process to be recalled out of the elements for the sudden peopling of the solitude!

"It is well," said I, scattering among them what small coin I had; "here comes Louis, and I am quite roused from my nap."

We journeyed on again, and I welcomed every new assurance that France stood where I had left it. There were the posting-houses, with their archways, dirty stable-yards, and clean post-masters' wives, bright women of business, looking on at the putting-to of the horses; there were the postilions counting what money they got, into their hats, and never making enough of it; there were the standard population of grey horses of Flanders descent, invariably biting one another when they got a chance; there were the fleecy sheepskins, looped on over their uniforms by the postilions, liked bibbed aprons, when it blew and rained; there were their jack-boots, and their cracking whips; there were the cathedrals that I got out to see, as under some cruel bondage, in no wise desiring to see them; there were the little towns that appeared to have no reason for being towns, since most of their houses were to let and nobody could be induced to look at them, except the people who couldn't let them and had nothing else to do but look at them all day. I lay a night upon the road and enjoyed delectable cookery of potatoes, and some other sensible things, adoption of which at home would inevitably be shown to be fraught with ruin, somehow or other, to that rickety national blessing, the British farmer; and at last I was rattled, like a single pill in a box, over leagues of stones, until – madly cracking, plunging, and flourishing two grey tails about – I made my triumphal entry into Paris.

At Paris, I took an upper apartment for a few days in one of the hotels of the Rue de Rivoli:[13] my front windows looking into the garden of the Tuileries (where the principal difference between the nursemaids and the flowers seemed to be that the former were locomotive and the latter not): my back windows looking at all the other back windows in the hotel, and deep down into a paved yard, where my German chariot had retired under a tight-fitting archway, to all appearance, for life, and where bells rang all day without anybody's minding them but certain chamberlains with feather brooms and green baize caps, who here and there leaned out of some high window placidly looking down, and where neat waiters with trays on their left shoulders passed and repassed from morning to night.

Whenever I am in Paris, I am dragged by invisible force into the Morgue.[14] I never want to go there, but am always pulled there. One Christmas Day, when I would rather have been anywhere else, I was attracted in, to see an old grey man lying all alone on his cold bed, with a tap of water turned on over his grey hair, and running, drip, drip, drip, down his wretched face until it got to the corner of his mouth, where it took a turn, and made him look sly. One New Year's Morning (by the same token, the sun was shining outside, and there was a mountebank[15] balancing a feather on his nose, within a yard of the gate), I was pulled in again to look at a flaxen-haired boy of eighteen with a heart hanging on his breast – "from his mother," was engraven on it – who had come into the net across the river, with a bullet-wound in his fair forehead and his hands cut with a knife, but whence or how was a blank mystery. This time, I was forced into the same dread place, to see a large dark man whose disfigurement by water was in a frightful manner, comic, and whose expression was that of a prize-fighter who had closed his eyelids under a heavy blow, but was going immediately to open them, shake his head, and "come up smiling." O what this large dark man cost me in that bright city!

It was very hot weather, and he was none the better for that, and I was much the worse. Indeed, a very neat and pleasant little woman, with the key of her lodging on her forefinger, who had been showing him to her little girl while she and the child ate sweetmeats, observed monsieur looking poorly as we came out together, and asked monsieur, with her wondering little eyebrows prettily raised, if there were anything the matter? Faintly replying in the negative, monsieur crossed the road to a wine-shop, got some brandy, and resolved to freshen himself with a dip in the great floating bath on the river.[16]

The bath was crowded in the usual airy manner, by a male population in striped drawers of various gay colours, who walked up and down arm in arm, drank coffee, smoked cigars, sat at little tables, conversed politely with the damsels who dispensed the towels, and every now and then pitched themselves into the river head foremost, and came out again to repeat this social routine. I made haste to participate in the water part of the entertainments, and was in full enjoyment of a delightful bath, when all in a moment I was seized with an unreasonable idea that the large dark body was floating straight at me.

I was out of the river, and dressing instantly. In the shock I had taken some water into my mouth, and it turned me sick, for I fancied that the contamination of the creature was in it. I had got back to my cool darkened room in the hotel, and was lying on a sofa there, before I began to reason with myself.

Of course, I knew perfectly well that the large dark creature was stone dead, and that I should no more come upon him out of the place where I had seen him dead, than I should come upon the cathedral of Notre-Dame in an entirely new situation. What troubled me was the picture of the creature; and that had so curiously and strongly painted itself upon my brain, that I could not get rid of it until it was worn out.

I noticed the peculiarities of this possession, while it was a real discomfort to me. That very day, at dinner, some morsel on my plate looked like a piece of him, and I was glad to get up and go out. Later in the evening, I was walking along the Rue St Honoré, when I saw a bill at a public room there, announcing a small-sword exercise, broad-sword exercise, wrestling, and other such feats. I went in, and some of the sword play being very skilful, remained. A specimen of our own national sport, The British Boaxe,[17] was announced to be given at the close of the evening. In an evil hour, I determined to wait for this Boaxe, as became a Briton. It was a clumsy specimen (executed by two English grooms out of place), but, one of the combatants, receiving a straight right-hander with the glove between his eyes, did exactly what the large dark creature in the Morgue had seemed going to do – and finished me for that night.

There was rather a sickly smell (not at all an unusual fragrance in Paris) in the little ante-room of my apartment at the hotel. The large dark creature in the Morgue was by no direct experience associated with my sense of smell, because, when I came to the knowledge of him, he lay behind a wall of thick plate-glass, as good as a wall of steel or marble for that matter. Yet the whiff of the room never failed to reproduce him. What was more curious was the capriciousness with which his portrait seemed to light itself up in my mind, elsewhere; I might be walking in the Palais Royal, lazily enjoying the shop windows,[18] and might be regaling myself with one of the ready-made clothes shops that are set out there. My eyes, wandering over impossible-waisted dressing-gowns and luminous waistcoats, would fall upon the master, or the shopman, or even the very dummy at the door, and would suggest to me, "Something like him!" – and instantly I was sickened again.

This would happen at the theatre, in the same manner. Often, it would happen in the street, when I was certainly not looking for the likeness, and when probably there was no likeness there. It was not because the creature was dead that I was so haunted, because I know that I have been (and I know it because I have been) equally attended by the image of a living aversion. This lasted about a week.

The picture did not fade by degrees, in the sense that it became a whit less forcible and distinct, but in the sense that it obtruded itself less and less frequently. The experience may be worth considering by some who have the care of children. It would be difficult to overstate the intensity and accuracy of an intelligent child's observation. At that impressible time of life, it must sometimes produce a fixed impression. If the fixed impression be of an object terrible to the child, it will be (for want of reasoning upon) inseparable from great fear. Force the child at such a time, be Spartan with it, send it into the dark against its will, leave it in a lonely bedroom against its will, and you had better murder it.

On a bright morning I rattled away from Paris, in the German chariot, and left the large dark creature behind me for good. I ought to confess, though, that I had been drawn back to the Morgue, after he was put under ground, to look at his clothes, and that I found them frightfully like him – particularly his boots. However, I rattled away for Switzerland, looking forward and not backward, and so we parted company.

Welcome again, the long long spell of France, with the queer country inns, full of vases of flowers and clocks, in the dull little towns, and with the little population not at all dull on the little Boulevard in the evening, under the little trees! Welcome Monsieur the Curé walking alone in the early morning a short way out of the town, reading that eternal Breviary of yours, which surely might be almost read, without book, by this time? Welcome Monsieur the Curé, later in the day, jolting through the highway dust (as if you had already ascended to the cloudy region), in a very big-headed cabriolet, with the dried mud of a dozen winters on it. Welcome again Monsieur the Curé, as we exchange salutations: you, straightening your back to look at the German chariot, while picking in your little village garden a vegetable or two for the day's soup; I, looking out of the German chariot window in that delicious traveller's-trance which knows no cares, no yesterdays, no tomorrows, nothing but the passing objects and the passing scents and sounds! And so I came, in due course of delight, to Strasbourg, where I passed a wet Sunday evening at a window, while an idle trifle of a vaudeville was played for me at the opposite house.

How such a large house came to have only three people living in it, was its own affair. There were at least a score of windows in its high roof alone; how many in its grotesque front, I soon gave up counting. The owner was a shopkeeper, by name Straudenheim; by trade – I couldn't make out what by trade, for he had forborne to write that up, and his shop was shut.

At first, as I looked at Straudenheim's through the steadily falling rain, I set him up in business in the goose-liver line.[19] But, inspection of Straudenheim, who became visible at a window on the second floor, convinced me that there was something more precious than liver in the case. He wore a black velvet skull-cap, and looked usurious and rich. A large-lipped, pear-nosed old man, with white hair, and keen eyes, though near-sighted. He was writing at a desk, was Straudenheim, and ever and again left off writing, put his pen in his mouth, and went through actions with his right hand, like a man steadying piles of cash. Five-franc pieces, Straudenheim, or golden Napoleons? A jeweller, Straudenheim, a dealer in money, a diamond merchant, or what?

Below Straudenheim, at a window on the first floor, sat his housekeeper – far from young, but of a comely presence, suggestive of a well-matured foot and ankle. She was cheerily dressed, had a fan in her hand, and wore large gold earrings and a large gold cross. She would have been out holiday-making (as I settled it) but for the pestilent rain. Strasbourg had given up holiday-making for that once, as a bad job, because the rain was jerking in gushes out of the old roof-spouts, and running in a brook down the middle of the street. The housekeeper, her arms folded on her bosom and her fan tapping her chin, was bright and smiling at her open window, but otherwise Straudenheim's house front was very dreary. The housekeeper's was the only open window in it; Straudenheim kept himself close, though it was a sultry evening when air is pleasant, and though the rain had brought into the town that vague refreshing smell of grass which rain does bring in the summer-time.

The dim appearance of a man at Straudenheim's shoulder, inspired me with a misgiving that somebody had come to murder that flourishing merchant for the wealth with which I had handsomely endowed him: the rather, as it was an excited man, lean and long of figure, and evidently stealthy of foot. But, he conferred with Straudenheim instead of doing him a mortal injury, and then they both softly opened the other window of that room – which was immediately over the housekeeper's – and tried to see her by looking down. And my opinion of Straudenheim was much lowered when I saw that eminent citizen spit out of window, clearly with the hope of spitting on the housekeeper.

The unconscious housekeeper fanned herself, tossed her head, and laughed. Though unconscious of Straudenheim, she was conscious of somebody else – of me? – there was nobody else.

After leaning so far out of window, that I confidently expected to see their heels tilt up, Straudenheim and the lean man drew their heads in and shut the window. Presently, the house door secretly opened, and they slowly and spitefully crept forth into the pouring rain. They were coming over to me (I thought) to demand satisfaction for my looking at the housekeeper, when they plunged into a recess in the architecture under my window and dragged out the puniest of little soldiers begirt with the most innocent of little swords.[20] The tall glazed head-dress of this warrior, Straudenheim instantly knocked off, and out of it fell two sugar-sticks, and three or four large lumps of sugar.

The warrior made no effort to recover his property or to pick up his shako,[21] but looked with an expression of attention at Straudenheim when he kicked him five times, and also at the lean man when *he* kicked him five times, and again at Straudenheim when he tore the breast of his (the warrior's) little coat open, and shook all his ten fingers in his face, as if they were ten thousand. When these outrages had been committed, Straudenheim and his man went into the house again and barred the door. A wonderful circumstance was, that the housekeeper who saw it all (and who could have taken six such warriors to her buxom bosom at once), only fanned herself and laughed as she had laughed before, and seemed to have no opinion about it, one way or other.

But, the chief effect of the drama was the remarkable vengeance taken by the little warrior. Left alone in the rain, he picked up his shako; put it on, all wet and dirty as it was; retired into a court, of which Straudenheim's house formed the corner; wheeled about; and bringing his two forefingers close to the top of his nose, rubbed them over one another, crosswise, in derision, defiance, and contempt of Straudenheim. Although Straudenheim could not possibly be supposed to be conscious of this strange proceeding, it so inflated and comforted the little warrior's soul, that twice he went away, and twice came back into the court to repeat it, as though it must goad his enemy to madness. Not only that, but he afterwards came back with two other small warriors, and they all three did it together. Not only that – as I live to tell the tale! – but just as it was falling quite dark, the three came back, bringing with them a huge, bearded Sapper, whom they moved, by recital of the original wrong, to go through the same performance, with the same complete absence of all possible knowledge of it on the part of Straudenheim. And then they all went away, arm in arm, singing.

I went away, too, in the German chariot, at sunrise, and rattled on, day after day, like one in a sweet dream; with so many clear little bells on the harness of the horses, that the nursery rhyme about Banbury Cross and the venerable lady who rode in state there, was always in my ears.[22] And now I came to the land of wooden houses, innocent cakes, thin butter soup, and spotless little inn bedrooms with a family likeness to Dairies. And now the Swiss marksmen were for ever rifle-shooting at marks across gorges,[23] so exceedingly near my ear, that I felt like a new Gesler in a Canton of Tells, and went in highly-deserved danger of my tyrannical life.[24] The prizes at these shootings, were watches, smart handkerchiefs, hats, spoons, and (above all) tea-trays; and at these contests I came upon a more than usually accomplished and amiable countryman of my own,[25] who had shot himself deaf in whole years of competition, and had won so many tea-trays that he went about the country with his carriage full of them, like a glorified Cheap-Jack.[26]

In the mountain country into which I had now travelled, a yoke of oxen were sometimes hooked on before the post-horses, and I went lumbering up, up, up, through mist and rain, with the roar of falling water for change of music. Of a sudden, mist and rain would clear away, and I would come down into picturesque little towns with gleaming spires and odd towers; and would stroll afoot into market-places in steep winding streets, where a hundred women in bodices, sold eggs and honey, butter and fruit, and suckled their children as they sat by their clean baskets, and had such enormous goitres (or glandular swellings in the throat) that it became a science to know where the nurse ended and the child began. About this time, I deserted my German chariot for the back of a mule (in colour and consistency so very like a dusty old hair trunk[27] I once had at school, that I half expected to see my initials in brass-headed nails on his backbone), and went up a thousand rugged ways, and looked down at

a thousand woods of fir and pine, and would on the whole have
preferred my mule's keeping a little nearer to the inside, and not
usually travelling with a hoof or two over the precipice – though much
consoled by explanation that this was to be attributed to his great
sagacity, by reason of his carrying broad loads of wood at other times,
and not being clear but that I myself belonged to that station of life,
and required as much room as they. He brought me safely, in his own
wise way, among the passes of the Alps, and here I enjoyed a dozen
climates a day; being now (like Don Quixote on the back of the
wooden horse[28]) in the region of wind, now in the region of fire, now
in the region of unmelting ice and snow. Here, I passed over
trembling domes of ice, beneath which the cataract was roaring; and
here was received under arches of icicles, of unspeakable beauty; and
here the sweet air was so bracing and so light, that at halting-times I
rolled in the snow when I saw my mule do it, thinking that he must
know best. At this part of the journey we would come, at mid-day,
into half an hour's thaw: when the rough mountain inn would be
found on an island of deep mud in a sea of snow, while the baiting
strings of mules, and carts full of casks and bales, which had been in
an Arctic condition a mile off, would steam again. By such ways and
means, I would come to a cluster of châlets where I had to turn out of
the track to see the waterfall; and then, uttering a howl like a young
giant, on espying a traveller – in other words, something to eat –
coming up the steep, the idiot lying on the wood-pile who sunned
himself and nursed his goitre, would rouse the woman-guide within
the hut, who would stream out hastily, throwing her child over one of
her shoulders and her goitre over the other, as she came along. I slept
at religious houses, and bleak refuges of many kinds, on this journey,
and by the stove at night heard stories of travellers who had perished
within call, in wreaths and drifts of snow. One night the stove within,

and the cold outside, awakened childish associations long forgotten, and I dreamed I was in Russia – the identical serf out of a picture-book I had, before I could read it for myself – and that I was going to be knouted[29] by a noble personage in a fur cap, boots, and earrings, who, I think, must have come out of some melodrama.

Commend me to the beautiful waters among these mountains! Though I was not of their mind: they, being inveterately bent on getting down into the level country, and I ardently desiring to linger where I was. What desperate leaps they took, what dark abysses they plunged into, what rocks they wore away, what echoes they invoked! In one part where I went, they were pressed into the service of carrying wood down, to be burnt next winter, as costly fuel, in Italy. But, their fierce savage nature was not to be easily constrained, and they fought with every limb of the wood; whirling it round and round, stripping its bark away, dashing it against pointed corners, driving it out of the course, and roaring and flying at the peasants who steered it back again from the bank with long stout poles. Alas! concurrent streams of time and water carried *me* down fast, and I came, on an exquisitely clear day, to the Lausanne shore of the Lake of Geneva, where I stood looking at the bright blue water, the flushed white mountains opposite, and the boats at my feet with their furled Mediterranean sails, showing like enormous magnifications of this goose-quill pen that is now in my hand.

—The sky became overcast without any notice; a wind very like the March east wind of England, blew across me; and a voice said, "How do you like it? Will it do?"

I had merely shut myself, for half a minute, in a German travelling chariot that stood for sale in the Carriage Department of the London Pantechnicon.[30] I had a commission to buy it, for a friend who was going abroad; and the look and manner of the chariot, as I tried the cushions and the springs, brought all these hints of travelling remembrance before me.

"It will do very well," said I, rather sorrowfully, as I got out at the other door, and shut the carriage up.

chapter four
HOLIDAYS IN BOULOGNE
("OUR FRENCH WATERING-PLACE")

"Our French Watering-Place" appeared in *Household Words* on 4 November 1854 and was subsequently included in *Reprinted Pieces*, 1858. It takes its title from an earlier article, "Our Watering Place" (*Household Words*, 2 August 1851), in which Dickens paints an affectionate portrait of Broadstairs on the Kent coast where he and his family spent many summers between 1837 and 1851. The two papers sit side by side in *Reprinted Pieces*, with the Broadstairs piece retitled "Our English Watering-Place."

Dickens and his family adopted Boulogne as their summer place of residence for 1853, 1854, and 1856, spending roughly four months there on the first two occasions (mid-June to early and mid-October respectively) and three months in 1856 (early June to early September, when their stay was cut short by a cholera epidemic). The idea of an article on Boulogne was conceived during the first of these stays, with Dickens writing to his Sub-Editor W.H. Wills in July that he was "getting capital materials together for the Autumnal article, our French Watering-Place" (*Pilgrim*, 7, p 113). In the event the piece was not written until the following year, a delay that no doubt enriched the final product as Dickens was then able to distill in it his experience of two long stays in the town.

Before these summer residences, there had been a scouting trip.

In October 1852 Dickens spent a fortnight in Boulogne with his wife Catherine and sister-in-law Georgina Hogarth to, in Forster's words, "try it as a resort for seaside holiday" (*Life*, 7, Chapter 2). His verdict was unequivocal – writing to Forster from Boulogne he extolled its attractions and criticized the snobbish English prejudice against it:

> I never saw a better instance of our countrymen than this place. Because it is accessible it is genteel to say it is of no character, quite English, nothing continental about it and so forth. It is as quaint, picturesque, good a place as I know; the boatmen and fishing-people quite a race apart, and some of their villages as good as the fishing-villages on the Mediterranean. The Haute Ville, with a walk all round it on the ramparts, charming. The country walks, delightful. It is the best mixture of town and country (with sea air into the bargain) I ever saw; everything cheap, everything good; and please God I shall be writing on those said ramparts next July! (*Life*, 7, Chapter 2.)

His conviction that English visitors tended to underestimate the charms of the town may well have been an important factor in Dickens's decision to write something in praise of it. He makes fun of their scant regard in the article itself (see the paragraph beginning "We have an old walled town...") and returns to the point repeatedly in correspondence. Before his departure for Boulogne in 1853, he tells W.J. Clement:

> It is in a country, and is in itself a place, the beauties of which are scarcely known to English people. (*Pilgrim*, 7, p 89.)

Shortly after his arrival in June 1853 he writes to Forster:

> If this were but 300 miles farther off, how the English would rave about it! (*Life*, 7, Chapter 4).

And in a letter to Mrs Watson of August 1853 he comments:

I think if you came to know the place (which I never did
myself until last October, often as I have been through it) you
could be but in one mind about it. (*Pilgrim*, 7, p 134.)

There is an echo of this last remark in the first sentence of "Our
French Watering-Place," in which Dickens refers to his own past
neglect of Boulogne, admitting that it was "once solely known to us
as a town with a very long street, beginning with an abattoir and
ending with a steamboat." Such is the fate of a cross-Channel port.
There was certainly no shortage of visitors, despite competition from
Calais and Dieppe. Murray's *Handbook for Travellers in France*, 1854
and Brunet's *New Guide to Boulogne-sur-Mer and its Environs*, 1862 both
put the annual inflow of passengers at over 100,000, and according to
Histoire de Boulogne-sur-Mer (Lottin, 1983) cross-Channel passengers
travelling via Boulogne increased from 86,000 in 1850 to 153,000 in
1867. But of course many of these visitors were just passing through
and, despite (or because of) its substantial English resident
population, fashion-conscious English travellers regarded Boulogne
as a rather unexciting port of call on their way to more exotic
destinations.

If the celebration of Boulogne, and by extension of French life
generally, in "Our French Watering-Place" is intended as a corrective
to this dismissive tendency, it is also a conscious rebuttal of more
deep-rooted Anglo–French prejudices. In a closing plea for mutual
understanding and respect, Dickens turns the strong English
presence in Boulogne to his advantage:

But, to us, it is not the least pleasant feature of our French
watering-place that a long and constant fusion of the two great
nations there, has taught each to like the other, and to learn
from the other, and to rise superior to the absurd prejudices
that have lingered among the weak and ignorant of both
countries equally.

In demonstration of the absurdity of those prejudices, "Our
French Watering-Place" presents a series of engaging vignettes of

Boulogne and its people – of, for example, the leafy walk around the ramparts of the Haute Ville, the town on market day, the fishing people's quarter, the popularity of sea-bathing and the local fêtes. In particular, there is an extended account of Ferdinand Beaucourt-Mutuel and his two holiday villas, at which the Dickens family stayed, respectively, in 1853 and 1854 (in 1856 they returned to the villa they had rented in 1853). Beaucourt appears in "Our French Watering-Place" under the fictitious name of Monsieur Loyal Devasseur, but there is no doubt that the character is drawn true to the original. Bringing the article to the attention of his friend W.C. Macready, Dickens told him that it included "an exact portrait of our Boulogne landlord" (*Pilgrim*, 7, p 452) and he wrote to Wilkie Collins,

> I am glad you like the portrait of Beaucourt so well. It was very pleasant to do, and I hope it may be of some service to him in the letting of his houses. (*Pilgrim*, 7, p 458.)

In a later comment to Forster, during his 1856 summer in Boulogne, Dickens said of Beaucourt "I never did see such a gentle, kind heart" (*Life*, 7, Chapter 4), words that were to be inscribed on Beaucourt's tomb in the cemetery at Condette, near Boulogne. Perhaps Beaucourt embodied for Dickens what he referred to elsewhere as French "gallantry and spirit" (*Pilgrim*, 7, p 439): in "Our French Watering-Place" he characterizes him as "one of the gentlest hearts that beat in a nation teeming with gentle people."

Beaucourt makes a curious reappearance as a character in the short story "His Boots," 1862 (included in this volume) and, in fact, continued to play a part in Dickens's life in the 1860s. Having sold his villas in Boulogne due to financial difficulties, Beaucourt bought a chalet in the neighboring village of Condette. Dickens stayed there during his later, more secretive travels in northern France and so, very probably, did Ellen Ternan and her mother (see, for example, Ackroyd's *Dickens*, 1990, Chapter 30 and W.J. Carlton's essay "Dickens's forgotten retreat in France," 1966). Janine Watrin fills in many details of Beaucourt's life and presents a careful analysis of the history of his relationship with Dickens in *Du Boulogne à Condette: une histoire d'amitié*, 1992. And for those interested in what may or may not have been the nature of Dickens's relationship with Ellen Ternan, and its French connections, Claire Tomalin's *The Invisible Woman*, 1991 and Peter Ackroyd's *Dickens*, 1990 offer scholarly speculation.

The Établissement des Bains at Boulogne, c 1845

OUR FRENCH WATERING-PLACE

Having earned, by many years of fidelity, the right to be sometimes inconstant to our English watering-place,[1] we have dallied for two or three seasons with a French watering-place: once solely known to us as a town with a very long street, beginning with an abattoir and ending with a steamboat,[2] which it seemed our fate to behold only at daybreak on winter mornings, when (in the days before continental railroads), just sufficiently awake to know that we were most uncomfortably asleep, it was our destiny always to clatter through it, in the coupé of the diligence from Paris,[3] with a sea of mud behind us, and a sea of tumbling waves before. In relation to which latter monster, our mind's eye now recalls a worthy Frenchman in a sealskin cap with a braided hood over it, once our travelling companion in the coupé aforesaid, who, waking up with a pale and crumpled visage, and looking ruefully out at the grim row of breakers enjoying themselves fanatically on an instrument of torture called "the Bar,"[4] inquired of us whether we were ever sick at sea? Both to prepare his mind for the abject creature we were presently to become, and also to afford him consolation, we replied, "Sir, your servant is always sick when it is possible to be so." He returned, altogether uncheered by the bright example, "Ah, Heaven, but I am always sick, even when it is *im*possible to be so."

The means of communication between the French capital and our French watering-place are wholly changed since those days; but, the Channel remains unbridged as yet, and the old floundering and knocking about go on there. It must be confessed that saving in reasonable (and therefore rare) sea-weather, the act of arrival at our French watering-place from England is difficult to be achieved with

Passengers landing at Boulogne from the Folkestone boat, 1858

dignity. Several little circumstances combine to render the visitor an object of humiliation. In the first place, the steamer no sooner touches the port, than all the passengers fall into captivity: being boarded by an overpowering force of Custom-house officers, and marched into a gloomy dungeon. In the second place, the road to this dungeon is fenced off with ropes breast-high, and outside those ropes all the English in the place who have lately been sea-sick and are now well, assemble in their best clothes to enjoy the degradation of their dilapidated fellow-creatures. "Oh, my gracious! How ill this one has been!" "Here's a damp one coming next!" "*Here's* a pale one!" "Oh! Ain't he green in the face, this next one!" Even we ourself (not deficient in natural dignity) have a lively remembrance of staggering up this detested lane one September day in a gale of wind, when we were received like an irresistible comic actor, with a burst of laughter and applause, occasioned by the extreme imbecility of our legs.

We were coming to the third place. In the third place, the captives, being shut up in the gloomy dungeon, are strained, two or three at a time, into an inner cell, to be examined as to passports; and across the doorway of communication, stands a military creature making a bar of his arm. Two ideas are generally present to the British mind during these ceremonies; first, that it is necessary to make for the cell with violent struggles, as if it were a life-boat and the dungeon a ship going down; secondly, that the military creature's arm is a national affront, which the government at home ought instantly to "take up." The British mind and body becoming heated by these fantasies, delirious answers are made to inquiries, and extravagant actions performed. Thus, Johnson persists in giving Johnson as his baptismal name, and substituting for his ancestral designation the national "Dam!" Neither can he by any means be brought to recognise the distinction between a portmanteau-key and a passport, but will obstinately persevere in tendering the one when asked for the other. This brings him to the fourth place, in a state of mere idiotcy; and when he is, in the fourth place, cast out at a little door into a howling wilderness of touters,[5] he becomes a lunatic with wild eyes and floating hair[6] until rescued and soothed. If friendless and unrescued, he is generally put into a railway omnibus and taken to Paris.

But, our French watering-place, when it is once got into, is a very enjoyable place. It has a varied and beautiful country around it, and many characteristic and agreeable things within it. To be sure, it might have fewer bad smells and less decaying refuse, and it might be better drained, and much cleaner in many parts, and therefore infinitely more healthy. Still, it is a bright, airy, pleasant, cheerful town; and if you were to walk down either of its three well-paved main streets, towards five o'clock in the afternoon, when delicate odours of cookery fill the air, and its hotel windows (it is full of hotels) give glimpses of long tables set out for dinner, and made to look sumptuous by the aid of napkins folded fan-wise, you would rightly judge it to be an uncommonly good town to eat and drink in.

We have an old walled town,[7] rich in cool public wells of water, on the top of a hill within and above the present business-town; and if it were some hundreds of miles further from England, instead of being, on a clear day, within sight of the grass growing in the crevices of the chalk-cliffs of Dover, you would long ago have been bored to death about that town. It is more picturesque and quaint than half the innocent places which tourists, following their leader like sheep, have made impostors of. To say nothing of its houses with grave courtyards, its queer by-corners, and its many-windowed streets white and quiet in the sunlight, there is an ancient belfry[8] in it that would have been in all the Annuals and Albums, going and gone, these hundred years, if it had but been more expensive to get at. Happily it has escaped so well, being only our French watering-place, that you may like it of your own accord in a natural manner, without being required to go into convulsions about it. We regard it as one of the later blessings of our life, that BILKINS,[9] the only authority on Taste, never took any notice that we can find out, of our French watering-place. Bilkins never wrote about it, never pointed out anything to be seen in it, never measured anything in it, always left it alone. For which relief, Heaven bless the town and the memory of the immortal Bilkins likewise!

There is a charming walk, arched and shaded by trees, on the old walls that form the four sides of this High Town, whence you get glimpses of the streets below, and changing views of the other town and of the river, and of the hills and of the sea.[10] It is made more agreeable and peculiar by some of the solemn houses that are rooted in the deep streets below, bursting into a fresher existence a-top, and having doors and windows, and even gardens, on these ramparts. A child going in at the courtyard gate of one of these houses, climbing up the many stairs, and coming out at the fourth-floor window, might conceive himself another Jack, alighting on enchanted ground from another bean-stalk. It is a place wonderfully populous in children; English children, with governesses reading novels as they walk down the shady lanes of trees, or nursemaids interchanging gossip on the seats; French children with their smiling bonnes in snow-white caps, and themselves – if little boys – in straw head-gear like bee-hives, work-baskets and church hassocks. Three years ago, there were three weazen old men, one bearing a frayed red ribbon[11] in his threadbare button-hole, always to be found walking together among these children, before dinner-time. If they walked for an appetite, they doubtless lived en pension – were contracted for – otherwise their poverty would have made it a rash action. They were stooping, blear-eyed, dull old men, slip-shod and shabby, in long-skirted short-waisted coats and meagre trousers, and yet with a ghost of gentility hovering in their company. They spoke little to each other, and looked as if they might have been politically discontented if they had had vitality enough. Once, we overheard red-ribbon feebly complain to the other two that somebody, or something, was "a Robber"; and then they all three set their mouths so that they would have ground their teeth if they had had any. The ensuing winter gathered red-ribbon unto the great company of faded ribbons, and next year the remaining two were there – getting themselves entangled with hoops and dolls – familiar mysteries to the children – probably in the eyes of most of them, harmless creatures who had never been like children, and whom children could never be like. Another winter came, and another old man went, and so, this present year, the last of the triumvirate left off walking – it was no good, now – and sat by himself on a little solitary bench, with the hoops and the dolls as lively as ever all about him.

Street in the "Quartier des Pêcheurs", Boulogne, 1858

In the Place d'Armes[12] of this town, a little decayed market is held, which seems to slip through the old gateway, like water, and go rippling down the hill, to mingle with the murmuring market in the lower town, and get lost in its movement and bustle. It is very agreeable on an idle summer morning to pursue this market-stream from the hill-top. It begins dozingly and dully, with a few sacks of corn; starts into a surprising collection of boots and shoes; goes brawling down the hill in a diversified channel of old cordage, old iron, old crockery, old clothes civil and military, old rags, new cotton goods, flaming prints of saints, little looking-glasses, and incalculable lengths of tape; dives into a backway, keeping out of sight for a little while, as streams will, or only sparkling for a moment in the shape of a market drinking-shop; and suddenly reappears behind the great church,[13] shooting itself into a bright confusion of white-capped women and blue-bloused men, poultry, vegetables, fruits, flowers, pots, pans, praying-chairs, soldiers, country butter, umbrellas and other sun-shades, girl-porters waiting to be hired with baskets at their backs, and one weazen little old man in a cocked hat, wearing a cuirass of drinking glasses and carrying on his shoulder a crimson temple fluttering with flags, like a glorified pavior's rammer without the handle, who rings a bell in all parts of the scene, and cries his cooling drink Hola, Hola, Ho-o-o! in a shrill cracked voice that somehow makes itself heard, above all the chaffering and vending hum.[14] Early in the afternoon, the whole course of the stream is dry. The praying-chairs are put back in the church, the umbrellas are folded up, the unsold goods are carried away, the stalls and stands disappear, the square is swept, the hackney coaches lounge there to be hired, and on all the country roads (if you walk about, as much as we do) you will see the peasant women, always neatly and comfortably dressed, riding home, with the pleasantest saddle-furniture of clean milk-pails, bright butter-kegs, and the like, on the jolliest little donkeys in the world.

We have another market in our French watering-place – that is to say, a few wooden hutches in the open street, down by the Port – devoted to fish. Our fishing-boats are famous everywhere; and our fishing people, though they love lively colours and taste is neutral (see Bilkins), are among the most picturesque people we ever encountered.[15] They have not only a Quarter of their own in the town itself, but they occupy whole villages of their own on the neighbouring cliffs. Their churches and chapels are their own; they consort with one another, they intermarry among themselves, their customs are their own, and their costume is their own and never changes. As soon as one of their boys can walk, he is provided with a long bright red nightcap; and one of their men would as soon as think of going afloat without his head, as without that indispensable appendage to it. Then, they wear the noblest boots, with the hugest tops – flapping and bulging over anyhow; above which, they encase themselves in such wonderful overalls and petticoat trousers, made to all appearance of tarry old sails, so additionally stiffened with pitch and salt, that the wearers have a walk of their own, and go straddling and swinging about, among the boats and barrels and nets and rigging, a sight to see. Then, their younger women, by dint of going down to the sea barefoot, to fling their baskets into the boats as they come in with the tide, and bespeak the first fruits of the haul with propitiatory promises to love and marry that dear fisherman who shall fill that basket like an Angel, have the finest legs ever carved by Nature in the brightest mahogany, and they walk like Juno.[16] Their eyes, too, are so lustrous that their long gold ear-rings turn dull beside those brilliant neighbours; and when they are dressed, what with these beauties, and their fine fresh faces, and their many petticoats – striped petticoats, red petticoats, blue petticoats, always clean and smart, and never too long – and their home-made stockings, mulberry-coloured, blue, brown, purple, lilac – which the older women, taking care of the Dutch-looking children, sit in all sorts of places knitting, knitting, knitting, from morning to night – and what with their little saucy bright blue jackets, knitted too, and fitting close to their handsome figures; and what with the natural grace with which they wear the commonest cap, or fold the commonest handkerchief round their luxuriant hair – we say, in a word and out of breath, that taking all these premises into our consideration, it has never been a matter of the least surprise to us that we have never once met, in the cornfields, on the dusty roads, by the breezy windmills, on the plots of short sweet grass overhanging the sea – anywhere – a young fisherman and fisherwoman of our French watering-place together, but the arm of that fisherman has invariably been, as a matter of course and without any absurd attempt to disguise so plain a necessity, round the neck or waist of that fisherwoman. And we have had no doubt whatever, standing looking at their uphill streets, house rising above house, and terrace above terrace, and bright garments here and there lying sunning on rough stone parapets, that the pleasant mist on all such objects, caused by their being seen through the brown nets hung across on poles to dry, is, in the eyes of every true young fisherman, a mist of love and beauty, setting off the goddess of his heart.

Moreover, it is to be observed that these are an industrious people, and a domestic people, and an honest people. And though we are aware that at the bidding of Bilkins it is our duty to fall down and worship the Neapolitans, we make bold very much to prefer the fishing people of our French watering-place – especially since our last visit to Naples within these twelvemonths, when we found only four conditions of men remaining in the whole city: to wit, lazzaroni,[17] priests, spies, and soldiers, and all of them beggars; the paternal government having banished all its subjects except the rascals.[18]

But we can never henceforth separate our French watering-place from our own landlord of two summers, M. Loyal Devasseur,[19] citizen and town-councillor. Permit us to have the pleasure of presenting M. Loyal Devasseur.

His own family name is simply Loyal; but, as he is married, and as in that part of France a husband always adds to his own name the family name of his wife, he writes himself Loyal Devasseur. He owns a compact little estate of some twenty or thirty acres on a lofty hill-side, and on it he has built two country houses which he lets furnished. They are by many degrees the best houses that are so let near our French watering-place; we have had the honour of living in both, and can testify. The entrance-hall of the first we inhabited,[20] was ornamented with a plan of the estate, representing it as about twice the size of Ireland; insomuch that when we were yet new to the Property (M. Loyal always speaks of it as "la propriété") we went three miles straight on end, in search of the bridge of Austerlitz[21] – which we afterwards found to be immediately outside the window. The Chateau of the Old Guard,[22] in another part of the grounds, and, according to the plan, about two leagues from the little dining room, we sought in vain for a week, until, happening

one evening to sit upon a bench in the forest (forest in the plan), a
few yards from the house-door, we observed at our feet, in the
ignominious circumstances of being upside down and greenly
rotten, the Old Guard himself: that is to say, the painted effigy of a
member of that distinguished corps, seven feet high, and in the act
of carrying arms, who had had the misfortune to be blown down in
the previous winter. It will be perceived that M. Loyal is a staunch
admirer of the great Napoleon. He is an old soldier himself – captain
of the National Guard,[23] with a handsome gold vase on his chimney-
piece, presented to him by his company – and his respect for the
memory of the illustrious general is enthusiastic. Medallions of him,
portraits of him, busts of him, pictures of him, are thickly sprinkled
all over the property. During the first month of our occupation, it
was our affliction to be constantly knocking down Napoleon: if we
touched a shelf in a dark corner, he toppled over with a crash; and
every door we opened, shook him to the soul. Yet M. Loyal is not a
man of mere castles in the air, or, as he would say, in Spain.[24] He has
a specially practical, contriving, clever, skilful eye and hand. His
houses are delightful. He unites French elegance and English
comfort, in a happy manner quite his own. He has an extraordinary
genius for making tasteful little bedrooms in angles of his roofs,
which an Englishman would as soon think of turning to any account,
as he would think of cultivating the Desert. We have ourself
reposed deliciously, in an elegant chamber of M. Loyal's
construction, with our head as nearly in the kitchen chimney-pot as
we can conceive it likely for the head of any gentleman, not by
profession a Sweep, to be. And, into whatsoever strange nook M.
Loyal's genius penetrates, it, in that nook, infallibly constructs a
cupboard and a row of pegs. In either of our houses, we could have
put away the knapsacks and hung up the hats of the whole regiment
of Guides.

Aforetime, M. Loyal was a tradesman in the town.[25] You can
transact business with no present tradesman in the town, and give
your card "chez M. Loyal," but a brighter face shines upon you
directly. We doubt if there ever is, ever was, or ever will be, a man so
universally pleasant in the minds of people as M. Loyal is in the
minds of the citizens of our French watering-place. They rub their
hands and laugh when they speak of him. Ah, but he is such a good
child, such a brave boy, such a generous spirit, that M. Loyal! It is the
honest truth. M. Loyal's nature is the nature of a gentleman. He
cultivates his ground with his own hands (assisted by one little
labourer, who falls into a fit now and then); and he digs and delves
from morn to eve in prodigious perspirations – "works always," as he
says – but, cover him with dust, mud, weeds, water, any stains you
will, you never can cover the gentleman in M. Loyal. A portly,
upright, broad-shouldered, brown-faced man, whose soldierly bearing
gives him the appearance of being taller than he is, look into the
bright eye of M. Loyal, standing before you in his working blouse and
cap, not particularly well shaved, and, it may be, very earthy, and you
shall discern in M. Loyal a gentleman whose true politeness is in
grain, and confirmation of whose word by his bond you would blush
to think of. Not without reason is M. Loyal when he tells that story,
in his own vivacious way, of his travelling to Fulham,[26] near London,
to buy all these hundreds and hundreds of trees you now see upon
the Property, then a bare, bleak hill; and of his sojourning in Fulham
three months; and of his jovial evenings with the market-gardeners;
and of the crowning banquet before his departure, when the market-
gardeners rose as one man, clinked their glasses all together (as the
custom at Fulham is), and cried, "Vive Loyal!"

M. Loyal has an agreeable wife, but no family; and he loves to
drill the children of his tenants, or run races with them, or do anything
with them, or for them, that is good-natured. He is of a highly

convivial temperament, and his hospitality is unbounded. Billet a soldier on him, and he is delighted. Five-and-thirty soldiers had M. Loyal billeted on him this present summer,[27] and they all got fat and red-faced in two days. It became a legend among the troops that whosoever got billeted on M. Loyal, rolled in clover; and so it fell out that the fortunate man who drew the billet "M. Loyal Devasseur" always leaped into the air, though in heavy marching order. M. Loyal cannot bear to admit anything that might seem by implication to disparage the military profession. We hinted to him once, that we were conscious of a remote doubt arising in our mind, whether a sou a day for pocket-money, tobacco, stockings, drink, washing, and social pleasures in general, left a very large margin for a soldier's enjoyment. Pardon! said Monsieur Loyal, rather wincing. It was not a fortune, but – à la bonne heure – it was better than it used to be! What, we asked him on another occasion, were all those neighbouring peasants, each living with his family in one room, and each having a soldier (perhaps two) billeted on him every other night, required to provide for those soldiers? "Faith!" said M. Loyal, reluctantly; "a bed, monsieur, and fire to cook with, and a candle. And they share their supper with those soldiers. It is not possible that they could eat alone." – "And what allowance do they get for this?" said we. M. Loyal drew himself up taller, took a step back, laid his hand upon his breast, and said, with majesty, as speaking for himself and all France, "Monsieur, it is a contribution to the State!"

It is never going to rain, according to M. Loyal. When it is impossible to deny that it is now raining in torrents, he says it will be fine – charming – magnificent – tomorrow. It is never hot on the Property, he contends. Likewise it is never cold. The flowers, he says, come out, delighting to grow there; it is like Paradise this morning; it is like the Garden of Eden. He is a little fanciful in his language: smilingly observing of Madame Loyal, when she is absent at vespers, that she is "gone to her salvation" – allée à son salut. He has a great enjoyment of tobacco, but nothing would induce him to continue smoking face to face with a lady. His short black pipe immediately goes into his breast pocket, scorches his blouse, and nearly sets him on fire. In the Town Council and on occasions of ceremony, he appears in a full suit of black, with a waistcoat of magnificent breadth across the chest, and a shirt-collar of fabulous proportions.[28] Good M. Loyal! Under blouse or waistcoat, he carries one of the gentlest hearts that beat in a nation teeming with gentle people. He has had losses, and has been at his best under them. Not only the loss of his way by night in the Fulham times – when a bad subject of an Englishman, under pretence of seeing him home, took him into all the night public-houses, drank "arfanarf"[29] in every one at his expense, and finally fled, leaving him shipwrecked at Cleefeeway, which we apprehend to be Ratcliffe Highway[30] – but heavier losses than that. Long ago, a family of children and a mother were left in one of his houses, without money, a whole year. M. Loyal – anything but as rich as we wish he had been – had not the heart to say "you must go;" so they stayed on and stayed on, and paying-tenants who would have come in couldn't come in, and at last they managed to get helped home across the water, and M. Loyal kissed the whole group, and said "Adieu, my poor infants!" and sat down in their deserted salon and smoked his pipe of peace. – "The rent, M. Loyal?" "Eh! well! The rent!" M. Loyal shakes his head. "Le bon Dieu," says M. Loyal presently, "will recompense me," and he laughs and smokes his pipe of peace. May he smoke it on the Property, and not be recompensed, these fifty years!

There are public amusements in our French watering-place, or it would not be French. They are very popular, and very cheap. The sea-bathing – which may rank as the most favoured daylight entertainment, inasmuch as the French visitors bathe all day long, and seldom appear to think of remaining less than an hour at a time in the water – is astoundingly cheap. Omnibuses convey you, if you please, from a convenient part of the town to the beach and back again; you have a clean and comfortable bathing-machine,[31] dress, linen, and all appliances; and the charge for the whole is half-a-franc, or fivepence. On the pier, there is usually a guitar, which seems presumptuously enough to set its tinkling against the deep hoarseness of the sea, and there is always some boy or woman who sings, without any voice, little songs without any tune: the strain we have most frequently heard being an appeal to "the sportsman" not to bag that choicest of game, the swallow. For bathing purposes, we have also a subscription establishment with an esplanade,[32] where people lounge about with telescopes, and seem to get a good deal of weariness for their money; and we have also an association of individual machine-proprietors combined against this formidable rival. M. Féroce,[33] our own particular friend in the bathing line, is one of these. How he ever came by his name, we cannot imagine. He is as gentle and polite a man as M. Loyal Devasseur himself; immensely stout withal, and of a beaming aspect. M. Féroce has saved so many people from drowning, and has been decorated with so many medals in consequence, that his stoutness seems a special dispensation of Providence to enable him to wear them; if his girth were the girth of an ordinary man, he could never hang them on, all at once. It is only on very great occasions that M. Féroce displays his shining honours. At other times they lie by, with rolls of manuscript testifying to the causes of their presentation, in a huge glass case in the red-sofa'd salon of his private residence on the beach, where M. Féroce also keeps his family pictures, his portraits of himself as he appears both in bathing life and in private life, his little boats that rock by clockwork, and his other ornamental possessions.

Then, we have a commodious and gay Theatre – or had, for it is burned down now[34] – where the opera was always preceded by a vaudeville,[35] in which (as usual) everybody, down to the little old man with the large hat and the little cane and tassel, who always played either my Uncle or my Papa, suddenly broke out of the dialogue into the mildest vocal snatches, to the great perplexity of unaccustomed strangers from Great Britain, who never could make out when they were singing and when they were talking – and indeed it was pretty much the same. But, the caterers in the way of entertainment to whom we are most beholden, are the Society of Welldoing,[36] who are active all the summer, and give the proceeds of their good works to the poor. Some of the most agreeable fêtes they contrive, are announced as "Dedicated to the children;" and the taste with which they turn a small public enclosure into an elegant garden beautifully illuminated; and the thorough-going heartiness and energy with which they personally direct the childish pleasures; are supremely delightful. For fivepence a head, we have on these occasions donkey races with English "Jokeis," and other rustic sports; lotteries for toys; roundabouts, dancing on the grass to the music of an admirable band, fire-balloons, and fireworks. Further, almost every week all through the summer – never mind, now, on what day of the week[37] – there is a fête in some adjoining village (called in that part of the country a Ducasse[38]), where the people – really *the people* – dance on the green turf in the open air, round a little orchestra, that seems itself to dance, there is such an airy motion of flags and streamers all about it. And we do not suppose that between the Torrid Zone and the North Pole there are to be found male dancers with such astonishingly loose legs, furnished with so many joints in wrong places, utterly unknown to Professor Owen,[39] as those who here disport themselves. Sometimes, the fête appertains to a particular trade; you will see among the cheerful young women at the joint Ducasse of the milliners and tailors, a wholesome knowledge of the art of making common and cheap things uncommon and pretty, by good sense and good taste, that is a practical lesson to any rank of society in a whole island we could mention. The oddest feature of these agreeable scenes is the everlasting Roundabout (we preserve an English word wherever we can, as we are writing the English language), on the wooden horses of which machine grown-up people of all ages are wound round and round with the utmost solemnity, while the proprietor's wife grinds an organ, capable of only one tune, in the centre.

As to the boarding-houses of our French watering-place, they are Legion, and would require a distinct treatise. It is not without a sentiment of national pride that we believe them to contain more bores from the shores of Albion than all the clubs in London.[40] As you walk timidly in their neighbourhood, the very neckcloths and hats of your elderly compatriots cry to you from the stones of the streets, "We are Bores – avoid us!" We have never overheard at street corners such lunatic scraps of political and social discussion as among these dear countrymen of ours. They believe everything that is impossible and nothing that is true. They carry rumours, and ask questions, and make corrections and improvements on one another, staggering to the human intellect. And they are for ever rushing into the English library,[41] propounding such incomprehensible paradoxes to the fair mistress of that establishment, that we beg to recommend her to her Majesty's gracious consideration as a fit object for a pension.

The English form a considerable part of the population of our French watering-place, and are deservedly addressed and respected in many ways. Some of the surface-addresses to them are odd enough, as when a laundress puts a placard outside her house announcing her possession of that curious British instrument, a "Mingle;" or when a tavern-keeper provides accommodation for the celebrated English game of "Nokemdon."[42] But, to us, it is not the least pleasant feature of our French watering-place that a long and constant fusion of the two great nations there, has taught each to like the other, and to learn from the other, and to rise superior to the absurd prejudices that have lingered among the weak and ignorant of both countries equally.

Drumming and trumpeting of course go on for ever in our French watering-place. Flag-flying is at a premium too; but, we cheerfully avow that we consider a flag a very pretty object, and that we take such outward signs of innocent liveliness to our heart of hearts. The people, in the town and in the country, are a busy people who work hard; they are sober, temperate, good-humoured, light-hearted, and generally remarkable for their engaging manners. Few just men, not immoderately bilious, could see them in their recreations without very much respecting the character that is so easily, so harmlessly, and so simply, pleased.

chapter five

GOING NORTH: COUNTRY WAYS, TRAVELLING PLAYERS, FUN AT THE FAIR

("IN THE FRENCH-FLEMISH COUNTRY")

"In the French-Flemish Country" was published in *All the Year Round* on 12 September 1863 as part of the second series of "Uncommercial Traveller" papers (see p 17). Seeking better acquaintance with a region he has often passed through, and tempted by a playbill and the prospect of a fair, the Uncommercial Traveller decides to stay in a small town in French Flanders, or the Département du Nord.

The town is not named and there are no clues to its identity (see further page 348, note 6). The reason for this is unclear. One possible explanation is that Dickens was protecting his privacy. He crossed the Channel frequently in the early 1860s – sometimes, it is now thought, accompanied by or to visit Ellen Ternan (see, for example, Tomalin, 1991, Chapter 9). Whether for this or some other reason, there is a recurrent vagueness in his correspondence from this period about his precise whereabouts. It may be that the town in "In the French-Flemish Country" owes its anonymity to this strategy of secrecy. Alternatively, perhaps Dickens simply wanted to portray a typical French-Flemish town and avoided naming it in order to generalize his description – or then again the town may be a composite, constructed from observations and experiences of several places in the region.

It seems, in any case, that an article on French Flanders was in Dickens's mind at least a year before "In the French-Flemish Country" was published. On 17 October 1862, writing from Hazebrouck, he told W.H. Wills that he was going to take advantage of some spare time to "have a look at Dunquerque – in the Uncommercial interest" (*Pilgrim*, 10, p 147). Slater and Drew (2000, pp xvii–xviii) suggest that Dickens may have sometimes referred to the "Uncommercial interest" in correspondence "as a coded periphrasis for visits of a more private nature – perhaps to Ellen Ternan." However, it seems reasonable to take his statement about Dunquerque at face value, regardless of whether there was an additional motive for the trip. It was not unknown for Dickens to take some time to bring an article from conception to fruition – "Our French Watering-Place," for example, appeared some 15 months after he first mentioned the notion of the article in correspondence (see p 55). Besides, as he was visiting or passing through northern France regularly it is likely to have occurred to him that it would make a fitting subject for the Uncommercial Traveller series.

If Dickens was planning an article on French Flanders as early as autumn 1862, the closing section of "The Calais Night Mail," published in May 1863, seems to have been a stage in its development. The brief portrait in that article of the countryside of the Nord and the subsequent recollection of a fair at Hazebrouck (see pp 31–32) prefigure the structure of "In the French-Flemish Country," which begins with an extended description of the rural landscape and then zooms in on the town with detailed accounts of a performance by a group of lowly travelling players and the amusements of a fair.

On 28 July 1863, Dickens wrote to his friend W.C. Macready that on 17 August he was "probably going away on an 'Uncommercial' trip that will occupy ten days or a fortnight" (*Pilgrim*, 10, p 276). On 9 August he told Wilkie Collins, "I have not been anywhere for ever and ever so long, but am thinking of evaporating for a fortnight on the

18th" (*Pilgrim*, 10, p 280). And on 31 August he wrote to Frederic Ouvry that he had "just come back from a fortnight's travelling abroad" (*Pilgrim*, 10, p 283). This must have been the trip on which Dickens finally fleshed out the article: it appeared in *All the Year Round* a couple of weeks after his return and the August visit is consistent with the season evoked in the text, with the wasps seeming "to have taken military possession of the town."

In a tone of unalloyed affection, "In the French-Flemish Country" articulates Dickens's admiration of the French ability to engage enthusiastically with life, making much out of little and finding real pleasure in cheap and accessible amusements – a theme to which he returns repeatedly in his writings on France. Here, the sparsely populated countryside is well cultivated; the hard-pressed farmers keep abundant and healthy livestock; the audience at the cheap and comically predictable theatrical performance could not be "more attentive or better behaved"; the ball after the fair is one "of great good humour and enjoyment" despite the poverty of the dancers; and the depressed young conscripts on their way to a military training camp find relief and hilarity in the antics of a performing dog.

Inside a weaver's cottage in the Département du Nord, 1866

IN THE FRENCH-FLEMISH COUNTRY

"It is neither a bold nor a diversified country," said I to myself, "this country which is three-quarters Flemish, and a quarter French; yet it has its attractions too. Though great lines of railway traverse it, the trains leave it behind, and go puffing off to Paris and the South, to Belgium and Germany, to the Northern Sea-Coast of France, and to England, and merely smoke it a little in passing. Then I don't know it, and that is a good reason for being here; and I can't pronounce half the long queer names I see inscribed over the shops, and that is another good reason for being here, since I surely ought to learn how." In short, I was "here," and I wanted an excuse for not going away from here, and I made it to my satisfaction, and stayed here.

What part in my decision was borne by Monsieur P. Salcy, is of no moment, though I own to encountering that gentleman's name on a red bill on the wall, before I made up my mind. Monsieur P. Salcy, "par permission de M. le Maire," had established his theatre in the whitewashed Hôtel de Ville, on the steps of which illustrious edifice I stood. And Monsieur P. Salcy, privileged director of such theatre, situate in "the first theatrical arrondissement of the department of the North,"[1] invited French-Flemish mankind to come and partake of the intellectual banquet provided by his family of dramatic artists, fifteen subjects in number. "La Famille P. SALCY, composée d'artistes dramatiques, au nombre de 15 sujets."

Neither a bold nor a diversified country, I say again, and withal an untidy country, but pleasant enough to ride in, when the paved roads over the flats and through the hollows, are not too deep in black mud. A country so sparely inhabited, that I wonder where the peasants who till and sow and reap the ground, can possibly dwell, and also by what invisible balloons they are conveyed from their distant homes into the fields at sunrise and back again at sunset. The occasional few poor cottages and farms in this region, surely cannot afford shelter to the numbers necessary to the cultivation, albeit the work is done so very deliberately, that on one long harvest day I have seen, in twelve miles, about twice as many men and women (all told) reaping and binding. Yet I have seen more cattle, more sheep, more pigs, and all in better case, than where there is purer French spoken, and also better ricks – round swelling peg-top ricks, well thatched: not a shapeless brown heap, like the toast out of a Giant's toast-and-water, pinned to the earth with one of the skewers out of his kitchen. A good custom they have about here, likewise, of prolonging the sloping tiled roof of farm or cottage, so that it overhangs three or four feet, carrying off the wet, and making a good drying place wherein to hang up herbs, or implements, or what not. A better custom than the popular one of keeping the refuse-heap and puddle close before the house door: which, although I paint my dwelling never so brightly blue (and it cannot be too blue for me, hereabouts), will bring fever inside my door. Wonderful poultry of the French-Flemish country, why take the trouble to *be* poultry? Why not stop short at eggs in the rising generation, and die out and have done with it? Parents of chickens have I seen this day, followed by their wretched young families, scratching nothing out of the mud with an air – tottering about on legs so scraggy and weak, that the valiant word drumsticks becomes a mockery when applied to them, and the crow of the lord and master has been a mere dejected case of croup. Carts have I seen, and other agricultural instruments, unwieldy, dislocated, monstrous. Poplar-trees by the thousand fringe the fields and fringe the end of the flat landscape, so that I feel, looking straight on before me, as if, when I pass the extremest fringe on the low horizon, I shall tumble over into space. Little whitewashed black holes of chapels, with barred doors and Flemish inscriptions, abound at roadside corners, and often they are garnished with a sheaf of wooden crosses, like children's swords; or, in their default, some hollow old tree with a saint roosting in it, is similarly decorated, or a pole with a very diminutive saint enshrined aloft in a sort of sacred pigeon-house. Not that we are deficient in such decoration in the town here, for, over at the church yonder, outside the building, is a scenic representation of the Crucifixion, built up with old bricks and stones, and made out with painted canvas and wooden figures: the whole surmounting the dusty skull of some holy personage (perhaps), shut up behind a little ashy iron grate, as if it were originally put there to be cooked, and the fire had long gone out. A windmilly country this, though the windmills are so damp and rickety, that they nearly knock themselves off their legs at every turn of their sails, and creak in loud complaint. A weaving country, too, for in the wayside cottages the loom goes wearily – rattle and click, rattle and click – and, looking in, I see the poor weaving peasant, man or woman, bending at the work, while the child, working too, turns a little handwheel put upon the ground to suit its height. An unconscionable monster, the loom in a small dwelling, asserting himself ungenerously as the bread-winner, straddling over the children's straw beds, cramping the family in space and air, and making himself generally objectionable and tyrannical. He is tributary, too, to ugly mills and factories and bleaching-grounds, rising out of the sluiced fields in an abrupt bare way, disdaining, like himself, to be ornamental or accommodating. Surrounded by these things, here I stood on the steps of the Hôtel de Ville, persuaded to remain by the P. Salcy family, fifteen dramatic subjects strong.

There was a Fair besides. The double persuasion being irresistible, and my sponge being left behind at the last Hotel, I made the tour of the little town to buy another. In the small sunny shops – mercers, opticians, and druggist-grocers, with here and there an emporium of religious images – the gravest of old spectacled Flemish husbands and wives sat contemplating one another across bare counters, while the wasps, who seemed to have taken military possession of the town, and to have placed it under wasp-martial law, executed warlike manoeuvres in the windows. Other shops the wasps had entirely to themselves, and nobody cared and nobody came when I beat with a five-franc piece upon the board of custom. What I sought was no more to be found than if I had sought a nugget of Californian gold: so I went, spongeless, to pass the evening with the Family P. Salcy.

The members of the Family P. Salcy were so fat and so like one another – fathers, mothers, sisters, brothers, uncles, and aunts – that I think the local audience were much confused about the plot of the piece under representation, and to the last expected that everybody must turn out to be the long-lost relative of everybody else. The Theatre was established on the top story of the Hôtel de Ville, and was approached by a long bare staircase, whereon, in an airy situation, one of the P. Salcy Family – a stout gentleman, imperfectly repressed by a belt – took the money. This occasioned the greatest excitement of the evening; for, no sooner did the curtain rise on the introductory Vaudeville,[2] and reveal in the person of the young lover (singing a very short song with his eyebrows) apparently the very same identical stout gentleman imperfectly repressed by a belt, than everybody rushed out to the paying-place, to ascertain whether he could possibly have put on that dress-coat, that clear complexion, and those arched black vocal eyebrows, in so short a space of time. It then became manifest that this was another stout gentleman imperfectly repressed by a belt: to whom, before the spectators had recovered their presence of mind, entered a third stout gentleman imperfectly repressed by a belt, exactly like him. These two "subjects," making with the money-taker three of the announced fifteen, fell into conversation touching a charming young widow: who, presently appearing, proved to be a stout lady altogether irrepressible by any means – quite a parallel case to the American Negro[3] – fourth of the fifteen subjects, and sister of the fifth who presided over the check-department.[4] In good time the whole of the fifteen subjects were dramatically presented, and we had the inevitable Ma Mère, Ma Mère! And also the inevitable malédiction d'un père, and likewise the inevitable Marquis, and also the inevitable provincial young man, weak-minded but faithful, who followed Julie to Paris, and cried and laughed and choked all at once. The story was wrought out with the help of a virtuous spinning-wheel in the beginning, a vicious set of diamonds in the middle, and a rheumatic blessing (which arrived by post) from Ma Mère towards the end; the whole resulting in a small sword in the body of one of the stout gentlemen imperfectly repressed by a belt, fifty thousand francs per annum and a decoration to the other stout gentleman imperfectly repressed by a belt, and an assurance from everybody to the provincial young man that if he were not supremely happy – which he seemed to have no reason whatever for being – he ought to be. This afforded him a final opportunity of crying and laughing and choking all at once, and sent the audience home sentimentally delighted. Audience more attentive or better behaved there could not possibly be, though the places of second rank in the Theatre of the Family P. Salcy were sixpence each in English money, and the places of the first rank a shilling. How the fifteen subjects ever got so fat upon it, the kind Heavens know.

What gorgeous china figures of knights and ladies, gilded till they gleamed again, I might have bought at the Fair for the garniture of my home, if I had been a French-Flemish peasant, and had had the money! What shining coffee-cups and saucers I might have won at the turntables, if I had had the luck! Ravishing perfumery also, and sweetmeats, I might have speculated in, or I might have fired for prizes at a multitude of little dolls in niches, and might have hit the doll of dolls, and won francs and fame. Or, being a French-Flemish youth, I might have been drawn in a hand-cart by my compeers, to tilt for municipal rewards at the water-quintain;[5] which, unless I sent my lance clean through the ring, emptied a full bucket over me; to fend off which, the competitors wore grotesque old scarecrow hats. Or, being French-Flemish man or woman, boy or girl, I might have circled all night on my hobby-horse in a stately cavalcade of hobby-horses four abreast, interspersed with triumphal cars, going round and round and round and round, we the goodly company singing a ceaseless chorus to the music of the barrel-organ, drum, and cymbals.[6] On the whole, not more monotonous than the Ring in Hyde Park,[7] London, and much merrier; for when do the circling company sing chorus, *there*, to the barrel-organ, when do the ladies embrace their horses round the neck with both arms, when do the gentlemen fan the ladies with the tails of their gallant steeds? On all these revolving delights, and on their own especial lamps and Chinese lanterns revolving with them, the thoughtful weaver-face brightens, and the Hôtel de Ville sheds an illuminated line of gas-light: while above it, the Eagle of France,[8] gas-outlined and apparently afflicted with the prevailing infirmities that have lighted on the poultry, is in a very undecided state of policy, and as a bird moulting. Flags flutter all around. Such is the prevailing gaiety that the keeper of the prison sits on the stone steps outside the prison-door, to have a look at the world that is not locked up; while that agreeable retreat, the wine-shop opposite to the prison in the prison-alley (its sign La Tranquillité, because of its charming situation), resounds with the voices of the shepherds and shepherdesses who resort there this festive night. And it reminds me that only this afternoon, I saw a shepherd in trouble, tending this way, over the jagged stones of a neighbouring street. A magnificent sight it was, to behold him in his blouse, a feeble little jog-trot rustic, swept along by the wind of two immense gendarmes, in cocked-hats for which the street was hardly wide enough, each carrying a bundle of stolen property that would not have held his shoulder-knot, and clanking a sabre that dwarfed the prisoner.

"Messieurs et Mesdames, I present to you at this Fair, as a mark of my confidence in the people of this so-renowned town, and as an act of homage to their good sense and fine taste, the Ventriloquist, the Ventriloquist! Further, Messieurs et Mesdames, I present to you the Face-Maker, the Physiognomist, the great Changer of Countenances, who transforms the features that Heaven has bestowed upon him into an endless succession of surprising and extraordinary visages, comprehending, Messieurs et Mesdames, all the contortions, energetic and expressive, of which the human face is capable, and all the passions of the human heart, as Love, Jealousy, Revenge, Hatred, Avarice, Despair! Hi hi, Ho ho, Lu lu, Come in!" To this effect, with an occasional smite upon a sonorous kind of tambourine – bestowed with a will, as if it represented the people who won't come in – holds forth a man of lofty and severe demeanour; a man in stately uniform, gloomy with the knowledge he possesses of the inner secrets of the booth. "Come in, come in! Your opportunity presents itself tonight; tomorrow it will be gone for ever. Tomorrow morning by the Express Train the railroad will reclaim the Ventriloquist and the Face-Maker! Algeria will reclaim the Ventriloquist and the Face-Maker! Yes! For the honour of their country they have accepted propositions of a magnitude incredible, to appear in Algeria. See them for the last time before their departure! We go to commence on the instant. Hi hi! Ho ho! Lu lu! Come in! Take the money that now ascends, Madame; but after that, no more, for we commence! Come in!"

Nevertheless, the eyes both of the gloomy Speaker and of Madame receiving sous in a muslin bower, survey the crowd pretty sharply after the ascending money has ascended, to detect any

lingering sous at the turning-point. "Come in! come in! Is there any
more money, Madame, on the point of ascending? If so, we wait for it.
If not, we commence!" The orator looks back over his shoulder to say
it, lashing the spectators with the conviction that he beholds through
the folds of the drapery into which he is about to plunge, the
Ventriloquist and the Face-Maker. Several sous burst out of pockets,
and ascend. "Come up, then, Messieurs!" exclaims Madame in a
shrill voice, and beckoning with a bejewelled finger. "Come up! This
presses. Monsieur has commanded that they commence!" Monsieur
dives into his Interior, and the last half-dozen of us follow. His
Interior is comparatively severe; his Exterior also. A true Temple of
Art needs nothing but seats, drapery, a small table with two moderator
lamps[9] hanging over it, and an ornamental looking-glass let into the
wall. Monsieur in uniform gets behind the table and surveys us with
disdain, his forehead becoming diabolically intellectual under the
moderators.   "Messieurs et Mesdames, I present to you the
Ventriloquist. He will commence with the celebrated Experience of
the bee in the window. The bee, apparently a veritable bee of Nature,
will hover in the window, and about the room. He will be with
difficulty caught in the hand of Monsieur the Ventriloquist – he will
escape – he will again hover – at length he will be recaptured by
Monsieur the Ventriloquist, and will be with difficulty put into a
bottle. Achieve then, Monsieur!" Here the Proprietor is replaced
behind the table by the Ventriloquist, who is thin and sallow, and of a
weakly aspect. While the bee is in progress, Monsieur the Proprietor
sits apart on a stool, immersed in dark and remote thought. The
moment the bee is bottled, he stalks forward, eyes us gloomily as we
applaud, and then announces, sternly waving his hand: "The
magnificent Experience of the child with the whooping-cough!" The
child disposed of, he starts up as before. "The superb and
extraordinary Experience of the dialogue between Monsieur

Tatambour in his dining-room, and his domestic, Jerome, in the cellar; concluding with the songsters of the grove, and the Concert of domestic Farm-yard animals." All this done, and well done, Monsieur the Ventriloquist withdraws, and Monsieur the Face-Maker bursts in, as if his retiring-room were a mile long instead of a yard. A corpulent little man in a large white waistcoat, with a comic countenance, and with a wig in his hand. Irreverent disposition to laugh, instantly checked by the tremendous gravity of the Face-Maker, who intimates in his bow that if we expect that sort of thing we are mistaken. A very little shaving-glass with a leg behind it is handed in, and placed on the table before the Face-Maker. "Messieurs et Mesdames, with no other assistance than this mirror and this wig, I shall have the honour of showing you a thousand characters." As a preparation, the Face-Maker with both hands gouges himself, and turns his mouth inside out. He then becomes frightfully grave again, and says to the Proprietor, "I am ready!" Proprietor stalks forth from baleful reverie, and announces "The Young Conscript!" Face-Maker claps his wig on, hind side before, looks in the glass, and appears above it as a conscript so very imbecile, and squinting so extremely hard, that I should think the State would never get any good of him. Thunders of applause. Face-Maker dips behind the looking-glass, brings his own hair forward, is himself again, is awfully grave. "A distinguished inhabitant of the Faubourg St Germain."[10] Face-Maker dips, rises, is supposed to be aged, blear-eyed, toothless, slightly palsied, supernaturally polite, evidently of noble birth. "The oldest member of the Corps of Invalides[11] on the fête-day of his master." Face-Maker dips, rises, wears the wig on one side, has become the feeblest military bore in existence, and (it is clear) would lie frightfully about his past achievements, if he were not confined to pantomime. "The miser!" Face-Maker dips, rises, clutches a bag, and every hair of the wig is on end to express that he lives in continual dread of thieves.

"The Genius of France!"[12] Face-Maker dips, rises, wig pushed back and smoothed flat, little cocked-hat (artfully concealed till now) put a-top of it, Face-Maker's white waistcoat much advanced, Face-Maker's left hand in bosom of white waistcoat, Face-Maker's right hand behind his back. Thunders. This is the first of three positions of the Genius of France. In the second position, the Face-Maker takes snuff; in the third, rolls up his right hand, and surveys illimitable armies through that pocket-glass. The Face-Maker then, by putting out his tongue, and wearing the wig nohow in particular, becomes the Village Idiot. The most remarkable feature in the whole of his ingenious performance, is, that whatever he does to disguise himself, has the effect of rendering him rather more like himself than he was at first.

There were peep-shows in this Fair, and I had the pleasure of recognising several fields of glory with which I became well acquainted a year or two ago as Crimean battles, now doing duty as Mexican victories.[13] The change was neatly effected by some extra smoking of the Russians, and by permitting the camp followers free range in the foreground to despoil the enemy of their uniforms. As no British troops had ever happened to be within sight when the artist took his original sketches, it followed fortunately that none were in the way now.

The Fair wound up with a ball. Respecting the particular night of the week on which the ball took place, I decline to commit myself;[14] merely mentioning that it was held in a stable-yard so very close to the railway, that it is a mercy the locomotive did not set fire to it. (In Scotland, I suppose it would have done so.[15]) There, in a tent prettily decorated with looking-glasses and a myriad of toy flags, the people danced all night. It was not an expensive recreation, the price of a double ticket for a cavalier and lady being one-and-threepence in English money, and even of that small sum fivepence was reclaimable for "consommation:" which word I venture to translate into refreshments of no greater strength, at the strongest, than ordinary wine made hot, with sugar and lemon in it. It was a ball of great good humour and of great enjoyment, though very many of the dancers must have been as poor as the fifteen subjects of the P. Salcy Family.

In short, not having taken my own pet national pint pot with me to this Fair, I was very well satisfied with the measure of simple enjoyment that it poured into the dull French-Flemish country life. How dull that is, I had an opportunity of considering when the Fair was over – when the tri-coloured flags were withdrawn from the windows of the houses on the Place where the Fair was held – when the windows were close shut, apparently until next Fair-time – when the Hôtel de Ville had cut off its gas and put away its eagle – when two paviours, whom I take to form the entire paving population of the town, were ramming down the stones which had been pulled up for the erection of decorative poles – when the jailer had slammed his gate, and sulkily locked himself in with his charges. But then, as I paced the ring which marked the track of the departed hobby-horses on the market-place, pondering in my mind how long some hobby-horses do leave their tracks in public ways, and how difficult they are to erase, my eyes were greeted with a goodly sight. I beheld four male personages thoughtfully pacing the Place together, in the sunlight, evidently not belonging to the town, and having upon them a certain loose cosmopolitan air of not belonging to any town. One was clad in a suit of white canvas, another in a cap and blouse, the third in an old military frock, the fourth in a shapeless dress that looked as if it had been made out of old umbrellas. All wore dust-coloured shoes. My heart beat high; for, in those four male personages, although complexionless and eyebrowless, I beheld the four subjects of the Family P. Salcy. Blue-bearded though they were, and bereft of the youthful smoothness of cheek which is imparted by what is termed in

Albion a "Whitechapel shave"[16] (and which is, in fact, whitening, judiciously applied to the jaws with the palm of the hand), I recognised them. As I stood admiring, there emerged from the yard of a lowly Cabaret,[17] the excellent Ma Mère, Ma Mère, with the words, "The soup is served;" words which so elated the subject in the canvas suit, that when they all ran in to partake, he went last, dancing with his hands stuck angularly into the pockets of his canvas trousers, after the Pierrot[18] manner. Glancing down the Yard, the last I saw of him was, that he looked in through a window (at the soup, no doubt) on one leg.

Full of this pleasure, I shortly afterwards departed from the town, little dreaming of an addition to my good fortune. But more was in reserve. I went by a train which was heavy with third-class carriages, full of young fellows (well guarded) who had drawn unlucky numbers in the last conscription, and were on their way to a famous French garrison town where much of the raw military material is worked up into soldiery.[19] At the station they had been sitting about, in their threadbare homespun blue garments, with their poor little bundles under their arms, covered with dust and clay, and the various soils of France; sad enough at heart, most of them, but putting a good face upon it, and slapping their breasts and singing choruses on the smallest provocation; the gayer spirits shouldering half loaves of black bread speared upon their walking-sticks. As we went along, they were audible at every station, chorusing wildly out of tune, and feigning the highest hilarity. After a while, however, they began to leave off singing, and to laugh naturally, while at intervals there mingled with their laughter the barking of a dog. Now, I had to alight short of their destination, and, as that stoppage of the train was attended with a quantity of horn blowing, bell ringing, and proclamation of what Messieurs les Voyageurs were to do, and were not to do, in order to reach their respective destinations, I had ample leisure to go forward on the platform to take a parting look at my recruits, whose heads were all out at window, and who were laughing like delighted children. Then I perceived that a large poodle with a pink nose, who had been their travelling companion and the cause of their mirth, stood on his hind-legs presenting arms on the extreme verge of the platform, ready to salute them as the train went off. This poodle wore a military shako[20] (it is unnecessary to add, very much on one side over one eye), a little military coat, and the regulation white gaiters. He was armed with a little musket and a little sword-bayonet, and he stood presenting arms in perfect attitude, with his unobscured eye on his master or superior officer, who stood by him. So admirable was his discipline, that, when the train moved, and he was greeted by the parting cheers of the recruits, and also with a shower of centimes, several of which struck his shako, and had a tendency to discompose him, he remained staunch on his post, until the train was gone. He then resigned his arms to his officer, took off his shako by rubbing his paw over it, dropped on four legs, bringing his uniform-coat into the absurdest relations with the overarching skies, and ran about the platform in his white gaiters, wagging his tail to an exceeding great extent. It struck me that there was more waggery than this in the poodle, and that he knew that the recruits would neither get through their exercises, nor get rid of their uniforms, as easily as he; revolving which in my thoughts, and seeking in my pockets some small money to bestow upon him, I casually directed my eyes to the face of his superior officer, and in him beheld the Face-Maker! Though it was not the way to Algeria, but quite the reverse, the military poodle's Colonel was the Face-Maker in a dark blouse, with a small bundle dangling over his shoulder at the end of an umbrella, and taking a pipe from his breast to smoke as he and the poodle went their mysterious way.

chapter six

AN AWAKENING IN A SLEEPY TOWN

("HIS BOOTS")

The short story "His Boots" appeared in *Somebody's Luggage*, the 1862 "Extra Christmas Number" of *All the Year Round*. It was Dickens's practice to invent a narrative context for the Christmas Numbers, within which a set of otherwise unrelated stories could be brought together. In *Somebody's Luggage*, a pile of unclaimed luggage left in a small hotel is found to contain the manuscripts of various tales, all untitled. As Christopher the Head Waiter, who narrates the framing story, explains,

> The writings are consequently called, here, by the names of the articles of Luggage to which they was found attached.

Hence the title "His Boots."

The story is set in a provincial fortified French town, drawn from Dickens's observations of many such small towns in northern France. Despite the fictional context, he was at pains to make his portrait of the town and its inhabitants true to life. On 4 October 1862 he told Wilkie Collins that he was working on "a little French story,"

...which reproduces (I think, to the Life) the ways and means of a dull fortified French town, full of French soldiers. (*Pilgrim*, 10, p 134.)

A few days later, when he had finished the story, he wrote again to Collins, telling him that he had tried to infuse into it "every conceivable feature of an old fortified French town" (*Pilgrim*, 10, p 137). In mid-October, on a visit to northern France, he double-checked the details of his fiction against the reality and wrote to W.H. Wills,

And by the bye I must say that I find the French fortified town in 'His Boots' to be amazingly accurate. I have been largely checking it off at two old Vauban defended towns since I came over yesterday. (*Pilgrim*, 10, p 147.)

And in a letter to Thomas Beard of 24 December 1862, shortly after the publication of *Somebody's Luggage*, he wondered how many of its purchasers would

... have any idea of the number of hours of steamboat, railway train, dusty French walk, and looking out of window, boiled down in 'His Boots'? (*Pilgrim*, 10, p 181.)

"His Boots" tells the story of Corporal Théophile, a young French soldier, Bebelle, a little girl he has befriended (born, it is implied, illegitimately), and Mr Langley, an Englishman living in the town in self-exile from his rejected daughter ("there was a child in that case too"). Explaining the original inspiration for the piece to John Forster, Dickens told him that he had made the story "a camera obscura of certain French places and styles of people; having founded it on something he had noticed in a French soldier" (*Life*, 9, Chapter 4). He was precise about what it was that he had noticed in the soldier in a letter to his acquaintance Mrs Brown on 24 October 1862:

It was put into my head by seeing a French soldier acting as a nurse to his master's – a captain's – little baby girl, and washing her and putting her to bed, and getting her up again in the morning, with the greatest gravity and gentleness. (*Pilgrim*, 10, p 150.)

The care and proficiency of the soldier in a domestic situation far removed from his professional duties would have struck Dickens as demonstrative of the courtesy and humanity that he had frequently observed in France and to which he often refers in his writing. A recurring theme in the pieces included in this volume is the contrast between the small-mindedness, discourtesy, and reserve of the English, and the good manners and open-heartedness of what Dickens calls in "Our French Watering-Place" a "nation teeming with gentle people." "His Boots" dramatizes these perceived cultural differences and draws its dynamic from them. In essence, it is the story of how a narrow-minded, inhibited Englishman learns gentleness and compassion through exposure to a culture characterized by openness and generosity.

The central character is clearly intended as a "type," representative of certain typically English weaknesses. His real name of Langley, which he is too reserved to enunciate properly in a foreign country, is heard as "L'Anglais" and so he becomes known as "Mr The Englishman," a comic misunderstanding that implicitly generalizes his characteristics. He also has no physical identity to individualize him: although there is much descriptive detail in the story, we are on exclusively psychological terms with Mr The Englishman. We know him only by his thoughts and we develop our acquaintance and familiarity with him through his growing responsiveness to the people of the town and to the events that unfold around him.

Théophile and Bebelle (illustration by Charles Green)

HIS BOOTS

"Eh! Well then, Monsieur Mutuel![1] What do I know, what can I say? I assure you that he calls himself Monsieur The Englishman."

"Pardon. But I think it is impossible," said Monsieur Mutuel. A spectacled, snuffy, stooping old gentleman in carpet shoes and a cloth cap with a peaked shade, a loose blue frock-coat reaching to his heels, a large limp white shirt-frill, and cravat to correspond, – that is to say, white was the natural colour of his linen on Sundays, but it toned down with the week.

"It is," repeated Monsieur Mutuel: his amiable old walnut-shell countenance, very walnut-shelly indeed as he smiled and blinked in the bright morning sunlight, "it is my cherished Madame Bouclet, I think, impossible."

"Hey!" (with a little vexed cry and a great many tosses of her head). "But it is not impossible that you are a Pig!" retorted Madame Bouclet: a compact little woman of thirty-five or so. "See then – look there – read! 'On the second floor Monsieur L'Anglais.' Is it not so?"

"It is so," said Monsieur Mutuel.

"Good. Continue your morning walk. Get out!" Madame Bouclet dismissed him with a lively snap of her fingers.

The morning walk of Monsieur Mutuel was in the brightest patch that the sun made in the Grande Place of a dull old fortified French town. The manner of his morning walk was with his hands crossed behind him: an umbrella, in figure the express image of himself, always in one hand: a snuff-box in the other. Thus, with the shuffling gait of the Elephant (who really does deal with the very worst trousers-maker employed by the Zoological world, and who appeared to have recommended him to Monsieur Mutuel), the old gentleman sunned himself daily when sun was to be had – of course, at the same time sunning a red ribbon at his button-hole;[2] for was he not an ancient Frenchman?

Being told by one of the angelic sex to continue his morning walk and get out, Monsieur Mutuel laughed a walnut-shell laugh, pulled off his cap at arm's length with the hand that contained his snuff-box, kept it off for a considerable period after he had parted from Madame Bouclet, and continued his morning walk and got out: like a man of gallantry as he was.

The documentary evidence to which Madame Bouclet had referred Monsieur Mutuel, was the list of her lodgers, sweetly written forth by her own Nephew and Book-keeper, who held the pen of an Angel, and posted up at the side of her gateway for the information of the Police. "Au second, M. L'Anglais, Propriétaire." On the second floor, Mr The Englishman, man of property. So it stood; nothing could be plainer.

Madame Bouclet now traced the line with her forefinger, as it were to confirm and settle herself in her parting snap at Monsieur Mutuel, and so, placing her right hand on her hip with a defiant air, as if nothing should ever tempt her to unsnap that snap, strolled out into the Place to glance up at the windows of Mr The Englishman. That worthy happening to be looking out of window at the moment, Madame Bouclet gave him a graceful salutation with her head, looked to the right and looked to the left to account to him for her being there, considered for a moment like one who accounted to herself for somebody she had expected not being there, and re-entered her own gateway. Madame Bouclet let all her house giving on the Place in furnished flats or floors, and lived up the yard behind, in company with Monsieur Bouclet her husband (great at billiards), an inherited brewing business, several fowls, two carts, a nephew, a little dog in a big kennel, a grape-vine, a counting-house, four horses, a married sister (with a share in the brewing business), the husband and two children of the married sister, a parrot, a drum (performed on by the little boy of the married sister), two billeted soldiers, a quantity of pigeons, a fife (played by the nephew in a ravishing manner), several domestics and supernumeraries, a perpetual flavour of coffee and soup, a terrific range of artificial rocks and wooden precipices at least four feet high, a small fountain, and half a dozen large sunflowers.

Now, the Englishman in taking his Appartement – or, as one might say on our side of the Channel, his set of chambers – had given his name, correct to the letter, LANGLEY. But as he had a British way of not opening his mouth very wide on foreign soil, except at meals, the Brewery had been able to make nothing of it but L'Anglais. So, Mr The Englishman he had become and he remained.

"Never saw such a people!" muttered Mr The Englishman, as he now looked out of window. "Never did, in my life!"

This was true enough, for he had never before been out of his own country – a right little island, a tight little island, a bright little island, a show-fight little island,[3] and full of merit of all sorts; but not the whole round world.

"These chaps," said Mr The Englishman to himself, as his eye rolled over the Place, sprinkled with military here and there, "are no more like soldiers — !" Nothing being sufficiently strong for the end of his sentence, he left it unended.

This again (from the point of view of his experience) was strictly correct; for, though there was a great agglomeration of soldiers in the town and neighbouring country, you might have held a grand Review and Field Day of them every one, and looked in vain among them all for a soldier choking behind his foolish stock,[4] or a soldier lamed by his ill-fitting shoes, or a soldier deprived of the use of his limbs by straps and buttons, or a soldier elaborately forced to be self-helpless in all the small affairs of life. A swarm of brisk bright active bustling handy odd skirmishing fellows, able to turn to cleverly at anything, from a siege to a soup, from great guns to needles and thread, from the broad-sword exercise to slicing an onion, from making war to making omelettes, was all you would have found.[5]

What a swarm! From the Great Place under the eye of Mr The Englishman, where a few awkward squads from the last conscription were doing the goose-step – some members of those squads still as to their bodies in the chrysalis peasant-state of Blouse, and only military butterflies as to their regimentally-clothed legs – from the Great Place, away outside the fortifications and away for miles along the dusty roads, soldiers swarmed. All day long, upon the grass-grown ramparts of the town, practising soldiers trumpeted and bugled; all day long, down in angles of dry trenches, practising soldiers drummed and drummed. Every forenoon, soldiers burst out of the great barracks into the sandy gymnasium-ground hard by, and flew over the wooden horse, and hung on to flying ropes, and dangled upside-down between parallel bars, and shot themselves off wooden platforms, splashes, sparks, coruscations, showers, of soldiers. At every corner of the town wall, every guard-house, every gateway, every sentry-box, every drawbridge, every reedy ditch and rushy dyke, soldiers soldiers soldiers. And the town being pretty well all wall, guard-house, gateway, sentry-box, drawbridge, reedy ditch and rushy dyke, the town was pretty well all soldiers.

What would the sleepy old town have been without the soldiers, seeing that even with them it had so overslept itself as to have slept its echoes hoarse, its defensive bars and locks and bolts and chains all rusty, and its ditches stagnant! From the days when VAUBAN[6] engineered it to that perplexing extent that to look at it was like being knocked on the head with it: the stranger becoming stunned and stertorous under the shock of its incomprehensibility – from the days when VAUBAN made it the express incorporation of every substantive and adjective in the art of military engineering, and not only twisted you into it and twisted you out of it, to the right, to the left, opposite, under here, over there, in the dark, in the dirt, by gateway, archway, covered way, dry way, wet way, fosse, portcullis, drawbridge, sluice, squat tower, pierced wall, and heavy battery, but likewise took a fortifying dive under the neighbouring country, and came to the surface three or four miles off, blowing out incomprehensible mounds and batteries among the quiet crops of chicory and beetroot – from those days to these, the town had been asleep, and dust and rust and must had settled on its drowsy Arsenals and Magazines, and grass had grown up in its silent streets.

On market-days alone, its Great Place suddenly leaped out of bed. On market-days, some friendly enchanter struck his staff upon the stones of the Great Place, and instantly arose the liveliest booths and stalls and sittings and standings, and a pleasant hum of chaffering and huckstering from many hundreds of tongues, and a pleasant though peculiar blending of colours – white caps, blue blouses, and green vegetables – and at last the Knight destined for the adventure seemed to have come in earnest, and all the Vaubanois sprang up awake. And now, by long low-lying avenues of trees, jolting in white-hooded donkey-cart, and on donkey-back, and in tumbril and waggon and cart and cabriolet, and a-foot with barrow and burden – and along the dykes and ditches and canals, in little peak-prowed country boats – came peasant men and women in flocks and crowds, bringing articles for sale. And here you had boots and shoes and sweetmeats and stuffs to wear, and here (in the cool shade of the Town Hall) you had milk and cream and butter and cheese, and here you had fruits and onions and carrots and all things needful for your soup, and here you had poultry and flowers and protesting pigs, and here new shovels axes spades and bill-hooks for your farming work, and here huge mounds of bread, and here your unground grain in sacks, and here your children's dolls, and here the cake-seller announcing his wares by beat and roll of drum. And hark! fanfaronade of trumpets, and here into the Great Place, resplendent in an open carriage with four gorgeously-attired servitors up behind, playing horns drums and cymbals, rolled "the Daughter of a Physician" in massive gold chains and ear-rings, and blue-feathered hat, shaded from the admiring sun by two immense umbrellas of artificial roses, to dispense (from motives of philanthropy) that small and pleasant dose which had cured so many thousands! Toothache earache headache heartache stomachache debility nervousness fits faintings fever ague, all equally cured by the small and pleasant dose of the great Physician's great daughter! The process was this: – she, the Daughter of a Physician, proprietress of the superb equipage you now admired, with its confirmatory blasts of trumpet drum and cymbal, told you so: – On the first day after taking the small and pleasant dose, you would feel no particular influence beyond a most harmonious sensation of indescribable and irresistible joy; on the second day, you would be so astonishingly better that you would think yourself changed into somebody else; on the third day, you would be entirely free from your disorder, whatever its nature and however long you had had it, and would seek out the Physician's daughter, to throw yourself at her feet, kiss the hem of her garment, and buy as many more of the small and pleasant doses as by the sale of all your few effects you could obtain; but she would be inaccessible – gone for herbs to the Pyramids of Egypt – and you would be (though cured) reduced to despair! Thus would the Physician's daughter drive her trade (and briskly too), and thus would the buying and selling and mingling of tongues and colours continue until the changing sunlight, leaving the Physician's Daughter in the shadow of high roofs, admonished her to jolt out westward, with a departing effect of gleam and glitter on the splendid equipage and brazen blast. And now the enchanter struck his staff upon the stones of the Great Place once more, and down went the booths the sittings and standings, and vanished the merchandise, and with it the barrows donkeys donkey-carts and tumbrils and all other things on wheels and feet, except the slow scavengers with unwieldy carts and meagre horses, clearing up the rubbish, assisted by the sleek town pigeons, better plumped out than on non-market days. While there was yet an hour or two to wane before the autumn sunset, the loiterer outside town-gate and drawbridge and postern and double-ditch, would see the last white-hooded cart lessening in the avenue of lengthening shadows of trees, or the last country boat, paddled by the last market-woman on her way home, showing black upon the reddening long low narrow dyke between him and the mill; and as the paddle-parted scum and weed closed over the boat's track, he might be comfortably sure that its sluggish rest would be troubled no more until next market-day.

As it was not one of the Great Place's days for getting out of bed when Mr The Englishman looked down at the young soldiers practising the goose-step there, his mind was left at liberty to take a military turn.

"These fellows are billeted everywhere about," said he, "and to see them lighting the people's fires, boiling the people's pots, minding the people's babies, rocking the people's cradles, washing the people's greens, and making themselves generally useful, in every sort of unmilitary way, is most ridiculous! – Never saw such a set of fellows; never did in my life!"

All perfectly true again. Was there not Private Valentine, in that very house, acting as sole housemaid, valet, cook, steward, and nurse, in the family of his captain, Monsieur le Capitaine De la Cour – cleaning the floors, making the beds, doing the marketing, dressing the captain, dressing the dinners, dressing the salads, and dressing the baby, all with equal readiness? Or, to put him aside, he being in loyal attendance on his Chief, was there not Private Hyppolite, billeted at the Perfumer's two hundred yards off, who, when not on duty, volunteered to keep shop while the fair Perfumeress stepped out to speak to a neighbour or so, and laughingly sold soap with his war sword girded on him? Was there not Emile, billeted at the Clockmaker's, perpetually turning to of an evening with his coat off, winding up the stock? Was there not Eugène, billeted at the Tinman's, cultivating, pipe in mouth, a garden four feet square for the Tinman, in the little court behind the shop, and extorting the fruits of the earth from the same, on his knees, with the sweat of his brow? Not to multiply examples, was there not Baptiste, billeted on the poor Water-Carrier, at that very instant sitting on the pavement in the sunlight, with his martial legs asunder, and one of the Water-Carrier's spare pails between them, which (to the delight and glory of the heart of the Water-Carrier coming across the Place from the fountain, yoked and burdened) he was painting bright green outside and bright red within? Or, to go no further than the Barber's at the very next door, was there not Corporal Théophile—

"No," said Mr The Englishman, glancing down at the Barber's, "he is not there at present. There's the child though."

A mere mite of a girl stood on the steps of the Barber's shop, looking across the Place. A mere baby, one might call her, dressed in the white linen cap which small French country-children wear (like the Children in Dutch pictures), and in a frock of homespun blue, that had no shape except where it was tied round her little fat throat. So that, being naturally short and round all over, she looked behind, as if she had been cut off at her natural waist, and had had her head neatly fitted on it.

"There's the child though."

To judge from the way in which the dimpled hand was rubbing the eyes, the eyes had been closed in a nap and were newly opened. But they seemed to be looking so intently across the Place, that the Englishman looked in the same direction.

"Oh!" said he, presently, "I thought as much. The Corporal's there."

The Corporal, a smart figure of a man of thirty: perhaps a thought under the middle size, but very neatly made – a sunburnt Corporal with a brown peaked beard – faced about at the moment, addressing voluble words of instruction to the squad in hand. Nothing was amiss or awry about the Corporal. A lithe and nimble Corporal, quite complete, from the sparkling dark eyes under his knowing uniform cap, to his sparkling white gaiters. The very image and presentment of a Corporal of his country's army, in the line of his shoulders, the line of his waist, the broadest line of his Bloomer trousers,[7] and their narrowest line at the calf of his leg.

Mr The Englishman looked on, and the child looked on, and the Corporal looked on (but the last-named at his men), until the drill ended a few minutes afterwards and the military sprinkling dried up directly and was gone. Then said Mr The Englishman to himself, "Look here! By George!" And the Corporal, dancing towards the Barber's with his arms wide open, caught up the child, held her over his head in a flying attitude, caught her down again, kissed her, and made off with her into the Barber's house.

Now, Mr The Englishman had had a quarrel with his erring and disobedient daughter, and there was a child in that case too. Had not his daughter been a child, and had she not taken angel-flights above his head as this child had flown above the Corporal's?

"He's a" – National Participled – "fool!" said the Englishman. And shut his window.

But the windows of the house of Memory, and the windows of the house of Mercy, are not so easily closed as windows of glass and wood. They fly open unexpectedly; they rattle in the night; they must be nailed up. Mr The Englishman had tried nailing them, but had not driven the nails quite home. So he passed but a disturbed evening and a worse night.

By nature a good-tempered man? No; very little gentleness, confounding the quality with weakness. Fierce and wrathful when crossed? Very, and stupendously unreasonable. Moody? Exceedingly so. Vindictive? Well; he *had* had scowling thoughts that he would formally curse his daughter, as he had seen it done on the stage. But remembering that the real Heaven is some paces removed from the mock one in the great chandelier of the Theatre, he had given that up.

And he had come abroad to be rid of his repudiated daughter for the rest of his life. And here he was.

At bottom, it was for this reason more than for any other that Mr The Englishman took it extremely ill that Corporal Théophile should be so devoted to little Bebelle, the child at the Barber's shop. In an unlucky moment he had chanced to say to himself, "Why, confound the fellow, he is not her father!" There was a sharp sting in the speech which ran into him suddenly and put him in a worse mood. So he had National Participled the unconscious Corporal with most hearty emphasis, and had made up his mind to think no more about such a mountebank.[8]

But it came to pass that the Corporal was not to be dismissed. If he had known the most delicate fibres of the Englishman's mind, instead of knowing nothing on earth about him, and if he had been the most obstinate Corporal in the Grand Army of France instead of being the most obliging, he could not have planted himself with more determined immovability plump in the midst of all the Englishman's thoughts. Not only so, but he seemed to be always in his view. Mr The Englishman had but to look out of window, to look upon the Corporal with Little Bebelle. He had but to go for walk, and there was the Corporal walking with Bebelle. He had but to come home again, disgusted, and the Corporal and Bebelle were at home before him. If he looked out at his back windows early in the morning, the

Corporal was in the Barber's back-yard, washing and dressing and brushing Bebelle. If he took refuge at his front windows, the Corporal brought his breakfast out into the Place, and shared it there with Bebelle. Always Corporal and always Bebelle. Never Corporal without Bebelle. Never Bebelle without Corporal.

Mr The Englishman was not particularly strong in the French language as a means of oral communication, though he read it very well. It is with languages as with people – when you only know them by sight, you are apt to mistake them; you must be on speaking terms before you can be said to have established an acquaintance.

For this reason, Mr The Englishman had to gird up his loins considerably, before he could bring himself to the point of exchanging ideas with Madame Bouclet on the subject of this Corporal and this Bebelle. But Madame Bouclet looking in apologetically one morning to remark, that O Heaven she was in a state of desolation because the lampmaker had not sent home that lamp confided to him to repair, but that truly he was a lampmaker against whom the whole world shrieked out, Mr The Englishman seized the occasion.

"Madame, that baby—"

"Pardon, monsieur. That lamp."

"No, no, that little girl."

"But, pardon!" said Madame Bouclet, angling for a clue; "one cannot light a little girl, or send her to be repaired?"

"The little girl – at the house of the barber."

"Ah-h-h!" cried Madame Bouclet, suddenly catching the idea, with her delicate little line and rod. "Little Bebelle? Yes, yes, yes! And her friend the Corporal? Yes, yes, yes, yes! So genteel of him; is it not?"

"He is not—?"

"Not at all; not at all! He is not one of her relations. Not at all!"

"Why then, he—"

"Perfectly!" cried Madame Bouclet, "you are right, monsieur. It is so genteel of him. The less relation, the more genteel. As you say."

"Is she—?"

"The child of the barber?" Madame Bouclet whisked up her skilful little line and rod again. "Not at all, not at all! She is the child of – in a word, of no one."

"The wife of the barber, then—?"

"Indubitably. As you say. The wife of the barber receives a small stipend to take care of her. So much by the month. Eh, then! It is without doubt very little, for we are all poor here."

"You are not poor, madame."

"As to my lodgers," replied Madame Bouclet, with a smiling and gracious bend of her head, "no. As to all things else, so-so."

"You flatter me, madame."

"Monsieur, it is you who flatter me in living here."

Certain fishy gasps on Mr The Englishman's part, denoting that he was about to resume his subject under difficulties, Madame Bouclet observed him closely, and whisked up her delicate line and rod again with triumphant success.

"Oh, no, monsieur, certainly not. The wife of the barber is not cruel to the poor child, but she is careless. Her health is delicate, and she sits all day, looking out at window. Consequently, when the Corporal first came, the poor little Bebelle was much neglected."

"It is a curious—" began Mr The Englishman.

"Name? That Bebelle? Again, you are right, monsieur. But it is a playful name for Gabrielle."

"And so the child is a mere fancy of the Corporal's?" said Mr The Englishman, in a gruffly disparaging tone of the voice.

"Eh well!" returned Madame Bouclet, with a pleading shrug: "one must love something. Human nature is weak."

("Devilish weak," muttered the Englishman in his own language.)

"And the Corporal," pursued Madame Bouclet, "being billeted at the barber's – where he will probably remain for a long time, for he is attached to the General – and finding the poor unowned child in need of being loved, and finding himself in need of loving – why, there you have it all, you see!"

Mr The Englishman accepted this interpretation of the matter with an indifferent grace, and observed to himself, in an injured manner, when he was again alone: "I shouldn't mind it so much, if these people were not such a" – National Participled – "sentimental people!"

There was a Cemetery outside the town, and it happened ill for the reputation of the Vaubanois in this sentimental connexion, that he took a walk there that same afternoon. To be sure there were some wonderful things in it (from the Englishman's point of view), and of a certainty in all Britain you would have found nothing like it. Not to mention the fanciful flourishes of hearts and crosses, in wood and iron, that were planted all over the place, making it look very like a Firework-ground where a most splendid pyrotechnic display might be expected after dark, there were so many wreaths upon the graves, embroidered, as it might be, "To my mother," "To my daughter," "To my father," "To my brother," "To my sister," "To my friend," and those many wreaths were in so many stages of elaboration and decay, from the wreath of yesterday all fresh colour and bright beads, to the wreath of last year, a poor mouldering wisp of straw! There were so many little gardens and grottos made upon graves, in so many tastes, with plants and shells and plaster figures and porcelain pitchers, and so many odds and ends! There were so many tributes of remembrance hanging up, not to be discriminated by the closest inspection from little round waiters,[9] whereon were depicted in glowing hues either a lady or a gentleman with a white pocket-handkerchief out of all proportion, leaning, in a state of the most faultless mourning and most profound affliction, on the most architectural and gorgeous urn! There were so many surviving wives who had put their names on the tombs of their deceased husbands with a blank for the date of their own departure from this weary world; and there were so many surviving husbands who had rendered the same homage to their deceased wives; and out of the number there must have been so many who had long ago married again! In fine, there was so much in the place that would have seemed mere frippery to a stranger, save for the consideration that the lightest paper flower that lay upon the poorest heap of earth was never touched by a rude hand, but perished there, a sacred thing.

"Nothing of the solemnity of Death, here," Mr The Englishman had been going to say; when this last consideration touched him with a mild appeal, and on the whole he walked out without saying it. "But these people are," he insisted, by way of compensation when he was well outside the gate, "they are so," Participled, "sentimental!"

His way back, lay by the military gymnasium-ground. And there he passed the Corporal glibly instructing young soldiers how to swing themselves over rapid and deep water-courses on their way to Glory, by means of a rope, and himself deftly plunging off a platform and flying a hundred feet or two as an encouragement to them to begin. And there he also passed, perched on a crowning eminence (probably by the Corporal's careful hands), the small Bebelle, with her round eyes wide open, surveying the proceeding like a wondering sort of blue and white bird.

"If that child was to die;" this was his reflection as he turned his back and went his way, " – and it would almost serve the fellow right for making such a fool of himself – I suppose we should have *him* sticking up a wreath and a waiter in that fantastic burying-ground."

Nevertheless, after another early morning or two of looking out of window, he strolled down into the Place, when the Corporal and Bebelle were walking there, and touching his hat to the Corporal (an immense achievement) wished him Good Day.

"Good day, monsieur."

"This is a rather pretty child you have here," said Mr The Englishman, taking her chin in his hand, and looking down into her astonished blue eyes.

"Monsieur, she is a very pretty child," returned the Corporal, with a stress on his polite correction of the phrase.

"And good?" said the Englishman.

"And very good. Poor little thing!"

"Hah!" The Englishman stooped down and patted her cheek: not without awkwardness, as if he were going too far in his conciliation. "And what is this medal round your neck, my little one?"

Bebelle having no other reply on her lips than her chubby right fist, the Corporal offered his services as interpreter.

"Monsieur demands, what is this, Bebelle?"

"It is the Holy Virgin," said Bebelle.

"And who gave it to you?" asked the Englishman.

"Théophile."

"And who is Théophile?"

Bebelle broke into a laugh, laughed merrily and heartily, clapped her chubby hands, and beat her little feet on the stone pavement of the Place.

"He doesn't know Théophile! Why he doesn't know any one! He doesn't know anything!" Then, sensible of a small solecism in her manners, Bebelle twisted her right hand in a leg of the Corporal's Bloomer trousers, and laying her cheek against the place, kissed it.

"Monsieur Théophile, I believe?" said the Englishman to the Corporal.

"It is I, monsieur."

"Permit me." Mr The Englishman shook him heartily by the hand and turned away. But he took it mighty ill that old Monsieur Mutuel in his patch of sunlight, upon whom he came as he turned, should pull off his cap to him with a look of pleased approval. And he muttered, in his own tongue, as he returned the salutation, "Well, walnut-shell! And what business is it of *yours?*"

Mr The Englishman went on for many weeks passing but disturbed evenings and worse nights, and constantly experiencing that those aforesaid windows in the houses of Memory and Mercy rattled after dark, and that he had very imperfectly nailed them up. Likewise, he went on for many weeks, daily improving the acquaintance of the Corporal and Bebelle. That is to say, he took Bebelle by the chin, and the Corporal by the hand, and offered Bebelle sous and the Corporal cigars, and even got the length of changing pipes with the Corporal and kissing Bebelle. But he did it all in a shamefaced way, and always took it extremely ill that Monsieur Mutuel in his patch of sunlight should note what he did. Whenever that seemed to be the case, he always growled in his own tongue, "There you are again, walnut-shell! What business is it of *yours?*"

In a word, it had become the occupation of Mr The Englishman's life to look after the Corporal and little Bebelle, and to resent old Monsieur Mutuel's looking after *him*. An occupation only varied by a fire in the town one windy night, and much passing of water-buckets from hand to hand (in which the Englishman rendered good service), and much beating of drums – when all of a sudden the Corporal disappeared.

Next, all of a sudden, Bebelle disappeared.

She had been visible a few days later than the Corporal – sadly deteriorated as to washing and brushing – but she had not spoken when addressed by Mr The Englishman, and had looked scared and had run away. And now it would seem that she had run away for good. And there lay the Great Place under the windows, bare and barren.

In his shamefaced and constrained way, Mr The Englishman asked no question of any one, but watched from his front windows, and watched from his back windows, and lingered about the Place, and peeped in at the Barber's shop, and did all this and much more with a whistling and tune-humming pretence of not missing anything, until one afternoon when Monsieur Mutuel's patch of sunlight was in shadow, and when according to all rule and precedent he had no right whatever to bring his red ribbon out of doors, behold here he was, advancing with his cap already in his hand twelve paces off!

Mr The Englishman had got as far into his usual objurgation as "What bu—si—" when he checked himself.

"Ah, it is sad, it is sad! Hélas, it is unhappy, it is sad!" Thus, old Monsieur Mutuel, shaking his grey head.

"What busin—at least, I would say what do you mean, Monsieur Mutuel?"

"Our Corporal. Hélas, our dear Corporal!"

"What has happened to him?"

"You have not heard?"

"No."

"At the fire. But he was so brave, so ready. Ah, too brave, too ready!"

"May the devil carry you away," the Englishman broke in impatiently; "I beg your pardon – I mean me – I am not accustomed to speak French – go on, will you!"

"And a falling beam—"

"Good God!" exclaimed the Englishman. "It was a private soldier who was killed?"

"No. A Corporal, the same Corporal, our dear Corporal. Beloved by all his comrades. The funeral ceremony was touching – penetrating. Monsieur The Englishman, your eyes fill with tears."

"What bu—si—"

"Monsieur The Englishman, I honour those emotions. I salute you with profound respect. I will not obtrude myself upon your noble heart."

Monsieur Mutuel, a gentleman in every thread of his cloudy linen, under whose wrinkled hand every grain in the quarter of an ounce of poor snuff in his poor little tin box became a gentleman's property, – Monsieur Mutuel passed on with his cap in his hand.

"I little thought," said the Englishman, after walking for several minutes, and more than once blowing his nose, "when I was looking round that Cemetery, – I'll go there!"

Straight he went there, and when he came within the gate he paused, considering whether he should ask at the lodge for some direction to the grave. But he was less than ever in a mood for asking questions, and he thought, "I shall see something on it, to know it by."

In search of the Corporal's grave, he went softly on, up this walk and down that, peering in among the crosses and hearts and columns and obelisks and tombstones for a recently disturbed spot. It troubled him now, to think how many dead there were in the cemetery – he had not thought them a tenth part so numerous before – and, after he had walked and sought for some time, he said to himself as he struck down a new vista of tombs, "I might suppose that every one was dead but I."

Not every one. A live child was lying on the ground asleep. Truly he had found something on the Corporal's grave to know it by, and the something was Bebelle.

With such a loving will had the dead soldier's comrades worked at his resting-place, that it was already a neat garden. On the green turf of the garden, Bebelle lay sleeping with her cheek touching it. A plain unpainted little wooden Cross was planted in the turf, and her short arm embraced this little Cross, as it had many a time embraced the Corporal's neck. They had put a tiny flag (the flag of France) at his head, and a laurel garland.

Mr The Englishman took off his hat, and stood for a while silent. Then, covering his head again, he bent down on one knee, and softly roused the child.

"Bebelle! My little one!"

Opening her eyes, on which the tears were still wet, Bebelle was at first frightened; but seeing who it was, she suffered him to take her in his arms, looking steadfastly at him.

"You must not lie here my little one. You must come with me."

"No, no. I can't leave Théophile. I want the good dear Théophile."

"We will go and seek him, Bebelle. We will go and look for him in England. We will go and look for him at my daughter's, Bebelle."

"Shall we find him there?"

"We shall find the best part of him there. Come with me, poor forlorn little one. Heaven is my witness," said the Englishman, in a low voice, as, before he rose, he touched the turf above the gentle Corporal's breast, "that I thankfully accept this trust!"

It was a long way for the child to have come unaided. She was soon asleep again, with her embrace transferred to the Englishman's neck. He looked at her worn shoes, and her galled feet, and her tired face, and believed that she had come there every day.

He was leaving the grave with the slumbering Bebelle in his arms, when he stopped, looked wistfully down at it, and looked wistfully at the other graves around. "It is the innocent custom of the people," said Mr The Englishman, with hesitation, "I think I should like to do it. No one sees."

Careful not to wake Bebelle as he went, he repaired to the lodge where such little tokens of remembrance were sold, and bought two wreaths. One, blue and white and glistening silver, "To my friend;" one of a soberer red and black and yellow, "To my friend." With these he went back to the grave, and so down on one knee again. Touching the child's lips with the brighter wreath, he guided her hand to hang it on the Cross; then hung his own wreath there. After all, the wreaths were not far out of keeping with the little garden. To my friend. To my friend.

Mr The Englishman took it very ill when he looked round a street-corner into the Great Place, carrying Bebelle in his arms, that old Mutuel should be there airing his red ribbon. He took a world of pains to dodge the worthy Mutuel, and devoted a surprising amount of time and trouble to skulking into his own lodging like a man pursued by Justice. Safely arrived there at last, he made Bebelle's toilette with as accurate a remembrance as he could bring to bear upon that work, of the way in which he had often seen the poor Corporal make it, and, having given her to eat and drink, laid her down on his own bed. Then, he slipped out into the barber's shop, and after a brief interview with the barber's wife and a brief recourse to his purse and card-case, came back again, with the whole of Bebelle's personal property in such a very little bundle that it was quite lost under his arm.

As it was irreconcilable with his whole course and character that he should carry Bebelle off in state, or receive any compliments or congratulations on that feat, he devoted the next day to getting his two portmanteaus out of the house by artfulness and stealth, and to comporting himself in every particular as if he were going to run away – except indeed that he paid his few debts in the town, and prepared a letter to leave for Madame Bouclet, enclosing a sufficient sum of money in lieu of notice. A railway train would come through at midnight, and by that train he would take away Bebelle to look for Théophile in England and at his forgiven daughter's.

At midnight on a moonlit night, Mr The Englishman came creeping forth like a harmless assassin, with Bebelle on his breast instead of a dagger. Quiet the Great Place, and quiet the never-stirring streets; closed the cafés; huddled together motionless their billiard-balls; drowsy the guard or sentinel on duty here and there; lulled for the time, by sleep, even the insatiate appetite of the Office of Town-dues.[10]

Mr The Englishman left the Place behind and left the streets behind, and left the civilian-inhabited town behind, and descended down among the military works of Vauban, hemming all in. As the shadow of the first heavy arch and postern fell upon him and was left behind, as the shadow of the second heavy arch and postern fell upon him and was left behind, as his hollow tramp over the first drawbridge was succeeded by a gentler sound, as his hollow tramp over the second drawbridge was succeeded by a gentler sound, as he overcame the stagnant ditches one by one, and passed out where the flowing waters were and where the moonlight, so the dark shades and the hollow sounds and the unwholesomely-locked currents of his soul, were vanquished and set free. See to it, Vaubans of your own hearts, who gird them in with triple walls and ditches, and with bolt and chain and bar and lifted bridge – raze those fortifications and lay them level with the all-absorbing dust, before the night cometh when no hand can work![11]

All went prosperously, and he got into an empty carriage in the train, where he could lay Bebelle on the seat over against him, as on a couch, and cover her from head to foot with his mantle. He had just drawn himself up from perfecting this arrangement, and had just leaned back in his own seat contemplating it with great satisfaction, when he became aware of a curious appearance at the open carriage-window – a ghostly little tin box floating up in the moonlight, and hovering there.

He leaned forward and put out his head. Down among the rails and wheels and ashes, Monsieur Mutuel, red ribbon and all!

"Excuse me, Monsieur The Englishman," said Monsieur Mutuel, holding up his box at arm's length; the carriage being so high and he so low; "but I shall reverence the little box for ever, if your so generous hand will take a pinch from it at parting."

Mr The Englishman reached out of the window before complying, and – without asking the old fellow what business it was of his – shook hands and said, "Adieu! God bless you!"

"And, Mr The Englishman, God bless *you*!" cried Madame Bouclet, who was also there among the rails and wheels and ashes. "And God will bless you in the happiness of the protected child now with you. And God will bless you in your own child at home. And God will bless you in your own remembrances. And this from me!"

He had barely time to catch a bouquet from her hand, when the train was flying through the night. Round the paper that enfolded it was bravely written (doubtless by the nephew who held the pen of an Angel), "Homage to the friend of the friendless."

"Not bad people, Bebelle!" said Mr The Englishman, softly drawing the mantle a little from her sleeping face, that he might kiss it, "though they are so—"

Too "sentimental" himself at the moment to get out that word, he added nothing but a sob, and travelled for some miles, through the moonlight, with his hand before his eyes.

chapter seven

A FLÂNEUR IN PARIS: CITY LIFE (AND DEATH)

("RAILWAY DREAMING"; "SOME RECOLLECTIONS OF MORTALITY"; EXTRACTS FROM *PICTURES FROM ITALY* AND "NEW YEAR'S DAY")

Dickens first saw Paris in July 1844, when he and his family were travelling through France on their way to Italy. He was instantly enthralled:

> I cannot tell you what an immense impression Paris made upon me. It is the most extraordinary place in the World. I was not prepared for, and really could not have believed in, its perfectly distinct and separate character. (Letter of 7 August 1844 to the Count d'Orsay, *Pilgrim*, 4, p 166.)

This first, fleeting visit marked the beginning of a friendship with the city that would last for the rest of his life. We know from his correspondence that Dickens visited Paris at least fifteen times between 1844 and 1868. He took up residence there on three of those occasions, renting apartments in the rue de Courcelles for two and a half months (November 1846–February 1847), on the avenue des

Champs-Élysées for six months (October 1855–April 1856), and in the rue du Faubourg Saint-Honoré for two months (October–December 1862). On his shorter trips he stayed at hotels in or near the rue de Rivoli until 1863 when, in Paris to give a series of readings, he switched allegiance to a hotel in the rue du Helder near the boulevard des Italiens, to which he returned on his last two recorded visits in 1865 and 1868.

All these locations were in the liveliest *quartiers* of mid-nineteenth century Paris. The main centers of fashion, shopping, dining, entertainment and nightlife were then to be found on the Right Bank. The Champs-Élysées, described in Murray's 1864 *Handbook for Visitors to Paris* as "one of the finest and most popular promenades," was both a parade ground for elegant carriages and a favorite walk for Parisians of all classes. With its stalls, cafés, and popular amusements it was a center of attraction day and night, perpetually buzzing with energy and activity. The section of the rue de Rivoli opposite the Tuileries was lined with hotels, including the famous Hôtel Meurice (which still exists). *Le Guide Parisien* of 1863 describes the street's covered gallery as constantly thronging with people. But it was the Grands Boulevards, especially the boulevard des Italiens, that provided the most dazzling spectacle of Parisian life. Crammed with famous cafés, fashionable shops, and popular theaters, these streets came alive at night:

> ...the hosts of people sitting outside cafés, the throng of loungers along the pavement, the lofty houses, the splendid shops, the brilliantly lighted cafés, and the numerous theatres form a scene which will be quite new to an Englishman. (*Handbook for Visitors to Paris*, 1864.)

Brilliance and splendor are words that frequently occur in descriptions of Paris under the Second Empire, the period that coincided with most of Dickens's visits. When he first saw the city in 1844 France was still governed by the constitutional monarchy of Louis-Philippe. This ended with the revolution of 1848, which established the short-lived Second Republic. Then, in 1852,

Louis-Napoléon was declared Emperor and became Napoléon III. His empire lasted until 1870, the year Dickens died.

Domestically, the Second Empire was characterized by radical urban development, rapid progress in transport and communications, and dramatic financial and industrial expansion. It was also associated with a particularly intense pursuit of wealth and pleasure, attributable partly to the financial expansion (which included the foundation of new banks and credit institutions) and partly to the glittering standard set by the Empress Eugénie and the Imperial Court.

Paris, at once the hub and symbol of this modernizing energy and assertive splendor, was itself transformed. At the beginning of the Second Empire it was a city in crisis, packed with haphazard networks of narrow streets darkened by high, often crumbling buildings, seriously overpopulated, and increasingly unsanitary. The over-population was stifling the city, the lack of major thoroughfares hindered commerce, the narrow streets were all too easy to barricade, the unsanitary conditions were conducive to cholera (an 1849 epidemic claimed some 16,000 Parisians), there was little space for modern stores and other new enterprises to develop and thrive – and the Second Empire needed a prestigious capital city appropriate to its aspirations. The pressure for change was urgent and there were to be no half measures. By 1870, Paris had become the spacious, elegant, joined-up city we know today.

It was transformed, under the aegis of Napoléon III, by Baron Georges Haussmann, Préfet de la Seine from 1853 to 1870. Haussmann had many of the old streets in central Paris demolished to make way for a system of long elegant boulevards that brought structural unity to the city. In addition, great avenues were constructed, radiating out from the place de l'Étoile; many smaller new streets were built, letting in light and facilitating traffic movements; the city boundaries were extended and the *arrondissements* increased from 12 to 20; striking new buildings rose up; new bridges were constructed; new parks and green spaces were created – and the list goes on. The transformation was rapid and dramatic. When the Exposition Universelle of 1867 took place in Paris, the magnificent new city itself was the main attraction.

Dickens witnessed the progress of this *Haussmannisation* at first hand. He told W.H. Wills in a letter of October 1862 that a group of theaters on the boulevard du Temple "that used to be so characteristic" had been demolished,

> ... and preparations for some amazing new street are in rapid progress. I couldn't find my way yesterday to the Poste Restante, without looking at a Map! – I suppose I have been there, at least 50 times before. Wherever I turn, I see some astounding new work, doing or done. When you come over here ... you shall see sights. (*Pilgrim*, 10, p 151.)

In "Some Recollections of Mortality," he stands in front of a "large open space" in front of Notre-Dame:

> A very little while gone, I had left that space covered with buildings densely crowded; and now it was cleared for some new wonder in the way of public Street, Place, Garden, Fountain, or all four.

But, fascinated though he was by the physical transformation of the city, what really attracted Dickens to Paris lay far beyond the influence of Haussmann. It was the spirit of the place, and the way people lived in it, that engaged him. In the words of the twentieth-century novelist Julian Green,

> The soul of a big city is not to be grasped so easily; in order to make contact with it, you have to have been bored, you have to have suffered a bit in those places that contain it. Anyone can get hold of a guide and tick off all the monuments, but within the very confines of Paris there is another city as difficult of access as Timbuktu once was. (*Paris*, 1991, p 49.)

Dickens, with his acute understanding of urban life and already adept at tapping the essence of London, recognized this "inner" city as soon as he set foot in Paris:

I cannot conceive any place so perfectly and wonderfully expressive of its own character; its secret character no less than that which is on its surface; as Paris is. (Letter of 7 August 1844 to the Count d'Orsay, *Pilgrim*, 4, p 166.)

On this first visit he "walked about the streets" for the two days he was there, feeling as if each person he saw was another page in the "enormous book" of the city. Never one for tourist sites, Dickens was a natural flâneur – he knew that it was in the streets, the cafés, the theaters that he would he would find the "secret" Paris. Towards the end of his six-month stay in 1854–55, he told W.H. Wills, "Paris is finer than ever, and I go wandering about it all day... I seem to be rather a free and easy sort of superior Vagabond" (*Pilgrim*, 7, p 542).

Dickens was not, though, unremittingly positive about Paris. His early impressions were not all good. During his first period of residence, in 1846–47, he wrote to Forster that it was a "wicked and detestable place, though wonderfully attractive" and complained about the unhelpful and procrastinating tradespeople (*Life*, 5, Chapter 7). By the end of that visit, however, his real affection for the city was clear:

About Paris! I am charmed with the place, and have a much greater respect for the French people than I had before. The general appreciation of, and respect for, Art, in its broadest and most universal sense, in Paris, is one of the finest national signs I know. They are 'specially intelligent people: and though there still lingers among them an odd mixture of refinement and coarseness, I believe them to be, in many high and great respects, the first people in the universe. (Letter to Émile de la Rue, 24 March 1847, *Pilgrim*, 5, p 42.)

Nevertheless, Dickens is still referring to the "wickedness" of Paris as late as 1863 in letters to Wilke Collins – "... Paris is more immeasurably wicked than ever" – and W.C. Macready – "Paris is about as wicked and extravagant as in the days of the Regency" (*Pilgrim*, 10, pp 200 and 215). The wickedness, of course, is part of the attraction. When he sees London for the first time, the young David Copperfield is fascinated by it and feels that it must be "fuller of wonders and wickedness than all the cities of the earth" (*David Copperfield*, Chapter 5). As Dickens's many evocations of London demonstrate, the wickedness and wonders walk side by side, and the darkness is as compelling as the light.

There was one dark aspect of Paris that Dickens found especially compelling. "Whenever I am in Paris," he admits in "Travelling Abroad," "I am dragged by invisible force into the Morgue." This may seem a bizarre compulsion indeed, but it was far from uncommon. The Morgue, situated on the Île de la Cité, was open to anyone who wished to step inside. It offered a ghoulish kind of window display:

> ... a glazed partition will be seen, behind which are exposed the bodies of men and women found dead or drowned, and unowned. They are naked with the exception of a piece of leather over the loins, and stretched upon black marble slabs; the clothes hang on pegs above them, and a stream of water is trickling over the bodies. (Murray's *Handbook for Visitors to Paris*, 1864.)

The fact that the Morgue justified a substantial entry in Murray's *Handbook* gives some indication of its notoriety – and the entry, despite its deprecating tone, inevitably arouses the curiosity. There was certainly no shortage of visitors. The *Handbook* refers to "... a perpetual stream of men, women and children" running in and out of the building. F. B. Head, who writes at length about the Morgue in *A Faggot of French Sticks*, 1852, was astonished at the variety and number of people he saw there:

> At first I endeavoured to write down, in short-hand, merely the sexes and apparent ages of the people who kept dropping in; the tide however, in and out was so great, the stream of coming-in faces and departing backs was so continuous and conflicting, that I found it to be utterly impossible... (2, p 46.)

And Émile Zola's description of the variety of its visitors in *Thérèse Raquin*, 1867, echoes Dickens's account in "Railway Dreaming" (see note 22, p 354).

Something about the Morgue clearly fascinated Dickens. It made an appearance in his writing even before he had seen it – at the end of *The Old Curiosity Shop*, 1840–41, the body of Frederick Trent is identified by someone at "that hospital in Paris where the dead are laid out to be owned." It is mentioned in the brief description of his first visit to Paris in *Pictures from Italy*. And it is described in detail in "Travelling Abroad," "Railway Dreaming," and "Some Recollections of Mortality." Perhaps, apart from its obvious appeal to morbid curiosity, it held symbolic significance for him. With its display of death in the midst of a city throbbing with energy and life, the Morgue brought wreckage from the dark side of Paris into the light. Its macabre display was at once a memento mori (to which the onlookers seemed largely oblivious) and bleak evidence of the wickedness that lurked behind the wonders:

> The number of bodies annually exposed for three days in La Morgue amount to about 300 … A considerable proportion of the corpses are those of suicides and of people who have been murdered. (Head, 1852, 2, p 51.)

The four pieces in this chapter are presented in alphabetical order. The short extract from *Pictures from Italy*, 1846, is the only published record of Dickens's first impressions of Paris. It describes his parting glimpse of the city on a Sunday morning as the family carriage heads south on its way to Genoa. "Railway Dreaming" appeared in *Household Words* on 10 May 1856 and was written shortly after Dickens's six-month residence in Paris. Using the traveller's sense of suspended reality and dreamy isolation to bestow an other-worldliness on it, he visualizes the city from the cocoon of his railway carriage as he travels home to England. He reflects on the Parisians' love of sitting outdoors, speculation fever, the pleasures and virtues of café life, and the dismal attractions of the Morgue. In the extract from "New Year's Day," published in *Household Words* on 1 January 1859 (and probably also drawing on memories of the winter of 1855–56), he soaks up the atmosphere of Paris in celebratory mood and wanders in and out of theaters on the boulevard du Temple. "Some Recollections of Mortality" (an ironic allusion to Wordsworth's "Intimations of Immortality") was published in *All the Year Round* on 16 May 1863 as part of the second series of Uncommercial Traveller papers (see p 17). The narrative picks up from the end of "The Calais Night Mail," which had appeared two weeks earlier, and we accompany the Uncommercial Traveller, newly arrived in Paris, on a stroll from the Île de la Cité, where he joins a crowd to see a new arrival at the Morgue, up to the Grands Boulevards. His experiences and observations en route prompt recollections of two incidents in London: one, as he leaves the Morgue, a dismal and pessimistic vision of suffering and indifference, and the other, as he heads towards the bright lights of the boulevards, a gentler and more optimistic tale of suffering and compassion.

Rue de Rivoli, c 1855

EXTRACT FROM PICTURES
FROM ITALY

(PARIS ON SUNDAY MORNING)

There was, of course, very little in the aspect of Paris – as we rattled near the dismal Morgue[1] and over the Pont Neuf – to reproach us for our Sunday travelling. The wine-shops (every second house) were driving a roaring trade; awnings were spreading, and chairs and tables arranging, outside the cafés, preparatory to the eating of ices, and drinking of cool liquids, later in the day; shoe-blacks were busy on the bridges; shops were open; carts and waggons clattered to and fro; the narrow, up-hill, funnel-like streets across the River,[2] were so many dense perspectives of crowd and bustle, parti-coloured night-caps, tobacco-pipes, blouses, large boots, and shaggy heads of hair; nothing at that hour denoted a day of rest, unless it were the appearance, here and there, of a family pleasure-party, crammed into a bulky old lumbering cab; or of some contemplative holiday maker in the freest and easiest dishabille, leaning out of a low garret window, watching the drying of his newly polished shoes on the little parapet outside (if a gentleman), or the airing of her stockings in the sun (if a lady), with calm anticipation.

RAILWAY DREAMING

When was I last in France all the winter, deducting the many hours I passed upon the wet and windy way between France and England? In what autumn and spring was it that those Champs Elysées trees were yellow and scant of leaf when I first looked at them out of my balcony, and were a bright and tender green when I last looked at them on a beautiful May morning?[1]

I can't make out. I am never sure of time or place upon a Railroad. I can't read, I can't think, I can't sleep – I can only dream. Rattling along in this railway carriage in a state of luxurious confusion, I take it for granted I am coming from somewhere, and going somewhere else. I seek to know no more. Why things come into my head and fly out again, whence they come and why they come, where they go and why they go, I am incapable of considering. It may be the guard's business, or the railway company's; I only know it is not mine. I know nothing about myself – for anything I know, I may be coming from the Moon.

If I am coming from the Moon, what an extraordinary people the Mooninians must be for sitting down in the open air! I have seen them wipe the hoar-frost off the seats in the public ways, on the faintest appearance of a gleam of sun, and sit down to enjoy themselves. I have seen them, two minutes after it has left off raining for the first time in eight-and-forty hours, take chairs in the midst of mud and water, and begin to chat. I have seen them by the roadside, easily reclining on iron couches, when their beards have been all but blown off their chins by the east wind. I have seen them with no protection from the black drizzle and dirt but a saturated canvas blind overhead, and a handful of sand under foot, smoke and drink new beer,[2] whole evenings. And the Mooninian babies. Heavens, what a surprising race are the Mooninian babies! Seventy-one of these innocents have I counted, with their nurses and chairs, spending the day outside the Café de la Lune,[3] in weather that would have satisfied Herod.[4] Thirty-nine have I beheld in that locality at once, with these eyes, partaking of their natural refreshment under umbrellas. Twenty-three have I seen engaged with skipping-ropes, in mire three inches thick. At three years old the Mooninian babies grow up. They are by that time familiar with coffee-houses, and used up as to truffles. They dine at six. Soup, fish, two entrées, a vegetable, a cold dish, or paté-de-foie-gras, a roast, a salad, a sweet, and a preserved peach or so, form (with occasional whets of sardines, radishes, and Lyons sausage) their frugal repast. They breakfast at eleven, on a light beefsteak with Madeira sauce, a kidney steeped in champagne, a trifle of sweet-bread, a plate of fried potatoes, and a glass or two of wholesome Bordeaux wine. I have seen a marriageable young female aged five, in a mature bonnet and crinoline, finish off at a public establishment with her amiable parents, on coffee that would consign a child of any other nation to the family undertaker in one experiment. I have dined at a friendly party, sitting next to a Mooninian baby, who ate of nine dishes besides ice and fruit, and, wildly stimulated by sauces, in all leisure moments flourished its spoon about its head in the manner of a pictorial glory.[5]

The Mooninian Exchange was a strange sight in my time.[6] The Mooninians of all ranks and classes were gambling at that period (whenever it was), in the wildest manner – in a manner, which, in its extension to all possible subjects of gambling, and in the prevalence of the frenzy among all grades, has few parallels that I can recall. The steps of the Mooninian Bourse were thronged every day with a vast, hot, mad crowd, so expressive of the desperate game in which the whole City were players, that one stood aghast. In the Mooninian Journals I read, any day, without surprise, how such a Porter had rushed out of such a house and flung himself into the river, "because of losses on the Bourse"; or how such a man had robbed such another, with the intent of acquiring funds for speculation on the Bourse. In the great Mooninian Public Drive,[7] every day, there were crowds of riders on blood-horses, and crowds of riders in dainty carriages red-velvet lined and white-leather harnessed, all of whom had the cards and counters in their pockets; who were all feeding the blood-horses on paper and stabling them on the board; who were leading a grand life at a great rate and with a mighty show; who were all profuse and prosperous while the cards could continue to be shuffled and the deals to go round.

In the same place, I saw, nearly every day, a curious spectacle. One pretty little child at a window, always waving his hand at, and cheering, an array of open carriages escorted by out-riders in green and gold;[8] and no one echoing the child's acclamation. Occasional deference in carriages, occasional curiosity on foot, occasional adulation from foreigners, I noticed in that connection, in that place; but, four great streams of determined indifference I always saw flowing up and down; and I never, in six months, knew a hand or heard a voice to come in real aid of the child.

I am not a lonely man, though I was once a lonely boy; but that was long ago. The Mooninian capital, however, is the place for lonely men to dwell in. I have tried it, and have condemned myself to solitary freedom expressly for the purpose. I sometimes like to pretend to be childless and companionless, and to wonder whether, if I were really so, I should be glad to find somebody to ask me out to dinner, instead of living under a constant terror of weakly making engagements that I don't want to make. Hence, I have been into many Mooninian restaurants as a lonely man. The company have regarded me as an unfortunate person of that description. The paternal character, occupying the next table with two little boys whose legs were difficult of administration in a narrow space, as never being the right legs in the right places, has regarded me, at first, with looks of envy. When the little boys have indecorously inflated themselves out of the seltzer-water bottle, I have seen discomfiture and social shame on that Mooninian's brow. Meanwhile I have sat majestically using my tooth-pick, in silent assertion of my counterfeit superiority. And yet it has been good to see how that family Mooninian has vanquished me in the long-run. I have never got so red in the face over my meat and wine, as he. I have never warmed up into such enjoyment of my meal as he has of his. I have never forgotten the legs of the little boys, whereas from that Mooninian's soul they have quickly walked into oblivion. And when, at last, under the ripening influence of the dinner, those boys have both together pulled at that Mooninian's waistcoat (imploring him, as I conceived, to take them to the play-house, next door but one), I have shrunk under the glance he has given me; so emphatically has it said, with the virtuous farmer in the English domestic comedy, "Dang it, Squoire, can'ee doa thic!"[9] (I may explain in a parenthesis that "thic," which the virtuous farmer can do and the squire can't, is to lay his hand upon his heart – a result opposed to my experience in actual life, where the humbugs are always able to lay their hands upon their hearts, and do it far oftener and much better than the virtuous men.)

In my solitary character I have walked forth after eating my dinner and paying my bill – in the Mooninian capital we used to call the bill "the addition" – to take my coffee and cigar at some separate establishment devoted to such enjoyments. And in the customs belonging to these, as in many other easy and gracious customs, the Mooninians are highly deserving of imitation among ourselves. I have never had far to go, unless I have been particularly hard to please; a dozen houses at the utmost. A spring evening is in my mind when I sauntered from my dinner into one of these resorts, hap-hazard. The thoroughfare in which it stood, was not as wide as the Strand in

London, by Somerset House;[10] the houses were no larger and no better than are to be found in that place; the climate (we find ours a convenient scape-goat) had been, for months, quite as cold and wet, and very very often almost as dark, as the climate in the Strand. The place into which I turned, had been there all the winter just as it was then. It was like a Strand-shop, with the front altogether taken away. Within, it was sanded, prettily painted and papered, decorated with mirrors and glass chandeliers for gas; furnished with little round stone tables, crimson stools, and crimson benches. It was made much more tasteful (at the cost of three and fourpence a-week) by two elegant baskets of flowers on pedestals. An inner raised-floor, answering to the back shop in the Strand, was partitioned off with glass, for those who might prefer to read the papers and play at dominoes, in an atmosphere free from tobacco-smoke. There, in her neat little tribune, sits the Lady of the Counter, surrounded at her needlework by lump-sugar and little punch-bowls. To whom I touch my hat; she graciously acknowledging the salute. Forth from her side comes a pleasant waiter, scrupulously clean, brisk, attentive, honest: a man to be very obliging to me, but expecting me to be obliging in return, and whom I cannot bully – which is no deprivation to me, as I don't at all want to do it. He brings me, at my request, my cup of coffee and cigar, and, of his own motion, a small decanter of brandy and a liqueur-glass. He gives me a light, and leaves me to my enjoyment. The place from which the shop-front has been taken makes a gay proscenium; as I sit and smoke, the street becomes a stage, with an endless procession of lively actors crossing and re-crossing. Women with children, carts and coaches, men on horseback, soldiers, water-carriers with their pails, family groups, more soldiers, lounging exquisites, more family groups (coming past, flushed, a little too late for the play), stone-masons leaving work on the new buildings and playing tricks with one another as they go along, two lovers, more soldiers, wonderfully neat

young women from shops, carrying flat boxes to customers; a seller of
cool drink, with the drink in a crimson velvet temple at his back,[11]
and a waistcoat of tumblers on; boys, dogs, more soldiers, horse-riders
strolling to the Circus[12] in amazing shirts of private life, and yellow
kid gloves; family groups; pickers-up of refuse, with baskets at their
backs and hooked rods in their hands to fill them with; more neat
young women, more soldiers. The gas begins to spring up in the
street; and my brisk waiter lighting our gas, enshrines me, like an idol,
in a sparkling temple. A family group come in: father and mother and
little child. Two short-throated old ladies come in, who will pocket
their spare sugar, and out of whom I foresee that the establishment
will get as little profit as possible. Workman in his common frock
comes in; orders his small bottle of beer, and lights his pipe. We are
all amused, sitting seeing the traffic in the street, and the traffic in the
street is in its turn amused by seeing us. It is surely better for me, and
for the family group, and for the two old ladies, and for the workman,
to have thus much of community with the city life of all degrees, than
to be getting bilious in hideous black-holes, and turning cross and
suspicious in solitary places! I may never say a word to any of these
people in my life, nor they to me; but we are all interchanging
enjoyment frankly and openly – not fencing ourselves off and boxing
ourselves up. We are forming a habit of mutual consideration and
allowance; and this institution of the café (for all my entertainment
and pleasure in which, I pay tenpence), is a part of the civilised
system that requires the giant to fall into his own place in a crowd,
and will not allow him to take the dwarf's; and which renders the
commonest person as certain of retaining his or her commonest seat
in any public assembly, as the marquis is of holding his stall at the
Opera through the evening.

There were many things among the Mooninians that might be
changed for the better, and there were many things that they might

learn from us. They could teach us, for all that, how to make and keep a Park – which we have been accustomed to think ourselves rather learned in – and how to trim up our ornamental streets, a dozen times a-day, with scrubbing-brushes, and sponges, and soap, and chloride of lime. As to the question of sweetness within doors, I would rather not have put my own residence, even under the perpetual influence of peat charcoal, in competition with the cheapest model lodging-house in England. And one strange sight, which I have contemplated many a time during the last dozen years, I think is not so well arranged in the Mooninian capital as in London, even though our coroners hold their dread courts at the little public-houses[13] – a custom which I am of course prepared to hear is, and which I know beforehand must be, one of the Bulwarks of the British Constitution.

I am thinking of the Mooninian Morgue[14] where the bodies of all persons discovered dead, with no clue to their identity upon them, are placed, to be seen by all who choose to go and look at them. All the world knows this custom, and perhaps all the world knows that the bodies lie on inclined planes within a great glass window, as though Holbein[15] should represent Death, in his grim Dance, keeping a shop, and displaying his goods like a Regent Street[16] or Boulevard linen-draper. But, all the world may not have had the means of remarking perhaps, as I by chance have had from time to time, some of the accidental peculiarities of the place. The keeper seems to be fond of birds. In fair weather, there is always a cage outside his little window, and a something singing within it as such a something sang, thousands of ages ago, before ever a man died on this earth.[17] The spot is sunny in the forenoon, and, there being a little open space there, and a market for fruit and vegetables close at hand, and a way to the Great Cathedral past the door,[18] is a reasonably good spot for mountebanks.[19] Accordingly, I have often found Paillasse[20] there, balancing a knife or a straw upon his nose, with such intentness

that he has almost backed himself in at the doorway. The learned
owls have elicited great mirth there, within my hearing, and once the
performing dog who had a wait in his part, came and peeped in, with
a red jacket on, while I was alone in the contemplation of five bodies,
one with a bullet through the temple.[21] It happened, on another
occasion, that a handsome youth lay in front in the centre of the
window, and that a press of people behind me rendered it a difficult
and slow process to get out. As I gave place to the man at my right
shoulder, he slipped into the position I had occupied, with his
attention so concentrated on the dead figure that he seemed unaware
of the change of place. I never saw a plainer expression than that
upon his features, or one that struck more enduringly into my
remembrance. He was an evil-looking fellow of two or three and
twenty, and had his left hand at the draggled ends of his cravat, which
he had put to his mouth, and his right hand feeling in his breast. His
head was a little on one side; his eyes were intently fixed upon the
figure. "Now, if I were to give that pretty young fellow, my rival, a
stroke with a hatchet on the back of the head, or were to tumble him
over into the river by night, he would look pretty much like that, I am
thinking!" He could not have said it more plainly; – I have always an
idea that he went away and did it.

It is wonderful to see the people at this place. Cheery married
women, basket in hand, strolling in, on their way to or from the
buying of the day's dinner; children in arms with little pointing
fingers; young girls; prowling boys; comrades in working, soldiering,
or what not.[22] Ninety-nine times in a hundred, nobody about to cross
the threshold, looking in the faces coming out, could form the least
idea, from anything in their expression, of the nature of the sight. I
have studied them attentively, and have reason for saying so.

But, I never derived so strange a sensation from this dismal
establishment as on going in there once, and finding the keeper

moving about among the bodies. I never saw any living creature in among them, before or since, and the wonder was that he looked so much more ghastly and intolerable than the dead, stark people. There is a strong light from above, and a general cold, clammy aspect; and I think that with the first start of seeing him must have come the impression that the bodies were all getting up! It was instantaneous; but he looked horribly incongruous there, even after it had departed. All about him was a library of mysterious books that I have often had my eyes on. From pegs and hooks and rods, hang, for a certain time, the clothes of the dead who have been buried without recognition.[23] They mostly have been taken off people who were found in the water, and are swollen (as the people often are) out of shape and likeness. Such awful boots, with turned-up toes, and sand and gravel clinging to them, shall be seen in no other collection of dress; nor, such neck-cloths, long and lank, still retaining the form of having been wrung out; nor, such slimy garments with puffed legs and arms; nor, such hats and caps that have been battered against pile and bridge; nor, such dreadful rags. Whose work ornaments that decent blouse; who sewed that shirt? And the man who wore it. Did he ever stand at this window wondering, as I do, what sleepers shall be brought to these beds, and whether wonderers as to who should occupy them, have come to be laid down here themselves?

London! Please to get your tickets ready, gentlemen! I must have a coach. And that reminds me, how much better they manage coaches for the public in the capital of the Mooninians![24] But, it is done by Centralisation! somebody shrieks to me from some vestry's topmost height.[25] Then, my good sir, let us have Centralisation. It is a long word, but I am not at all afraid of long words when they represent efficient things. Circumlocution[26] is a long word, but it represents inefficiency; inefficiency in everything; inefficiency from the state coach to my hackney cab.

The Grands Boulevards: Porte St Denis and boulevard St Denis, 1858

EXTRACT FROM NEW YEAR'S DAY

Narrative context: The arrival of another New Year's Day acts like a magic wand on Dickens's imagination and takes him back in time to New Year's Days in his past. After recollections from his childhood and early adulthood, he draws on more recent memories to end the article with colorful and atmospheric descriptions of New Year's Day in Italy and, finally, in Paris.

And here is another New Year's Day invoked by the Wand of the time, and this New Year's Day is a French one, and a bitter, bitter cold one. All Paris is out of doors. Along the line of the Boulevards[1] runs a double row of stalls, like the stalls at an English fair; and surely those are hard to please, in all small wares and all small gambling, who cannot be pleased here. Paris is out of doors in its newest and brightest clothes. Paris is making presents to the Universe – which is well known to be in Paris.[2] Paris will eat more bons-bons this day, than in the whole bon-bon eating year. Paris will dine out this day, more than ever. In homage to the day, the peculiar glory of the always-glorious plate-glass windows of the Restorers[3] in the Palais Royal, where rare summer-vegetables from Algiers contend with wonderful great pears from the richest soils of France, and with little plump birds of exquisite plumage, direct from the skies. In homage to the day, the glittering brilliancy of the sweet-shops, teeming with beautiful arrangement of colours, and with beautiful tact and taste in trifles. In homage to the day, the new Review – Dramas at the Theatre of Varieties, and the Theatre of Vaudevilles, and the Theatre of the Palais Royal.[4] In homage to the day, the new Drama in seven acts, and incalculable pictures, at the Ambiguously Comic Theatre, the Theatre of the Gate of St Martin, and the Theatre of Gaiety: at which last establishment particularly, a brooding Englishman can, by intensity of interest, get himself made wretched for a fortnight.[5] In homage to the day, the extra-announcing of these Theatres, and fifty more, and the queues of blouses already, at three o'clock in the afternoon, penned up in the cold wind on the cold stone pavement outside them.[6] Spite of wind and frost, the Elysian Fields and the Wood of Boulogne are filled with equipages, equestrians, and pedestrians: while the strange, rackety, rickety, up-all-night looking world of eating house, tomb-stone maker, ball room, cemetery, and wine-shop, outside the Barriers,[7] is as thickly-peopled as the Paris streets themselves; with one universal tendency observable in both hemispheres, to sit down upon any public seat at a risk of being frozen to death, and to go round and round on a hobby-horse in any roundabout, to the music of a barrel organ, as a severe act of duty. And now, this New Year's Day tones down into night, and the brilliantly lighted city shines out like the gardens of the Wonderful Lamp,[8] and the penned blouses flutter into the Theatres in orderly line, and the confidential men, not unaccustomed to lean on umbrellas as they survey mankind of an afternoon, who have tickets to sell cheap, are very busy among them,[9] and the women money-takers shut up in strong iron-cages are busy too, and the three men all of a row behind a breast-work who take the checks are busy too, and the women box-openers with their footstools begin to be busy too, but as yet not very, and the curtain goes up for the curtain-rising piece, and the gloomy young gentleman with the tight black head and the new black moustache is as much in love as ever with the young lady whose eyebrows are very arched and whose voice is very thin, and the gloomy young gentleman's experienced friend (generally chewing something, by the bye, and I wonder what), who leans his back against the chimney-piece and reads him lessons of life, is just as cool as he always was, and an amazing circumstance to me is, that they are

always doing this thing and no other thing, and that I don't find them
to have any place in the great event of the evening, and that I want to
know whether they go home when they have done it, or what
becomes of them. Meanwhile, gushes of cookery rise with the night
air from the Restorer's kitchens; and the guests at the Café of Paris,
and the Café of the Three Provincial Brothers, and the Café Vefour,
and the Café Verey, and the Gilded House, and others of first class,
are reflected in wildernesses of looking glass, and sit on red velvet
and order dinner out of red velvet books;[10] while the citizens at the
Café Champeaux[11] near the Bourse, and others of second class, sit on
rush-bottomed chairs, and have their dinner-library bound in plain
leather, though they dine well too; while both kinds of company have
plenty of children with them (which is pleasant to me, though I think
they begin life biliously), and both unite in eating everything that is
set before them. But, now it is eight o'clock upon this New Year's
evening. The new Dramas being about to begin, bells ring violently
in the Theatre lobbies and rooms, and cigars, coffee cups, and small
glasses are hastily abandoned, and I find myself assisting at one of the
Review-pieces: where I notice that the English gentleman's stomach
isn't very like, because it doesn't fit him, and wherein I doubt the
accurate nationality of the English lady's walking on her toes with an
upward jerk behind. The Review is derived from various times and
sources, and when I have seen David the Psalmist in his droll scene
with Mahomet and Abd-el-Kader,[12] and have heard the best joke and
best song that Eve (a charming young lady, but liable, I should fear,
to take cold) has in her part (which occurs in her scene with the Sieur
Framboisie[13]), I think I will step out to the Theatre of the Gaiety,[14]
and see what they are about there. I am so fortunate as to arrive in the
nick of time to find the very estimable man just eloped with the wife
of the much less estimable man whom Destiny has made a bore, and
to find her honest father just arriving from the country by one door,

encountering the father of the very estimable man just arriving from the country by another door, and to hear them launch cross-curses – her father at him: his father at her – which so deeply affects a martial gentleman of tall stature and dark complexion, in the next stall to mine, that, taking out his handkerchief from his hat to dry his eyes, he pulls out with it several very large lumps of sugar which he abstracted when he took his coffee, and showers them over my legs – exceedingly to my confusion, but not at all to his. The drop-curtain being, to appearance, down for a long time, I think I will step on a little further – say to the Theatre of the Scavengers[15] – and see what they are doing there. At the Theatre of the Scavengers, I find Pierrot on a voyage. I know he is aboard ship, because I can see nothing but sky; and I infer that the crew are aloft from the circumstance of two rope-ladders crossing the stage and meeting at top; about mid-way on each of which hangs, contemplating the public, an immovable young lady in male attire, with highly unseamanlike pink legs. This spectacle reminds me of another New Year's Day at home in England, where I saw the brave William, lover of Black Eyed Susan, tried by a Court Martial[16] composed entirely of ladies, wearing perceptible combs in their heads: with the exception of the presiding Admiral, who was so far gone in liquor that I trembled to think what could possibly be done respecting the catastrophe, if he should take it in his head to record the verdict "Not guilty." On this present New Year's Day, I find Pierrot suffering, in various ways, so very much from sea-sickness, that I soon leave the congregated Scavengers in possession of him; but not before I have gathered from the bill that in the case even of his drama, as of every French piece, it takes at least two men to write it.[17] So, I pass this New Year's evening, which is a French one, looking about me until midnight: when, going into a Boulevard café on my way home, I find the elderly men who are always playing dominoes there, or always looking on at one another playing dominoes there, hard at it still, not in the least moved by the stir and novelty of the day, not in the least minding the New Year.

Franconi's Circus, Champs-Élysées, 1843

SOME RECOLLECTIONS OF MORTALITY

I had parted from the small bird[1] at somewhere about four o'clock in the morning, when he had got out at Arras, and had been received by two shovel-hats[2] in waiting at the station, who presented an appropriately ornithological and crow-like appearance. My compatriot and I had gone on to Paris; my compatriot enlightening me occasionally with a long list of the enormous grievances of French railway travelling: every one of which, as I am a sinner, was perfectly new to me, though I have as much experience of French railways as most uncommercials.[3] I had left him at the terminus (through his conviction, against all explanation and remonstrance, that his baggage-ticket was his passenger-ticket), insisting in a very high temper to the functionary on duty, that in his own personal identity he was four packages weighing so many kilogrammes – as if he had been Cassim Baba![4] I had bathed and breakfasted, and was strolling on the bright quays. The subject of my meditations was the question whether it is positively in the essence and nature of things, as a certain school of Britons would seem to think it, that a Capital must be ensnared and enslaved before it can be made beautiful: when I lifted up my eyes, and found that my feet, straying like my mind, had brought me to Notre-Dame.

That is to say, Notre-Dame was before me, but there was a large open space between us. A very little while gone, I had left that space covered with buildings densely crowded; and now it was cleared for some new wonder in the way of public Street, Place, Garden, Fountain, or all four.[5] Only the obscene little Morgue, slinking on the brink of the river and soon to come down,[6] was left there, looking mortally ashamed of itself, and supremely wicked. I had but glanced at this old acquaintance, when I beheld an airy procession coming round in front of Notre-Dame, past the great hospital.[7] It had something of a Masaniello[8] look, with fluttering striped curtains in the midst of it, and it came dancing round the cathedral in the liveliest manner.

I was speculating on a marriage in Blouse-life, or a Christening, or some other domestic festivity which I would see out, when I found, from the talk of a quick rush of Blouses past me, that it was a Body coming to the Morgue. Having never before chanced upon this initiation, I constituted myself a Blouse likewise, and ran into the Morgue with the rest. It was a very muddy day, and we took in a quantity of mire with us, and the procession coming in upon our heels brought a quantity more. The procession was in the highest spirits, and consisted of idlers who had come with the curtained litter from its starting-place, and all of the reinforcements it had picked up on the way. It set the litter down in the midst of the Morgue, and then two Custodians proclaimed aloud that we were all "invited" to go out. This invitation was rendered the more pressing, if not the more flattering, by our being shoved out, and the folding-gates being barred upon us.

Those who have never seen the Morgue, may see it perfectly, by presenting to themselves an indifferently paved coach-house accessible from the street by a pair of folding-gates; on the left of the coach-house, occupying its width, any large London tailor's or linendraper's plate-glass window reaching to the ground; within the window, on two rows of inclined planes, what the coach-house has to show; hanging above, like irregular stalactites from the roof of a cave, a quantity of clothes – the clothes of the dead and buried shows of the coach-house.[9]

We had been excited in the highest degree by seeing the Custodians pull off their coats and tuck up their shirt-sleeves, as the procession came along. It looked so interestingly like business. Shut out in the muddy street, we now became quite ravenous to know all about it. Was it river, pistol, knife, love, gambling, robbery, hatred, how many stabs, how many bullets, fresh or decomposed, suicide or murder? All wedged together, and all staring at one another with our heads thrust forward, we propounded these inquiries and a hundred more such. Imperceptibly, it came to be known that Monsieur the tall and sallow mason yonder, was acquainted with the facts. Would Monsieur the tall and sallow mason, surged at by a new wave of us, have the goodness to impart? It was but a poor old man, passing along the street under one of the new buildings, on whom a stone had fallen, and who had tumbled dead. His age? Another wave surged up against the tall and sallow mason, and our wave swept on and broke, and he was any age from sixty-five to ninety.

An old man was not much: moreover, we could have wished he had been killed by human agency – his own, or somebody else's: the latter, preferable – but our comfort was, that he had nothing about him to lead to his identification, and that his people must seek him here. Perhaps they were waiting dinner for him even now? We liked that. Such of us as had pocket-handkerchiefs took a slow intense protracted wipe at our noses, and then crammed our handkerchiefs into the breast of our blouses. Others of us who had no handkerchiefs administered a similar relief to our overwrought minds, by means of prolonged smears or wipes of our mouths on our sleeves. One man with a gloomy malformation of brow – a homicidal worker in white-lead, to judge from his blue tone of colour, and a certain flavour of paralysis pervading him – got his coat-collar between his teeth, and bit at it with an appetite. Several decent women arrived upon the outskirts of the crowd, and prepared to launch themselves into the dismal coach-house when opportunity should come; among them, a pretty young mother, pretending to bite the forefinger of her baby-boy, kept it between her rosy lips that it might be handy for guiding to point at the show. Meantime, all faces were turned towards the building, and we men waited with a fixed and stern resolution: – for the most part with folded arms. Surely, it was the only public French sight these uncommercial eyes had seen, at which the expectant people did not form *en queue*. But there was no such order of arrangement here; nothing but a general determination to make a rush for it, and a disposition to object to some boys who had mounted on the two stone posts by the hinges of the gates, with the design of swooping in when the hinges should turn.

Now, they turned, and we rushed! Great pressure, and a scream or two from the front. Then a laugh or two, some expressions of disappointment, and a slackening of the pressure and subsidence of the struggle. – Old man not there.

"But what would you have?" the Custodian reasonably argues, as he looks out at his little door. "Patience, patience! We make his toilette, gentlemen. He will be exposed presently. It is necessary to proceed according to rule. His toilette is not made all at a blow. He will be exposed in good time, gentlemen, in good time." And so retires, smoking, with a wave of his sleeveless arm towards the window, importing, "Entertain yourselves in the meanwhile with the other curiosities. Fortunately the Museum is not empty today."

Who would have thought of public fickleness even at the Morgue? But there it was, on that occasion. Three lately popular articles that had been attracting greatly when the litter was first descried coming dancing round the corner by the great cathedral, were so completely deposed now, that nobody save two little girls (one showing them to a doll) would look at them. Yet the chief of the three, the article in the front row, had received jagged injury of the left temple; and the other two in the back row, the drowned two lying side by side with their heads very slightly turned towards each other, seemed to be comparing notes about it. Indeed, those two of the back row were so furtive of appearance, and so (in their puffed way) assassinatingly knowing as to the one of the front, that it was hard to think the three had never come together in their lives, and were only chance companions after death. Whether or no this was the general, as it was the uncommercial, fancy, it is not to be disputed that the group had drawn exceedingly within ten minutes. Yet now, the inconstant public turned its back upon them, and even leaned its elbows carelessly against the bar outside the window and shook off the mud from its shoes, and also lent and borrowed fire for pipes.

Custodian re-enters from his door, "Again once, gentlemen, you are invited —" No further invitation necessary. Ready dash into the street. Toilette finished. Old man coming out.

This time, the interest was grown too hot to admit of toleration of the boys on the stone posts. The homicidal white-lead worker made a pounce upon one boy who was hoisting himself up, and brought him to earth amidst general commendation. Closely stowed as we were, we yet formed into groups – groups of conversation, without separation from the mass – to discuss the old man. Rivals of the tall and sallow mason sprang into being, and here again was popular inconstancy. These rivals attracted audiences, and were greedily listened to; and whereas they had derived their information solely from the tall and sallow one, officious members of the crowd now sought to enlighten *him* on their authority. Changed by this social experience into an iron-visaged and inveterate misanthrope, the mason glared at mankind, and evidently cherished in his breast the wish that the whole of the present company could change places with the deceased old man. And now listeners became inattentive, and people made a start forward at a slight sound, and an unholy fire kindled in the public eye, and those next the gates beat at them impatiently, as if they were of the cannibal species and hungry.

Again the hinges creaked, and we rushed. Disorderly pressure for some time ensued before the uncommercial unit got figured into the front row of the sum. It was strange to see so much heat and uproar seething about one poor spare white-haired old man, quiet for evermore. He was calm of feature and undisfigured, as he lay on his back – having been struck upon the hinder part of the head, and thrown forward – and something like a tear or two had started from the closed eyes, and lay wet upon the face. The uncommercial interest, sated at a glance, directed itself upon the striving crowd on either side and behind: wondering whether one might have guessed, from the expression of those faces merely, what kind of sight they were looking at. The differences of expression were not many. There was a little pity, but not much, and that mostly with a selfish touch in it – as who would say, "Shall I, poor I, look like that, when the time comes!" There was more of a secretly brooding contemplation and curiosity, as "That man I don't like, and have the grudge against; would such be his appearance, if some one – not to mention names – by any chance gave him an ugly knock?" There was a wolfish stare at the object, in which the homicidal white-lead worker shone conspicuous. And there was a much more general, purposeless, vacant staring at it – like looking at waxwork, without a catalogue, and not knowing what to make of it. But all these expressions concurred in possessing the one underlying expression of *looking at something that could not return a look*. The uncommercial notice had established this as very remarkable, when a new pressure all at once coming up from the street pinioned him ignominiously, and hurried him into the arms (now sleeved again) of the Custodian smoking at his door, and answering questions, between-puffs, with a certain placid meritorious air of not being proud, though high in office. And mentioning pride, it may be observed, by the way, that one could not well help investing the original sole occupant of the front row with an air depreciatory of the legitimate attraction of the poor old man: while the two in the second row seemed to exult at his superseded popularity.

Pacing presently round the garden of the Tower of St Jacques de la Boucherie,[10] and presently again in front of the Hôtel de Ville, I called to mind a certain desolate open-air Morgue that I happened to light upon in London, one day in the hard winter of 1861, and which seemed as strange to me, at the time of seeing it, as if I had found it in China. Towards that hour of a winter's afternoon when the lamplighters are beginning to light the lamps in the streets a little before they are wanted, because the darkness thickens fast and soon, I was walking in from the country on the northern side of Regent's Park – hard frozen and deserted – when I saw an empty Hansom cab drive up to the lodge at Gloucester-gate,[11] and the driver with great agitation call to the man there: who quickly reached a long pole from a tree, and, deftly collared by the driver, jumped to the step of his little seat, and so the Hansom rattled out at the gate, galloping over the iron-bound road.[12] I followed running, though not so fast but that when I came to the right-hand Canal Bridge, near the cross-path to Chalk Farm,[13] the Hansom was stationary, the horse was smoking hot, the long pole was idle on the ground, and the driver and the park-keeper were looking over the bridge parapet. Looking over too, I saw, lying on the towing-path with her face turned up towards us, a woman, dead a day or two, and under thirty, as I guessed, poorly dressed in black. The feet were lightly crossed at the ankles, and the dark hair, all pushed back from the face, as though that had been the last action of her desperate hands, streamed over the ground. Dabbled all about her, was the water and the broken ice that had dropped from her dress, and had splashed as she was got out. The policeman who had just got her out, and the passing costermonger who had helped him, were standing near the body; the latter with that stare at it which I have likened to being at a waxwork exhibition without a catalogue; the former, looking over his stock, with professional stiffness and coolness, in the direction in which the bearers he had sent for were expected. So dreadfully forlorn, so dreadfully sad, so dreadfully mysterious, this spectacle of our dear sister here departed![14] A barge came up, breaking the floating ice and the silence, and a woman steered it. The man with the horse that towed it, cared so little for the body, that the stumbling hoofs had been among the hair, and the tow-rope had caught and turned the head, before our cry of horror took him to the bridle. At which sound the steering woman looked up at us on the bridge, with contempt unutterable, and then looking down at the body with a similar expression – as if it were made in another likeness from herself, had been informed with other passions, had been lost by other chances, had had another nature dragged down to perdition – steered a spurning streak of mud at it, and passed on.

A better experience, but also of the Morgue kind, in which chance happily made me useful in a slight degree, arose to my remembrance as I took my way by the Boulevard de Sébastopol to the brighter scenes of Paris.[15]

The thing happened, say, five-and-twenty years ago. I was a modest young uncommercial then, and timid and inexperienced. Many suns and winds have browned me in the line, but those were my pale days. Having newly taken the lease of a house in a certain distinguished metropolitan parish[16] – a house which then appeared to me to be a frightfully first-class Family Mansion, involving awful responsibilities – I became the prey of a Beadle.[17] I think the Beadle must have seen me going in or coming out, and must have observed that I tottered under the weight of my grandeur. Or he may have been hiding under straw when I bought my first horse (in the desirable stable-yard attached to the first-class Family Mansion), and when the vendor remarked to me, in an original manner, on bringing him for approval, taking his cloth off and smacking him, "There Sir! *There's* a Orse!" And when I said gallantly, "How much do you want for him?" and when the vendor said, "No more than sixty guineas, from you," and when I said smartly, "Why not more than sixty from *me*?" And when he said crushingly, "Because upon my soul and body he'd be considered cheap at seventy, by one who understood the subject – but you don't." – I say, the Beadle may have been in hiding under straw, when this disgrace befell me, or he may have noted that I was too raw and young an Atlas to carry the first-class Family Mansion in a knowing manner. Be this as it may, the Beadle did what Melancholy did to the youth in Gray's Elegy[18] – he marked me for his own. And the way in which the Beadle did it, was this: he summoned me as a Juryman on his Coroner's Inquests.[19]

In my first feverish alarm I repaired "for safety and for succour" – like those sagacious Northern shepherds who, having had no previous reason whatever to believe in young Norval, very prudently did not originate the hazardous idea of believing in him[20] – to a deep householder. This profound man informed me that the Beadle counted on my buying him off; on my bribing him not to summon me; and that if I would attend an Inquest with a cheerful countenance, and profess alacrity in that branch of my country's service, the Beadle would be disheartened, and would give up the game.

I roused my energies, and the next time the wily Beadle summoned me, I went. The Beadle was the blankest Beadle I have ever looked on when I answered to my name; and his discomfiture gave me courage to go through with it.

We were impannelled to inquire concerning the death of a very little mite of a child. It was the old miserable story. Whether the mother had committed the minor offence of concealing the birth, or whether she had committed the major offence of killing the child, was the question on which we were wanted. We must commit her on one of the two issues.

The Inquest came off in the parish workhouse, and I have yet a lively impression that I was unanimously received by my brother Jurymen as a brother of the utmost conceivable insignificance. Also, that before we began, a broker who had lately cheated me fearfully in the matter of a pair of card-tables, was for the utmost rigour of the law. I remember that we sat in a sort of board-room, on such very large square horse-hair chairs that I wondered what race of Patagonians[21] they were made for; and further, that an undertaker gave me his card when we were in the full moral freshness of having just been sworn, as "an inhabitant that was newly come into the parish, and was likely to have a young family." The case was then stated to us by the Coroner, and then we went down-stairs – led by the plotting Beadle – to view the body. From that day to this, the poor little figure, on which that sounding legal appellation was bestowed, has lain in the same place and with the same surroundings, to my thinking. In a kind of crypt devoted to the warehousing of the parochial coffins, and in the midst of a perfect Panorama of coffins of all sizes, it was stretched on a box; the mother had put it in her box – this box – almost as soon as it was born, and it had been presently found there. It had been opened, and neatly sewn up, and regarded from that point of view, it looked like a stuffed creature. It rested on a clean white cloth, with a surgical instrument or so at hand, and regarded from that point of view, it looked as if the cloth were "laid," and the Giant were coming to dinner. There was nothing repellant about the poor piece of innocence, and it demanded a mere form of looking at. So, we looked at an old pauper who was going about among the coffins with a foot rule, as if he were a case of Self-Measurement; and we looked at one another; and we said the place was well whitewashed anyhow; and then our conversational powers as a British Jury flagged, and the foreman said, "All right, gentlemen? Back again, Mr Beadle!"

The miserable young creature who had given birth to this child within a very few days, and who had cleaned the cold wet door-steps immediately afterwards, was brought before us when we resumed our horse-hair chairs, and was present during the proceedings. She had a horse-hair chair herself, being very weak and ill; and I remember how she turned to the unsympathetic nurse who attended her, and who might have been the figure-head of a pauper-ship, and how she hid her face and sobs and tears upon that wooden shoulder. I remember, too, how hard her mistress was upon her (she was a servant-of-all-work), and with what a cruel pertinacity that piece of Virtue[22] spun her thread of evidence double, by intertwisting it with the sternest thread of construction. Smitten hard by the terrible low wail from the utterly friendless orphan girl, which never ceased during the whole inquiry, I took heart to ask this witness a question or two, which hopefully admitted of an answer that might give a favourable turn to the case. She made the turn as little favourable as it could be, but it did some good, and the Coroner, who was nobly patient and humane (he was the late Mr Wakley[23]), cast a look of strong encouragement in my direction. Then, we had the doctor who had made the examination, and the usual tests as to whether the child was born alive; but he was a timid muddle-headed doctor, and got confused and contradictory, and wouldn't say this, and couldn't answer for that, and the immaculate broker was too much for him, and our side slid back again. However, I tried again, and the Coroner backed me again, for which I ever afterwards felt grateful to him as I do now to his memory; and we got another favourable turn, out of some other witness, some member of the family with a strong prepossession against the sinner; and I think we had the doctor back again; and I know that the Coroner summed up for our side, and that

I and my British brothers turned round to discuss our verdict, and get ourselves into great difficulties with our large chairs and the broker. At that stage of the case I tried hard again, being convinced that I had cause for it; and at last we found for the minor offence of only concealing the birth; and the poor desolate creature, who had been taken out during our deliberation, being brought in again to be told of the verdict, then dropped upon her knees before us, with protestations that we were right – protestations among the most affecting that I have ever heard in my life – and was carried away insensible.

(In private conversation after this was all over, the Coroner showed me his reasons as a trained surgeon, for perceiving it to be impossible that the child could, under the most favourable circumstances, have drawn many breaths, in the very doubtful case of its ever having breathed at all; this, owing to the discovery of some foreign matter in the windpipe, quite irreconcilable with many moments of life.)

When the agonised girl had made those final protestations, I had seen her face, and it was in unison with her distracted heartbroken voice, and it was very moving. It certainly did not impress me by any beauty that it had, and if I ever see it again in another world I shall only know it by the help of some new sense or intelligence. But it came to me in my sleep that night,[24] and I selfishly dismissed it in the most efficient way I could think of. I caused some extra care to be taken of her in the prison, and counsel to be retained for her defence when she was tried at the Old Bailey;[25] and her sentence was lenient, and her history and conduct proved that it was right. In doing the little I did for her, I remember to have had the kind help of some gentle-hearted functionary to whom I addressed myself – but what functionary I have long forgotten – who I suppose was officially present at the Inquest.

I regard this as a very notable uncommercial experience, because this good came of a Beadle. And to the best of my knowledge, information, and belief, it is the only good that ever did come of a Beadle since the first Beadle put on his cocked-hat.[26]

chapter eight

GOING SOUTH: LYON, THE RHÔNE, AND AVIGNON

(EXTRACT FROM *PICTURES FROM ITALY*)

On 2 July 1844 Dickens and his family left London in an "English travelling-carriage of considerable proportions" to spend a year in Italy. There were twelve in the party – Dickens, his wife Catherine, their five children (including a six-month-old baby), his wife's sister Georgina Hogarth, three servants, and a courier. They spent twelve days travelling through France to Marseille where, on 15 July, they boarded a steamer bound for Genoa.

This coach journey through France is the subject of the early chapters of *Pictures from Italy*, the travel book that records Dickens's impressions and observations during his year of residence in Italy. Published in May 1846, the book was based on letters that Dickens had written to John Forster and other friends while on his travels. The text therefore has the quality of immediacy, as if the traveller-writer is jotting down what he sees and feels in the freshness of the experience.

Dickens was keen to convey this sense of immediacy to his readers. Earlier versions of the first few chapters of *Pictures from Italy* had appeared in the newly launched *Daily News* in January–March 1846. That series of articles was tagged "Travelling Letters. *Written on the Road.*" (emphasis added.) In *Pictures from Italy*, Dickens explains the origin of the text in a foreword entitled "The Reader's Passport" and offers it as a kind of certificate of authenticity:

> The greater part of the descriptions were written on the spot, and sent home, from time to time, in private letters. I do not mention the circumstance as an excuse for any defects they may present, for it would be none; but as a guarantee to the Reader that they were at least penned in the fulness of the subject, and with the liveliest impressions of novelty and freshness.

Pictures from Italy, then, reads like a travel diary written on the move – a collection of subjective, sometimes whimsical accounts of people and places, and incidents connected with them, infused with the traveller's personal perceptions and responses. Dickens is interested in communicating the experience of the journey and the reflections it engenders – and he sees it as no part of his business to be bothering with factual detail that does not relate directly to this purpose. As he tells his readers,

> If you would know all about the architecture of this church, or any other, its dates, dimensions, endowments and history, is it not written in Mr Murray's Guide-Book, and may you not read it there, with thanks to him, as I did!

The extract that follows includes the whole of the "Lyons, the Rhone, and the Goblin of Avignon" chapter of *Pictures from Italy* and the first few paragraphs of "Avignon to Genoa." We join Dickens at Lyon, a city with which he is less than impressed, and accompany him down the Rhône to Avignon. At Avignon he visits the Cathedral where he muses on humble pictures hung up as votive offerings, and the immense Palais des Papes where, listening to dismal tales of imprisonment and torture, he sees rays of hope in the sunlight that shines through cracks in dungeon walls.

Lyon, c 1850

EXTRACT FROM PICTURES FROM ITALY

(LYON, THE RHÔNE, AVIGNON)

What a city Lyons is! Talk about people feeling, at certain unlucky times, as if they had tumbled from the clouds! Here is a whole town that has tumbled, anyhow, out of the sky; having been first caught up, like other stones that tumble down from that region, out of fens and barren places, dismal to behold! The two great streets through which the two great rivers dash,[1] and all the little streets whose name is Legion,[2] were scorching, blistering, and sweltering. The houses, high and vast, dirty to excess, rotten as old cheeses, and as thickly peopled. All up the hills that hem the city in, these houses swarm; and the mites inside were lolling out of the windows, and drying their ragged clothes on poles, and crawling in and out at the doors, and coming out to pant and gasp upon the pavement, and creeping in and out among huge piles and bales of fusty, musty, stifling goods; and living, or rather not dying till their time should come, in an exhausted receiver.[3] Every manufacturing town, melted into one, would hardly convey an impression of Lyons as it presented itself to me: for all the undrained, unscavengered,[4] qualities of a foreign town, seemed grafted, there, upon the native miseries of a manufacturing one; and it bears such fruit as I would go some miles out of my way to avoid encountering again.[5]

In the cool of the evening: or rather in the faded heat of the day: we went to see the Cathedral, where divers old women, and a few dogs, were engaged in contemplation. There was no difference, in point of cleanliness, between its stone pavement and that of the streets; and there was a wax saint, in a little box like a berth aboard ship, with a glass front to it, whom Madame Tussaud[6] would have nothing to say to, on any terms, and which even Westminster Abbey[7] might be ashamed of. If you would know all about the architecture of this church, or any other, its dates, dimensions, endowments, and history, is it not written in Mr Murray's Guide-Book,[8] and may you not read it there, with thanks to him, as I did!

For this reason, I should abstain from mentioning the curious clock in Lyons Cathedral, if it were not for a small mistake I made, in connection with that piece of mechanism.[9] The keeper of the church was very anxious it should be shown; partly for the honour of the establishment and the town; and, partly, perhaps, because of his deriving a percentage from the additional consideration. However that may be, it was set in motion, and thereupon a host of little doors flew open, and innumerable little figures staggered out of them, and jerked themselves back again, with that special unsteadiness of purpose, and hitching in the gait, which usually attaches to figures that are moved by clock-work. Meanwhile, the Sacristan stood explaining these wonders, and pointing them out, severally, with a wand. There was a centre puppet of the Virgin Mary; and close to her, a small pigeon-hole, out of which another and a very ill-looking puppet made one of the most sudden plunges I ever saw accomplished: instantly flopping back again at sight of her, and banging his little door, violently, after him. Taking this to be emblematic of the victory over Sin and Death, and not at all unwilling to show that I perfectly understood the subject, in anticipation of the showman, I rashly said, "Aha! The Evil Spirit. To be sure. He is very soon disposed of." "Pardon, Monsieur," said the Sacristan, with a polite motion of his hand towards the little door, as if introducing somebody – " The Angel Gabriel!"

Soon after daybreak next morning, we were steaming down the Arrowy Rhone,[10] at the rate of twenty miles an hour, in a very dirty vessel full of merchandise, and with only three or four other passengers for our companions: among whom, the most remarkable was a silly, old, meek-faced, garlic-eating, immeasurably polite Chevalier,[11] with a dirty scrap of red ribbon hanging at his button-hole, as if he had tied it there, to remind himself of something: as Tom Noddy, in the farce, ties knots in his pocket-handkerchief.[12]

For the last two days, we had seen great sullen hills, the first indications of the Alps, lowering in the distance. Now, we were rushing on beside them: sometimes close beside them: sometimes with an intervening slope, covered with vineyards. Villages and small towns hanging in mid-air, with great woods of olives seen through the light open towers of their churches, and clouds moving slowly on, upon the steep acclivity behind them; ruined castles perched on every eminence; and scattered houses in the clefts and gullies of the hills; made it very beautiful. The great height of these, too, making the buildings look so tiny, that they had all the charm of elegant models; their excessive whiteness, as contrasted with the brown rocks, or the sombre, deep, dull, heavy green of the olive-tree; and the puny size, and little slow walk of the Lilliputian men and women on the bank; made a charming picture. There were ferries out of number, too; bridges; the famous Pont d'Esprit, with I don't know how many arches;[13] towns where memorable wines are made; Valence, where Napoleon studied;[14] and the noble river, bringing, at every winding turn, new beauties into view.

There lay before us, that same afternoon, the broken bridge of Avignon,[15] and all the city baking in the sun; yet with an under-done-pie-crust, battlemented wall, that never will be brown, though it bake for centuries.

The grapes were hanging in clusters in the streets, and the brilliant Oleander was in full bloom everywhere. The streets are old and very narrow, but tolerably clean, and shaded by awnings stretched from house to house. Bright stuffs and handkerchiefs, curiosities, ancient frames of carved wood, old chairs, ghostly tables, saints, virgins, angels, and staring daubs of portraits, being exposed for sale beneath, it was very quaint and lively. All this was much set off, too, by the glimpses one caught, through rusty gates standing ajar, of quiet sleepy court-yards, having stately old houses within, as silent as tombs. It was all very like one of the descriptions in the Arabian Nights. The three one-eyed Calendars might have knocked at any one of those doors till the street rang again, and the porter who persisted in asking questions – the man who had the delicious purchases put into his basket in the morning – might have opened it quite naturally.[16]

After breakfast next morning, we sallied forth to see the lions.[17] Such a delicious breeze was blowing in, from the north, as made the walk delightful: though the pavement-stones, and stones of the walls and houses, were far too hot to have a hand laid on them comfortably.

We went, first of all, up a rocky height, to the cathedral: where Mass was performing to an auditory very like that of Lyons, namely, several old women, a baby, and a very self-possessed dog, who had marked out for himself a little course or platform for exercise, beginning at the altar-rails and ending at the door, up and down which constitutional walk he trotted, during the service, as methodically and calmly, as any old gentleman out of doors. It is a bare old church, and the paintings in the roof are sadly defaced by time and damp weather; but the sun was shining in, splendidly, through the red curtains of the windows, and glittering on the altar furniture; and it looked as bright and cheerful as need be.

Going apart, in this church, to see some painting which was being executed in fresco by a French artist and his pupil,[18] I was led to observe more closely than I might otherwise have done, a great number of votive offerings with which the walls of the different chapels were profusely hung. I will not say decorated, for they were very roughly and comically got up: most likely by poor sign-painters, who eke out their living in that way. They were all little pictures: each representing some sickness or calamity from which the person placing it there, had escaped, through the interposition of his or her patron saint, or of the Madonna; and I may refer to them as good specimens of the class generally. They are abundant in Italy.

In a grotesque squareness of outline, an impossibility of perspective, they were not unlike the woodcuts in old books; but they were oil-paintings, and the artist, like the painter of the Primrose family,[19] had not been sparing of his colours. In one, a lady was having a toe amputated – an operation which a saintly personage had sailed into the room, upon a couch, to superintend. In another, a lady was lying in bed; tucked up very tight and prim, and staring with much composure at a tripod, with a slop-basin on it: the usual form of washing-stand, and the only piece of furniture, besides the bedstead, in her chamber. One would never have supposed her to be labouring under any complaint, beyond the inconvenience of being miraculously wide awake, if the painter had not hit upon the idea of putting all her family on their knees in one corner, with their legs sticking out behind them on the floor, like boot-trees. Above whom, the Virgin, on a kind of blue divan, promised to restore the patient. In another case, a lady was in the very act of being run over, immediately outside the city walls, by a sort of piano-forte van. But the Madonna was there again. Whether the supernatural appearance had startled the horse (a bay griffin), or whether it was invisible to him, I don't know; but he was galloping away, ding-dong, without the smallest reverence or compunction. On every picture "Ex voto" was painted in yellow capitals in the sky.

Though votive offerings were not unknown in Pagan Temples, and are evidently among the many compromises made between the false religion and the true, when the true was in its infancy, I could wish that all the other compromises were as harmless. Gratitude and Devotion are Christian qualities; and a grateful, humble, Christian spirit may dictate the observance.

Hard by the cathedral stands the ancient Palace of the Popes,[20] of which one portion is now a common jail, and another a noisy barrack: while gloomy suites of state apartments, shut up and deserted, mock their own old state and glory, like the embalmed bodies of kings. But we neither went there, to see state rooms, nor soldiers' quarters, nor a common jail, though we dropped some money into a prisoners' box outside, whilst the prisoners, themselves, looked through the iron bars, high up, and watched us eagerly. We went to see the ruins of the dreadful rooms in which the Inquisition used to sit.[21]

A little, old, swarthy woman, with a pair of flashing black eyes, – proof that the world hadn't conjured down the devil within her, though it had had between sixty and seventy years to do it in, – came out of the Barrack Cabaret,[22] of which she was the keeper, with some large keys in her hands, and marshalled us the way that we should go. How she told us, on the way, that she was a Government Officer (*concierge du palais apostolique*), and had been, for I don't know how many years; and how she had shown these dungeons to princes; and how she was the best of dungeon demonstrators; and how she had resided in the palace from an infant, – had been born there, if I recollect right, – I needn't relate. But such a fierce, little, rapid, sparkling, energetic she-devil I never beheld. She was alight and flaming, all the time. Her action was violent in the extreme. She never spoke, without stopping expressly for the purpose. She stamped her feet, clutched us by the arms, flung herself into attitudes, hammered against walls with her keys, for mere emphasis: now whispered as if the Inquisition were there still: now shrieked as if she were on the rack herself; and had a mysterious, hag-like way with her forefinger, when approaching the remains of some new horror – looking back and walking stealthily, and making horrible grimaces – that might alone have qualified her to walk up and down a sick man's counterpane, to the exclusion of all other figures, through a whole fever.

Passing through the court-yard, among groups of idle soldiers, we turned off by a gate, which this She-Goblin unlocked for our admission, and locked again behind us: and entered a narrow court, rendered narrower by fallen stones and heaps of rubbish; part of it choking up the mouth of a ruined subterranean passage, that once communicated (or is said to have done so) with another castle on the opposite bank of the river. Close to this court-yard is a dungeon – we stood within it, in another minute – in the dismal tower *des oubliettes*,[23] where Rienzi[24] was imprisoned, fastened by an iron chain to the very wall that stands there now, but shut out from the sky which now looks down upon it. A few steps brought us to the Cachots,[25] in which the prisoners of the Inquisition were confined for forty-eight hours after their capture, without food or drink, that their constancy might be shaken, even before they were confronted with their gloomy judges. The day has not got in there yet. They are still small cells, shut in by four unyielding, close, hard walls; still profoundly dark; still massively doored and fastened, as of old.

Goblin, looking back as I have described, went softly on, into a vaulted chamber, now used as a store-room: once the chapel of the Holy Office.[26] The place where the tribunal sat, was plain. The platform might have been removed but yesterday. Conceive the parable of the Good Samaritan having been painted on the wall of one of these Inquisition chambers! But it was, and may be traced there yet.

High up in the jealous wall, are niches where the faltering replies of the accused were heard and noted down. Many of them had been brought out of the very cell we had just looked into, so awfully; along the same stone passage. We had trodden in their very footsteps.

I am gazing round me, with the horror that the place inspires, when Goblin clutches me by the wrist, and lays, not her skinny finger, but the handle of a key, upon her lip. She invites me, with a jerk, to follow her. I do so. She leads me out into a room adjoining – a rugged room, with a funnel-shaped, contracting roof, open at the top, to the bright day. I ask her what it is. She folds her arms, leers hideously, and stares. I ask again. She glances round, to see that all the little company are there; sits down upon a mound of stones; throws up her arms, and yells out, like a fiend, "La Salle de la Question!"[27]

The Chamber of Torture! And the roof was made of that shape to stifle the victim's cries! Oh Goblin, Goblin, let us think of this awhile, in silence. Peace, Goblin! Sit with your short arms crossed on your short legs, upon that heap of stones, for only five minutes, and then flame out again.

Minutes! Seconds are not marked upon the Palace clock, when, with her eyes flashing fire, Goblin is up, in the middle of the chamber, describing, with her sunburnt arms, a wheel of heavy blows. Thus it ran round! cries Goblin. Mash, mash, mash! An endless routine of heavy hammers. Mash, mash, mash! upon the sufferer's limbs. See the stone trough! says Goblin. For the water torture! Gurgle, swill, bloat, burst, for the Redeemer's honour! Suck the bloody rag, deep down into your unbelieving body, Heretic, at every breath you draw! And when the executioner plucks it out, reeking with the smaller mysteries of God's own Image, know us for His chosen servants, true believers in the Sermon on the Mount, elect disciples of Him who never did a miracle but to heal: who never struck a man with palsy, blindness, deafness, dumbness, madness, any one affliction of mankind; and never stretched His blessed hand out, but to give relief and ease!

See! cries Goblin. There the furnace was. There they made the irons red-hot. Those holes supported the sharp stake, on which the tortured persons hung poised: dangling with their whole weight from the roof. "But;" and Goblin whispers this; "Monsieur has heard of this tower? Yes? Let Monsieur look down, then!"

A cold air, laden with an earthy smell, falls upon the face of Monsieur; for she has opened, while speaking, a trap-door in the wall. Monsieur looks in. Downward to the bottom, upward to the top, of a steep, dark, lofty tower: very dismal, very dark, very cold. The Executioner of the Inquisition, says Goblin, edging in her head to look down also, flung those who were past all further torturing, down here. "But look! does Monsieur see the black stains on the wall?" A glance, over his shoulder, at Goblin's keen eye, shows Monsieur – and would without the aid of the directing-key – where they are. "What are they?" "Blood!"

In October, 1791, when the Revolution was at its height here, sixty persons: men and women ("and priests," says Goblin, "priests"): were murdered, and hurled, the dying and the dead, into this dreadful pit, where a quantity of quick-lime was tumbled down upon their bodies.[28] Those ghastly tokens of the massacre were soon no more; but while one stone of the strong building in which the deed was done, remains upon another, there they will lie in the memories of men, as plain to see as the splashing of their blood upon the wall is now.

Was it a portion of the great scheme of Retribution, that the cruel deed should be committed in this place! That a part of the atrocities and monstrous institutions, which had been, for scores of years, at work, to change men's nature, should in its last service, tempt them with the ready means of gratifying their furious and beastly rage! Should enable them to show themselves, in the height of their frenzy, no worse than a great, solemn, legal establishment, in the height of its power! No worse! Much better. They used the Tower of the Forgotten, in the name of Liberty – their liberty; an earth-born creature, nursed in the black mud of the Bastille moats and dungeons, and necessarily betraying many evidences of its unwholesome bringing-up – but the Inquisition used it in the name of Heaven.

Goblin's finger is lifted; and she steals out again, into the Chapel of the Holy Office. She stops at a certain part of the flooring. Her great effect is at hand. She waits for the rest. She darts at the brave Courier,[29] who is explaining something; hits him a sounding rap on the hat with the largest key; and bids him be silent. She assembles us all, round a little trap-door in the floor, as round as a grave.

"Voilà!" she darts down at the ring, and flings the door open with a crash, in her goblin energy, though it is no light weight. "Voilà les oubliettes! Voilà les oubliettes! Subterranean! Frightful! Black! Terrible! Deadly! Les oubliettes de l'Inquisition!"

My blood ran cold, as I looked from Goblin, down into the vaults, where those forgotten creatures, with recollections of the world outside: of wives, friends, children, brothers: starved to death, and made the stones ring with their unavailing groans. But, the thrill I felt on seeing the accursed wall below, decayed and broken through, and the sun shining in through its gaping wounds, was like a sense of victory and triumph. I felt exalted with the proud delight of living in these degenerate times, to see it. As if I were the hero of some high achievement! The light in the doleful vaults was typical of the light that has streamed in, on all persecution in God's name, but which is not yet at its noon! It cannot look more lovely to a blind man newly restored to sight, than to a traveller who sees it, calmly and majestically, treading down the darkness of that Infernal Well.[30]

Goblin, having shown *les oubliettes*, felt that her great *coup* was struck. She let the door fall with a crash, and stood upon it with her arms a-kimbo, sniffing prodigiously.

When we left the place, I accompanied her into her house, under the outer gateway of the fortress, to buy a little history of the building. Her cabaret, a dark low room, lighted by small windows, sunk in the thick wall – in the softened light, and with its forge-like chimney; its little counter by the door, with bottles, jars, and glasses on it; its household implements and scraps of dress against the walls; and a sober-looking woman (she must have a congenial life of it, with Goblin,) knitting at the door – looked exactly like a picture by OSTADE.[31]

I walked round the building on the outside, in a sort of dream, and yet with a delightful sense of having awakened from it, of which the light, down in the vaults, had given me the assurance. The immense thickness and giddy height of the walls, the enormous strength of the massive towers, the great extent of the building, its gigantic proportions, frowning aspect, and barbarous irregularity, awaken awe and wonder. The recollection of its opposite old uses: an impregnable fortress, a luxurious palace, a horrible prison, a place of torture, the court of the Inquisition: at one and the same time, a house of feasting, fighting, religion, and blood: gives to every stone in its huge form a fearful interest, and imparts new meaning to its incongruities. I could think of little, however, then, or long afterwards, but the sun in the dungeons. The palace coming down to be the lounging-place of noisy soldiers, and being forced to echo their rough talk, and common oaths, and to have their garments fluttering from its dirty windows, was some reduction of its state, and something to rejoice at; but the day in its cells, and the sky for the roof of its chambers of cruelty – that was its desolation and defeat! If I had seen it in a blaze from ditch to rampart, I should have felt that not that light, nor all the light in all the fire that burns, could waste it, like the sunbeams in its secret council-chamber, and its prisons.

chapter nine

FROM TRAVELOGUE TO
FICTION

(EXTRACTS FROM *PICTURES FROM ITALY, DOMBEY AND
SON, LITTLE DORRIT*, AND *MRS LIRRIPER'S LEGACY*)

This chapter juxtaposes three extracts from Dickens's description of
his 1844 journey through France in *Pictures from Italy*, 1846, with
corresponding episodes from his fiction. The comparisons thus
invited provide examples of how he used his actual experiences and
impressions of France in his fiction and suggest explanations for his
choice of particular French settings in *Dombey and Son*, 1846–48, *Little
Dorrit*, 1855–57, and *Mrs Lirriper's Legacy*, 1864.

The first extract, an impressionistic account of travelling through
France by coach, is from the "Going through France" chapter of
Pictures from Italy. It begins as Dickens and his family leave Paris on
their way south to Marseille and describes the journey between Paris
and Chalon-sur-Saône. It is paired with the description in *Dombey and
Son* of Carker's frenzied flight back to England following Edith's
rejection of him at Dijon. On the surface, Dickens's choice of Dijon
as the location for the meeting between Edith and Carker seems a
random one. He makes no mention of ever having visited it, most of
the action there takes place in an interior setting, and what little
description he provides of the city could easily have been gleaned

from Murray's *Handbook*. However, the choice of Dijon does put Carker in the right part of France for a journey north to Paris (and on to the coast) that is similar in route and distance to the journey south from Paris to Chalon-sur-Saône described in *Pictures*. Dickens travelled the whole distance from Boulogne to Chalon by coach (from Chalon he went by steamboat to Lyon and then to Avignon). That part of his journey would therefore have provided an appropriate model for Carker's tormented dash along the roads of France. The selection of Dijon rather than, for example, Chalon may have been motivated simply by Dickens's desire to avoid the association of a potentially adulterous liaison with a place he was known to have visited. He needed to set Carker on a long journey that he could describe from his own experience, but would hardly have been keen to imply any closer connection with the story.

Various details in the *Pictures* passage resurface in the extract from *Dombey and Son* – such as the postilion's verbal abuse of his horses, the crumbling out-houses of the village inns, the old chateau with its extinguisher-like turrets – but we see everything in a bleaker aspect. The "innumerable beggars" mentioned in passing in *Pictures* become "blind men with quivering eyelids, led by old women holding candles to their faces; idiot girls; the lame; the epileptic, and the palsied..." In *Pictures* Dickens describes dispassionately the monotony of travelling on the long French roads, "from a dreary plain, to an interminable avenue." In *Dombey and Son* the monotony becomes a "wheel of fear, regret, and passion" and the "long roads, that stretched away to an horizon, always receding and never gained..." are a tormenting symbol of failed ambition.

The narrative of Carker's flight takes the normal responses and sensations of the traveller and colors them dark. That sense of "otherness," of isolation from the world outside, used to humorous and celebratory effect in articles like "A Flight" and "Railway Dreaming," here fuels Carker's psychological disorientation. The foreignness of the environment and the blur of the landscape as the carriage rushes through it heighten his confusion – "Nothing clear without, and nothing clear within." Dickens fuses the general experience of travel with the particular psychology of the traveller, producing "a fevered vision of things past and present all confounded together; of his life and journey blended into one."

The next extract from *Pictures from Italy*, taken from the "Avignon to Genoa" chapter, features a colourful description of Marseille and is paired with the famous evocation of that city in the opening paragraphs of *Little Dorrit*. Both extracts portray Marseille at its hottest – the visit recorded in *Pictures* took place in July and *Little Dorrit* opens on "a fierce August day." There are many similarities of detail, but for the fictional piece Dickens focuses on the intense heat he experienced in Aix and Marseille and works with it to produce an atmospheric and thematically significant evocation of the city. For the opening of *Little Dorrit*, a novel of physical and psychological oppression, he mixes an exotic cocktail with the heat, light, and dust described in his travelogue to evoke a city caught and stultified in the merciless glare of the sun. The brief perception in *Pictures* of the country houses as "staring white" is developed in *Little Dorrit* into the "universal stare" that bewitches Marseille as it stews in its own heat – "Everything that lived or grew was oppressed by the glare..."

In the final extract from *Pictures* we return to the "Going through France" chapter and the three-day journey between Paris and Chalon-sur-Saône. Here, after a day on the road, the travelling party arrives at the town where it is to spend the night. On this section of the journey, the family stopped overnight at Sens, Avallon, and Chalon. Dickens does not specify which of these he has in mind, intending his description to be taken as representative – "A sketch of one day's proceedings is a sketch of all three..." However, such details as the name of the hotel, the cathedral tower overlooking the courtyard of the inn and the market in front of the cathedral indicate that this is at least predominantly an account of the overnight stay in Sens.

And Sens is the destination of Mrs Lirriper in *Mrs Lirriper's Legacy*. In the extract presented here, after spending a day in Paris ("I feel as if it was beautiful fireworks being let off in my head") Mrs Lirriper and her companions arrive at Sens in search of the mysterious dying man who has named her as his legatee. They stay at the Hotel de l'Écu, recognizable from Dickens's description of it in *Pictures* –

with the balcony overlooking the courtyard where the servants have their supper and its proximity to the market and, most significantly, to the cathedral. In *Pictures*, Dickens mentions the cathedral's "massive tower" which "frowns down upon the courtyard of the inn." Mrs Lirriper describes the inn as situated "right under the two towers, with their shadows a changing upon it all day like a kind of sundial" and later recalls,

> But every evening at a regular time we all three sat out in the balcony of the hotel at the end of the court-yard, looking up at the golden and rosy light as it changed on the great towers, and looking at the shadows of the towers as they changed on all about us ourselves included...

The "massive tower" to which Dickens refers in *Pictures* is presumably the taller of the cathedral's two towers, La Tour de Pierre, which is topped by the campanile that fascinates Mrs Lirriper and becomes associated with the theme of redemption in her story:

> I had been a fancying as I sat in the balcony of the hotel that an Angel might light there and call down to the people to be good, but I little thought what Jemmy all unknown to himself was a calling down from that high place to some one in the town.

Dickens has turned his perception of the cathedral as something "solemn and grand" in the midst of a bustling and colorful provincial town to symbolic effect. At the end of the extract from *Pictures* he describes the busy and picturesque market in front of the "grim, and swarthy, and mouldering, and cold" cathedral. This grave and gloomy presence in the midst of color and merriment becomes in *Mrs Lirriper's Legacy* a still grave but now hopeful symbol of reverence and redemption – casting its benign shadow over the bustle of the market and the comings and goings in the courtyard of the inn.

This chapter ends with a short extract from *Little Dorrit* describing the arrival of the fugitive Rigaud at Chalon-sur-Saône. Dickens devotes only one short paragraph to Chalon in *Pictures*:

Chalons is a fair resting-place, in right of its good inn on the bank of the river, and the little steam-boats, gay with green and red paint, that come and go upon it: which make up a pleasant and refreshing scene after the dusty roads. But, unless you would like to dwell on an enormous plain, with jagged rows of irregular poplars on it, that look like so many combs with broken teeth: and unless you would like to pass your life without the possibility of going up-hill, or going up anything but stairs: you would hardly approve of Chalons as a place of residence.

The first paragraph of the *Little Dorrit* extract reflects the less complimentary aspect of this description, using the monotony of the landscape to evoke a dreary and hostile environment for the secretive journey of Rigaud. Then, as Rigaud approaches the town, Dickens brings into play the experience he describes in *Pictures* as he heads towards Sens after a long day's travelling, weary and hungry and anticipating the comfort of a good hotel and a hearty dinner,

...when, down at the end of the long avenue of trees through which you are travelling, the first indication of a town appears, in the shape of some straggling cottages: and the carriage begins to rattle and roll over a horribly uneven pavement... and here we are in the yard of the Hôtel de l'Ecu d'Or...

Rigaud, tired and hungry after his long journey on foot, is filled not with hopeful anticipation as the lights of Chalon come into sight, but with envy and spite. There is to be no warm welcome for him. The town is his enemy. Even the uneven pavement, "jagged" beneath his feet, seems hostile. The "hotel with its gateway, and its savoury smell of cooking," which provided Dickens with rest and sustenance, is closed to him. He wanders past it and on through the town until he chances on a humble tavern in a squalid back street. In *Little Dorrit*, the simple travel experience recorded in an engaging and light-hearted episode of *Pictures from Italy* has been transformed into a dark vision of alienation and malice.

Sens Cathedral, 1866, showing the campanile on the Tour de Pierre (right) which features in *Mrs Lirriper's Legacy*. When Dickens visited Sens in 1844 the Tour de Plomb (left) was surmounted by a lead-covered timbered belfry, but it was destroyed in 1848.

EXTRACT FROM PICTURES FROM ITALY

(TRAVELLING THROUGH FRANCE)

We have four horses, and one postilion, who has a very long whip, and drives his team, something like the Courier of Saint Petersburg in the circle at Astley's or Franconi's:[1] only he sits his own horse instead of standing on him. The immense jack-boots worn by these postilions, are sometimes a century or two old; and are so ludicrously disproportionate to the wearer's foot, that the spur, which is put where his own heel comes, is generally halfway up the leg of the boots. The man often comes out of the stable-yard, with his whip in his hand and his shoes on, and brings out, in both hands, one boot at a time, which he plants on the ground by the side of his horse, with great gravity, until everything is ready. When it is – and oh Heaven! the noise they make about it! – he gets into the boots, shoes and all, or is hoisted into them by a couple of friends; adjusts the rope harness, embossed by the labours of innumerable pigeons in the stables; makes all the horses kick and plunge; cracks his whip like a madman; shouts "En route – Hi!" and away we go. He is sure to have a contest with his horse before we have gone very far; and then he calls him a Thief, and a Brigand, and a Pig, and what not; and beats him about the head as if he were made of wood.

There is little more than one variety in the appearance of the country, for the first two days. From a dreary plain, to an interminable avenue; and from an interminable avenue, to a dreary plain again. Plenty of vines there are, in the open fields, but of a short low kind, and not trained in festoons, but about straight sticks. Beggars innumerable there are, everywhere; but an extraordinarily scanty population, and fewer children than I ever encountered. I don't

believe we saw a hundred children between Paris and Chalons.[2]
Queer old towns, draw-bridged and walled: with odd little towers at
the angles, like grotesque faces, as if the wall had put a mask on, and
were staring down into the moat; other strange little towers, in
gardens and fields, and down lanes, and in farm-yards: all alone, and
always round, with a peaked roof, and never used for any purpose at
all; ruinous buildings of all sorts; sometimes an hôtel de ville,
sometimes a guard-house, sometimes a dwelling-house, sometimes a
château with a rank garden, prolific in dandelion, and watched over
by extinguisher-topped turrets,[3] and blink-eyed little casements; are
the standard objects, repeated over and over again. Sometimes we
pass a village inn, with a crumbling wall belonging to it, and a perfect
town of out-houses: and painted over the gateway, "Stabling for Sixty
Horses;" as indeed there might be stabling for sixty score, were there
any horses to be stabled there, or anybody resting there, or anything
stirring about the place but a dangling bush, indicative of the wine
inside:[4] which flutters idly in the wind, in lazy keeping with
everything else, and certainly is never in a green old age,[5] though
always so old as to be dropping to pieces. And all day long, strange
little narrow waggons, in strings of six or eight, bringing cheese from
Switzerland, and frequently in charge, the whole line, of one man, or
even boy – and he very often asleep in the foremost cart – come
jingling past: the horses drowsily ringing the bells upon their harness,
and looking as if they thought (no doubt they do) their great blue
woolly furniture, of immense weight and thickness, with a pair of
grotesque horns growing out of the collar, very much too warm for the
Midsummer weather.

Then there is the Diligence,[6] twice or thrice a-day; with the
dusty outsides in blue frocks, like butchers; and the insides in white
nightcaps; and its cabriolet head[7] on the roof, nodding and shaking,
like an idiot's head; and its Young-France[8] passengers staring out of

window, with beards down to their waists, and blue spectacles awfully shading their warlike eyes, and very big sticks clasped in their National grasp. Also the Malle Poste,[9] with only a couple of passengers, tearing along at a real good dare-devil pace, and out of sight in no time. Steady old Curés come jolting past, now and then, in such ramshackle, rusty, musty, clattering coaches as no Englishman would believe in; and bony women dawdle about in solitary places, holding cows by ropes while they feed, or digging and hoeing or doing field-work of a more laborious kind, or representing real shepherdesses with their flocks – to obtain an adequate idea of which pursuit and its followers, in any country, it is only necessary to take any pastoral poem, or picture, and imagine to yourself whatever is most exquisitely and widely unlike the descriptions therein contained.

EXTRACT FROM DOMBEY AND SON

(CARKER'S FLIGHT FROM DIJON)

Narrative context: Carker has put into action his scheme to deceive and humiliate his employer Mr Dombey by ruining his firm and eloping with his wife. Edith and he, having travelled separately to the Continent, meet as agreed at Dijon where Carker has rented an apartment for the purpose. Edith, however, has spurned Carker and fled from the building. At the same time Mr Dombey, in hot pursuit, has arrived in Dijon and is now beating at the main door of the apartment. Defeated in his schemes and panic-stricken, Carker forces open the door to a back staircase that Edith used for her escape and locked behind her. He makes his way out into the street. The extract is from Chapter 55.

The porter at the iron gate which shut the court-yard from the street, had left the little wicket of his house open, and was gone away; no doubt to mingle in the distant noise at the door on the great staircase. Lifting the latch softly, Carker crept out, and shutting the jangling gate after him with as little noise as possible, hurried off.

In the fever of his mortification and unavailing rage, the panic that had seized upon him mastered him completely. It rose to such a height that he would have blindly encountered almost any risk, rather than meet the man of whom, two hours ago, he had been utterly regardless. His fierce arrival, which he had never expected; the sound of his voice; their having been so near a meeting, face to face; he would have braved out this, after the first momentary shock of alarm, and would have put as bold a front upon his guilt as any villain. But the springing of his mine upon himself, seemed to have rent and shivered all his hardihood and self-reliance. Spurned like any reptile; entrapped and mocked; turned upon, and trodden down by the proud woman whose mind he had slowly poisoned, as he thought, until she had sunk into the mere creature of his pleasure; undeceived in his deceit, and with his fox's hide stripped off, he sneaked away, abashed, degraded, and afraid.

Some other terror came upon him quite removed from this of being pursued, suddenly, like an electric shock, as he was creeping through the streets. Some visionary terror, unintelligible and inexplicable, associated with a trembling of the ground, – a rush and sweep of something through the air, like Death upon the wing. He shrunk, as if to let the thing go by. It was not gone, it had never been there, yet what a startling horror it had left behind.[1]

He raised his wicked face, so full of trouble, to the night sky where the stars, so full of peace, were shining on him as they had been when he first stole out into the air; and stopped to think what he should do. The dread of being hunted in a strange remote place, where the laws might not protect him – the novelty of the feeling that it *was* strange and remote, originating in his being left alone so suddenly amid the ruins of his plans – his greater dread of seeking refuge now, in Italy or in Sicily, where men might be hired to assassinate him, he thought, at any dark street corner – the waywardness of guilt and fear – perhaps some sympathy of action with the turning back of all his schemes – impelled him to turn back too, and go to England.

"I am safer there, in any case. If I should not decide," he thought, "to give this fool a meeting, I am less likely to be traced there, than abroad here, now. And if I should (this cursed fit being over), at least I shall not be alone, without a soul to speak to, or advise with, or stand by me. I shall not be run in upon and worried like a rat."

He muttered Edith's name, and clenched his hand. As he crept along, in the shadow of the massive buildings, he set his teeth, and muttered dreadful imprecations on her head, and looked from side to side, as if in search of her. Thus, he stole on to the gate of an inn-yard. The people were a-bed; but his ringing at the bell soon produced a man with a lantern, in company with whom he was presently in a dim coach-house, bargaining for the hire of an old phaeton,[2] to Paris.

The bargain was a short one; and the horses were soon sent for. Leaving word that the carriage was to follow him when they came, he stole away again, beyond the town, past the old ramparts, out on the open road, which seemed to glide away along the dark plain, like a stream!

Whither did it flow? What was the end of it? As he paused, with some such suggestion within him, looking over the gloomy flat where the slender trees marked out the way, again that flight of Death came rushing up, again went on, impetuous and resistless, again was nothing but a horror in his mind, dark as the scene and undefined as its remotest verge.

There was no wind; there was no passing shadow on the deep shade of the night; there was no noise. The city lay behind him, lighted here and there, and starry worlds were hidden by the masonry of spire and roof that hardly made out any shapes against the sky. Dark and lonely distance lay around him everywhere, and the clocks were faintly striking two.

He went forward for what appeared a long time, and a long way; often stopping to listen. At last the ringing of horses' bells greeted his anxious ears. Now softer, and now louder, now inaudible, now ringing very slowly over bad ground, now brisk and merry, it came on; until with a loud shouting and lashing, a shadowy postilion muffled to the eyes, checked his four struggling horses at his side.

"Who goes there! Monsieur?"

"Yes."

"Monsieur has walked a long way in the dark midnight."

"No matter. Every one to his taste. Were there any other horses ordered at the post-house?"[3]

"A thousand devils! – and pardons! other horses? at this hour? No."

"Listen, my friend. I am much hurried. Let us see how fast we can travel! The faster, the more money there will be to drink. Off we go then! Quick!"

"Halloa! whoop! Halloa! Hi!" Away, at a gallop, over the black landscape, scattering the dust and dirt like spray!

The clatter and commotion echoed to the hurry and discordance of the fugitive's ideas. Nothing clear without, and nothing clear within. Objects flitting past, merging into one another, dimly descried, confusedly lost sight of, gone! Beyond the changing scraps of fence and cottage immediately upon the road, a lowering waste. Beyond the shifting images that rose up in his mind and vanished as they showed themselves, a black expanse of dread and rage and baffled villainy. Occasionally, a sigh of mountain air came from the distant Jura, fading along the plain. Sometimes that rush which was so furious and horrible, again came sweeping through his fancy, passed away, and left a chill upon his blood.

The lamps, gleaming on the medley of horses' heads, jumbled with the shadowy driver, and the fluttering of his cloak, made a thousand indistinct shapes, answering to his thoughts. Shadows of familiar people, stooping at their desks and books, in their remembered attitudes; strange apparitions of the man whom he was flying from, or of Edith; repetitions in the ringing bells and rolling wheels, of words that had been spoken; confusions of time and place, making last night a month ago, a month ago last night – home now distant beyond hope, now instantly accessible; commotion, discord, hurry, darkness, and confusion in his mind, and all around him. – Hallo! Hi! away at a gallop over the black landscape; dust and dirt flying like spray, the smoking horses snorting and plunging as if each of them were ridden by a demon, away in a frantic triumph on the dark road – whither!

Again the nameless shock comes speeding up, and as it passes, the bells ring in his ears "whither?" The wheels roar in his ears "whither?" All the noise and rattle shapes itself into that cry. The lights and shadows dance upon the horses' heads like imps. No stopping now: no slackening! On, on! Away with him upon the dark road wildly!

He could not think to any purpose. He could not separate one subject of reflection from another, sufficiently to dwell upon it, by itself, for a minute at a time. The crash of his project for the gaining of a voluptuous compensation for past restraint; the overthrow of his treachery to one who had been true and generous to him, but whose least proud word and look he had treasured up, at interest, for years – for false and subtle men will always secretly despise and dislike the object upon which they fawn, and always resent the payment and receipt of homage that they know to be worthless; these were the themes uppermost in his mind. A lurking rage against the woman who had so entrapped him and avenged herself was always there; crude and misshapen schemes of retaliation upon her, floated in his brain; but nothing was distinct. A hurry and contradiction pervaded all his thoughts. Even while he was so busy with this fevered, ineffectual thinking, his one constant idea was, that he would postpone reflection until some indefinite time.

Then, the old days before the second marriage rose up in his remembrance.[4] He thought how jealous he had been of the boy, how jealous he had been of the girl,[5] how artfully he had kept intruders at a distance, and drawn a circle round his dupe that none but himself should cross; and then he thought, had he done all this to be flying now, like a scared thief, from only the poor dupe?

He could have laid hands upon himself for his cowardice, but it was the very shadow of his defeat, and could not be separated from it. To have his confidence in his own knavery so shattered at a blow – to be within his own knowledge such a miserable tool – was like being paralysed. With an impotent ferocity he raged at Edith, and hated Mr Dombey and hated himself, but still he fled, and could do nothing else.

Again and again he listened for the sound of wheels behind. Again and again his fancy heard it, coming on louder and louder. At last he was so persuaded of this, that he cried out, "Stop!" preferring even the loss of ground to such uncertainty.

The word soon brought carriage, horses, driver, all in a heap together, across the road.

"The devil!" cried the driver, looking over his shoulder, "what's the matter!"

"Hark! What's that?"

"What?"

"That noise."

"Ah Heaven, be quiet, cursed brigand!" to a horse who shook his bells. "What noise?"

"Behind. Is it not another carriage at a gallop? There! what's that?"

"Miscreant with a pig's head, stand still!" to another horse, who bit another, who frightened the other two, who plunged and backed. "There is nothing coming."

"Nothing?"

"No, nothing but the day yonder."

"You are right, I think. I hear nothing now, indeed. Go on!"

The entangled equipage, half hidden in the reeking cloud from the horses, goes on slowly at first, for the driver, checked unnecessarily in his progress, sulkily takes out a pocket knife, and puts a new lash to his whip. Then "Hallo, whoop! Hallo, hi!" Away once more, savagely.

And now the stars faded, and the day glimmered, and standing in the carriage, looking back, he could discern the track by which he had come, and see that there was no traveller within view, on all the heavy expanse. And soon it was broad day, and the sun began to shine on corn-fields and vineyards; and solitary labourers, risen from little temporary huts by heaps of stones upon the road, were, here and there, at work repairing the highway, or eating bread. By and by, there were peasants going to their daily labour, or to market, or lounging at the doors of poor cottages, gazing idly at him as he passed. And then there was a postyard, ankle-deep in mud, with steaming dunghills and vast outhouses half ruined; and looking on this dainty prospect, an immense, old, shadeless, glaring, stone chateau, with half its windows blinded, and green damp crawling lazily over it, from the balustraded terrace to the taper tips of the extinguishers upon the turrets.[6]

Gathered up moodily in a corner of the carriage, and only intent on going fast – except when he stood up, for a mile together, and looked back; which he would do whenever there was a piece of open country – he went on, still postponing thought indefinitely, and still always tormented with thinking to no purpose.

Shame, disappointment, and discomfiture gnawed at his heart; a constant apprehension of being overtaken, or met – for he was groundlessly afraid even of travellers, who came towards him by the way he was going – oppressed him heavily. The same intolerable awe and dread that had come upon him in the night, returned unweakened in the day. The monotonous ringing of the bells and tramping of the horses; the monotony of his anxiety, and useless rage; the monotonous wheel of fear, regret, and passion, he kept turning round and round; made the journey like a vision, in which nothing was quite real but his own torment.

It was a vision of long roads, that stretched away to an horizon, always receding and never gained; of ill-paved towns, up hill and down, where faces came to dark doors and ill-glazed windows, and where rows of mud-bespattered cows and oxen were tied up for sale in the long narrow streets, butting and lowing, and receiving blows on their blunt heads from bludgeons that might have beaten them in; of bridges, crosses, churches, postyards, new horses being put in against their wills, and the horses of the last stage reeking, panting, and laying their drooping heads together dolefully at stable doors; of little cemeteries with black crosses settled sideways in the graves, and withered wreaths upon them dropping away; again of long, long roads, dragging themselves out, up hill and down, to the treacherous horizon.

Of morning, noon, and sunset; night, and the rising of an early moon. Of long roads temporarily left behind, and a rough pavement reached; of battering and clattering over it, and looking up, among house-roofs, at a great church-tower; of getting out and eating hastily, and drinking draughts of wine that had no cheering influence; of coming forth afoot, among a host of beggars – blind men with quivering eyelids, led by old women holding candles to their faces; idiot girls; the lame, the epileptic, and the palsied – of passing through the clamour, and looking from his seat at the upturned countenances and outstretched hands, with a hurried dread of recognising some pursuer pressing forward – of galloping away again, upon the long, long road, gathered up, dull and stunned, in his corner, or rising to see where the moon shone faintly on a patch of the same endless road miles away, or looking back to see who followed.

Of never sleeping, but sometimes dozing with unclosed eyes, and springing up with a start, and a reply aloud to an imaginary voice. Of cursing himself for being there, for having fled, for having let her go, for not having confronted and defied him. Of having a deadly quarrel with the whole world, but chiefly with himself. Of blighting everything with his black mood as he was carried on and away.

It was a fevered vision of things past and present all confounded together; of his life and journey blended into one. Of being madly hurried somewhere, whither he must go. Of old scenes starting up among the novelties through which he travelled. Of musing and brooding over what was past and distant, and seeming to take no notice of the actual objects he encountered, but with a wearisome exhausting consciousness of being bewildered by them, and having their images all crowded in his hot brain after they were gone.

A vision of change upon change, and still the same monotony of bells and wheels, and horses' feet, and no rest. Of town and country, postyards, horses, drivers, hill and valley, light and darkness, road and pavement, height and hollow, wet weather and dry, and still the same monotony of bells and wheels, and horses' feet, and no rest. A vision of tending on at last, towards the distant capital, by busier roads, and sweeping round, by old cathedrals, and dashing through small towns and villages, less thinly scattered on the road than formerly, and sitting shrouded in his corner, with his cloak up to his face, as people passing by looked at him.

Of rolling on and on, always postponing thought, and always racked with thinking; of being unable to reckon up the hours he had been upon the road, or to comprehend the points of time and place in his journey. Of being parched and giddy, and half mad. Of pressing on, in spite of all, as if he could not stop, and coming into Paris, where the turbid river held its swift course undisturbed, between two brawling streams of life and motion.

A troubled vision, then, of bridges, quays, interminable streets; of wine-shops, water-carriers, great crowds of people, soldiers, coaches, military drums, arcades. Of the monotony of bells and wheels and horses' feet being at length lost in the universal din and uproar. Of the gradual subsidence of that noise as he passed out in another carriage, by a different barrier[7] from that by which he had entered. Of the restoration, as he travelled on towards the sea-coast, of the monotony of bells, and wheels, and horses' feet, and no rest.

Of sunset once again, and nightfall. Of long roads again, and dead of night, and feeble lights in windows by the road-side; and still the old monotony of bells, and wheels, and horses' feet, and no rest. Of dawn, and daybreak, and the rising of the sun. Of toiling slowly up a hill, and feeling on its top the fresh sea-breeze; and seeing the morning light upon the edges of the distant waves. Of coming down into a harbour when the tide was at its full, and seeing fishing-boats float in, and glad women and children waiting for them. Of nets and seamen's clothes spread out to dry upon the shore; of busy sailors, and their voices high among ships' masts and rigging; of the buoyancy and brightness of the water, and the universal sparkling.

Of receding from the coast, and looking back upon it from the deck when it was a haze upon the water, with here and there a little opening of bright land where the Sun struck. Of the swell, and flash, and murmur of the calm sea. Of another grey line on the ocean, on the vessel's track, fast growing clearer and higher. Of cliffs, and buildings, and a windmill, and a church, becoming more and more visible upon it. Of steaming on at last into smooth water, and mooring to a pier whence groups of people looked down, greeting friends on board. Of disembarking, passing among them quickly, shunning every one; and of being at last again in England.

EXTRACT FROM PICTURES FROM ITALY

(MARSEILLE)

After seeing the churches (I will not trouble you with churches just now), we left Avignon that afternoon. The heat being very great, the roads outside the walls were strewn with people fast asleep in every little slip of shade, and with lazy groups, half asleep and half awake, who were waiting until the sun should be low enough to admit of their playing bowls among the burnt-up trees, and on the dusty road. The harvest here, was already gathered in, and mules and horses were treading out the corn in the fields. We came, at dusk, upon a wild and hilly country, once famous for brigands: and travelled slowly up a steep ascent. So we went on, until eleven at night, when we halted at the town of Aix (within two stages[1] of Marseilles) to sleep.

The hotel, with all the blinds and shutters closed to keep the light and heat out, was comfortable and airy next morning, and the town was very clean; but so hot, and so intensely light, that when I walked out at noon it was like coming suddenly from the darkened room into crisp blue fire. The air was so very clear, that distant hills and rocky points appeared within an hour's walk; while the town immediately at hand – with a kind of blue wind between me and it – seemed to be white hot, and to be throwing off a fiery air from the surface.

We left this town towards evening, and took the road to Marseilles. A dusty road it was; the houses shut up close; and the vines powdered white. At nearly all the cottage doors, women were peeling and slicing onions into earthen bowls for supper. So they had been doing last night all the way from Avignon. We passed one or two shady dark châteaux, surrounded by trees, and embellished with cool basins of water: which were the more refreshing to behold, from the great scarcity of such residences on the road we had travelled. As we approached Marseilles, the road began to be covered with holiday people. Outside the public-houses were parties smoking, drinking, playing draughts and cards, and (once) dancing. But dust, dust, dust, everywhere. We went on, through a long, straggling, dirty suburb, thronged with people; having on our left a dreary slope of land, on which the country-houses of the Marseilles merchants, always staring white, are jumbled and heaped without the slightest order: backs, fronts, sides, and gables towards all points of the compass;[2] until, at last, we entered the town.

I was there, twice or thrice afterwards, in fair weather and foul;[3] and I am afraid there is no doubt that it is a dirty and disagreeable place. But the prospect, from the fortified heights, of the beautiful Mediterranean, with its lovely rocks and islands, is most delightful.[4] These heights are a desirable retreat, for less picturesque reasons – as an escape from a compound of vile smells perpetually arising from a great harbour full of stagnant water, and befouled by the refuse of innumerable ships with all sorts of cargoes: which, in hot weather, is dreadful in the last degree.[5]

There were foreign sailors, of all nations, in the streets; with red shirts, blue shirts, buff shirts, tawny shirts, and shirts of orange colour; with red caps, blue caps, green caps, great beards, and no beards; in Turkish turbans, glazed English hats, and Neapolitan head-dresses. There were the townspeople sitting in clusters on the pavement, or airing themselves on the tops of their houses, or walking up and down the closest and least airy of the Boulevards; and there were crowds of fierce-looking people of the lower sort, blocking up the way, constantly. In the very heart of all this stir and uproar, was the common madhouse; a low, contracted, miserable building, looking straight upon the street, without the smallest screen or court-yard; where chattering madmen and mad-women were peeping out, through rusty bars, at the staring faces below, while the sun, darting fiercely aslant into their little cells, seemed to dry up their brains, and worry them, as if they were baited by a pack of dogs.

We were pretty well accommodated at the Hôtel du Paradis,[6] situated in a narrow street of very high houses, with a hairdresser's shop opposite, exhibiting in one of its windows two full-length waxen ladies, twirling round and round: which so enchanted the hairdresser himself, that he and his family sat in arm-chairs, and in cool undresses, on the pavement outside, enjoying the gratification of the passers-by, with lazy dignity. The family had retired to rest when we went to bed, at midnight; but the hairdresser (a corpulent man, in drab slippers) was still sitting there, with his legs stretched out before him, and evidently couldn't bear to have the shutters put up.[7]

Next day we went down to the harbour, where the sailors of all nations were discharging and taking in cargoes of all kinds: fruits, wines, oils, silks, stuffs, velvets, and every manner of merchandise.

Taking one of a great number of lively little boats with gay-striped awnings, we rowed away, under the sterns of great ships, under tow-ropes and cables, against and among other boats, and very much too near the sides of vessels that were faint with oranges, to the *Marie Antoinette*, a handsome steamer bound for Genoa, lying near the mouth of the harbour. By-and-by, the carriage, that unwieldy "trifle from the Pantechnicon,"[8] on a flat barge, bumping against everything, and giving occasion for a prodigious quantity of oaths and grimaces, came stupidly alongside; and by five o'clock we were steaming out in the open sea. The vessel was beautifully clean; the meals were served under an awning on deck; the night was calm and clear; the quiet beauty of the sea and sky unspeakable.

EXTRACT FROM LITTLE DORRIT

(MARSEILLE)

Thirty years ago, Marseilles lay burning in the sun, one day.[1]

A blazing sun upon a fierce August day was no greater rarity in southern France then, than at any other time, before or since. Everything in Marseilles, and about Marseilles, had stared at the fervid sky, and been stared at in return, until a staring habit had become universal there. Strangers were stared out of countenance by staring white houses, staring white walls, staring white streets, staring tracts of arid road, staring hills from which verdure was burnt away. The only things to be seen not fixedly staring and glaring were the vines drooping under their load of grapes. These did occasionally wink a little, as the hot air barely moved their faint leaves.[2]

There was no wind to make a ripple on the foul water within the harbour,[3] or on the beautiful sea without. The line of demarcation between the two colours, black and blue, showed the point which the pure sea would not pass; but it lay as quiet as the abominable pool, with which it never mixed. Boats without awnings were too hot to touch; ships blistered at their moorings; the stones of the quays had not cooled, night or day, for months. Hindoos, Russians, Chinese, Spaniards, Portuguese, Englishmen, Frenchmen, Genoese, Neapolitans, Venetians, Greeks, Turks, descendants from all the builders of Babel,[4] come to trade at Marseilles, sought the shade alike – taking refuge in any hiding-place from a sea too intensely blue to be looked at, and a sky of purple, set with one great flaming jewel of fire.

The universal stare made the eyes ache. Towards the distant line of Italian coast, indeed, it was a little relieved by light clouds of mist, slowly rising from the evaporation of the sea; but it softened nowhere else. Far away the staring roads, deep in dust, stared from the hillside, stared from the hollow, stared from the interminable plain. Far away the dusty vines overhanging wayside cottages, and the monotonous wayside avenues of parched trees without shade, drooped beneath the stare of earth and sky. So did the horses with drowsy bells, in long files of carts, creeping slowly towards the interior; so did their recumbent drivers, when they were awake, which rarely happened; so did the exhausted labourers in the fields. Everything that lived or grew, was oppressed by the glare; except the lizard, passing swiftly over rough stone walls, and the cicala,[5] chirping his dry hot chirp, like a rattle. The very dust was scorched brown, and something quivered in the atmosphere as if the air itself were panting.

Blinds, shutters, curtains, awnings, were all closed and drawn to keep out the stare. Grant it but a chink or keyhole, and it shot in like a white-hot arrow. The churches were the freest from it. To come out of the twilight of pillars and arches – dreamily dotted with winking lamps, dreamily peopled with ugly old shadows piously dozing, spitting, and begging – was to plunge into a fiery river, and swim for life to the nearest strip of shade. So, with people lounging and lying wherever shade was, with but little hum of tongues or barking of dogs, with occasional jangling of discordant church bells, and rattling of vicious drums, Marseilles, a fact to be strongly smelt and tasted, lay broiling in the sun one day.

EXTRACT FROM PICTURES FROM ITALY

(SENS)

You have been travelling along, stupidly enough, as you generally do in the last stage[1] of the day; and the ninety-six bells upon the horses – twenty-four apiece – have been ringing sleepily in your ears for half an hour or so; and it has become a very jog-trot, monotonous, tiresome sort of business; and you have been thinking deeply about the dinner you will have at the next stage; when, down at the end of the long avenue of trees through which you are travelling, the first indication of a town appears, in the shape of some straggling cottages: and the carriage begins to rattle and roll over a horribly uneven pavement. As if the equipage were a great firework, and the mere sight of a smoking cottage chimney had lighted it, instantly it begins to crack and splutter, as if the very devil were in it. Crack, crack, crack, crack. Crack-crack-crack. Crick-crack. Crick-crack. Helo! Hola! Vite! Voleur! Brigand! Hi hi hi! En r-r-r-r-route! Whip, wheels, driver, stones, beggars, children; crack, crack, crack; helo! hola! charité pour l'amour de Dieu! crick-crack-crick-crack; crick, crick, crick; bump, jolt, crack, bump, crick-crack; round the corner, up the narrow street, down the paved hill on the other side; in the gutter; bump, bump; jolt, jog, crick, crick, crick; crack, crack, crack; into the shop-windows on the left-hand side of the street, preliminary to a sweeping turn into the wooden archway on the right; rumble, rumble, rumble; clatter, clatter, clatter; crick, crick, crick; and here we are in the yard of the Hôtel de l'Ecu d'Or;[2] used up, gone out, smoking, spent, exhausted; but sometimes making a false start unexpectedly, with nothing coming of it – like a firework to the last!

The landlady of the Hôtel de l'Ecu d'Or is here; and the landlord of the Hôtel de l'Ecu d'Or is here; and the femme de chambre of the Hôtel de l'Ecu d'Or is here; and a gentleman in a glazed cap, with a red beard like a bosom friend, who is staying at the Hôtel de l'Ecu d'Or, is here; and Monsieur le Curé is walking up and down in a corner of the yard by himself, with a shovel hat upon his head, and a black gown upon his back, and a book in one hand, and an umbrella in the other; and everybody, except Monsieur le Curé, is open-mouthed and open-eyed, for the opening of the carriage-door. The landlord of the Hôtel de l'Ecu d'Or, dotes to that extent upon the Courier,[3] that he can hardly wait for his coming down from the box, but embraces his very legs and boot-heels as he descends. "My Courier! My brave Courier! My friend! My brother!" The landlady loves him, the femme de chambre blesses him, the garçon worships him. The Courier asks if his letter has been received? It has, it has. Are the rooms prepared? They are, they are. The best rooms for my noble Courier. The rooms of state for my gallant Courier; the whole house is at the service of my best of friends! He keeps his hands upon the carriage-door, and asks some other question to enhance the expectation. He carries a green leathern purse outside his coat, suspended by a belt. The idlers look at it; one touches it. It is full of five-franc pieces. Murmurs of admiration are heard among the boys. The landlord falls upon the Courier's neck, and folds him to his breast. He is so much fatter than he was, he says! He looks so rosy and so well!

The door is opened. Breathless expectation. The lady of the family gets out.[4] Ah sweet lady! Beautiful lady! The sister of the lady of the family gets out. Great Heaven, Ma'amselle is charming! First little boy gets out. Ah, what a beautiful little boy! First little girl gets out. Oh, but this is an enchanting child! Second little girl gets out. The landlady, yielding to the finest impulse of our common nature, catches her up in her arms! Second little boy gets out. Oh, the sweet boy! Oh, the tender little family! The baby is handed out. Angelic baby! The baby has topped everything. All the rapture is expended on the baby! Then the two nurses tumble out; and the enthusiasm swelling into madness, the whole family are swept upstairs as on a cloud; while the idlers press about the carriage, and look into it, and walk round it, and touch it. For it is something to touch a carriage that has held so many people. It is a legacy to leave one's children.

The rooms are on the first floor, except the nursery for the night, which is a great rambling chamber, with four or five beds in it: through a dark passage, up two steps, down four, past a pump, across a balcony, and next door to the stable. The other sleeping apartments are large and lofty; each with two small bedsteads, tastefully hung, like the windows, with red and white drapery. The sitting-room is famous. Dinner is already laid in it for three; and the napkins are folded in cocked-hat fashion. The floors are of red tile. There are no carpets, and not much furniture to speak of; but there is abundance of looking-glass, and there are large vases under glass shades, filled with artificial flowers; and there are plenty of clocks. The whole party are in motion. The brave Courier, in particular, is everywhere: looking after the beds, having wine poured down his throat by his dear brother the landlord, and picking up green cucumbers – always cucumbers; Heaven knows where he gets them – with which he walks about, one in each hand, like truncheons.

Dinner is announced. There is very thin soup; there are very large loaves – one apiece; a fish; four dishes afterwards; some poultry afterwards; a dessert afterwards; and no lack of wine. There is not much in the dishes, but they are very good, and always ready instantly. When it is nearly dark, the brave Courier, having eaten the two cucumbers, sliced up in the contents of a pretty large decanter of oil, and another of vinegar, emerges from his retreat below, and proposes a visit to the Cathedral, whose massive tower frowns down upon the courtyard of the inn.[5] Off we go; and very solemn and grand it is, in the dim light: so dim at last, that the polite, old, lanthorn-jawed Sacristan has a feeble little bit of candle in his hand, to grope among the tombs with – and looks among the grim columns, very like a lost ghost who is searching for his own.

Underneath the balcony, when we return, the inferior servants of the inn are supping in the open air, at a great table; the dish a stew of meat and vegetables, smoking hot, and served in the iron cauldron it was boiled in. They have a pitcher of thin wine, and are very merry; merrier than the gentleman with the red beard, who is playing billiards in the light room on the left of the yard, where shadows, with cues in their hands, and cigars in their mouths, cross and recross the window, constantly. Still the thin Curé walks up and down alone, with his book and umbrella. And there he walks, and there the billiard-balls rattle, long after we are fast asleep.

We are astir at six next morning. It is a delightful day, shaming yesterday's mud upon the carriage, if anything could shame a carriage, in a land where carriages are never cleaned. Everybody is brisk; and as we finish breakfast, the horses come jingling into the yard from the Post-house.[6] Everything taken out of the carriage is put back again. The brave Courier announces that all is ready, after walking into every room, and looking all round it, to be certain that nothing is left behind. Everybody gets in. Everybody connected with the Hôtel de l'Ecu d'Or is again enchanted. The brave Courier runs into the house for a parcel containing cold fowl, sliced ham, bread, and biscuits, for lunch; hands it into the coach; and runs back again.

What has he got in his hand now? More cucumbers? No. A long strip of paper. It's the bill.

The brave Courier has two belts on, this morning: one supporting the purse; another, a mighty good sort of leathern bottle, filled to the throat with the best light Bordeaux wine in the house. He never pays the bill till this bottle is full. Then he disputes it.

He disputes it now, violently. He is still the landlord's brother, but by another father or mother. He is not so nearly related to him as he was last night. The landlord scratches his head. The brave Courier points to certain figures in the bill, and intimates that if they remain there, the Hôtel de l'Ecu d'Or is thenceforth and for ever an Hôtel de l'Ecu de cuivre. The landlord goes into a little counting-house. The brave Courier follows, forces the bill and a pen into his hand, and talks more rapidly than ever. The landlord takes the pen. The Courier smiles. The landlord makes an alteration. The Courier cuts a joke. The landlord is affectionate, but not weakly so. He bears it like a man. He shakes hands with his brave brother, but he don't hug him. Still, he loves his brother; for he knows that he will be returning that way, one of these fine days, with another family, and he foresees that his heart will yearn towards him again. The brave Courier traverses all round the carriage once, looks at the drag,[7] inspects the wheels, jumps up, gives the word, and away we go!

It is market morning. The market is held in the little square outside, in front of the cathedral.[8] It is crowded with men and women, in blue, in red, in green, in white; with canvassed stalls; and fluttering merchandise. The country people are grouped about, with their clean baskets before them. Here, the lace-sellers; there the butter and egg-sellers; there, the fruit-sellers; there, the shoe-makers. The whole place looks as if it were the stage of some great theatre, and the curtain had just run up, for a picturesque ballet. And there is the cathedral to boot: scene-like: all grim, and swarthy, and mouldering, and cold; just splashing the pavement in one place with faint purple drops, as the morning sun, entering by a little window on the eastern side, struggles through some stained glass panes, on the western.

In five minutes we have passed the iron cross, with a little ragged kneeling-place of turf before it, in the outskirts of the town; and are again upon the road.

EXTRACT FROM
MRS LIRRIPER'S LEGACY

(MRS LIRRIPER GOES TO SENS)

Narrative context: Mrs Lirriper, an elderly London landlady with a boarding house off the Strand, made her first appearance in Mrs Lirriper's Lodgings, the 1863 Christmas Number of All the Year Round. In the opening story she talks directly to the reader about her life and recounts various episodes involving her lodgers and neighbors. The most important thread in her narrative is the account of how she and her long-term boarder Major Jackman adopt and raise the child of a young woman who dies after her callous lover has abandoned her. Mrs Lirriper's Lodgings was such a success that Dickens brought Mrs Lirriper and company back for the 1864 Christmas Number of All the Year Round, entitled Mrs Lirriper's Legacy, which continues and concludes the story relating to Jemmy, the adopted child. This extract picks up the narrative from the moment

Mrs Lirriper learns that an unknown Englishman, then dying at Sens, has named her as his legatee.

And now my dear I really am a going to tell you about my Legacy if you're inclined to favour me with your attention, and I did fully intend to have come straight to it only one thing does so bring up another. It was the month of June and the day before Midsummer Day when my girl Winifred Madgers – she was what is termed a Plymouth Sister, and the Plymouth Brother[1] that made away with her was quite right, for a tidier young woman for a wife never came into a house and afterwards called with the beautifullest Plymouth Twins – it was the day before Midsummer Day when Winifred Madgers comes and says to me "A gentleman from the Consul's wishes particular to speak to Mrs Lirriper." If you'll believe me my dear the Consols[2] at the bank where I have a little matter for Jemmy got into my head, and I says "Good gracious I hope he ain't had any dreadful fall!" Says Winifred, "He don't look as if he had ma'am." And I says "Show him in."

The gentleman came in dark and with his hair cropped what I should consider too close, and he says very polite "Madame Lirrwiper!" I says "Yes sir. Take a chair." "I come," says he "frrwom the Frrwench Consul's." So I saw at once that it wasn't the Bank of England. "We have rrweceived," says the gentleman turning his r's very curious and skilful, "frrwom the Mairrwie"[3] at Sens, a communication which I will have the honour to rrwead. Madame Lirrwiper understands Frrwench?" "Oh dear no sir!" says I. "Madame Lirriper don't understand anything of the sort." "It matters not," says the gentleman, "I will trrwanslate."

With that my dear the gentleman after reading something about a Department[4] and a Mairie (which Lord forgive me I supposed till the Major came home was Mary, and never was I more puzzled than to think how that young woman came to have so much to do with it)

translated a lot with the most obliging pains, and it came to this:–
That in the town of Sens in France, an unknown Englishman lay a
dying. That he was speechless and without motion. That in his
lodging there was a gold watch and a purse containing such and such
money and a trunk containing such and such clothes, but no passport
and no papers, except that on his table was a pack of cards and that
he had written in pencil on the back of the ace of hearts: "To the
authorities. When I am dead, pray send what is left, as a last Legacy,
to Mrs Lirriper Eighty-one Norfolk-street Strand London."[5] When
the gentleman had explained all this, which seemed to be drawn up
much more methodical than I should have given the French credit
for, not at that time knowing the nation, he put the document into my
hand. And much the wiser I was for that you may be sure, except that
it had the look of being made out upon grocery-paper and was
stamped all over with eagles.[6]

"Does Madame Lirrwiper" says the gentleman "believe she
rrwecognises her unfortunate compatrrwiot?"

You may imagine the flurry it put me into my dear to be talked to
about my compatriots.

I says "Excuse me. Would you have the kindness sir to make your
language as simple as you can?"

"This Englishman unhappy, at the point of death. This
compatrrwiot afflicted," says the gentleman.

"Thank you sir" I says "I understand you now. No sir I have not
the least idea who this can be."

"Has Madame Lirrwiper no son, no nephew, no godson, no
frrwiend, no acquaintance of any kind in Frrwance?"

"To my certain knowledge" says I "no relation or friend, and to
the best of my belief no acquaintance."

"Pardon me. You take Locataires?" says the gentleman.

My dear fully believing he was offering me something with his obliging foreign manners – snuff for anything I knew – I gave a little bend of my head and I says if you'll credit it, "No I thank you. I have not contracted the habit."

The gentleman looks perplexed and says "Lodgers?"

"Oh!" says I laughing. "Bless the man! Why yes to be sure!"

"May it not be a former lodger?" says the gentleman. "Some lodger that you pardoned some rrwent? You have pardoned lodgers some rrwent?"

"Hem! It has happened sir" says I, "but I assure you I can call to mind no gentleman of that description that this is at all likely to be."

In short my dear we could make nothing of it, and the gentleman noted down what I said and went away. But he left me the paper of which he had two with him, and when the Major comes in I says to the Major as I put it in his hand "Major here's Old Moore's Almanack[7] with the hieroglyphic complete, for your opinion."

It took the Major a little longer to read than I should have thought, judging from the copious flow with which he seemed to be gifted when attacking the organ-men,[8] but at last he got through it and stood a gazing at me in amazement.

"Major" I says "you're paralysed."

"Madam" says the Major, "Jemmy Jackman is doubled up."

Now it did so happen that the Major had been out to get a little information about rail-roads and steam-boats, as our boy was coming home for his Midsummer holidays next day and we were going to take him somewhere for a treat and a change. So while the Major stood a gazing it came into my head to say to him "Major I wish you'd go and look at some of your books and maps, and see whereabouts this same town of Sens is in France."

The Major he roused himself and he went into the Parlours and he poked about a little, and he came back to me and he says, "Sens my dearest madam is seventy odd miles south of Paris."

With what I may truly call a desperate effort "Major" I says "we'll go there with our blessed boy!"

If ever the Major was beside himself it was at the thoughts of that journey. All day long he was like the wild man of the woods[9] after meeting with an advertisement in the papers telling him something to his advantage, and early next morning hours before Jemmy could possibly come home he was outside in the street ready to call out to him that we was all a going to France. Young Rosy-cheeks you may believe was as wild as the Major, and they did carry on to that degree that I says "If you two children ain't more orderly I'll pack you both off to bed." And then they fell to cleaning up the Major's telescope to see France with, and went out and bought a leather bag with a snap to hang round Jemmy, and him to carry the money like a little Fortunatus with his purse.[10]

If I hadn't passed my word and raised their hopes, I doubt if I could have gone through with the undertaking but it was too late to go back now. So on the second day after Midsummer Day we went off by the morning mail.[11] And when we came to the sea which I had never seen but once in my life and that when my poor Lirriper was courting me, the freshness of it and the deepness and the airiness and to think that it had been rolling ever since and that it was always a rolling and so few of us minding, made me feel quite serious. But I felt happy too and so did Jemmy and the Major and not much motion on the whole, though me with a swimming in the head and a sinking but able to take notice that the foreign insides appear to be constructed hollower than the English, leading to much more tremenjous noises when bad sailors.

But my dear the blueness and the lightness and the coloured look of everything and the very sentry-boxes striped and the shining rattling drums and the little soldiers with their waists and tidy gaiters, when we got across to the Continent – it made me feel as if I don't know what – as if the atmosphere had been lifted off me. And as to lunch why bless you if I kept a man-cook and two kitchen-maids I couldn't get it done for twice the money, and no injured young women a glaring at you and grudging you and acknowledging your patronage by wishing that your food might choke you, but so civil and so hot and attentive and every way comfortable except Jemmy pouring wine down his throat by tumblers-full and me expecting to see him drop under the table.

And the way in which Jemmy spoke his French was a real charm. It was often wanted of him, for whenever anybody spoke a syllable to me I says "Noncomprenny, you're very kind but it's no use – Now Jemmy!" and then Jemmy he fires away at 'em lovely, the only thing wanting in Jemmy's French being as it appeared to me that he hardly ever understood a word of what they said to him which made it scarcely of the use it might have been though in other respects a perfect Native, and regarding the Major's fluency I should have been of the opinion judging French by English that there might have been a greater choice of words in the language though still I must admit that if I hadn't known him when he asked a military gentleman in a grey cloak what o'clock it was I should have took him for a Frenchman born.

Before going on to look after my Legacy we were to make one regular day in Paris, and I leave you to judge my dear what a day *that* was with Jemmy and the Major and the telescope and me and the prowling young man at the inn door (but very civil too) that went along with us to show the sights. All along the railway to Paris Jemmy and the Major had been frightening me to death by stooping down on the platforms at stations to inspect the engines underneath their mechanical stomachs, and by creeping in and out I don't know where all, to find improvements for the United Grand Junction Parlour,[12] but when we got out into the brilliant streets on a bright morning they gave up all their London improvements as a bad job and gave their minds to Paris. Says the prowling young man to me, "Will I speak Inglis No?" So I says "If you can young man I shall take it as a favour," but after half an hour of it when I fully believed the man had gone mad and me too I says "Be so good as fall back on your French sir," knowing that then I shouldn't have the agonies of trying to understand him which was a happy release.[13] Not that I lost much more than the rest either, for I generally noticed that when he had described something very long indeed and I says to Jemmy "What does he say Jemmy?" Jemmy says looking at him with vengeance in his eye "He is so jolly indistinct!" and that when he had described it longer all over again and I says to Jemmy "Well Jemmy what's it all about?" Jemmy says "He says the building was repaired in seventeen hundred and four, Gran."

Wherever that prowling young man formed his prowling habits I cannot be expected to know, but the way in which he went round the corner while we had our breakfasts and was there again when we swallowed the last crumb was most marvellous, and just the same at dinner and at night, prowling equally at the theatre and the inn gateway and the shop-doors when we bought a trifle or two and everywhere else but troubled with a tendency to spit. And of Paris I can tell you no more my dear than that it's town and country both in one, and carved stone and long streets of high houses and gardens and fountains and statues and trees and gold, and immensely big soldiers and immensely little soldiers and the pleasantest nurses with the whitest caps a playing at skipping-rope with the bunchiest babies in the flattest caps, and clean tablecloths spread everywhere for dinner and people sitting out of doors smoking and sipping all day long and little plays being acted in the open air for little people and every shop a complete and elegant room, and everybody seeming to play at everything in this world. And as to the sparkling lights my dear after dark, glittering high up and low down and on before and on behind and all round, and the crowd of theatres and the crowd of people and the crowd of all sorts, it's pure enchantment. And pretty well the only thing that grated on me was that whether you pay your fare at the railway or whether you change your money at a money-dealer's or whether you take your ticket at the theatre, the lady or gentleman is caged up (I suppose by Government) behind the strongest iron bars having more of a Zoological appearance than a free country.[14]

Well to be sure when I did after all get my precious bones to bed that night, and my Young Rogue came in to kiss me and asks "What do you think of this lovely lovely Paris, Gran?" I says "Jemmy I feel as if it was beautiful fireworks being let off in my head." And very cool and refreshing the pleasant country was the next day when we went on to look after my Legacy, and rested me much and did me a deal of good.

So at length and at last my dear we come to Sens, a pretty little town with a great two-towered cathedral and the rooks flying in and out of the loopholes and another tower atop of one of the towers like a sort of a stone pulpit.[15] In which pulpit with the birds skimming below him if you'll believe me, I saw a speck while I was resting at the inn before dinner which they made signs to me was Jemmy and which really was. I had been a fancying as I sat in the balcony of the hotel that an Angel might light there and call down to the people to be good, but I little thought what Jemmy all unknown to himself was a calling down from that high place to some one in the town.

The pleasantest-situated inn my dear![16] Right under the two towers, with their shadows a changing upon it all day like a kind of a sundial,[17] and country people driving in and out of the court-yard in carts and hooded cabriolets and such-like, and a market outside in front of the cathedral,[18] and all so quaint and like a picter. The Major and me agreed that whatever came of my Legacy this was the place to stay in for our holiday, and we also agreed that our dear boy had best not be checked in his joy that night by the sight of the Englishman if he was still alive, but that we would go together and alone. For you are to understand that the Major not feeling himself quite equal in his wind to the heighth to which Jemmy had climbed, had come back to me and left him with the Guide.

So after dinner when Jemmy had set off to see the river, the Major went down to the Mairie, and presently came back with a military character in a sword and spurs and a cocked-hat and a yellow shoulder-belt and long tags about him that he must have found inconvenient. And the Major says "The Englishman still lies in the same state dearest madam. This gentleman will conduct us to his lodging." Upon which the military character pulled off his cocked-hat to me, and I took notice that he had shaved off his forehead in imitation of Napoleon Bonaparte but not like.

We went out at the court-yard gate and past the great doors of the cathedral and down a narrow High Street where the people were sitting chatting at their shop-doors and the children were at play. The military character went in front and he stopped at a pork-shop with a little statue of a pig sitting up, in the window, and a private door that a donkey was looking out of.

When the donkey saw the military character he came slipping out on the pavement to turn round and then clattered along the passage into a back-yard. So the coast being clear, the Major and me were conducted up the common stair and into the front room on the second, a bare room with a red tiled floor and the outside lattice blinds pulled close to darken it. As the military character opened the blinds I saw the tower where I had seen Jemmy, darkening as the sun got low, and I turned to the bed by the wall and saw the Englishman.

It was some kind of brain fever he had had, and his hair was all gone, and some wetted folded linen lay upon his head. I looked at him very attentive as he lay there all wasted away with his eyes closed, and I says to the Major

"I never saw this face before."

The Major looked at him very attentive too, and he says

"*I* never saw this face before."

When the Major explained our words to the military character, that gentleman shrugged his shoulders and showed the Major the card on which it was written about the Legacy for me. It had been written with a weak and trembling hand in bed, and I knew no more of the writing than of the face. Neither did the Major.

Though lying there alone, the poor creetur was as well taken care of as could be hoped, and would have been quite unconscious of any one's sitting by him then. I got the Major to say that we were not going away at present and that I would come back tomorrow and watch a bit by the bedside. But I got him to add – and I shook my head hard to make it stronger – "We agree that we never saw this face before."

Our boy was greatly surprised when we told him sitting out in the balcony in the starlight, and he ran over some of those stories of former Lodgers, of the Major's putting down,[19] and asked wasn't it possible that it might be this lodger or that lodger. It was not possible and we went to bed.

In the morning just at breakfast-time the military character came jingling round, and said that the doctor thought from the signs he saw there might be some rally before the end. So I says to the Major and Jemmy, "You two boys go and enjoy yourselves, and I'll take my Prayer-Book and go sit by the bed." So I went, and I sat there some hours, reading a prayer for him poor soul now and then, and it was quite on in the day when he moved his hand.

He had been so still, that the moment he moved I knew of it, and I pulled off my spectacles and laid down my book and rose and looked at him. From moving one hand he began to move both, and then his action was the action of a person groping in the dark. Long after his eyes had opened, there was a film over them and he still felt for his way out into light. But by slow degrees his sight cleared and his hands stopped. He saw the ceiling, he saw the wall, he saw me. As his sight cleared, mine cleared too, and when at last we looked in one another's faces, I started back and I cries passionately:

"O you wicked wicked man! Your sin has found you out!"[20]

For I knew him, the moment life looked out of his eyes, to be Mr Edson, Jemmy's father who had so cruelly deserted Jemmy's young unmarried mother who had died in my arms, poor tender creetur, and left Jemmy to me.

"You cruel wicked man! You bad black traitor!"

With the little strength he had, he made an attempt to turn over on his wretched face to hide it. His arm dropped out of the bed and his head with it, and there he lay before me crushed in body and in mind. Surely the miserablest sight under the summer sun!

"O blessed Heaven" I says a crying, "teach me what to say to this broken mortal! I am a poor sinful creetur, and the Judgment is not mine."

As I lifted my eyes up to the clear bright sky, I saw the high tower where Jemmy had stood above the birds, seeing that very window; and the last look of that poor pretty young mother when her soul brightened and got free, seemed to shine down from it.[21]

"O man, man, man!" I says, and I went on my knees beside the bed; "if your heart is rent asunder and you are truly penitent for what you did, Our Saviour will have mercy on you yet!"[22]

As I leaned my face against the bed, his feeble hand could just move itself enough to touch me. I hope the touch was penitent. It tried to hold my dress and keep hold, but the fingers were too weak to close.

I lifted him back upon the pillows, and I says to him:

"Can you hear me?"

He looked yes.

"Do you know me?"

He looked yes, even yet more plainly.

"I am not here alone. The Major is with me. You recollect the Major?"

Yes. That is to say he made out yes, in the same way as before.

"And even the Major and I are not alone. My grandson – his godson – is with us. Do you hear? My grandson."

The fingers made another trial to catch at my sleeve, but could only creep near it and fall.

"Do you know who my grandson is?"

Yes.

"I pitied and loved his lonely mother. When his mother lay a dying I said to her, 'My dear this baby is sent to a childless old woman.' " He has been my pride and joy ever since. I love him as dearly as if he had drunk from my breast. Do you ask to see my grandson before you die?"

Yes.

"Show me, when I leave off speaking, if you correctly understand what I say. He has been kept unacquainted with the story of his birth. He has no knowledge of it. No suspicion of it. If I bring him here to the side of this bed, he will suppose you to be a perfect stranger. It is more than I can do, to keep from him the knowledge that there is such wrong and misery in the world; but that it was ever so near him in his innocent cradle, I have kept from him, and I do keep from him, and I ever will keep from him. For his mother's sake, and for his own."

He showed me that he distinctly understood, and the tears fell from his eyes.

"Now rest, and you shall see him."

So I got him a little wine and some brandy and I put things straight about his bed. But I began to be troubled in my mind lest Jemmy and the Major might be too long of coming back. What with this occupation for my thoughts and hands, I didn't hear a foot upon the stairs, and was startled when I saw the Major stopped short in the middle of the room by the eyes of the man upon the bed, and knowing him then, as I had known him a little while ago.

There was anger in the Major's face, and there was horror and repugnance and I don't know what. So I went up to him and I led him to the bedside and when I clasped my hands and lifted of them up, the Major did the like.

"O Lord" I says "Thou knowest what we two saw together of the sufferings and sorrows of that young creetur now with Thee. If this dying man is truly penitent, we two together humbly pray Thee to have mercy on him!"

The Major says "Amen!" and then after a little stop I whispers him, "Dear old friend fetch our beloved boy." And the Major, so clever as to have got to understand it all without being told a word, went away and brought him.

Never never never, shall I forget the fair bright face of our boy when he stood at the foot of the bed, looking at his unknown father. And O so like his dear young mother then!

"Jemmy" I says, "I have found out all about this poor gentleman who is so ill, and he did lodge in the old house once. And as he wants to see all belonging to it, now that he is passing away, I sent for you."

"Ah poor man!" says Jemmy stepping forward and touching one of his hands with great gentleness. "My heart melts for him. Poor, poor, man!"

The eyes that were so soon to close for ever, turned to me, and I was not that strong in the pride of my strength that I could resist them.

"My darling boy, there is a reason in the secret history of this fellow-creetur, lying as the best and worst of us must all lie one day, which I think would ease his spirit in his last hour if you would lay your cheek against his forehead and say 'May God forgive you!' "

"O Gran," says Jemmy with a full heart "I am not worthy!" But he leaned down and did it. Then the faltering fingers made out to catch hold of my sleeve at last, and I believe he was a trying to kiss me when he died.

❋ ❋ ❋

There my dear! There you have the story of my Legacy in full, and it's worth ten times the trouble I have spent upon it if you are pleased to like it.

You might suppose that it set us against the little French town of Sens, but no we didn't find that. I found myself that I never looked up at the high tower atop of the other tower, but the days came back again when that fair young creetur with her pretty bright hair trusted in me like a mother, and the recollection made the place so peaceful to me as I can't express. And every soul about the hotel down to the pigeons in the court-yard made friends with Jemmy and the Major, and went lumbering away with them on all sorts of expeditions in all sorts of vehicles drawn by rampagious cart-horses – with heads and without[23] – mud for paint and ropes for harness – and every new friend dressed in blue like a butcher, and every new horse standing on his hind legs wanting to devour and consume every other horse, and every man that had a whip to crack crack-crack-crack-crack-cracking it as if it was a schoolboy with his first.

As to the Major my dear that man lived the greater part of his time with a little tumbler in one hand and a bottle of small wine[24] in the other, and whenever he saw anybody else with a little tumbler, no matter who it was – the military character with the tags, or the inn servants at their supper in the court-yard, or towns-people a chatting on a bench, or country-people a starting home after market – down rushes the Major to clink his glass against their glasses and cry – Hola! Vive Somebody! or Vive Something! as if he was beside himself. And though I could not quite approve of the Major's doing it, still the ways of the world are the ways of the world varying according to different parts of it, and dancing at all in the open Square with a lady that kept a barber's shop my opinion is that the Major was right to dance his best and to lead off with a power that I did not think was in him, though I was a little uneasy at the Barricading sound of the cries that were set up by the other dancers and the rest of the company, until when I says "What are they ever calling out Jemmy?" Jemmy says "They're calling out Gran, Bravo the Military English! Bravo the Military English!" which was very gratifying to my feelings as a Briton and became the name the Major was known by.

But every evening at a regular time we all three sat out in the balcony of the hotel at the end of the court-yard, looking up at the golden and rosy light as it changed on the great towers, and looking at the shadows of the towers as they changed on all about us ourselves included, and what do you think we did there? My dear if Jemmy hadn't brought some other of those stories of the Major's taking down from the telling of former lodgers at Eighty-one Norfolk-street,[25] and if he didn't bring 'em out with this speech:

"Here you are Gran! Here you are Godfather! More of 'em! *I*'ll read. And though you wrote 'em for me, Godfather, I know you won't disapprove of my making 'em over to Gran; will you?"

"No my dear boy," says the Major. "Everything we have is hers, and we are hers."

"Hers ever affectionately and devotedly J. Jackman, and J. Jackman Lirriper," cries the Young Rogue giving me a close hug. "Very well then Godfather. Look here. As Gran is in the Legacy way just now, I shall make these stories a part of Gran's Legacy. I'll leave 'em to her. What do you say Godfather?"

"Hip hip Hurrah!" says the Major.

"Very well then" cries Jemmy all in a bustle. "Vive the Military English! Vive the Lady Lirriper! Vive the Jemmy Jackman Ditto! Vive the Legacy! Now, you look out, Gran. And you look out, Godfather. I'll read! And I'll tell you what I'll do besides. On the last night of our holiday here when we are all packed and going away, I'll top up with something of my own."

"Mind you do sir" says I.

"Don't you be afraid, Gran" cries Young Sparkles. "Now then! I'm going to read. Once, twice, three and away. Open your mouths and shut your eyes, and see what Fortune sends you. All in to begin. Look out Gran. Look out Godfather!"

So in his lively spirits Jemmy began a reading, and he read every evening while we there, and sometimes we were about it late enough to have a candle burning quite steady out in the balcony in the still air. And so here is the rest of my Legacy my dear that I now hand over to you in this bundle of papers all in the Major's plain round writing. I wish I could hand you the church towers over too, and the pleasant air and the inn yard and the pigeons often coming and perching on the rail by Jemmy and seeming to be critical with their heads on one side, but you'll take as you find.[26]

MRS LIRRIPER RELATES HOW JEMMY TOPPED UP

Well my dear and so the evening readings of these jottings of the Major's brought us round at last to the evening when we were all packed and going away next day, and I do assure you that by that time though it was deliciously comfortable to look forward to the dear old house in Norfolk-street again, I had formed quite a high opinion of the French nation and had noticed them to be much more homely and domestic in their families and far more simple and amiable in their lives than I had ever been led to expect, and it did strike me between ourselves that in one particular they might be imitated to advantage by another nation which I will not mention, and that is in the courage with which they take their little enjoyments on little means and with little things and don't let solemn big-wigs stare them out of countenance or speechify them dull, of which said solemn big-wigs I have ever had the one opinion that I wish they were all made comfortable separately in coppers[27] with the lids on and never let out any more.

"Now young man," I says to Jemmy when we brought our chairs into the balcony that last evening, "you please to remember who was to 'top up.' "

"All right Gran" says Jemmy. "I am the illustrious personage."

But he looked so serious after he had made me that light answer, that the Major raised his eyebrows at me and I raised mine at the Major.

"Gran and Godfather," says Jemmy, "you can hardly think how much my mind has run on Mr Edson's death."

It gave me a little check. "Ah! It was a sad scene my love" I says, "and sad remembrances come back stronger than merry. But this" I says after a little silence, to rouse myself and the Major and Jemmy all together, "is not topping up. Tell us your story my dear."

"I will" says Jemmy.

"What is the date sir?" says I. "Once upon a time when pigs drank wine?"[28]

"No Gran," says Jemmy, still serious; "once upon a time when the French drank wine."

Again I glanced at the Major, and the Major glanced at me.

"In short, Gran and Godfather," says Jemmy, looking up, "the date is this time, and I'm going to tell you Mr Edson's story."

The flutter that it threw me into. The change of colour on the part of the Major!

"That is to say, you understand," our bright-eyed boy says, "I am going to give you my version of it. I shall not ask whether it's right or not, firstly because you said you knew very little about it, Gran, and secondly because what little you did know was a secret."

I folded my hands in my lap and I never took my eyes off Jemmy as he went running on.

"The unfortunate gentleman" Jemmy commences, "who is the subject of our present narrative was the son of Somebody, and was born Somewhere, and chose a profession Somehow. It is not with those parts of his career that we have to deal; but with his early attachment to a young and beautiful lady."

I thought I should have dropped. I durstn't look at the Major; but I knew what his state was, without looking at him.

"The father of our ill-starred hero" says Jemmy, copying as it seemed to me the style of some of his story-books, "was a worldly man who entertained ambitious views for his only son and who firmly set his face against the contemplated alliance with a virtuous but penniless orphan. Indeed he went so far as roundly to assure our hero that unless he weaned his thoughts from the object of his devoted affection, he would disinherit him. At the same time, he proposed as a suitable match, the daughter of a neighbouring gentleman of a good estate, who was neither ill favoured nor unamiable, and whose eligibility in a pecuniary point of view could not be disputed. But young Mr Edson, true to the first and only love that had inflamed his breast, rejected all considerations of self-advancement, and, deprecating his father's anger in a respectful letter, ran away with her."

My dear I had begun to take a turn for the better, but when it come to running away I began to take another turn for the worse.

"The lovers" says Jemmy "fled to London and were united at the altar of Saint Clement's Danes.[29] And it is at this period of their simple but touching story, that we find them inmates of the dwelling of a highly respected and beloved lady of the name of Gran, residing within a hundred miles of Norfolk-street."

I felt that we were almost safe now, I felt that the dear boy had no suspicion of the bitter truth, and I looked at the Major for the first time and drew a long breath. The Major gave me a nod.

"Our hero's father" Jemmy goes on "proving implacable and carrying his threat into unrelenting execution, the struggles of the young couple in London were severe, and would have been far more so, but for their good angel's having conducted them to the abode of Mrs Gran: who, divining their poverty (in spite of their endeavours to conceal it from her), by a thousand delicate arts smoothed their rough way, and alleviated the sharpness of their first distress."

Here Jemmy took one of my hands in one of his, and began a marking the turns of his story by making me give a beat from time to time upon his other hand.

"After a while, they left the house of Mrs Gran, and pursued their fortunes through a variety of successes and failures elsewhere. But in all reverses, whether for good or evil, the words of Mr Edson to the fair young partner of his life, were: 'Unchanging Love and Truth will carry us through all!' "

My hand trembled in the dear boy's, those words were so wofully unlike the fact.

"Unchanging Love and Truth" says Jemmy over again, as if he had a proud kind of a noble pleasure in it, "will carry us through all! Those were his words. And so they fought their way, poor but gallant and happy, until Mrs Edson gave birth to a child."

"A daughter," I says.

"No" says Jemmy, " a son. And the father was so proud of it that he could hardly bear it out of his sight. But a dark cloud overspread the scene. Mrs Edson sickened, drooped, and died."

"Ah! Sickened, drooped, and died!" I says.

"And so Mr Edson's only comfort, only hope on earth, and only stimulus to action, was his darling boy. As the child grew older, he grew so like his mother that he was her living picture. It used to make him wonder why his father cried when he kissed him. But unhappily he was like his mother in constitution as well as in face, and he died too before he had grown out of childhood. Then Mr Edson, who had good abilities, in his forlornness and despair threw them all to the winds. He became apathetic, reckless, lost. Little by little he sank down, down, down, down, until at last he almost lived (I think) by gaming. And so sickness overtook him in the town of Sens in France, and he lay down to die. But now that he had laid him down when all was done, and looked back upon the green Past beyond the time when he had covered it with ashes, he thought gratefully of the good Mrs Gran long lost sight of, who had been so kind to him and his young wife in the early days of their marriage, and he left the little that he had as a last Legacy to her. And she, being brought to see him, at first no more knew him than she would know from seeing the ruin of a Greek or Roman Temple, what it used to be before it fell; but at length she remembered him. And then he told her with tears, of his regret for the misspent part of his life, and besought her to think as mildly of it as she could, because it was the poor fallen Angel of his unchanging Love and Constancy after all. And because she had her grandson with her, and he fancied that his own boy, if he had lived, might have grown to be something like him, he asked her to let him touch his forehead with his cheek and say certain parting words."

Jemmy's voice sank low when it got to that, and tears filled my eyes, and filled the Major's.

"You little Conjuror" I says, "how did you ever make it all out? Go in and write it every word down, for it's a wonder."

Which Jemmy did, and I have repeated it to you my dear from his writing.

Then the Major took my hand and kissed it, and said "Dearest madam all has prospered with us."

"Ah Major" I says drying my eyes, "we needn't have been afraid. We might have known it. Treachery don't come natural to beaming youth; but trust and pity, love and constancy – they do, thank God!"

EXTRACT FROM LITTLE DORRIT

(RIGAUD AT CHALON-SUR-SAÔNE)

Narrative context: The notorious criminal Rigaud, accused of murdering his wife and released from prison at Marseille because of insufficient evidence, is making his way to Paris and then on to England. Forced to leave Marseille in secrecy and with very little money, he travels on foot and, in fear of attack as the news of his release spreads, under an assumed name. Hungry and tired, he approaches Chalon as night falls. The extract is from Book 1, Chapter 11.

A late, dull autumn night, was closing in upon the river Saone. The stream, like a sullied looking-glass in a gloomy place, reflected the clouds heavily; and the low banks leaned over here and there, as if they were half curious, and half afraid, to see their darkening pictures in the water. The flat expanse of country about Chalons lay a long heavy streak, occasionally made a little ragged by a row of poplar trees against the wrathful sunset. On the banks of the river Saone it was wet, depressing, solitary; and the night deepened fast.

One man, slowly moving on towards Chalons, was the only visible figure in the landscape. Cain might have looked as lonely and avoided.[1] With an old sheepskin knapsack at his back, and a rough, unbarked stick cut out of some wood in his hand; miry, footsore, his shoes and gaiters trodden out, his hair and beard untrimmed; the cloak he carried over his shoulder, and the clothes he wore, soddened with wet; limping along in pain and difficulty; he looked as if the clouds were hurrying from him, as if the wail of the wind and the shuddering of the grass were directed against him, as if the low mysterious plashing of the water murmured at him, as if the fitful autumn night were disturbed by him.

He glanced here, and he glanced there, sullenly but shrinkingly; and sometimes stopped and turned about, and looked all round him. Then he limped on again, toiling and muttering:

"To the devil with this plain that has no end! To the devil with these stones that cut like knives! To the devil with this dismal darkness, wrapping itself about one with a chill! I hate you!"

And he would have visited his hatred upon it all with the scowl he threw about him, if he could. He trudged a little further; and looking into the distance before him, stopped again.

"I, hungry, thirsty, weary. You, imbeciles, where the lights are yonder, eating and drinking, and warming yourselves at fires! I wish I had the sacking of your town, I would repay you, my children!"

But the teeth he set at the town, and the hand he shook at the town, brought the town no nearer; and the man was yet hungrier, and thirstier, and wearier, when his feet were on its jagged pavement, and he stood looking about him.

There was the hotel with its gateway, and its savoury smell of cooking; there was the café, with its bright windows, and its rattling of dominoes; there was the dyer's, with its strips of red cloth on the doorposts; there was the silversmith's, with its ear-rings, and its offerings for altars; there was the tobacco dealer's, with its lively group of soldier customers coming out pipe in mouth; there were the bad odours of the town, and the rain and refuse in the kennels,[2] and the faint lamps slung across the road, and the huge Diligence,[3] and its mountain of luggage, and its six grey horses with their tails tied up, getting under weigh at the coach office. But no small cabaret[4] for a straitened traveller being within sight, he had to seek one round the dark corner, where the cabbage leaves lay thickest, trodden about the public cistern at which women had not yet left off drawing water. There, in the back street he found one, the Break of Day. The curtained windows clouded the Break of Day, but it seemed light and warm, and it announced in legible inscriptions with appropriate pictorial embellishment of billiard cue and ball, that at the Break of Day one could play billiards; that there one could find meat, drink, and lodging, whether one came on horseback, or came on foot; and that it kept good wines, liqueurs, and brandy. The man turned the handle of the Break of Day door, and limped in.

He touched his discoloured slouched hat, as he came in at the door, to a few men who occupied the room. Two were playing dominoes at one of the little tables; three or four were seated round the stove, conversing as they smoked; the billiard-table in the centre was left alone for the time; the landlady of the Daybreak sat behind her little counter among her cloudy bottles of syrups, baskets of cakes, and leaden drainage for glasses, working at her needle.

Making his way to an empty little table, in a corner of the room behind the stove, he put down his knapsack and his cloak upon the ground. As he raised his head from stooping to do so, he found the landlady beside him.

"One can lodge here tonight, madame?"

chapter ten

THE FRENCH REVOLUTION

("JUDICIAL SPECIAL PLEADING"; EXTRACTS FROM *A TALE OF TWO CITIES*)

"Judicial Special Pleading" appeared on the front page of the 23 December 1848 edition of *The Examiner*, the weekly paper then edited by John Forster. Dickens had first written for the paper as a reviewer in the late 1830s and early 1840s but in 1848–49 he contributed a wider range of articles, from reviews to editorial leaders on social and political issues. Like all contributions to *The Examiner* these articles were published without bylines – Michael Slater lists those now firmly attributed to Dickens in Volume 2 of his edition of the journalism (Slater, 1996, pp 375–377).

The unhappy target of "Judicial Special Pleading" is Sir Edward Hall Alderson, a presiding judge in the political trials that followed the large-scale arrests of Chartists during the summer of 1848 (see note 1, p 373, for details). Alderson's opening address to the jury at the Chester Assizes, with all its blatant political bias and moralizing middle-class conservatism, was reported at length in *The Times* on 8 December (see note 6, p 375, for a summary of the speech). The main thrust of his argument was that significant political or systemic change was not the way to alleviate the sufferings of the poor. In support of this contention he alluded to the example of the French Revolution, claiming that there was documentary evidence to suggest that the French people were worse off after the Revolution than they had been before it. It is this part of Alderson's address that Dickens ridicules in *The Examiner*, ripping into his flimsy historical "evidence" and thus implying that his overall position is based on irrationality and ignorance. The judge's attempt to influence the jury – "a kind of judicial special-constableism by no means edifying" – is exposed as nonsensical as well as objectionable.

Dickens's primary source for the historical details and counterargument in "Judicial Special Pleading" was the first volume of *Histoire de la Révolution française*, 1823–27 by Adolphe Thiers (English translation, 1838). With Thiers as his authority, he argues that the French Revolution and its bloody aftermath were the direct consequences of deep-rooted intolerance and injustice:

> It was a struggle on the part of the people for social recognition and existence. It was a struggle for vengeance against intolerable oppressors. It was a struggle for the overthrow of a system of oppression, which in its contempt of all humanity, decency, and natural rights, and its systematic degradation of the people, had trained them to be the demons that they showed themselves, when they rose up and cast it down for ever.

Eleven years later, in *A Tale of Two Cities*, 1859, this view of the Revolution as the inevitable consequence of sustained social and economic injustice, and of the brutalizing effects of oppression, is expressed in vivid and dramatic detail. In the novel's closing chapter, Dickens articulates his theme in similar terms:

> All the devouring and insatiate Monsters imagined since imagination could record itself, are fused into the one realisation, Guillotine. And yet there is not in France, with its rich variety of soil and climate, a blade, a leaf, a root, a sprig, a peppercorn, which will grow to maturity under conditions more certain than those that have produced this horror. Crush humanity out of shape once more, under similar hammers, and

it will twist itself into the same tortured forms. Sow the same seed of rapacious licence and oppression ever again, and it will surely yield the same fruit according to its kind.

The five extracts presented here track the historical narrative of *A Tale of Two Cities* from the early rumblings of rebellion to the height of The Terror. The first portrays life in the working-class *quartier* of Saint-Antoine in 1775, fourteen years before the outbreak of the Revolution. Dickens brings into play his often-voiced perception of the readiness of French people to derive enjoyment from simple pleasures, but here adds a sinister undercurrent of deprivation and latent violence. In the second extract, set several years later, he turns his attention to the luxury and power of the aristocracy, the decadence of the regime and, in one of the novel's most memorable incidents, the callous indifference of the rich and privileged to the sufferings of the poor. The third extract is the dramatic account of the storming of the Bastille, in which the power of the novel's marriage of fiction and history is at its height, with the personal drama of the characters at once influenced by and illuminating the greater drama that unfolds around them. The fourth extract, with its extreme narrative compression, a breathless race through key historical events, conveys the pace of change and the headlong descent into The Terror, evoking Thomas Carlyle's vision of a "rushing down" into the "black precipitous Abyss" (*The French Revolution*, Part 3, 5, Chapter 1). The final extract, another outstanding example of the novel's fusion of the micro-drama of its characters with the macro-drama of history, is from the closing chapter and portrays Paris in the grip of The Terror, deep down in the depths of Carlyle's Abyss.

Dickens had long known and admired Carlyle's *The French Revolution*, published in 1837 – he told Forster in 1849 that he had been "reading that wonderful book the *French Revolution* again for the 500th time" (*Life*, 6, Chapter 3) – and he mined it deeply in his research for *A Tale of Two Cities*. In the Preface to the first volume edition of the novel he acknowledges his debt to "Mr Carlyle's wonderful book." But if *The French Revolution* was the principal source for *A Tale*, in relation both to its interpretation of history and its historical narrative, it was by no means the only one. Dickens took his research seriously and strove for accuracy and authenticity. In his Preface he assures his readers,

> Whenever any reference (however slight) is made here to the condition of the French people before or during the Revolution, it is truly made, on the faith of trustworthy witnesses.

He was at pains to immerse himself in the period. "All the time I was at work on the Two Cities, I read no books but such as had the air of the time in them," he wrote to John Forster in May 1860 (*Pilgrim*, 9, p 245). He consulted Carlyle, who sent him a large selection of further reading: in a letter of 24 March 1859 he thanks Carlyle for his help and advice and for "the books received from the London Library, and suggested by you" (*Pilgrim*, 9, p 41). And in a letter to Bulwer-Lytton of 5 June 1860 (*Pilgrim*, 9, pp 258–260) he names several sources as his authority for various characters and events in the novel, mentioning in particular Louis-Sébastien Mercier's *Tableau de Paris*, 1782–88. Mercier's 12-volume apparently haphazard, often acerbic and always minutely detailed account of life in Paris in the years immediately preceding the Revolution is no easy book to negotiate, and Dickens must have labored hard to use it as effectively as he did. Next to Carlyle, it appears to have been the work on which he most relied.

The annotation to the extracts presented here gives an indication of the extent to which Dickens drew on his principal sources, points to other books to which he may have referred and demonstrates his concern to be historically accurate. For extensive information on the sources for the novel as a whole, see Andrew Sanders's *The Companion to A Tale of Two Cities*, 2002. Sanders's 1998 Oxford World's Classics edition of the novel also provides valuable detail on its sources, as does Richard Maxwell's 2000 Penguin Classics edition.

The arrest of the Marquis de Launay, Governor of the Bastille, 14 July 1789

JUDICIAL SPECIAL PLEADING

It is unnecessary for us to observe that we have not the least sympathy with physical-force chartism in the abstract, or with the tried and convicted physical-force chartists in particular.[1] Apart from the atrocious designs to which these men, beyond all question, willingly and easily subscribed, even if it be granted that such extremes of wickedness were mainly suggested by the spies in whom their dense ignorance confided,[2] they have done too much damage to the cause of rational liberty and freedom all over the world to be regarded in any other light than as enemies of the common weal, and the worst foes of the common people.

But, for all this, we would have the language of common-sense and knowledge addressed to these offenders – especially from the Bench. They need it very much; and besides that the truth should be spoken at all times, it is desirable that it should always appear in conjunction with the gravity and authority of the judicial ermine.

Mr Baron Alderson,[3] we regret to observe, opened the late special commission for the county of Chester[4] with a kind of judicial special-constableism by no means edifying. In sporting phrase, he "went in"[5] upon the subject of Revolution with a determination to win; and as nothing is easier than for a man, wigged or unwigged, to say what he pleases when he has all the talk to himself and there is nobody to answer him, he improved the occasion after a somewhat startling manner.[6] It is important that it should not be left wholly unnoticed. On Mr Isaac Bickerstaff's magic thermometer, at his apartment in Shoe Lane, the Church was placed between zeal and moderation;[7] and Mr Bickerstaff observed that if the enchanted liquor rose from the central point, Church, too high in zeal, it was in danger of going up to wrath, and from wrath to persecution. The substitution of "Bench" for "Church" by the wise old censor of

Great Britain, would no doubt have been attended with the same result.

Mr Baron Alderson informed the grand jury, for their edification, that "previous to the Revolution in France, of 1790, the physical comforts possessed by the poor greatly exceeded those possessed by them subsequent to that event." Before we pass to Mr Baron Alderson's proof in support of this allegation, we would inquire whether, at this time of day, any rational man supposes that the first Revolution in France was an event that could be avoided, or that is difficult to be accounted for, on looking back? Whether it was not the horrible catastrophe of a drama, which had already passed through every scene and shade of progress, inevitably leading on to that fearful conclusion? Whether there is any record, in the world's history, of a people among whom the arts and sciences and the refinements of civilised life existed, so oppressed, degraded, and utterly miserable, as the mass of the French population were before that Revolution? Physical comforts! No such thing was known among the French people – among *the people* – for years before the Revolution. They had died of sheer want and famine, in numbers. The hunting-trains of their kings had ridden over their bodies in the Royal Forests. Multitudes had gone about, crying and howling for bread, in the streets of Paris. The line of road from Versailles to the capital had been blocked up by starvation and nakedness pouring in from the departments.[8] The tables spread by Egalité Orleans[9] in the public streets, had been beseiged by the foremost stragglers of a whole nation of paupers, on the face of every one of whom the shadow of the coming guillotine was black. An infamous feudality and a corrupt government had plundered and ground them down, year after year, until they were reduced to a condition of distress which has no parallel. As their wretchedness deepened, the wantonness and luxury of their oppressors heightened, until the very fashions and customs of the upper classes ran mad from being unrestrained, and became monstrous.

"All," says Thiers,[10] "was monopolised by a few hands, and the burdens bore upon a single class. The nobility and the clergy possessed nearly two-thirds of the landed property. The other third, belonging to the people, paid taxes to the king, a multitude of feudal dues to the nobility, the tithe to the clergy, and was, moreover, liable to the devastations of noble sportsmen and their game. The taxes on consumption weighed heavily on the great mass, and consequently on the people. The mode in which they were levied was vexatious. The gentry might be in arrear with impunity; the people, on the other hand, ill-treated and imprisoned, were doomed to suffer in body, in default of goods. They defended with their blood the upper classes of society, without being able to subsist themselves."

Bad as the state of things was which succeeded to the Revolution and must always follow any such dire convulsion, if there be anything in history that is certain, it is certain that the French people had NO physical comforts when the Revolution occurred. And when Mr Baron Alderson talks to the grand jury of that Revolution being a mere struggle for "political rights," he talks (with due submission to him) nonsense, and loses an opportunity of pointing his discourse to the instruction of the chartists. It was a struggle on the part of the people for social recognition and existence. It was a struggle for vengeance against intolerable oppressors. It was a struggle for the overthrow of a system of oppression, which in its contempt of all humanity, decency, and natural rights, and in its systematic degradation of the people, had trained them to be the demons that they showed themselves, when they rose up and cast it down for ever.

Mr Baron Alderson's proof of his position would be a strange one, by whomsoever adduced, but it is an especially strange one to be put forward by a high functionary, one of whose most important duties is the examination and sifting of evidence, with a view to its being the better understood by minds unaccustomed to such investigations.

It had been assumed, on very competent authority, that the physical comforts of the poor might be safely judged of by the quantity of meat consumed by the population; and, taking this as the criterion, the statistics of Paris gave the following result: – In 1789, during the period of the old monarchy, the quantity of meat consumed was 147lb. per man; in 1817, after the Bourbon dynasty had been restored to the throne, subsequent to the revolution, it was 110lb. 2oz. per man; and in 1827, the medium period between the restoration of the Bourbons and the present time, the average was still about 110lb.; while, after the revolution of 1830, it fell to 98lb. 11oz., and at this period it was in all probability still less.

The statistics, *of Paris*, in 1789! When the Court, displaying extraordinary magnificence, was in Paris; when the three orders, all the great dignitaries of the state, and their immense trains of followers and dependants, were in Paris;[11] when the aristocracy, making their last effort at accommodation with the king, were in Paris, and remained there until the close of the year;[12] when there was the great procession to the church of Notre Dame, in Paris;[13] when the opening of the States-General took place, in Paris;[14] when the Commons constituted themselves the National Assembly, in Paris;[15] when the electors, assembled from sixty districts, refused to depart from Paris;[16] when the garden of the Palais Royal was the scene of the nightly assemblage of more foreigners, debauchees, and loungers, than had ever been seen in Paris;[17] when people came into Paris from all parts of France; when there was all the agitation, uproar, revelling, banquetting, and delirium in Paris, which distinguished that year of great events; – when, in short, the meat-eating classes were all in Paris, and all at high-feasting in the whirl and fury of such a time!

Mr Baron Alderson takes this very year of 1789, and dividing the quantity of meat consumed, by the population of Paris, sets before the grand jury the childish absurdity of there having been 147lb. of meat per man, as a proof of the physical comforts of the people! This year of 1789 being on record as the hardest ever known by the French people since the disasters of Louis XIV and the immortal charity of Fenelon![18] This year of 1789 being the year when Mirabeau was speaking in the assembly of "famished Paris";[19] when the king was forced to receive deputations of women, who demanded bread; and when they rang out to all Paris "Bread! rise up for bread!" with the great bell of the Hôtel de Ville![20]

It would be idle to dissect such evidence more minutely. It is too gross and palpable. We will conclude with a final and grave reason, as it seems to us, for noticing this serious mistake on the part of Mr Baron Alderson.

That learned judge is much deceived if he imagines that there are not, among the chartists, men possessed of sufficient information to detect such juggling, and make the most of it. Those active and mischievous agents of the chartists who live by lecturing, will do more with such a charge as this, than they could do with all the misery in England for the next twelve months. In any common history of the French Revolution, they have the proof against Mr Baron Alderson under their hands. The grade of education and intellect they address is particularly prone to accept a brick as a specimen of a house; and its ready conclusion from such an exposition is, that the whole system which rules and restrains it is a falsehood and a cheat.

It was but the other day that Mr Baron Alderson stated to some chartist prisoners, as a fact which everybody knew, that any man in England who was industrious and persevering could obtain political power. Are there no industrious and persevering men in England on whom this comfortable doctrine casts a slur? We rather think the chartist lecturers might find out some.

EXTRACTS FROM A TALE OF TWO CITIES

(QUARTIER SAINT ANTOINE)

Narrative context: This is the novel's first scene in Paris. Set in 1775, it introduces the working-class quartier of Saint Antoine, a center of deprivation and discontent (the demonstrations and rioting here in spring 1789 foreshadowed the storming of the Bastille in July). The wine-shop keeper who makes a brief appearance at the end is Ernest Defarge, who is to play a prominent role in the story. The extract is from Book 1, Chapter 5, "The Wine Shop."

A large cask of wine had been dropped and broken, in the street. The accident had happened in getting it out of a cart; the cask had tumbled out with a run, the hoops had burst, and it lay on the stones just outside the door of the wine-shop, shattered like a walnut-shell.

All the people within reach had suspended their business, or their idleness, to run to the spot and drink the wine. The rough, irregular stones of the street, pointing every way, and designed, one might have thought, expressly to lame all living creatures that approached them,[1] had dammed it into little pools; these were surrounded, each by its own jostling group or crowd, according to its size. Some men kneeled down, made scoops of their two hands joined, and sipped, or tried to help women, who bent over their shoulders, to sip, before the wine had all run out between their fingers. Others, men and women, dipped in the puddles with little mugs of mutilated earthenware, or even with handkerchiefs from women's heads, which were squeezed dry into infants' mouths; others made small mud-embankments, to stem the wine as it ran; others, directed by lookers-on up at high windows, darted here and there, to cut off little streams of wine that started away in new directions; others devoted themselves to the sodden and lee-dyed pieces of the cask, licking, and even champing the moister wine-rotted fragments with eager relish. There was no drainage to carry off the wine, and not only did it all get taken up, but so much mud had got taken up along with it, that there might have been a scavenger[2] in the street, if anybody acquainted with it could have believed in such a miraculous presence.

A shrill sound of laughter and of amused voices – voices of men, women, and children – resounded in the street while this wine-game lasted. There was a little roughness in the sport, and much playfulness. There was special companionship in it, an observable inclination on the part of every one to join some other one, which led, especially among the luckier or lighter-hearted, to frolicsome embraces, drinking of healths, shaking of hands, and even joining of hands and dancing, a dozen together. When the wine was gone, and the places where it had been most abundant were raked into a gridiron-pattern by fingers, these demonstrations ceased, as suddenly as they had broken out. The man who had left his saw sticking in the firewood he was cutting,[3] set it in motion again; the woman who had left on a door-step the little pot of hot ashes, at which she had been trying to soften the pain in her own starved fingers and toes, or in those of her child, returned to it; men with bare arms, matted locks, and cadaverous faces, who had emerged into the winter light from cellars, moved away to descend again; and a gloom gathered on the scene that appeared more natural to it than sunshine.

The wine was red wine, and had stained the ground of the narrow street in the suburb of Saint Antoine,[4] in Paris, where it was spilled. It had stained many hands, too, and many faces, and many naked feet, and many wooden shoes. The hands of the man who sawed the wood, left red marks on the billets; and the forehead of the woman who nursed her baby, was stained with the stain of the old rag she wound about her head again. Those who had been greedy with the staves of the cask, had acquired a tigerish smear about the mouth; and one tall joker so besmirched, his head more out of a long squalid bag of a nightcap than in it, scrawled upon a wall with his finger dipped in muddy wine lees – BLOOD.

The time was to come, when that wine too would be spilled on the street-stones, and when the stain of it would be red upon many there.

And now that the cloud settled on Saint Antoine, which a momentary gleam had driven from his sacred countenance, the darkness of it was heavy – cold, dirt, sickness, ignorance, and want, were the lords in waiting on the saintly presence – nobles of great power all of them; but, most especially the last. Samples of a people that had undergone a terrible grinding and re-grinding in the mill, and certainly not in the fabulous mill which ground old people young,[5] shivered at every corner, passed in and out at every doorway, looked from every window, fluttered in every vestige of a garment that the wind shook. The mill which had worked them down, was the mill that grinds young people old; the children had ancient faces and grave voices; and upon them, and upon the grown faces, and ploughed into every furrow of age and coming up afresh, was the sign, Hunger. It was prevalent everywhere. Hunger was pushed out of the tall houses, in the wretched clothing that hung upon poles and lines; Hunger was patched into them with straw and rag and wood and paper; Hunger was repeated in every fragment of the small modicum of firewood that the man sawed off; Hunger stared down from the smokeless chimneys, and started up from the filthy street that had no offal, among its refuse, of anything to eat. Hunger was the inscription on the baker's shelves, written in every small loaf of his scanty stock of bad bread; at the sausage-shop, in every dead-dog preparation that was offered for sale. Hunger rattled its dry bones among the roasting chestnuts in the turned cylinder; Hunger was shred into atomies in every farthing porringer of husky chips of potato, fried with some reluctant drops of oil.

Its abiding-place was in all things fitted to it. A narrow winding street, full of offence and stench, with other narrow winding streets diverging, all peopled by rags and nightcaps, and all smelling of rags and nightcaps, and all visible things with a brooding look upon them that looked ill. In the hunted air of the people there was yet some wild-beast thought of the possibility of turning at bay. Depressed and slinking though they were, eyes of fire were not wanting among them; nor compressed lips, white with what they suppressed; nor foreheads knitted into the likeness of the gallows-rope they mused about enduring, or inflicting. The trade signs (and they were almost as many as the shops) were, all, grim illustrations of Want. The butcher and the porkman painted up, only the leanest scrags of meat; the baker, the coarsest of meagre loaves. The people rudely pictured as drinking in the wine-shops, croaked over their scanty measures of thin wine and beer, and were gloweringly confidential together. Nothing was represented in a flourishing condition, save tools and weapons; but, the cutler's knives and axes were sharp and bright, the smith's hammers were heavy, and the gunmaker's stock was murderous. The crippling stones of the pavement, with their many little reservoirs of mud and water, had no footways, but broke off abruptly at the doors. The kennel, to make amends, ran down the middle of the street – when it ran at all: which was only after heavy rains, and then it ran, by many eccentric fits, into the houses.[6] Across the streets, at wide intervals, one clumsy lamp was slung by a rope and pulley;[7] at night, when the lamplighter had let these down, and lighted, and hoisted them again, a feeble grove of dim wicks swung in a sickly manner overhead, as if they were at sea. Indeed they were at sea, and the ship and crew were in peril of tempest.

For, the time was to come, when the gaunt scarecrows of that region should have watched the lamplighter, in their idleness and hunger, so long, as to conceive the idea of improving on his method, and hauling up men by those ropes and pulleys, to flare upon the darkness of their condition. But, the time was not come yet; and every wind that blew over France shook the rags of the scarecrows in vain, for the birds, fine of song and feather, took no warning.

The wine-shop was a corner shop, better than most others in its appearance and degree, and the master of the wine-shop had stood outside it, in a yellow waistcoat and green breeches, looking on at the struggle for the lost wine. "It's not my affair," said he, with a final shrug of his shoulders. "The people from the market did it. Let them bring another."

(THE ARISTOCRACY)

Narrative context: The action has moved forward to 1780. This passage describes the extravagance, decadence, and influence of the ruling class, as represented by the unidentified "Monseigneur." It also introduces the Marquis St Evrémonde ("Monsieur the Marquis"), the callous uncle of Charles Darnay, who, speeding through the Paris streets on his way home from Monseigneur's reception, becomes involved in one of the novel's most significant incidents. The extract is from Book 2, Chapter 7, entitled "Monsieur the Marquis in Town" in the original weekly part (from which this text is taken) and subsequently retitled "Monseigneur in Town."

Monseigneur,[1] one of the great lords in power at the Court, held his fortnightly reception in his grand hotel in Paris. Monseigneur was in his inner room, his sanctuary of sanctuaries, the Holiest of Holies to the crowd of worshippers in the suite of rooms without.[2] Monseigneur was about to take his chocolate. Monseigneur could swallow a great many things with ease, and was by some few sullen minds supposed to be rather rapidly swallowing France; but, his morning's chocolate could not so much as get into the throat of Monseigneur, without the aid of four strong men besides the Cook.

Yes. It took four men, all four a-blaze with gorgeous decoration, and the Chief of them unable to exist with fewer than two gold watches in his pocket, emulative of the noble and chaste fashion set by Monseigneur,[3] to conduct the happy chocolate to Monseigneur's lips. One lacquey carried the chocolate-pot into the sacred presence; a second, milled and frothed the chocolate with the little instrument he bore for that function; a third, presented the favoured napkin; a fourth (he of the two gold watches) poured the chocolate out. It was impossible for Monseigneur to dispense with one of these attendants on the chocolate and hold his high place under the admiring Heavens. Deep would have been the blot upon his escutcheon if his chocolate had been ignobly waited on by only three men; he must have died of two.

Monseigneur had been out at a little supper last night, where the Comedy and the Grand Opera were charmingly represented.[4] Monseigneur was out at a little supper most nights, with fascinating company. So polite and so impressible was Monseigneur, that the Comedy and the Grand Opera had far more influence with him in the tiresome articles of state affairs and state secrets, than the needs of all France. A happy circumstance for France, as the like always is for all countries similarly favoured! – always was for England (by way of example), in the regretted days of the merry Stuart who sold it.[5]

Monseigneur had one truly noble idea of general public business, which was, to let everything go on in its own way; of particular public business, Monseigneur had the other truly noble idea that it must all go his way – tend to his own power and pocket. Of his pleasures, general and particular, Monseigneur had the other truly noble idea, that the world was made for them. The text of his order (altered from the original by only a pronoun, which is not much) ran: "The earth and the fulness thereof are mine, saith Monseigneur."[6]

Yet, Monseigneur had slowly found that vulgar embarrassments crept into his affairs, both private and public; and he had, as to both classes of affairs, allied himself perforce with a Farmer-General.[7] As to finances public, because Monseigneur could not make anything at all of them, and must consequently let them out to somebody who could; as to finances private, because Farmer-Generals were rich, and Monseigneur, after generations of great luxury and expense, was growing poor. Hence, Monseigneur had taken his sister from a convent, while there was yet time to ward off the impending veil, the cheapest garment she could wear, and had bestowed her as a prize upon a very rich Farmer-General, poor in family. Which Farmer-General, carrying an appropriate cane with a golden apple on the top of it,[8] was now among the company in the outer rooms, much prostrated before by mankind – always excepting superior mankind of the blood of Monseigneur, who, his own wife included, looked down upon him with the loftiest contempt.[9]

A sumptuous man was the Farmer-General. Thirty horses stood in his stables, twenty-four male domestics sat in his halls, six body-women waited on his wife.[10] As one who pretended to do nothing but plunder and forage where he could, the Farmer-General – howsoever his matrimonial relations conduced to social morality – was at least the greatest reality among the personages who attended at the hotel of Monseigneur that day.

For, the rooms, though a beautiful scene to look at, and adorned with every device of decoration that the taste and skill of the time could achieve, were, in truth, not a sound business; considered with any reference to the scarecrows in the rags and nightcaps elsewhere (and not so far off, either, but that the watching towers of Notre Dame, almost equidistant from the two extremes,[11] could see them both), they would have been an exceedingly uncomfortable business – if that could have been anybody's business, at the house of Monseigneur. Military officers destitute of military knowledge; naval officers with no idea of a ship; civil officers without a notion of affairs; brazen ecclesiastics, of the worst world worldly, with sensual eyes, loose tongues, and looser lives; all totally unfit for their several callings, all lying horribly in pretending to belong to them, but all nearly or remotely of the order of Monseigneur, and therefore foisted on all public employments from which anything was to be got; these were to be told off by the score and the score.[12] People not immediately connected with Monseigneur or the State, yet equally unconnected with anything that was real, or with lives passed in travelling by any straight road to any true earthly end, were no less abundant. Doctors who made great fortunes out of dainty remedies for imaginary disorders that never existed, smiled upon their courtly patients in the ante-chambers of Monseigneur.[13] Projectors[14] who had discovered every kind of remedy for the little evils with which the State was touched, except the remedy of setting to work in earnest to root out a single sin, poured their distracting babble into any ears they could lay hold of, at the reception of Monseigneur. Unbelieving Philosophers who were remodelling the world with words, and making card-towers of Babel to scale the skies with, talked with Unbelieving Chemists who had an eye on the transmutation of metals, at this wonderful gathering accumulated by Monseigneur.[15] Exquisite gentlemen of the finest breeding, which was at that remarkable time – and has been since – to be known by its fruits of indifference to every natural subject of human interest, were in the most exemplary state of exhaustion, at the hotel of Monseigneur. Such homes had these various notabilities left behind them in the fine world of Paris, that the spies[16] among the assembled devotees of Monseigneur – forming a goodly half of the polite company – would have found it hard to discover among the angels of that sphere, one solitary wife, who, in her manners and appearance, owned to being a Mother. Indeed, except for the mere act of bringing a troublesome creature into this world – which does not go far towards the realisation of the name of mother – there was no such thing known to the fashion. Peasant women kept the unfashionable babies close, and brought them up, and charming grandmammas of sixty dressed and supped as at twenty.[17]

The leprosy of unreality disfigured every human creature in attendance upon Monseigneur. In the outermost room were half a dozen exceptional people who had had, for a few years, some vague misgiving in them that things in general were going rather wrong. As a promising way of setting them right, half of the half-dozen had become members of a fantastic sect of Convulsionists,[18] and were even then considering within themselves whether they should foam, rage, roar, and turn cataleptic on the spot – thereby setting up a highly intelligible finger-post to the Future, for Monseigneur's guidance. Beside these Dervishes,[19] were other three who had rushed into another sect, which mended matters with a jargon about "the Centre of Truth:"[20] holding that Man had got out of the Centre of Truth – which did not need much demonstration – but had not got out of the Circumference, and that he was to be kept from flying out of the Circumference, and was even to be shoved back into the Centre, by fasting and seeing of spirits. Among these, accordingly, much discoursing with spirits went on – and it did a world of good which never became manifest.

But, the comfort was, that all the company at the grand hotel of Monseigneur were perfectly dressed. If the Day of Judgment had only been ascertained to be a dress day, everybody there would have been eternally correct. Such frizzling and powdering and sticking up of hair, such delicate complexions artificially preserved and mended, such gallant swords to look at, and such delicate honour to the sense of smell, would surely keep anything going, for ever and ever. The exquisite gentlemen of the finest breeding wore little pendent trinkets that chinked as they languidly moved; these golden fetters rang like precious little bells; and what with that ringing, and with the rustle of silk and brocade and fine linen, there was a flutter in the air that fanned Saint Antoine and his devouring hunger far away.

Dress was the one unfailing talisman and charm used for keeping all things in their places. Everybody was dressed for a Fancy Ball that was never to leave off. From the Palace of the Tuileries,[21] through Monseigneur and the whole Court, through the Chambers, the Tribunals of Justice, and all society (except the scarecrows), the Fancy Ball descended to the Common Executioner: who, in pursuance of the charm, was required to officiate "frizzled, powdered, in a gold-laced coat, pumps, and white silk stockings."[22] At the gallows and the wheel – the axe was a rarity – Monsieur Paris, as it was the episcopal mode among his brother Professors of the provinces, Monsieur Orleans, and the rest, to call him, presided in this dainty dress.[23] And who among the company at Monseigneur's reception in that seventeen hundred and eightieth year of our Lord, could possibly doubt, that a system rooted in a frizzled hangman, powdered, gold-laced, pumped, and white-silk stockinged, would see the very stars out!

Monseigneur having eased his four men of their burdens and taken his chocolate, caused the doors of the Holiest of Holiests to be thrown open, and issued forth. Then, what submission, what cringing and fawning, what servility, what abject humiliation! As to bowing down in body and spirit, nothing in that way was left for Heaven – which may have been one among other reasons why the worshippers of Monseigneur never troubled it.[24]

Bestowing a word of promise here and a smile there, a whisper on one happy slave and a wave of the hand on another, Monseigneur affably passed through his rooms to the remote region of the Circumference of Truth. There, Monseigneur turned, and came back again, and so in due course of time got himself shut up in his sanctuary by the chocolate sprites, and was seen no more.

The show being over, the flutter in the air became quite a little storm, and the precious little bells went ringing down stairs. There was soon but one person left of all the crowd, and he, with his hat under his arm and his snuff-box in his hand, slowly passed among the mirrors on his way out.

"I devote you," said this person, stopping at the last door on his way, and turning in the direction of the sanctuary, "to the Devil!"

With that, he shook the snuff from his fingers as if he had shaken the dust from his feet,[25] and quietly walked down stairs.

He was a man of about sixty, handsomely dressed, haughty in manner, and with a face like a fine mask. A face of transparent paleness; every feature in it clearly defined; one set expression on it. The nose, beautifully formed otherwise, was very slightly pinched at the top of each nostril. In those two compressions, or dints, the only little change that the face ever showed, resided. They persisted in changing colour sometimes, and they would be occasionally dilated and contracted by something like a faint pulsation; then, they gave a look of treachery, and cruelty, to the whole countenance. Examined with attention, its capacity of helping such a look was to be found in the line of the mouth, and the lines of the orbits of the eyes, being much too horizontal and thin; still, in the effect the face made, it was a handsome face, and a remarkable one.

Its owner went down stairs into the court-yard, got into his carriage, and drove away. Not many people had talked with him at the reception; he had stood in a little space apart, and Monseigneur might have been warmer in his manner. It appeared, under the circumstances, rather agreeable to him to see the common people dispersed before his horses, and often barely escaping from being run down. His man drove as if he were charging an enemy, and the furious recklessness of the man brought no check into the face, or to the lips, of the master. The complaint had sometimes made itself audible, even in that deaf city and dumb age, that, in the narrow streets without footways, the fierce patrician custom of hard driving endangered and maimed the mere vulgar in a barbarous manner.[26] But, few cared enough for that to think of it a second time, and, in this matter, as in all others, the common wretches were left to get out of their difficulties as they could.

With a wild rattle and clatter, and an inhuman abandonment of consideration not easy to be understood in these days, the carriage dashed through streets and swept round corners, with women screaming before it, and men clutching each other and clutching children out of its way. At last, swooping at a street corner by a fountain, one of its wheels came to a sickening little jolt, and there was a loud cry from a number of voices, and the horses reared and plunged.

But for the latter inconvenience, the carriage probably would not have stopped; carriages were often known to drive on, and leave their wounded behind, and why not? But, the frightened valet had got down in a hurry, and there were twenty hands at the horses' bridles.

"What has gone wrong?" said Monsieur, calmly looking out.

A tall man in a nightcap had caught up a bundle from among the feet of the horses, and had laid it on the basement of the fountain, and was down in the mud and wet, howling over it like a wild animal.

"Pardon, Monsieur the Marquis!" said a ragged and submissive man, "it is a child."[27]

"Why does he make that abominable noise? Is it his child?"

"Excuse me, Monsieur the Marquis – it is a pity – yes."

The fountain was a little removed; for the street opened, where it was, into a space some ten or twelve yards square. As the tall man suddenly got up from the ground, and came running at the carriage, Monsieur the Marquis clapped his hand for an instant on his sword-hilt.

"Killed!" shrieked the man, in wild desperation, extending both arms at their length above his head, and staring at him. "Dead!"

The people closed round, and looked at Monsieur the Marquis. There was nothing revealed by the many eyes that looked at him but watchfulness and eagerness; there was no visible menacing or anger. Neither did the people say anything; after the first cry, they had been silent, and they remained so. The voice of the submissive man who had spoken, was flat and tame in its extreme submission. Monsieur the Marquis ran his eyes over them all, as if they had been mere rats come out of their holes.

He took out his purse.

"It is extraordinary to me," said he, "that you people cannot take care of yourselves and your children. One or the other of you is for ever in the way. How do I know what injury you have done my horses? See! Give him that."

He threw out a gold coin for the valet to pick up, and all the heads craned forward that all the eyes might look down at it as it fell. The tall man called out again with a most unearthly cry, "Dead!"

He was arrested by the quick arrival of another man, for whom the rest made way. On seeing him, the miserable creature fell upon his shoulder, sobbing and crying, and pointing to the fountain, where some women were stooping over the motionless bundle, and moving gently about it. They were as silent, however, as the men.

"I know all, I know all," said that last comer. "Be a brave man, my Gaspard! It is better for the poor little plaything to die so, than to live. It has died in a moment without pain. Could it have lived an hour as happily?"

"You are a philosopher, you there," said the Marquis, smiling. "How do they call you?"

"They call me Defarge."

"Of what trade?"

"Monsieur the Marquis, vendor of wine."

"Pick up that, philosopher and vendor of wine," said the Marquis throwing him another gold coin, "and spend it as you will. The horses there; are they right?"

Without deigning to look at the assemblage a second time, Monsieur the Marquis leaned back in his seat, and was just being driven away with the air of a gentleman who had accidentally broken some common thing, and had paid for it, and could afford to pay for it; when his ease was suddenly disturbed by a coin flying into his carriage, and ringing on its floor.

"Hold!" said Monsieur the Marquis. "Hold the horses! Who threw that?"

He looked to the spot where Defarge the vendor of wine had stood, a moment before; but the wretched father was grovelling on his face on the pavement in that spot, and the figure that stood beside him was the figure of a dark stout woman, knitting.[28]

"You dogs!" said the Marquis, but smoothly, and with an unchanged front, except as to the spots on his nose: "I would ride over any of you very willingly, and exterminate you from the earth. If I knew which rascal threw at the carriage, and if that brigand were sufficiently near it, he should be crushed under the wheels."

So cowed was their condition, and so long and so hard their

experience of what such a man could do to them, within the law and beyond it, that not a voice, or a hand, or even an eye, was raised. Among the men, not one. But, the woman who stood knitting looked up steadily, and looked the Marquis in the face. It was not for his dignity to notice it; his contemptuous eyes passed over her, and over all the other rats; and he leaned back in his seat again, and gave the word "Go on!"

He was driven on, and other carriages came whirling by in quick succession; the Minister, the State-Projector, the Farmer-General, the Doctor, the Lawyer, the Ecclesiastic, the Grand Opera, the Comedy, the whole Fancy Ball in a bright continuous flow, came whirling by. The rats had crept out of their holes to look on, and they remained looking on for hours; soldiers and police often passing between them and the spectacle, and making a barrier behind which they slunk, and through which they peeped. The father had long ago taken up his bundle and hidden himself away with it, when the women who had tended the bundle while it lay on the base of the fountain, sat there watching the running of the water and the rolling of the Fancy Ball – when the one woman who had stood conspicuous, knitting, still knitted on with the steadfastness of Fate. The water of the fountain ran, the swift river ran, the day ran into evening, so much life in the city ran into death according to rule, time and tide waited for no man, the rats were sleeping close together in their dark holes again, the Fancy Ball was lighted up at supper, all things ran their course.

(THE STORMING OF THE BASTILLE)

Narrative context: It is 14 July 1789 and the Bastille is stormed. In the thick of the fighting, Defarge seeks out the cell in which Dr Manette was imprisoned for eighteen years. There he finds the doctor's hidden account of the events leading to his incarceration, with its incriminating evidence against the St Evrémonde family. The extract is from Book 2, Chapter 21, "Echoing Footsteps."

Saint Antoine[1] had been, that morning, a vast dusky mass of scarecrows heaving to and fro, with frequent gleams of light above the billowy heads, where steel blades and bayonets shone in the sun. A tremendous roar arose from the throat of Saint Antoine, and a forest of naked arms struggled in the air like shrivelled branches of trees in a winter wind: all the fingers convulsively clutching at every weapon that was thrown up from the depths below, no matter how far off.

Who gave them out, whence they last came, where they began, through what agency they crookedly quivered and jerked, scores at a time, over the heads of the crowd, like a kind of lightning, no eye in the throng could have told; but, muskets were being distributed – so were cartridges, powder, and ball, bars of iron and wood, knives, axes, pikes, every weapon that distracted ingenuity could discover or devise. People who could lay hold of nothing else, set themselves with bleeding hands to force stones and bricks out of their places in walls. Every pulse and heart in Saint Antoine was on high-fever strain and at high-fever heat. Every living creature there held life as of no account, and was demented with a passionate readiness to sacrifice it.[2]

As a whirlpool of boiling waters has a centre point, so, all this raging circled round Defarge's wine-shop, and every human drop in the caldron had a tendency to be sucked towards the vortex where Defarge himself, already begrimed with gunpowder and sweat, issued orders, issued arms, thrust this man back, dragged this man forward, disarmed one to arm another, laboured and strove in the thickest of the uproar.

"Keep near to me, Jacques Three,"[3] cried Defarge; "and do you, Jacques One and Two, separate and put yourselves at the head of as many of these patriots as you can. Where is my wife?"

"Eh, well! Here you see me!" said madame, composed as ever, but not knitting today. Madame's resolute right hand was occupied with an axe, in place of the usual softer implements, and in her girdle were a pistol and a cruel knife.

"Where do you go, my wife?"

"I go," said madame, "with you at present. You shall see me at the head of women, by-and-by."

"Come, then!" cried Defarge, in a resounding voice. "Patriots and friends, we are ready! The Bastille!"

With a roar that sounded as if all the breath in France had been shaped into the detested word, the living sea rose, wave on wave, depth on depth, and overflowed the city to that point.[4] Alarm-bells ringing, drums beating, the sea raging and thundering on its new beach, the attack begun.

Deep ditches, double drawbridge, massive stone walls, eight great towers,[5] cannon, muskets, fire and smoke. Through the fire and through the smoke – in the fire and in the smoke, for the sea cast him up against a cannon, and on the instant he became a cannonier – Defarge of the wine-shop worked like a manful soldier, Two fierce hours.[6]

Deep ditch, single drawbridge, massive stone walls, eight great towers, cannon, muskets, fire and smoke. One drawbridge down! "Work, comrades all, work! Work, Jacques One, Jacques Two, Jacques One Thousand, Jacques Two Thousand, Jacques Five-and-Twenty Thousand; in the name of all the Angels or the Devils – which you prefer – work!" Thus Defarge of the wine-shop, still at his gun, which had long grown hot.

"To me, women!" cried his wife. "What! We can kill as well as the men when the place is taken!" And to her, with a shrill thirsty cry, trooping women variously armed, but all armed alike in hunger and revenge.

Cannon, muskets, fire and smoke; but, still the deep ditch, the single drawbridge, the massive stone walls, and the eight great towers. Slight displacements of the raging sea, made by the falling wounded. Flashing weapons, blazing torches, smoking waggon-loads of wet straw, hard work at neighbouring barricades in all directions, shrieks, volleys, execrations, bravery without stint, boom, smash and rattle, and the furious sounding of the living sea; but, still the deep ditch, and the single drawbridge, and the massive stone walls, and the eight great towers, and still Defarge of the wine-shop at his gun, grown doubly hot by the service of Four fierce hours.

A white flag from within the fortress, and a parley – this dimly perceptible through the raging storm, nothing audible in it – suddenly the sea rose immeasurably wider and higher, and swept Defarge of the wine-shop over the lowered drawbridge, past the massive stone outer walls, in among the eight great towers surrendered!

So resistless was the force of the ocean bearing him on, that even to draw his breath or turn his head was as impracticable as if he been struggling in the surf of the South Sea,[7] until he was landed in the outer court-yard of the Bastille. There, against an angle of a wall, he made a struggle to look about him. Jacques Three was nearly at his side; Madame Defarge, still heading some of her women, was visible in the inner distance, and her knife was in her hand. Everywhere was tumult, exultation, deafening and maniacal bewilderment, astounding noise, yet furious dumb-show.

"The Prisoners!"

"The Records!"[8]

"The secret cells!"

"The instruments of torture!"

"The Prisoners!"

Of all these cries, and ten thousand incoherencies, "The Prisoners!" was the cry most taken up by the sea that rushed in, as if there were an eternity of people, as well as of time and space. When the foremost billows rolled past, bearing the prison officers with them, and threatening them all with instant death if any secret nook remained undisclosed, Defarge laid his strong hand on the breast of one of these men – a man with a grey head, who had a lighted torch in his hand – separated him from the rest, and got him between himself and the wall.

"Show me the North Tower!"[9] said Defarge. "Quick!"

"I will faithfully," replied the man, "if you will come with me. But there is no one there."

"What is the meaning of One Hundred and Five, North Tower?"[10] asked Defarge. "Quick!"

"The meaning, monsieur?"

"Does it mean a captive, or a place of captivity? Or do you mean that I shall strike you dead?"

"Kill him!" croaked Jacques Three, who had come close up.

"Monsieur, it is a cell."

"Show it me!"

"Pass this way, then."

Jacques Three, with his usual craving on him, and evidently disappointed by the dialogue taking a turn that did not seem to promise bloodshed, held by Defarge's arm as he held by the turnkey's. Their three heads had been close together during this brief discourse, and it had been as much as they could do to hear one another, even then: so tremendous was the noise of the living ocean, in its irruption into the Fortress, and its inundation of the courts and passages and staircases. All around outside, too, it beat the walls with a deep, hoarse roar, from which, occasionally, some partial shouts of tumult broke and leaped into the air like spray.

Through gloomy vaults where the light of day had never shone, past hideous doors of dark dens and cages, down cavernous flights of steps, and again up rugged ascents of stone and brick, more like dry waterfalls than staircases, Defarge, the turnkey, and Jacques Three, linked hand and arm, went with all the speed they could make. Here and there, especially at first, the inundation started on them and swept by; but, when they had done descending, and were winding and climbing up a tower, they were alone. Hemmed in here by the massive thickness of walls and arches, the storm within the fortress and without was only audible to them in a dull, subdued way, as if the noise out of which they had come had almost destroyed their sense of hearing.

The turnkey stopped at a low door, put a key in a clashing lock, swung the door slowly open, and said, as they all bent their heads and passed in:

"One hundred and five, North Tower!"

There was a small, heavily-grated, unglazed window high in the wall, with a stone screen before it, so that the sky could be only seen by stooping low and looking up. There was a small chimney, heavily barred across, a few feet within. There was a heap of old feathery wood-ashes on the hearth. There was a stool, and table, and a straw bed. There were four blackened walls, and a rusted iron ring in one of them.[11]

"Pass that torch slowly along these walls, that I may see them," said Defarge to the turnkey.

The man obeyed, and Defarge followed the light closely with his eyes.

"Stop! – Look here, Jacques!"

"A.M.!" croaked Jacques Three, as he read greedily.

"Alexandre Manette," said Defarge in his ear, following the letters with his swart forefinger, deeply engrained with gunpowder. "And here he wrote 'a poor physician.'[12] And it was he, without doubt, who scratched a calendar on this stone. What is that in your hand? A crowbar? Give it me!"

He had still the linstock of his gun in his own hand. He made a sudden exchange of the two instruments, and turning on the wormeaten stool and table, beat them to pieces in a few blows.

"Hold the light higher!" he said, wrathfully, to the turnkey. "Look among those fragments with care, Jacques. And see! Here is my knife," throwing it to him; "rip open that bed, and search the straw. Hold the light higher, you!"

With a menacing look at the turnkey he crawled upon the hearth, and, peering up the chimney, struck and prised at its sides with the crowbar, and worked at the iron grating across it. In a few minutes, some mortar and dust came dropping down, which he averted his face to avoid; and in it, and in the old wood-ashes, and in a crevice in the chimney into which his weapon had slipped or wrought itself, he groped with a cautious touch.

"Nothing in the wood, and nothing in the straw, Jacques?"

"Nothing."

"Let us collect them together, in the middle of the cell. So! Light them, you!"

The turnkey fired the little pile, which blazed high and hot. Stooping again to come out at the low-arched door, they left it burning, and retraced their way to the court-yard: seeming to recover their sense of hearing as they came down, until they were in the raging flood once more.

They found it surging and tossing, in quest of Defarge himself.

Saint Antoine was clamorous to have its wine-shop-keeper foremost in the guard upon the governor[13] who had defended the Bastille and shot the people. Otherwise, the governor would not be marched to the Hôtel de Ville for judgment. Otherwise, the governor would escape, and the people's blood (suddenly of some value, after many years of worthlessness) be unavenged.

In the howling universe of passion and contention that seemed to encompass this grim old officer conspicuous in his grey coat and red decoration,[14] there was but one quite steady figure, and that was a woman's. "See, there is my husband!" she cried, pointing him out. "See Defarge!" She stood immovable close to the grim old officer, and remained immovable close to him; remained immovable close to him through the streets, as Defarge and the rest bore him along; remained immovable close to him when he was got near his destination, and began to be struck at from behind; remained immovable close to him when the long-gathering rain of stabs and blows fell heavy; was so close to him when he dropped dead under it, that, suddenly animated, she put her foot upon his neck, and with her cruel knife – long ready – hewed off his head.[15]

The hour was come, when Saint Antoine was to execute his horrible idea of hoisting up men for lamps[16] to show what he could be and do. Saint Antoine's blood was up, and the blood of tyranny and domination by the iron hand was down – down on the steps of the Hôtel de Ville where the governor's body lay – down on the sole of the shoe of Madame Defarge where she had trodden on the body to steady it for mutilation. "Lower the lamp yonder!" cried Saint Antoine, after glaring round for a new means of death; "here is one of his soldiers to be left on guard!" The swinging sentinel was posted, and the sea rushed on.

The sea of black and threatening waters, and of destructive upheavings of wave against wave, whose depths were yet unfathomed and whose forces were yet unknown. The remorseless sea of turbulently swaying shapes, voices of vengeance, and faces hardened in the furnaces of suffering until the touch of pity could make no mark on them.

But, in the ocean of faces where every fierce and furious expression was in vivid life, there were two groups of faces – each seven in number – so fixedly contrasting with the rest, that never did sea roll which bore more memorable wrecks with it. Seven faces of prisoners,[17] suddenly released by the storm that had burst their tomb, were carried high over head; all scared, all lost, all wondering and amazed, as if the Last Day were come, and those who rejoiced around them were lost spirits.[18] Other seven faces there were, carried higher, seven dead faces, whose drooping eyelids and half-seen eyes awaited the Last Day. Impassive faces, yet with a suspended – not an abolished – expression on them; faces, rather, in a fearful pause, as having yet to raise the dropped lids of the eyes, and bear witness with the bloodless lips, "THOU DIDST IT!"

Seven prisoners released, seven gory heads on pikes, the keys of the accursed fortress of the eight strong towers, some discovered letters and other memorials of prisoners of old time, long dead of broken hearts, – such, and such-like, the loudly echoing footsteps of Saint Antoine escort through the Paris streets in mid-July, one thousand seven hundred and eighty-nine.[19] Now, Heaven defeat the fancy of Lucie Darnay, and keep these feet far out of her life![20] For, they are headlong, mad, and dangerous; and in the years so long after the breaking of the cask at Defarge's wine-shop door,[21] they are not easily purified when once stained red.

(THE TERROR)

Narrative context: Here Dickens races through the key events of 1793, conveying the pace of change in the wake of the Revolution and the rapidity of the descent into ever-increasing cruelty and violence that culminated in the institution of The Terror. The extract is from Book 3, Chapter 4, "Calm in Storm."

The new era began;[1] the king was tried, doomed, and beheaded;[2] the Republic of Liberty, Equality, Fraternity, or Death, [3] declared for victory or death against the world in arms; the black flag waved night and day from the great towers of Notre-Dame; three hundred thousand men, summoned to rise against the tyrants of the earth,[4] rose from all the varying soils of France, as if the dragon's teeth had been sown broadcast,[5] and had yielded fruit equally on hill and plain, on rock, in gravel, and alluvial mud, under the bright sky of the South and under the clouds of the North, in fell and forest, in the vineyards and the olive-grounds and among the cropped grass and the stubble of the corn, along the fruitful banks of the broad rivers, and in the sand of the sea-shore. What private solicitude could rear itself against the deluge of the Year One of Liberty[6] – the deluge rising from below, not falling from above, and with the windows of Heaven shut, not opened![7]

There was no pause, no pity, no peace, no interval of relenting rest, no measurement of time. Though days and nights circled as regularly as when time was young, and the evening and the morning were the first day,[8] other count of time there was none. Hold of it was lost in the raging fever of a nation, as it is in the fever of one patient. Now, breaking the unnatural silence of a whole city, the executioner showed the people the head of the king[9] – and now, it seemed almost in the same breath, the head of his fair wife which had had eight weary months of imprisoned widowhood and misery, to turn it grey.[10]

And yet, observing the strange law of contradiction which obtains in all such cases, the time was long, while it flamed by so fast. A revolutionary tribunal in the capital, and forty or fifty thousand revolutionary committees all over the land;[11] a law of the Suspected, which struck away all security for liberty or life, and delivered over any good and innocent person to any bad and guilty one;[12] prisons gorged with people who had committed no offence, and could obtain no hearing; these things became the established order and nature of appointed things, and seemed to be ancient usage before they were many weeks old. Above all, one hideous figure grew as familiar as if it had been before the general gaze from the foundations of the world – the figure of the sharp female called La Guillotine.[13]

It was the popular theme for jests;[14] it was the best cure for headache, it infallibly prevented the hair from turning grey, it imparted a peculiar delicacy to the complexion, it was the National Razor which shaved close: who kissed La Guillotine, looked through the little window and sneezed into the sack. It was the sign of the regeneration of the human race. It superseded the Cross. Models of it were worn on breasts from which the Cross was discarded, and it was bowed down to and believed in where the Cross was denied.[15]

It sheared off heads so many, that it, and the ground it most polluted, were a rotten red. It was taken to pieces, like a toy-puzzle for a young Devil, and was put together again where the occasion wanted it. It hushed the eloquent, struck down the powerful, abolished the beautiful and good. Twenty-two friends of high public mark, twenty-one living and one dead, it had lopped the heads off, in one morning, in as many minutes.[16] The name of the strong man of Old Scripture had descended to the chief functionary who worked it; but, so armed, he was stronger than his namesake, and blinder, and tore away the gates of God's own Temple every day.[17]

(THE GUILLOTINE)

Narrative context: Paris is in the grip of The Terror. Charles Darnay (real name Evrémonde) has been sentenced to death but Sydney Carton, determined to carry out his plan of self-sacrifice, has disguised himself as Darnay and is on his way to the Guillotine in his place. He has befriended a fellow prisoner, a young seamstress, and he comforts her as their tumbril heads towards the place of execution. The extract is from Book 3, Chapter 15, "The Footsteps Die Out For Ever."

Along the Paris streets, the death-carts rumble, hollow and harsh. Six tumbrils[1] carry the day's wine to La Guillotine.[2] All the devouring and insatiate Monsters imagined since imagination could record itself, are fused in the one realisation, Guillotine. And yet there is not in France, with its rich variety of soil and climate, a blade, a leaf, a root, a sprig, a peppercorn, which will grow to maturity under conditions more certain than those that have produced this horror. Crush humanity out of shape once more, under similar hammers, and it will twist itself into the same tortured forms. Sow the same seed of rapacious licence and oppression ever again, and it will surely yield the same fruit according to its kind.

Six tumbrils roll along the streets. Change these back again to what they were, thou powerful enchanter, Time, and they shall be seen to be the carriages of absolute monarchs, the equipages of feudal nobles, the toilettes of flaring Jezebels, the churches that are not my father's house but dens of thieves,[3] the huts of millions of starving peasants! No; the great magician who majestically works out the appointed order of the Creator, never reverses his transformations. "If thou be changed into this shape by the will of God," say the seers to the enchanted, in the wise Arabian stories, "then remain so! But, if thou wear this form through mere passing conjuration, then resume thy former aspect!"[4] Changeless and hopeless, the tumbrils roll along.

As the sombre wheels of the six carts go round, they seem to plough up a long crooked furrow among the populace in the streets.[5] Ridges of faces are thrown to this side and to that, and the ploughs go steadily onward. So used are the regular inhabitants of the houses to the spectacle, that in many windows there are no people, and in some the occupation of the hands is not so much as suspended, while the eyes survey the faces in the tumbrils. Here and there, the inmate has visitors to see the sight; then he points his finger, with something of the complacency of a curator or authorised exponent, to this cart and to this, and seems to tell who sat here yesterday, and who there the day before.

Of the riders in the tumbrils, some observe these things, and all things on their last roadside, with an impassive stare; others, with a lingering interest in the ways of life and men. Some, seated with drooping heads, are sunk in silent despair; again, there are some so heedful of their looks that they cast upon the multitude such glances as they have seen in theatres, and in pictures. Several close their eyes, and think, or try to get their straying thoughts together. Only one, and he a miserable creature of a crazed aspect, is so shattered and made drunk by horror that he sings, and tries to dance. Not one of the whole number appeals, by look or gesture, to the pity of the people.[6]

There is a guard of sundry horsemen riding abreast of the tumbrils, and faces are often turned up to some of them and they are asked some question. It would seem to be always the same question, for, it is always followed by a press of people towards the third cart. The horsemen abreast of that cart, frequently point out one man in it with their swords. The leading curiosity is, to know which is he; he stands at the back of the tumbril with his head bent down, to converse with a mere girl who sits on the side of the cart, and holds his hand. He has no curiosity or care for the scene about him, and always speaks to the girl. Here and there in the long Street of St Honoré,[7] cries are raised against him. If they move him at all, it is only to a quiet smile, as he shakes his hair a little more loosely about his face. He cannot easily touch his face, his arms being bound.

On the steps of a church, awaiting the coming-up of the tumbrils, stands the Spy and prison-sheep.[8] He looks into the first of them: not there. He looks into the second: not there. He already asks himself, "Has he sacrificed me?" when his face clears, as he looks into the third.

"Which is Evrémonde?"[9] says a man behind him.

"That. At the back there."

"With his hand in the girl's?"

"Yes."

The man cries "Down, Evrémonde! To the Guillotine all aristocrats! Down, Evrémonde!"

"Hush, hush!" the Spy entreats him, timidly.

"And why not, citizen?"

"He is going to pay the forfeit: it will be paid in five minutes more. Let him be at peace."

But, the man continuing to exclaim, "Down, Evrémonde!" the face of Evrémonde is for a moment turned towards him. Evrémonde then sees the Spy, and looks attentively at him, and goes his way.

The clocks are on the stroke of three, and the furrow ploughed among the populace is turning round, to come on into the place of execution, and end.[10] The ridges thrown to this side and to that, now crumble in and close behind the last plough as it passes on, for all are following to the Guillotine. In front of it, seated in chairs, as in a garden of public diversion, are a number of women, busily knitting.[11] On one of the foremost chairs, stands The Vengeance,[12] looking about for her friend.

"Thérèse!" she cries, in her shrill tones. "Who has seen her? Thérèse Defarge!"

"She never missed before," says a knitting-woman of the sisterhood.

"No; nor will she miss now," cries The Vengeance, petulantly. "Thérèse!"

"Louder," the woman recommends.

Ay! Louder, Vengeance, much louder, and still she will scarcely hear thee. Louder yet, Vengeance, with a little oath or so added, and yet it will hardly bring her. Send other women up and down to seek her, lingering somewhere; and yet, although the messengers have done dread deeds, it is questionable whether of their own wills they will go far enough to find her![13]

"Bad Fortune!" cries The Vengeance, stamping her foot in the chair, "and here are the tumbrils! And Evrémonde will be despatched in a wink, and she not here! See her knitting in my hand, and her empty chair ready for her. I cry with vexation and disappointment!"

As The Vengeance descends from her elevation to do it, the tumbrils begin to discharge their loads. The ministers of Sainte Guillotine[14] are robed and ready. Crash! – A head is held up, and the knitting-women who scarcely lifted their eyes to look at it a moment ago when it could think and speak, count One.

The second tumbril empties and moves on; the third comes up. Crash! – And the knitting-women, never faltering or pausing in their work, count Two.

The supposed Evrémonde descends, and the seamstress is lifted out next after him. He has not relinquished her patient hand in getting out, but still holds it as he promised. He gently places her with her back to the crashing engine that constantly whirrs up and falls, and she looks into his face and thanks him.

"But for you, dear stranger, I should not be so composed, for I am naturally a poor little thing, faint of heart; nor should I have been able to raise my thoughts to Him who was put to death, that we might have hope and comfort here today. I think you were sent to me by Heaven."

"Or you to me," says Sydney Carton. "Keep your eyes upon me, dear child, and mind no other object."

"I mind nothing while I hold your hand. I shall mind nothing when I let it go, if they are rapid."

"They will be rapid. Fear not!"

The two stand in the fast-thinning throng of victims, but they speak as if they were alone. Eye to eye, voice to voice, hand to hand, heart to heart, these two children of the Universal Mother, else so wide apart and differing, have come together on the dark highway, to repair home together, and to rest in her bosom.

"Brave and generous friend, will you let me ask you one last question? I am very ignorant, and it troubles me – just a little."

"Tell me what it is."

"I have a cousin, an only relative and an orphan, like myself, whom I love very dearly. She is five years younger than I, and she lives in a farmer's house in the south country. Poverty parted us, and she knows nothing of my fate – for I cannot write – and if I could, how should I tell her! It is better as it is."

"Yes, yes: better as it is."

"What I have been thinking as we came along, and what I am still thinking now, as I look into your kind strong face which gives me so much support, is this: – If the Republic really does good to the poor, and they come to be less hungry, and in all ways to suffer less, she may live a long time: she may even live to be old."

"What then, my gentle sister?"

"Do you think:" the uncomplaining eyes in which there is so

much endurance, fill with tears, and the lips part a little more and tremble: "that it will seem long to me, while I wait for her in the better land where I trust both you and I will be mercifully sheltered?"

"It cannot be, my child; there is no Time there, and no trouble there."

"You comfort me so much! I am so ignorant. Am I to kiss you now? Is the moment come?"

"Yes."

She kisses his lips; he kisses hers; they solemnly bless each other. The spare hand does not tremble as he releases it; nothing worse than a sweet, bright constancy is in the patient face. She goes next before him – is gone; the knitting-women count Twenty-Two.

"I am the Resurrection and the Life, saith the Lord: he that believeth in me, though he were dead, yet shall he live: and whosoever liveth and believeth in me shall never die."[15]

The murmuring of many voices, the upturning of many faces, the pressing on of many footsteps in the outskirts of the crowd, so that it swells forward in a mass, like one great heave of water, all flashes away. Twenty-Three.

chapter eleven

SLAUGHTERHOUSES, RAILWAY CATERING, AND OTHER FRENCH LESSONS

("A MONUMENT OF FRENCH FOLLY"; "THE BOY AT MUGBY"; "INSULARITIES")

"They order, said I, this matter better in France." While Dickens would not have found the opening words of Sterne's *A Sentimental Journey* invariably applicable, they will certainly serve as generally representative of his opinion. Readers of this book will by now be familiar with his frequent comparisons of the traditions and attitudes of the French with those of the British, usually to the detriment of the latter. In "Railway Dreaming," for example, he refers to many "easy and gracious customs" in which Parisians "are highly deserving of imitation among ourselves." In "Our French Watering-Place" he praises the ability of working-class people in Boulogne to make "common and cheap things uncommon and pretty, by good sense and good taste, that is a practical lesson to any rank of society in a whole island we could mention." And Mrs Lirriper, having "formed quite a high opinion of the French nation," admires the capacity of its people to enjoy life unaffected by the pronouncements of speechifying "big-wigs" and thinks that this quality "might be imitated to advantage by another nation which I will not mention."

The campaigning and satirical pieces in this chapter all make their points through a comparison of French and British attitudes and practices. The demonstration that "they order this matter better in France" serves to highlight what is wrong with the British system and ridicules the dismissive and xenophobic assumption of British superiority that Dickens noted all too frequently among his compatriots.

The ironically entitled "A Monument of French Folly" was inspired by just such John Bull arrogance. Published in *Household Words* on 8 March 1851 (and subsequently included in *Reprinted Pieces*, 1858) it was Dickens's latest contribution to the anti-Smithfield campaign. The famous livestock market at Smithfield, in the City of London, had become one of London's most notorious running sores. According to Peter Cunningham, average weekly sales of cattle and sheep in 1850 amounted to 3,000 and 30,000 respectively, and around a quarter of a million pigs changed hands annually (*Hand-Book of London*, 1850). The animals were driven through busy city streets to the market's overcrowded pens and the densely populated area around Smithfield had been colonized by its associated industries. Writing in 1855, the year in which the livestock market finally ceased to trade, John Timbs summarized the problem:

> This over-crowding has led to dreadful cruelties to the poor animals by drovers and others; whilst the market is surrounded by slaughter-houses and knackers' yards, tallow-melting, bone-boiling, tripe-washing, and other offensive trades; and over-peopled and ill-drained alleys, yards, and lanes, – a pestilential nuisance to the City... (*Curiosities of London*, 1855.)

Dickens refers to the market several times in his fiction, most famously in his nightmarish evocation of Smithfield on market-morning as Oliver passes through it with Bill Sikes in chapter 21 of *Oliver Twist*. He also includes brief but damning descriptions in chapter 20 of *Great Expectations* ("the shameful place, being all asmear with filth and fat and blood and foam") and chapter 16 of *Bleak House* ("the blinded oxen, over-goaded, over-driven, never guided, run into wrong places and are beaten out; and plunge, red-eyed and foaming, at stone walls").

The danger, disruption, cruelty and threats to health of "crowded pens and reeking slaughter-houses and over-driven beasts in the heart of a populous city" (*The Times*, 3 June 1850) should have led to the relocation of the livestock market many years earlier. However, tradition and the self-interest of the Common Council of the Corporation of London (the governing body of the City of London) had beaten off several concerted efforts to move it away from the city center. Despite the failure of the most recent of these attempts in 1849, the anti-Smithfield campaign, with *The Times* as one of its prominent voices, fought back with renewed vigour in 1850. Its arguments gained additional force in June, when the Royal Commission on Smithfield reported its conclusions, recommending that the livestock market be removed to a suburban site.

Dickens contributed two anti-Smithfield pieces to *Household Words* during 1850. The first, "The Heart of Mid-London," appeared on 4 May. Co-written with W.H. Wills, it focuses on the horrifying cruelty with which the animals were treated. The second, published in the 26 October issue, was "Lively Turtle," a sharply satirical response to an "intolerably asinine speech" (*Pilgrim*, 6, p 129) given in defense of Smithfield by Common Councillor H.L. Taylor (see note 2, p 392 for details).

Taylor's address to the Court of the Common Council also provided the inspiration for "A Monument of French Folly." The Paris system, with its out-of-town livestock markets and purpose-built abattoirs away from the city center, had been praised by the anti-Smithfield campaigners and recommended as a suitable model for London. Taylor vented his frustration at this suggestion through die-hard nationalistic rhetoric, disparaging the French nation in general and insisting that

...he would prefer remaining English. (Cheers.) He did not want to go to France to learn how to live. (Continued cheering.) The citizens of London did not want to have any trees of liberty planted in Cheapside. (Loud cheers.) They would rather remain as they are. (*The Times*, 12 July 1850, p 8.)

Dickens ridicules this aspect of the speech in the opening paragraphs of "A Monument of French Folly" and for the rest of the article works ironically with the bigotry of Taylor and his colleagues to subvert the "comparison, in these particulars of civilisation, between the capital of England, and the capital of that frog-eating and wooden-shoe wearing country, which the illustrious Common Councilman so sarcastically settled."

By way of research, he made a short trip to Paris in February 1851, visiting the cattle market at Poissy – "an expedition to a market 13 miles away, which involved the necessity of getting up at 5" (*Pilgrim*, 6, p 289) – and the abattoirs at Montmartre and Grenelle. His vivid and atmospheric descriptions in "A Monument of French Folly" derive from this recent first-hand experience. The many advantages of the Poissy market and Paris abattoirs over their London equivalents are powerfully conveyed (although Dickens is not indiscriminate in his praise of the French system, repeatedly criticizing the treatment of calves at Poissy), but the article goes beyond this immediate journalistic brief, frequently highlighting social behavior to draw out a comparison of deeper cultural significance. Each instance of courtesy or friendly humour that Dickens encounters in France is contrasted implicitly or explicitly with the typical experience at home. A French market porter, for example, politely asks him to move out of the way and "on he staggers, calf and all, and makes no allusion whatever either to my eyes or limbs." In this broader cultural context, Smithfield thus becomes a monument to a very British kind of folly.

"The Boy at Mugby" takes a similarly ironic approach in a less serious but nonetheless worthwhile cause. The story, which mercilessly satirizes the poor standard of railway catering in Britain, was included in *Mugby Junction*, the 1866 Christmas Number of *All the Year Round*. The subject had long been a sore point with Dickens: in an 1856 article, for example, he had complained about the bad service at railway refreshment rooms:

Why does a young woman of prepossessing appearance, glossy hair, and neat attire, taken from any station of life and put behind the counter of a Refreshment Room on an English Railroad, conceive the idea that her mission in life is to treat me with scorn? ("Why?", *Household Words*, 1 March 1856.)

However, according to George Dolby, his readings manager from 1866 to 1870, "The Boy at Mugby" was inspired by a specific incident at Rugby ("Mugby") station, which provided the prototypes for the characters of the Boy and Our Missis:

Entering the refreshment room, he and Mr Wills had each asked for a cup of coffee, which was supplied to them. While Wills was feeling in his pocket for some small change wherewith to pay, Mr Dickens reached across the counter for the sugar and milk, when both articles were suddenly snatched away from him and placed beneath the counter, while his ears were greeted with the remark, made in shrill and shrewish tones, 'You shan't have any milk and sugar 'till you two fellows have paid for your coffee.'

This speech was delivered by the woman whom he had pointed out to me as 'our Missis,' and it gave infinite amusement to a page in buttons, who, with that demoniacal spirit which seems to seize some boys at the idea of somebody else 'catching it,' was so overjoyed that he burst out into an uncontrollable fit of laughter. The discomfited travellers left their coffee on the counter, after an apology for making so free with the sugar-basin. (*Charles Dickens As I Knew Him*, 1885, pp 30–31.)

Dickens got his own back in fine style. The Boy's comic narrative demonstrates the gross inadequacy of British railway catering by comparison with the high quality of food and service available on the other side of the Channel. The contrast must indeed have been striking. Murray's 1864 *Handbook for Visitors to Paris* describes the refreshment room at Folkestone station as "very indifferent," noting a couple of sentences later that there is "a very good refreshment room at the Boulogne station, where persons proceeding to London or Paris will be able to dine without going to the hotels in the town." For Dickens it provided yet another example of how life in Britain was impoverished by a lack of the courtesy, hospitality, and *joie de vivre* that he found in abundance on the Continent, and particularly in France. In relation to railway catering, he had put this perception into the mouth of Mrs Lirriper two years earlier in *Mrs Lirriper's Legacy*. Her account of her first meal on French soil reads like a thematic synopsis of "The Boy at Mugby":

> And as to lunch why bless you if I kept a man-cook and two kitchen-maids I couldn't get it done for twice the money, and no injured young women a glaring at you and grudging you and acknowledging your patronage by wishing that your food might choke you, but so civil and so hot and attentive and every way comfortable...

"The Boy at Mugby" certainly had at least one immediate effect. In a letter to Dolby of 19 December 1866 Dickens comments,

> I have just heard from Mr Ryland of Birmingham that 'Our Missis and our Young Ladies' at Mugby are going to give up their places, declaring that 'they cannot bear the public facetiousness occasioned by Mr D's show up.' (*Pilgrim*, 11, p 284.)

In "Insularities," published in *Household Words* on 19 January 1856, Dickens turns his gun on further instances of "unreasonable ways of acting and thinking," comparing in each case the "insular" culture of the English with the more open-minded and rational attitudes in evidence on the Continent (here almost always represented by France). Ranging over social, political, and artistic issues, the article is especially revealing about Dickens's profound discomfort with the state of his nation, heightened by his respect for what he finds in France and elsewhere. The England he portrays is steeped in prejudice, deeply resistant to change, bound and blinkered by an unthinking adherence to convention, and culturally diminished by stultifying social snobbery and an obsequious obsession with its aristocracy. Like the other pieces in this chapter, "Insularities" makes the case that there is much to be learned "through our intercourse with other nations" and that the key to learning is an open mind.

Le Marché de Poissy, 1859

A MONUMENT OF FRENCH FOLLY

It was profoundly observed by a witty member of the Court of Common Council,[1] in Council assembled in the City of London, in the year of our Lord one thousand eight hundred and fifty, that the French are a frog-eating people, who wear wooden shoes.[2]

We are credibly informed, in reference to the nation whom this choice spirit so happily disposed of, that the caricatures and stage representations which were current in England some half a century ago, exactly depict their present condition. For example, we understand that every Frenchman, without exception, wears a pigtail and curl-papers. That he is extremely sallow, thin, long-faced, and lantern-jawed. That the calves of his legs are invariably undeveloped; that his legs fail at the knees, and that his shoulders are always higher than his ears. We are likewise assured that he rarely tastes any food but soup maigre, and an onion; that he always says, "By Gar! Aha! Vat you tell me, Sare?"[3] at the end of every sentence he utters; and that the true generic name of his race is the Mounseers, or the Parly-voos. If he be not a dancing-master, or a barber, he must be a cook; since no other trades but those three are congenial to the tastes of the people, or permitted by the Institutions of the country. He is a slave, of course. The ladies of France (who are also slaves) invariably have their heads tied up in Belcher handherchiefs,[4] wear long ear-rings, carry tambourines, and beguile the weariness of their yoke by singing in head voices through their noses – principally to barrel-organs.

It may be generally summed up, of this inferior people, that they have no idea of anything.

Of a great Institution like Smithfield,[5] they are unable to form the least conception. A Beast Market in the heart of Paris would be regarded as an impossible nuisance. Nor have they any notion of slaughter-houses in the midst of a city. One of these benighted frog-eaters would scarcely understand your meaning, if you told him of the existence of such a British bulwark.

It is agreeable, and perhaps pardonable, to indulge in a little self-complacency when our right to it is thoroughly established. At the present time, to be rendered memorable by a final attack on that good old market which is the (rotten) apple of the Corporation's eye, let us compare ourselves, to our national delight and pride, as to these two subjects of slaughter-house and beast-market, with the outlandish foreigner.

The blessings of Smithfield are too well understood to need recapitulation; all who run (away from mad bulls and pursuing oxen) may read.[6] Any market-day, they may be beheld in glorious action. Possibly, the merits of our slaughter-houses are not yet quite so generally appreciated.

Slaughter-houses, in the large towns of England, are always (with the exception of one or two enterprising towns) most numerous in the most densely crowded places, where there is the least circulation of air. They are often underground, in cellars; they are sometimes in close back yards; sometimes (as in Spitalfields[7]) in the very shops where the meat is sold. Occasionally, under good private management, they are ventilated and clean. For the most part, they are unventilated and dirty; and, to the reeking walls, putrid fat and other offensive animal matter clings with a tenacious hold. The busiest slaughter-houses in London are in the neighbourhood of Smithfield, in Newgate Market, in Whitechapel, in Newport Market, in Leadenhall Market, in Clare Market.[8] All these places are surrounded by houses of a poor description, swarming with inhabitants. Some of them are close to the worst burial-grounds in London. When the slaughter-house is below the ground, it is a

common practice to throw the sheep down areas,[9] neck and crop –
which is exciting, but not at all cruel. When it is on the level surface,
it is often extremely difficult of approach. Then, the beasts have to be
worried, and goaded, and pronged, and tail-twisted, for a long time
before they can be got in – which is entirely owing to their natural
obstinacy. When it is not difficult of approach, but is in a foul
condition, what they see and scent makes them still more reluctant to
enter – which is their natural obstinacy again. When they do get in at
last, after no trouble and suffering to speak of (for, there is nothing in
the previous journey into the heart of London, the night's endurance
in Smithfield, the struggle out again, among the crowded multitude,
the coaches, carts, waggons, omnibuses, gigs, chaises, phaetons, cabs,
trucks, dogs, boys, whoopings, roarings, and ten thousand other
distractions), they are represented to be in a most unfit state to be
killed, according to microscopic examinations made of their fevered
blood by one of the most distinguished physiologists in the world,
PROFESSOR OWEN[10] – but that's humbug. When they *are* killed, at
last, their reeking carcases are hung in impure air, to become, as the
same Professor will explain to you, less nutritious and more
unwholesome – but he is only an *un*common counsellor, so don't
mind *him*. In half a quarter of a mile's length of Whitechapel, at one
time, there shall be six hundred newly slaughtered oxen hanging up,
and seven hundred sheep – but, the more the merrier – proof of
prosperity. Hard by Snow Hill and Warwick Lane,[11] you shall see the
little children, inured to sights of brutality from their birth, trotting
along the alleys, mingled with troops of horribly busy pigs, up to their
ankles in blood – but it makes the young rascals hardy. Into the
imperfect sewers of this overgrown city, you shall have the immense
mass of corruption, engendered by these practices, lazily thrown out
of sight, to rise, in poisonous gases, into your house at night, when
your sleeping children will most readily absorb them, and to find its

languid way, at last, into the river that you drink – but, the French are
a frog-eating people who wear wooden shoes, and it's O the roast beef
of England, my boy, the jolly old English roast beef![12]

It is quite a mistake – a new-fangled notion altogether – to
suppose that there is any natural antagonism between putrefaction
and health. They know better than that, in the Common Council. You
may talk about Nature, in her wisdom, always warning man through
his sense of smell, when he draws near to something dangerous; but,
that won't go down in the city. Nature very often don't mean
anything. Mrs Quickly says that prunes are ill for a green wound;[13]
but whosoever says that putrid animal substances are ill for a green
wound, or for robust vigour, or for any thing or for any body, is a
humanity-monger and a humbug. Britons never, never, never, &c.,
therefore.[14] And prosperity to cattle-driving, cattle-slaughtering,
bone-crushing, blood-boiling, trotter-scraping, tripe-dressing,
paunch-cleaning, gut-spinning, hide-preparing, tallow-melting, and
other salubrious proceedings, in the midst of hospitals, churchyards,
workhouses, schools, infirmaries, refuges, dwellings, provision-shops,
nurseries, sick-beds, every stage and baiting-place in the journey
from birth to death!

These *un*common counsellors, your Professor Owens and fellows,
will contend that to tolerate these things in a civilised city, is to
reduce it to a worse condition than BRUCE found to prevail in
ABYSSINIA.[15] For, there (say they) the jackals and wild dogs came at
night to devour the offal; whereas here there are no such natural
scavengers, and quite as savage customs. Further, they will
demonstrate that nothing in Nature is intended to be wasted, and that
besides the waste which such abuses occasion in the articles of health
and life – main sources of the riches of any community – they lead to
a prodigious waste of changing matters, which might, with proper
preparation, and under scientific direction, be safely applied to the

increase of the fertility of the land. Thus (they argue) does Nature ever avenge infractions of her beneficent laws, and so surely as Man is determined to warp any of her blessings into curses, shall they become curses, and shall he suffer heavily. But, this is cant. Just as it is cant of the worst description to say to the London Corporation, "How can you exhibit to the people so plain a spectacle of dishonest equivocation, as to claim the right of holding a market in the midst of the great city, for one of your vested privileges, when you know that when your last market-holding charter was granted to you by King Charles the First, Smithfield stood IN THE SUBURBS OF LONDON, and is in that very charter so described in those five words?"[16] – which is certainly true, but has nothing to do with the question.

Now to the comparison, in these particulars of civilisation, between the capital of England, and the capital of that frog-eating and wooden-shoe wearing country, which the illustrious Common Councilman so sarcastically settled.

In Paris, there is no Cattle Market. Cows and calves are sold within the city, but, the Cattle Markets are at Poissy, about thirteen miles off, on a line of railway; and at Sceaux, about five miles off.[17] The Poissy market is held every Thursday; the Sceaux market, every Monday. In Paris, there are no slaughter-houses, in our acceptation of the term. There are five public Abattoirs – within the walls, though in the suburbs – and in these all the slaughtering of the city must be performed.[18] They are managed by a Syndicat or Guild of Butchers, who confer with the Minister of the Interior on all matters affecting the trade, and who are consulted when any new regulations are contemplated for its government. They are, likewise, under the vigilant superintendence of the police. Every butcher must be licensed: which proves him at once to be a slave, for we don't license butchers in England – we only license apothecaries, attorneys, postmasters, publicans, hawkers, retailers of tobacco, snuff, pepper, and vinegar – and one or two other little trades not worth mentioning. Every arrangement in connexion with the slaughtering and sale of meat, is matter of strict police regulation. (Slavery again, though we certainly have a general sort of a Police Act here.[19])

But, in order that the reader may understand what a monument of folly these frog-eaters have raised in their abattoirs and cattle markets, and may compare it with what common counselling has done for us all these years, and would still do but for the innovating spirit of the times, here follows a short account of a recent visit to these places:[20]

It was as sharp a February morning[21] as you would desire to feel at your fingers' ends when I turned out – tumbling over a chiffonier[22] with his little basket and rake, who was picking up the bits of coloured paper that had been swept out, overnight, from a Bon-Bon shop – to take the Butchers' Train to Poissy. A cold dim light just touched the high roofs of the Tuileries which have seen such changes, such distracted crowds, such riot and bloodshed;[23] and they looked as calm, and as old, all covered with white frost, as the very Pyramids. There was not light enough, yet, to strike upon the towers of Notre Dame across the water; but I thought of the dark pavement of the old Cathedral as just beginning to be streaked with grey; and of the lamps in the "House of God," the Hospital close to it,[24] burning low and being quenched; and of the keeper of the Morgue going about with a fading lantern, busy in the arrangement of his terrible waxwork for another sunny day.[25]

The sun was up, and shining merrily when the butchers and I, announcing our departure with an engine-shriek to sleepy Paris, rattled away for the Cattle Market. Across the country, over the Seine, among a forest of scrubby trees – the hoar frost lying cold in shady places, and glittering in the light – and here we are at Poissy! Out leap the butchers who have been chattering all the way like madmen, and off they straggle for the Cattle Market (still chattering, of course, incessantly), in hats and caps of all shapes, in coats and blouses, in calf-skins, cow-skins, horse-skins, furs, shaggy mantles, hairy coats, sacking, baize, oil-skin, anything you please that will keep a man and a butcher warm, upon a frosty morning.

Many a French town have I seen, between this spot of ground and Strasburgh or Marseilles, that might sit for your picture, little Poissy! Barring the details of your old church, I know you well, albeit we make acquaintance, now, for the first time. I know your narrow, straggling, winding streets, with a kennel[26] in the midst, and lamps slung across. I know your picturesque street-corners, winding up-hill Heaven knows why or where! I know your tradesmen's inscriptions, in letters not quite fat enough; your barbers' brazen basins dangling over little shops; your Cafés and Estaminets, with cloudy bottles of stale syrup in the windows, and pictures of crossed billiard-cues outside.[27] I know this identical grey horse with his tail rolled up in a knot like the "back hair" of an untidy woman, who won't be shod, and who makes himself heraldic by clattering across the street on his hind legs, while twenty voices shriek and growl at him as a Brigand, an accursed Robber, and an everlastingly-doomed Pig.[28] I know your sparkling town-fountain too, my Poissy, and am glad to see it near a cattle market, gushing so freshly, under the auspices of a gallant little sublimated Frenchman wrought in metal, perched upon the top. Through all the land of France I know this unswept room at The Glory, with its peculiar smell of beans and coffee, where the butchers crowd about the stove, drinking the thinnest of wine from the smallest of tumblers; where the thickest of coffee-cups mingle with the longest of loaves, and the weakest of lump sugar; where Madame at the counter easily acknowledges the homage of all entering and departing butchers; where the billiard-table is covered up in the midst like a great bird-cage – but the bird may sing by-and-by!

A bell! The Calf Market! Polite departure of butchers. Hasty payment and departure on the part of amateur Visitor. Madame reproaches Ma'amselle for too fine a susceptibility in reference to the devotion of a Butcher in a bear-skin. Monsieur, the landlord of The Glory, counts a double handful of sous, without an unobliterated inscription, or an undamaged crowned head, among them.

There is little noise without, abundant space, and no confusion. The open area devoted to the market, is divided into three portions: the Calf Market, the Cattle Market, the Sheep Market. Calves at eight, cattle at ten, sheep at mid-day. All is very clean.

The Calf Market is a raised platform of stone, some three or four feet high, open on all sides, with a lofty over-spreading roof, supported on stone columns, which give it the appearance of a sort of vineyard from Northern Italy. Here, on the raised pavement, lie innumerable calves, all bound hind-legs and fore-legs together, and all trembling violently – perhaps with cold, perhaps with fear, perhaps with pain; for, this mode of tying, which seems to be an absolute superstition with the peasantry, can hardly fail to cause great suffering. Here, they lie, patiently in rows, among the straw, with their stolid faces and inexpressive eyes, superintended by men and women, boys and girls; here, they are inspected by our friends, the butchers, bargained for, and bought. Plenty of time; plenty of room; plenty of good humour. "Monsieur François in the bear-skin, how do you do, my friend? You come from Paris by the train? The fresh air does you good. If you are in want of three or four fine calves this market-morning, my angel, I, Madame Doche, shall be happy to deal with you. Behold these calves, Monsieur François! Great Heaven, you are doubtful! Well, sir, walk round and look about you. If you find better for the money, buy them. If not, come to me!" Monsieur

François goes his way leisurely, and keeps a wary eye upon the stock. No other butcher jostles Monsieur François; Monsieur François jostles no other butcher. Nobody is flustered and aggravated. Nobody is savage. In the midst of the country blue frocks and red handkerchiefs, and the butchers' coats, shaggy, furry, and hairy: of calf-skin, cow-skin, horse-skin, and bear-skin: towers a cocked hat and a blue cloak. Slavery! For *our* Police wear great coats and glazed hats.

But now the bartering is over, and the calves are sold. "Ho! Gregorie, Antoine, Jean, Louis! Bring up the carts, my children! Quick, brave infants![29] Hola! Hi!"

The carts, well littered with straw, are backed up to the edge of the raised pavement, and various hot infants carry calves upon their heads, and dexterously pitch them in, while other hot infants, standing in the carts, arrange the calves, and pack them carefully in straw. Here is a promising young calf, not sold, whom Madame Doche unbinds. Pardon me, Madame Doche, but I fear this mode of tying the four legs of a quadruped together, though strictly à la mode, is not quite right. You observe, Madame Doche, that the cord leaves deep indentations in the skin, and that the animal is so cramped at first as not to know, or even remotely suspect, that he *is* unbound, until you are so obliging as to kick him, in your delicate little way, and pull his tail like a bell-rope. Then, he staggers to his knees, not being able to stand, and stumbles about like a drunken calf, or the horse at Franconi's,[30] whom you may have seen, Madame Doche, who is supposed to have been mortally wounded in battle. But, what is this rubbing against me, as I apostrophise Madame Doche? It is another heated infant, with a calf upon his head. "Pardon, Monsieur, but will you have the politeness to allow me to pass?" "Ah, Sir, willingly. I am vexed to obstruct the way." On he staggers, calf and all, and makes no allusion whatever either to my eyes or limbs.

Now, the carts are full. More straw, my Antoine, to shake over these top rows; then, off we will clatter, rumble, jolt, and rattle, a long row of us, out of the first town-gate, and out at the second town-gate, and past the empty sentry-box, and the little thin square bandbox of a guardhouse, where nobody seems to live; and away for Paris, by the paved road, lying, a straight straight line, in the long long avenue of trees. We can neither choose our road, nor our pace, for that is all prescribed to us. The public convenience demands that our carts should get to Paris by such a route, and no other (Napoleon had leisure to find that out, while he had a little war with the world upon his hands[31]), and woe betide us if we infringe orders.

Droves of oxen stand in the Cattle Market, tied to iron bars fixed into posts of granite. Other droves advance slowly down the long avenue, past the second town-gate, and the first town-gate, and the sentry-box, and the bandbox, thawing the morning with their smoky breath as they come along. Plenty of room; plenty of time. Neither man nor beast is driven out of his wits by coaches, carts, waggons, omnibuses, gigs, chaises, phaetons, cabs, trucks, boys, whoopings, roarings, and multitudes. No tail-twisting is necessary – no iron pronging is necessary.[32] There are no iron prongs here. The market for cattle is held as quietly as the market for calves. In due time, off the cattle go to Paris; the drovers can no more choose their road, nor their time, nor the numbers they shall drive, than they can choose their hour for dying in the course of nature.

Sheep next. The sheep-pens are up here, past the Branch Bank of Paris established for the convenience of the butchers,[33] and behind the two pretty fountains they are making in the Market. My name is Bull: yet I think I should like to see as good twin fountains – not to say in Smithfield, but in England anywhere. Plenty of room; plenty of time. And here are sheep-dogs, sensible as ever, but with a certain French air about them – not without a suspicion of dominoes – with a kind of flavour of moustache and beard – demonstrative dogs, shaggy and loose where an English dog would be tight and close – not so troubled with business calculations as our English drovers' dogs, who have always got their sheep upon their minds, and think about their work, even resting, as you may see by their faces; but, dashing, showy, rather unreliable dogs: who might worry me instead of their legitimate charges if they saw occasion – and might see it somewhat suddenly. The market for sheep passes off like the other two; and away they go, by *their* allotted road to Paris. My way being the Railway, I make the best of it at twenty miles an hour; whirling through the now high-lighted landscape; thinking that the inexperienced green buds will be wishing before long, they had not been tempted to come out so soon; and wondering who lives in this or that château, all window and lattice, and what the family may have for breakfast this sharp morning.

After the Market comes the Abattoir. What abattoir shall I visit first? Montmartre is the largest. So, I will go there.

The abattoirs are all within the walls of Paris, with an eye to the receipt of the octroi duty;[34] but, they stand in open places in the suburbs, removed from the press and bustle of the city.[35] They are managed by the Syndicat or Guild of Butchers under the inspection of the Police. Certain smaller items of the revenue derived from them are in part retained by the Guild for the payment of their expenses, and in part devoted by it to charitable purposes in connexion with the trade. They cost six hundred and eighty thousand pounds; and they return to the city of Paris an interest on that outlay, amounting to nearly six and a-half per cent.

Here, in a sufficiently dismantled space is the Abattoir of Montmartre, covering nearly nine acres of ground, surrounded by a high wall, and looking from the outside like a calvary barrack.[36] At the iron gates is a small functionary in a large cocked hat. "Monsieur desires to see the abattoir? Most certainly."[37] State being inconvenient in private transactions, and Monsieur being already aware of the cocked hat, the functionary puts it into a little official bureau which it almost fills, and accompanies me in the modest attire – as to his head – of ordinary life.

Many of the animals from Poissy have come here. On the arrival of each drove, it was turned into yonder ample space, where each butcher who had bought, selected his own purchases. Some, we see now, in these long perspectives of stalls with a high overhanging roof of wood and open tiles rising above the walls. While they rest here, before being slaughtered, they are required to be fed and watered, and the stalls must be kept clean. A stated amount of fodder must always be ready in the loft above; and the supervision is of the strictest kind. The same regulations apply to sheep and calves; for which, portions of these perspectives are strongly railed off. All the buildings are of the strongest and most solid description.

After traversing these lairs, through which, besides the upper provision for ventilation just mentioned, there may be a thorough current of air from opposite windows in the side walls, and from doors at either end, we traverse the broad, paved, court-yard until we come to the slaughter-houses. They are all exactly alike, and adjoin each other, to the number of eight or nine together, in blocks of solid building. Let us walk into the first.

It is firmly built and paved with stone. It is well lighted, thoroughly aired, and lavishly provided with fresh water. It has two doors opposite each other; the first, the door by which I entered from the main yard; the second, which is opposite, opening on another smaller yard, where the sheep and calves are killed on benches. The pavement of that yard, I see, slopes downward to a gutter, for its being more easily cleansed. The slaughter-house is fifteen feet high, sixteen feet and a-half wide, and thirty-three feet long. It is fitted

with a powerful windlass, by which one man at the handle can bring
the head of an ox down to the ground to receive the blow from the
pole-axe that is to fell him – with the means of raising the carcass and
keeping it suspended during the after-operation of dressing – and
with hooks on which carcasses can hang, when completely prepared,
without touching the walls. Upon the pavement of this first stone
chamber, lies an ox scarcely dead. If I except the blood draining from
him, into a little stone well in a corner of the pavement, the place is
free from offence as the Place de la Concorde. It is infinitely purer
and cleaner, I know, my friend the functionary, than the Cathedral of
Notre Dame. Ha, ha! Monsieur is pleasant, but, truly, there is reason,
too, in what he says.

I look into another of these slaughter-houses. "Pray enter," says
a gentleman in bloody boots. "This is a calf I have killed this
morning. Having a little time on my hands, I have cut and punctured
this lace pattern in the coats of his stomach. It is pretty enough. I did
it to divert myself." – "It is beautiful, Monsieur, the slaughterer!" He
tells me I have the gentility to say so.

I look into rows of slaughter-houses. In many, retail dealers, who
have come here for the purpose, are making bargains for meat. There
is killing enough, certainly, to satiate an unused eye; and there are
steaming carcasses enough, to suggest the expediency of a fowl and
salad for dinner; but, everywhere, there is an orderly, clean, well-
systematised routine of work in progress – horrible work at the best,
if you please; but, so much the greater reason why it should be made
the best of. I don't know (I think I have observed, my name is Bull)
that a Parisian of the lowest order is particularly delicate, or that his
nature is remarkable for an infinitesimal infusion of ferocity; but, I do
know, my potent, grave, and common counselling Signors,[38] that he is
forced, when at this work, to submit himself to a thoroughly good
system, and to make an Englishman very heartily ashamed of you.

Here, within the walls of the same abattoir, in other roomy and commodious buildings, are a place for converting the fat into tallow and packing it for market – a place for cleansing and scalding calves' heads and sheeps' feet – a place for preparing tripe – stables and coach-houses for the butchers – innumerable conveniences, aiding in the diminution of offensiveness to its lowest possible point, and the raising of cleanliness and supervision to their highest. Hence, all the meat that goes out of the gate is sent away in clean covered carts. And if every trade connected with the slaughtering of animals were obliged by law to be carried on in the same place, I doubt, my friend, now reinstated in the cocked hat (whose civility these two francs imperfectly acknowledge, but appear munificently to repay), whether there could be better regulations than those which are carried out at the Abattoir of Montmartre. Adieu, my friend, for I am away to the other side of Paris, to the Abattoir of Grenelle![39] And there, I find exactly the same thing on a smaller scale, with the addition of a magnificent Artesian well,[40] and a different sort of conductor, in the person of a neat little woman with neat little eyes, and a neat little voice, who picks her neat little way among the bullocks in a very neat little pair of shoes and stockings.

Such is the Monument of French Folly which a foreigneering people have erected, in a national hatred and antipathy for common counselling wisdom. That wisdom, assembled in the City of London, having distinctly refused, after a debate three days long, and by a majority of nearly seven to one, to associate itself with any Metropolitan Cattle Market unless it be held in the midst of the City, it follows that we shall lose the inestimable advantages of common counselling protection, and be thrown, for a market, on our own wretched resources. In all human probability we shall thus come, at last, to erect a monument of folly very like this French monument. If that be done, the consequences are obvious. The leather trade will be ruined, by the introduction of American timber, to be manufactured into shoes for the fallen English; the Lord Mayor will be required, by the popular voice, to live entirely on frogs; and both these changes will (how, is not at present quite clear, but certainly somehow or other) fall on that unhappy landed interest which is always being killed, yet is always found to be alive – and kicking.

THE BOY AT MUGBY

I am The Boy at Mugby. That's about what *I* am.

You don't know what I mean? What a pity! But I think you do. I think you must. Look here. I am the Boy at what is called The Refreshment Room at Mugby Junction, and what's proudest boast is, that it never yet refreshed a mortal being.[1]

Up in a corner of the Down Refreshment Room at Mugby Junction, in the height of twenty-seven cross draughts (I've often counted 'em while they brush the First Class hair twenty-seven ways), behind the bottles, among the glasses, bounded on the nor'-west by the beer, stood pretty far to the right of a metallic object that's at times the tea-urn and at times the soup-tureen, according to the nature of the last twang imparted to its contents which are the same groundwork, fended off from the traveller by a barrier of stale sponge-cakes erected atop of the counter, and lastly exposed sideways to the glare of Our Missis's eye – you ask a Boy so sitiwated, next time you stop in a hurry at Mugby, for anything to drink; you take particular notice that he'll try to seem not to hear you, that he'll appear in a absent manner to survey the Line through a transparent medium composed of your head and body, and that he won't serve you as long as you can possibly bear it. That's Me.

What a lark it is! We are the Model Establishment, we are, at
Mugby. Other Refreshment Rooms send their imperfect young ladies
up to be finished off by Our Missis. For some of the young ladies,
when they're new to the business, come into it mild! Ah! Our Missis,
she soon takes that out of 'em. Why, I originally come into the
business meek myself. But Our Missis she soon took that out of *me*.

What a delightful lark it is! I look upon us Refreshmenters as
ockipying the only proudly independent footing on the Line. There's
Papers for instance – my honourable friend if he will allow me to call
him so – him as belongs to Smith's bookstall.[2] Why he no more dares
to be up to our Refreshmenting games, than he dares to jump atop of
a locomotive with her steam at full pressure, and cut away upon her
alone, driving himself, at limited-mail[3] speed. Papers, he'd get his
head punched at every compartment, first second and third, the
whole length of the train, if he was to ventur to imitate my
demeanour. It's the same with the porters, the same with the guards,
the same with the ticket clerks, the same the whole way up to the
secretary, traffic manager, or very chairman. There ain't a one among
'em on the nobly independent footing we are. Did you ever catch one
of *them*, when you wanted anything of him, making a system of
surveying the Line through a transparent medium composed of your
head and body? I should hope not.

You should see our Bandolining[4] Room at Mugby Junction. It's
led to, by the door behind the counter which you'll notice usually
stands ajar, and it's the room where Our Missis and our young ladies
Bandolines their hair. You should see 'em at it, betwixt trains,
Bandolining away, as if they was anointing themselves for the combat.
When you're telegraphed,[5] you should see their noses all a going up
with scorn, as if it was a part of the working of the same Cooke and
Wheatstone electrical machinery.[6] You should hear Our Missis give
the word "Here comes the Beast to be Fed!" and then you should see

'em indignantly skipping across the Line, from the Up to the Down, or Wicer Warsaw, and begin to pitch the stale pastry into the plates, and chuck the sawdust sangwiches under the glass covers, and get out the – ha ha ha! – the Sherry – O my eye, my eye! – for your Refreshment.

It's only in the Isle of the Brave and Land of the Free[7] (by which of course I mean to say Britannia) that Refreshmenting is so effective, so 'olesome, so constitutional, a check upon the public. There was a foreigner, which having politely, with his hat off, beseeched our young ladies and Our Missis for "a leetel gloss hoff prarndee," and having had the Line surveyed through him by all and no other acknowledgment, was a proceeding at last to help himself, as seems to be the custom in his own country, when Our Missis with her hair almost a coming un-Bandolined with rage, and her eyes omitting sparks, flew at him, cotched the decanter out of his hand, and said: "Put it down! I won't allow that!" The foreigner turned pale, stepped back with his arms stretched out in front of him, his hands clasped, and his shoulders riz, and exclaimed: "Ah! Is it possible this! That these disdaineous females and this ferocious old woman are placed here by the administration, not only to empoison the voyagers, but to affront them! Great Heaven! How arrives it? The English people. Or is he then a slave? Or idiot?" Another time, a merry wideawake American gent had tried the sawdust and spit it out, and had tried the Sherry and spit that out, and had tried in vain to sustain exhausted natur upon Butter-Scotch,[8] and had been rather extra Bandolined and Line-surveyed through, when, as the bell was ringing and he paid Our Missis, he says, very loud and good-tempered: "I tell yew what 'tis, ma'arm. I la'af. Theer! I la'af. I Dew. I oughter ha' seen most things, for I hail from the Onlimited side of the Atlantic Ocean, and I haive travelled right slick over the Limited, head on through Jeerusalemm and the East, and likeways France and Italy, Europe Old

World, and am now upon the track to the Chief Europian Village;[9] but such an Institution as Yew, and Yewer young ladies, and Yewer fixin's solid and liquid, afore the glorious Tarnal[10] I never did see yet! And if I hain't found the eighth wonder of monarchical Creation, in finding Yew, and Yewer young ladies, and Yewer fixin's solid and liquid, all as aforesaid, established in a country where the people air not absolute Loo-naticks, I am Extra Double Darned with a Nip and Frizzle to the innermostest grit! Wheerfur – Theer! – I la'af! I Dew, ma'arm. I la'af!" And so he went, stamping and shaking his sides, along the platform all the way to his own compartment.

I think it was her standing up agin the Foreigner, as giv' Our Missis the idea of going over to France, and droring a comparison betwixt Refreshmenting as followed among the frog-eaters, and Refreshmenting as triumphant in the Isle of the Brave and Land of the Free (by which of course I mean to say agin, Britannia). Our young ladies, Miss Whiff, Miss Piff, and Mrs Sniff, was unanimous opposed to her going; for, as they says to Our Missis one and all, it is well beknown to the hends of the herth as no other nation except Britain has a idea of anythink, but above all of business. Why then should you tire yourself to prove what is already proved? Our Missis however (being a teazer at all pints) stood out grim obstinate, and got a return pass by South-Eastern Tidal,[11] to go right through, if such should be her dispositions, to Marseilles.

Sniff is husband to Mrs Sniff, and is a regular insignificant cove. He looks arter the sawdust department in a back room, and is sometimes when we are very hard put to it let in behind the counter with a corkscrew; but never when it can be helped, his demeanour towards the public being disgusting servile. How Mrs Sniff ever come so far to lower herself as to marry him, I don't know; but I suppose *he* does, and I should think he wished he didn't, for he leads a awful life. Mrs Sniff couldn't be much harder with him if he was the public.

Similarly, Miss Whiff and Miss Piff, taking the tone of Mrs Sniff, they shoulder Sniff about when he *is* let in with a corkscrew, and they whisk things out of his hands when in his servility he is a going to let the public have 'em, and they snap him up when in the crawling baseness of his spirit he is a going to answer a public question, and they drore more tears into his eyes than ever the mustard does which he all day long lays on to the sawdust. (But it ain't strong.) Once, when Sniff had the repulsiveness to reach across to get the milk-pot to hand over for a baby, I see Our Missis in her rage catch him by both his shoulders and spin him out into the Bandolining Room.

But Mrs Sniff. How different! She's the one! She's the one as you'll notice to be always looking another way from you, when you look at her. She's the one with the small waist buckled in tight in front, and with the lace cuffs at her wrists, which she puts on the edge of the counter before her, and stands a smoothing while the public foams. This smoothing the cuffs and looking another way while the public foams, is the last accomplishment taught to the young ladies as come to Mugby to be finished by Our Missis; and it's always taught by Mrs Sniff.

When Our Missis went away upon her journey, Mrs Sniff was left in charge. She did hold the public in check most beautiful! In all my time, I never see half so many cups of tea given without milk to people as wanted it with, nor half so many cups of tea with milk given to people as wanted it without. When foaming ensued, Mrs Sniff would say: "Then you'd better settle it among yourselves, and change with one another." It was a most highly delicious lark. I enjoyed the Refreshmenting business more than ever, and was so glad I had took to it when young.

Our Missis returned. It got circulated among the young ladies, and it as it might be penetrated to me through the crevices of the Bandolining Room, that she had Orrors to reveal, if revelations so contemptible could be dignified with the name. Agitation become awakened. Excitement was up in the stirrups. Expectation stood a tiptoe. At length it was put forth that on our slackest evening in the week, and at our slackest time of that evening betwixt trains, Our Missis would give her views of foreign Refreshmenting, in the Bandolining Room.

It was arranged tasteful for the purpose. The Bandolining table and glass was hid in a corner, a arm-chair was elevated on a packing-case for Our Missis's ockypation, a table and a tumbler of water (no sherry in it, thankee) was placed beside it. Two of the pupils, the season being autumn, and hollyhocks and dahlias being in, ornamented the wall with three devices in those flowers. On one might be read, "MAY ALBION NEVER LEARN;" on another "KEEP THE PUBLIC DOWN;" on another, "OUR REFRESHMENTING CHARTER." The whole had a beautiful appearance, with which the beauty of the sentiments corresponded.

On Our Missis's brow was wrote Severity, as she ascended the fatal platform.[12] (Not that that was anythink new.) Miss Whiff and Miss Piff sat at her feet. Three chairs from the Waiting Room might have been perceived by a average eye, in front of her, on which the pupils was accommodated. Behind them, a very close observer might have discerned a Boy. Myself.

"Where," said Our Missis, glancing gloomily around, "is Sniff?"

"I thought it better," answered Mrs Sniff, "that he should not be let to come in. He is such an Ass."

"No doubt," assented Our Missis. "But for that reason is it not desirable to improve his mind?"

"O! Nothing will improve *him*," said Mrs Sniff.

"However," pursued Our Missis, "call him in, Ezekiel."

I called him in. The appearance of the low-minded cove was hailed with disapprobation from all sides, on account of his having brought his corkscrew with him. He pleaded "the force of habit."

"The force!" said Mrs Sniff. "Don't let us have you talking about force, for Gracious sake. There! Do stand still where you are, with your back against the wall."

He is a smiling piece of vacancy, and he smiled in the mean way in which he will even smile at the public if he gets a chance (language can say no meaner of him), and he stood upright near the door with the back of his head agin the wall, as if he was a waiting for somebody to come and measure his heighth for the Army.

"I should not enter, ladies," says Our Missis, "on the revolting disclosures I am about to make, if it was not in the hope that they will cause you to be yet more implacable in the exercise of the power you wield in a constitutional country, and yet more devoted to the constitutional motto which I see before me;"[13] it was behind her, but the words sounded better so; " 'May Albion never learn!' "

Here the pupils as had made the motto, admired it, and cried, "Hear! Hear! Hear!" Sniff, showing an inclination to join in chorus, got himself frowned down by every brow.

"The baseness of the French," pursued Our Missis, "as displayed in the fawning nature of their Refreshmenting, equals, if not surpasses, anythink as was ever heard of the baseness of the celebrated Buonaparte."

Miss Whiff, Miss Piff and me, we drored a heavy breath, equal to saying, "We thought as much!" Miss Whiff and Miss Piff seeming to object to my droring mine along with theirs, I drored another, to aggravate 'em.

"Shall I be believed," says Our Missis, with flashing eyes, "when I tell you that no sooner had I set my foot upon that treacherous shore—"

Here Sniff, either busting out mad, or thinking aloud, says, in a low voice: "Feet. Plural, you know."

The cowering that come upon him when he was spurned by all eyes, added to his being beneath contempt, was sufficient punishment for a cove so grovelling. In the midst of a silence rendered more impressive by the turned-up female noses with which it was pervaded, Our Missis went on:

"Shall I be believed when I tell you that no sooner had I landed," this word with a killing look at Sniff, "on that treacherous shore, than I was ushered into a Refreshment Room where there were, I do not exaggerate, actually eatable things to eat?"[14]

A groan burst from the ladies. I not only did myself the honour of jining, but also of lengthening it out.

"Where there were," Our Missis added, "not only eatable things to eat, but also drinkable things to drink?"

A murmur, swelling almost into a scream, ariz. Miss Piff, trembling with indignation, called out: "Name!"

"I *will* name," said Our Missis. "There was roast fowls, hot and cold; there was smoking roast veal surrounded with browned potatoes; there was hot soup with (again I ask shall I be credited?) nothing bitter in it, and no flour to choke off the consumer; there was a variety of cold dishes set off with jelly; there was salad; there was – mark me! – *fresh* pastry, and that of a light construction; there was a luscious show of fruit. There was bottles and decanters of sound small wine,[15] of every size and adapted to every pocket; the same odious statement will apply to brandy; and these were set out upon the counter so that all could help themselves."

Our Missis's lips so quivered, that Mrs Sniff, though scarcely less convulsed than she were, got up and held the tumbler to them.

"This," proceeds Our Missis, "was my first unconstitutional experience. Well would it have been, if it had been my last and worst. But no. As I proceeded further into that enslaved and ignorant land, its aspect became more hideous. I need not explain to this assembly, the ingredients and formation of the British Refreshment sangwich?"

Universal laughter – except from Sniff, who, as sangwich-cutter, shook his head in a state of the utmost dejection as he stood with it agin the wall.

"Well!" said Our Missis, with dilated nostrils. "Take a fresh crisp long crusty penny loaf made of the whitest and best flour. Cut it longwise through the middle. Insert a fair and nicely fitting slice of ham. Tie a smart piece of ribbon round the middle of the whole to bind it together. Add at one end a neat wrapper of clean white paper by which to hold it. And the universal French Refreshment sangwich busts on your disgusted vision."

A cry of "Shame!" from all – except Sniff, which rubbed his stomach with a soothing hand.

"I need not," said Our Missis, "explain to this assembly, the usual formation and fitting of the British Refreshment Room?"

No, no, and laughter. Sniff agin shaking his head in low spirits agin the wall.

"Well," said Our Missis, "what would you say to a general decoration of everythink, to hangings (sometimes elegant), to easy velvet furniture, to abundance of little tables, to abundance of little seats, to brisk bright waiters, to great convenience, to a pervading cleanliness and tastefulness positively addressing the public and making the Beast thinking itself worth the pains?"

Contemptuous fury on the part of all the ladies. Mrs Sniff looking as if she wanted somebody to hold her, and everybody else looking as if they'd rayther not.

"Three times," said Our Missis, working herself into a truly terrimenjious state, "three times did I see these shameful things, only between the coast and Paris, and not counting either: at Hazebroucke, at Arras, at Amiens. But worse remains. Tell me, what would you call a person who should propose in England that there should be kept, say at our own model Mugby Junction, pretty baskets, each holding an assorted cold lunch and dessert for one, each at a certain fixed price, and each within a passenger's power to take away, to empty in the carriage at perfect leisure, and to return at another station fifty or a hundred miles further on?"

There was disagreement what such a person should be called. Whether revolutionist, atheist, Bright[16] (*I* said him), or Un-English. Miss Piff screeched her shrill opinion last, in the words: "A malignant maniac!"

"I adopt," says Our Missis, "the brand set upon such a person by the righteous indignation of my friend Miss Piff. A malignant maniac. Know then, that that malignant maniac has sprung from the congenial soil of France, and that his malignant madness was in unchecked action on this same part of my journey."

I noticed that Sniff was a rubbing his hands, and that Mrs Sniff had got her eye upon him. But I did not take more particular notice, owing to the excited state in which the young ladies was, and to feeling myself called upon to keep it up with a howl.

"On my experience south of Paris," said Our Missis, in a deep tone, "I will not expatiate. Too loathsome were the task! But fancy this. Fancy a guard coming round, with the train at full speed, to inquire how many for dinner. Fancy his telegraphing forward, the number of dinners. Fancy every one expected, and the table elegantly laid for the complete party. Fancy a charming dinner, in a charming room, and the head-cook, concerned for the honour of every dish, superintending in his clean white jacket and cap. Fancy the Beast travelling six hundred miles on end, very fast, and with great punctuality, yet being taught to expect all this to be done for it!"

A spirited chorus of "The Beast!"

I noticed that Sniff was agin a rubbing his stomach with a soothing hand, and that he had drored up one leg. But agin I didn't take particular notice, looking on myself as called upon to stimilate public feeling. It being a lark besides.

"Putting everything together," said Our Missis, "French Refreshmenting comes to this, and O it comes to a nice total! First: eatable things to eat, and drinkable things to drink."

A groan from the young ladies, kep' up by me.

"Second: convenience and even elegance."

Another groan from the young ladies, kep' up by me.

"Third: moderate charges."

This time, a groan from me, kep' up by the young ladies.

"Fourth: – and here," says Our Missis, "I claim your angriest sympathy – attention, common civility, nay, even politeness!"

Me and the young ladies regularly raging mad all together.

"And I cannot in conclusion," says Our Missis, with her spitefullest sneer, "give you a completer pictur of that despicable nation (after what I have related), than assuring you that they wouldn't bear our constitutional ways and noble independence at Mugby Junction, for a single month, and that they would turn us to the right-about and put another system in our places, as soon as look at us; perhaps sooner, for I do not believe they have the good taste to care to look at us twice."

The swelling tumult was arrested in its rise. Sniff, bore away by his servile disposition, had drored up his leg with a higher and a higher relish, and was now discovered to be waving his corkscrew over his head. It was at this moment that Mrs Sniff, who had kep' her eye upon him like the fabled obelisk,[17] descended on her victim. Our Missis followed them both out, and cries was heard in the sawdust department.

You come into the Down Refreshment Room, at the Junction, making believe you don't know me, and I'll pint you out with my right thumb over my shoulder which is Our Missis, and which is Miss

Whiff, and which is Miss Piff, and which is Mrs Sniff. But you won't get a chance to see Sniff, because he disappeared that night. Whether he perished, tore to pieces, I cannot say; but his corkscrew alone remains, to bear witness to the servility of his disposition.

INSULARITIES

It is more or less the habit of every country – more or less commendable in every case – to exalt itself and its institutions above every other country, and be vainglorious. Out of the partialities thus engendered and maintained, there has arisen a great deal of patriotism, and a great deal of public spirit. On the other hand, it is of paramount importance to every nation that its boastfulness should not generate prejudice, conventionality, and a cherishing of unreasonable ways of acting and thinking, which have nothing in them deserving of respect, but are ridiculous or wrong.

We English people, owing in a great degree to our insular position, and in a small degree to the facility with which we have permitted electioneering lords and gentlemen to pretend to think for us, and to represent our weaknesses to us as our strength, have been in particular danger of contracting habits which we will call for our present purpose, Insularities. Our object in this paper, is to string together a few examples.

On the continent of Europe, generally, people dress according to their personal convenience and inclinations. In that capital which is supposed to set the fashion in affairs of dress, there is an especial independence in this regard. If a man in Paris have an idiosyncrasy on the subject of any article of attire between his hat and his boots, he gratifies it without the least idea that it can be anybody's affair but his; nor does anybody else make it his affair. If, indeed, there be anything

obviously convenient or tasteful in the peculiarity, then it soon ceases
to be a peculiarity, and is adopted by others. If not, it is let alone. In
the meantime, the commonest man in the streets does not consider it
at all essential to his character as a true Frenchman, that he should
howl, stare, jeer, or otherwise make himself offensive to the author of
the innovation. That word has ceased to be Old Boguey[1] to him since
he ceased to be a serf, and he leaves the particular sample of
innovation to come in or go out upon its merits.

Our strong English prejudice against anything of this kind that is
new to the eye, forms one of our decided insularities. It is
disappearing before the extended knowledge of other countries
consequent upon steam and electricity, but it is not gone yet. The
hermetically-sealed, black, stiff, chimney-pot, a foot and a half high,
which we call a hat,[2] is generally admitted to be neither convenient
nor graceful; but, there are very few middle-aged gentlemen within
two hours' reach of the Royal Exchange,[3] who would bestow their
daughters on wide-awakes,[4] however estimable the wearers. Smith
Payne and Smith, or Ransom and Co.,[5] would probably consider a run
upon the house not at all unlikely, in the event of their clerks coming
to business in caps, or with such felt-fashions on their heads as didn't
give them the head-ache, and as they could wear comfortably and
cheaply. During the dirt and wet of at least half the year in London,
it would be a great comfort and a great saving of expense to a large
class of persons, to wear the trousers gathered up about the leg, as a
Zouave does,[6] with a long gaiter below – to shift which, is to shift the
whole mud-encumbered part of the dress, and to be dry and clean
directly. To such clerks, and others with much out-door work to do, as
could afford it, Jack-boots, a much more costly article, would, for
similar reasons, be excellent wear. But what would Griggs and Bodger
say to Jack-boots? They would say, "This sort of thing, sir, is not the
sort of thing the house has been accustomed to, you will bring the

house into the Gazette,[7] you must ravel out four inches of trousers daily, sir, or you must go."

Some years ago, we, the writer, not being in Griggs and Bodger's, took the liberty of buying a great coat which we saw exposed for sale in the Burlington Arcade,[8] London, and which appeared to be in our eyes the most sensible great coat we had ever seen. Taking the further liberty to wear this great coat after we had bought it, we became a sort of Spectre, eliciting the wonder and terror of our fellow creatures as we flitted along the streets. We accompanied the coat to Switzerland for six months; and, although it was perfectly new there, we found it was not regarded as a portent of the least importance. We accompanied it to Paris for another six months; and, although it was perfectly new there too, nobody minded it. This coat so intolerable to Britain, was nothing more nor less than the loose wide-sleeved mantle, easy to put on, easy to put off, and crushing nothing beneath it, which everybody now wears.

During hundreds of years, it was the custom in England to wear beards. It became, in course of time, one of our Insularities to shave close. Whereas, in almost all the other countries of Europe, more or less of moustache and beard was habitually worn, it came to be established in this speck of an island, as an Insularity from which there was no appeal, that an Englishman, whether he liked it or not, must hew, hack, and rasp his chin and upper lip daily. The inconvenience of this infallible test of British respectability was so widely felt, that fortunes were made by razors, razor-strops, hones, pastes, shaving-soaps, emollients for the soothing of the tortured skin, all sorts of contrivances to lessen the misery of the shaving process and diminish the amount of time it occupied. This particular Insularity even went some miles further on the broad highway of Nonsense than other Insularities; for it not only tabooed unshorn civilians, but claimed for one particular and very limited military class the sole right to dispense with razors as to their upper lips. We ventured to suggest in this journal that the prohibition was ridiculous,[9] and to show some reasons why it was ridiculous. The Insularity having no sense in it, has since been losing ground every day.

One of our most remarkable Insularities is a tendency to be firmly persuaded that what is not English is not natural. In the Fine Arts department of the French Exhibition,[10] recently closed, we repeatedly heard, even from the more educated and reflective of our countrymen, that certain pictures which appeared to possess great merit – of which not the lowest item was, that they possessed the merit of a vigorous and bold Idea – were all very well, but were "theatrical."[11] Conceiving the difference between a dramatic picture and a theatrical picture, to be, that in the former case a story is strikingly told, without apparent consciousness of a spectator, and that in the latter case the groups are obtrusively conscious of a spectator, and are obviously dressed up, and doing (or not doing) certain things with an eye to the spectator, and not for the sake of the story; we sought in vain for this defect. Taking further pains then, to find out what was meant by the term theatrical, we found that the actions and gestures of the figures were not English. That is to say, – the figures expressing themselves in the vivacious manner natural in a greater or less degree to the whole great continent of Europe, were overcharged and out of the truth, because they did not express themselves in the manner of our little Island – which is so very exceptional, that it always places an Englishman at a disadvantage, out of his own country, until his fine sterling qualities shine through his external formality and constraint. Surely nothing can be more unreasonable, say, than that we should require a Frenchman of the days of Robespierre,[12] to be taken out of his jail to the guillotine with the calmness of Clapham or the respectability of Richmond Hill,[13] after a trial at the Central Criminal Court in eighteen hundred and fifty-six.[14] And yet this exactly illustrates the requirement of the particular Insularity under consideration.

When shall we get rid of the Insularity of being afraid to make the most of small resources, and the best of scanty means of enjoyment? In Paris (as in innumerable other places and countries) a man who has six square feet of yard, or six square feet of housetop, adorns it in his own poor way, and sits there in fine weather because he likes to do it, because he chooses to do it, because he has got nothing better of his own, and has never been laughed out of the enjoyment of what he has got. Equally, he will sit at his door, or in his balcony, or out on the pavement, because it is cheerful and pleasant and he likes to see the life of the city. For the last seventy years his family have not been tormenting their lives with continual enquiries and speculations whether other families, above and below, to the right and to the left, over the way and round the corner, would consider these recreations genteel, or would do the like, or would not do the like. That abominable old Tyrant, Madame Grundy,[15] has never been of his acquaintance. The result is, that, with a very small income and in a very dear city, he has more innocent pleasure than fifty Englishmen of the same condition; and is distinctly, in spite of our persuasion to the contrary (another Insularity!) a more domestic man than the Englishman, in regard of his simple pleasures being, to a much greater extent, divided with his wife and children. It is a natural consequence of their being easy and cheap, and profoundly independent of Madame Grundy.

But, this Insularity rests, not to the credit of England, on a more palpable foundation than perhaps any other. The old school of Tory[16] writers did so pertinaciously labour to cover all easily available recreations and cheap reliefs from the monotony of common life, with ridicule and contempt, that great numbers of English people got scared into being dull, and are only now beginning to recover their courage. The object of these writers, when they had any object beyond an insolent disparagement of the life-blood of the nation, was to jeer the weaker members of the middle class into making themselves a poor fringe on the skirts of the class above them, instead of occupying their own honest, honourable, independent place. Unfortunately they succeeded only too well, and to this grievous source may be traced many of our present political ills. In no country but England have the only means and scenes of relaxation within the reach of some million or two of people been systematically lampooned and derided. This disgraceful Insularity exists no longer. Still, some weak traces of its contemptuous spirit may occasionally be found, even in very unlikely places. The accomplished Mr Macaulay, in the third volume of his brilliant History,[17] writes loftily about "the thousands of clerks and milliners who are now thrown into raptures by the sight of Loch Katrine and Loch Lomond."[18] No such responsible gentleman, in France or Germany, writing history – writing anything – would think it fine to sneer at any inoffensive and useful class of his fellow subjects. If the clerks and milliners – who pair off arm in arm, by thousands, for Loch Katrine and Loch Lomond, to celebrate the Early Closing Movement,[19] we presume – will only imagine their presence poisoning those waters to the majestic historian as he roves along the banks, looking for Whig Members of Parliament[20] to sympathise with him in admiration of the beauties of Nature, we think they will be amply avenged in the absurdity of the picture.

Not one of our Insularities is so astonishing in the eyes of an intelligent foreigner, as the Court Newsman. He is one of the absurd little obstructions perpetually in the way of our being understood abroad. The quiet greatness and independence of the national character seems so irreconcilable with its having any satisfaction in the dull slipslop about the slopes and the gardens, and about the Prince Consort's[21] going a-hunting and coming back to lunch, and about Mr Gibbs[22] and the ponies, and about the Royal Highnesses on horseback and the Royal infants taking carriage exercise, and about the slopes and the gardens again, and the Prince Consort again, and Mr Gibbs and the ponies again, and the Royal Highnesses on horseback again, and the Royal infants taking carriage exercise again, and so on for every day in the week and every week in the year,[23] that in questions of importance the English as a people, really miss their just recognition. Similar small beer is chronicled[24] with the greatest care about the nobility in their country-houses. It is in vain to represent that the English people don't care about these insignificant details, and don't want them; that aggravates the misunderstanding. If they don't want them, why do they have them? If they feel the effect of them to be ridiculous, why do they consent to be made ridiculous? If they can't help it, why, then the bewildered foreigner submits that he was right at first, and that it is not the English people that is the power, but Lord Aberdeen, or Lord Palmerston, or Lord Aldborough,[25] or Lord Knowswhom.

It is an Insularity well worth general consideration and correction, that the English people are wanting in self-respect. It would be difficult to bear higher testimony to the merits of the English aristocracy than they themselves afford in not being very arrogant or intolerant, with so large a public always ready to abase themselves before titles. On all occasions, public and private, where the opportunity is afforded, this readiness is to be observed. So long as it obtains so widely, it is impossible that we should be justly appreciated and comprehended, by those who have the greatest part in ruling us. And thus it happens that now we are facetiously pooh-poohed by our Premier in the English capital,[26] and now the accredited representatives of our arts and sciences are disdainfully slighted by our Ambassador in the French capital,[27] and we wonder to find ourselves in such curious and disadvantageous comparison with the people of other countries. Those people may, through many causes, be less fortunate and less free; but, they have more social self-respect: and that self-respect must, through all their changes, be deferred to, and will assert itself. We apprehend that few persons are disposed to contend that Rank does not receive its due share of homage on the continent of Europe; but, between the homage it receives there, and the homage it receives in our island, there is an immense difference. Half-a-dozen dukes and lords, at an English county ball, or public dinner, or any tolerably miscellaneous gathering, are painful and disagreeable company; not because they have any disposition unduly to exalt themselves, or are generally otherwise than cultivated and polite gentlemen, but, because too many of us are prone to twist ourselves out of shape before them, into contortions of servility and adulation. Elsewhere, Self-respect usually steps in to prevent this; there is much less toadying and tuft-hunting;[28] and the intercourse between the two orders is infinitely more agreeable to both, and far more edifying to both.

It is one of our Insularities, if we have a royal or titled visitor among us, to use expressions of slavish adulation in our public addresses that have no response in the heart of any breathing creature, and to encourage the diffusion of details respecting such visitor's devout behaviour at church, courtly behaviour in reception-rooms, decent behaviour at dinner-tables, implying previous acquaintance with the uses of knife, fork, spoon, and wine-glass, – which would really seem to denote that we had expected Orson.[29] These doubtful compliments are paid nowhere else, and would not be paid by us if we had a little more self-respect. Through our intercourse with other nations, we cannot too soon import some. And when we have left off representing, fifty times a day, to the King of

Brentford[30] and the Chief Tailor of Tooley Street,[31] that their smiles are necessary to our existence, those two magnificent persons will begin to doubt whether they really are so, and we shall have begun to get rid of another Insularity.

chapter twelve

LANGUAGE SKILLS AND THE ENGLISH

(EXTRACTS FROM *NICHOLAS NICKLEBY* AND *OUR MUTUAL FRIEND*)

"It were bootless to add that if languages were required to be jabbered and English is not good enough, both families and gentlemen had better go somewhere else," warns Christopher the Head Waiter in *Somebody's Luggage*. The characteristic unwillingness of the English to learn other languages, and the corresponding expectation that any self-respecting foreigner will speak English, come in for various satirical treatments in Dickens's fiction. In *Little Dorrit*, the kind-hearted inhabitants of Bleeding Heart Yard have some trouble accommodating to the foreignness of the Italian John Baptist Cavaletto:

> They spoke to him in very loud voices as if he were stone deaf. They constructed sentences, by way of teaching him the language in its purity, such as were addressed by the savages to Captain Cook, or by Friday to Robinson Crusoe. Mrs Plornish was particularly ingenious in this art; and attained so much celebrity for saying 'Me ope you leg well soon,' that it was

considered in the Yard but a very short remove indeed from speaking Italian. (*Little Dorrit*, Book 1, Chapter 25.)

In the same novel Mr Meagles, "who never by any accident acquired any knowledge whatever of the language of any country into which he travelled," has a similar approach to communication with foreigners,

> ... it being another of his habits to address individuals of all nations in idiomatic English, with a perfect conviction that they were bound to understand it somehow. (Book 1, Chapter 2.)

And in the extract presented here from *Our Mutual Friend*, Podsnap and his dinner guests treat the French visitor "as if he were a child who was hard of hearing."

For Dickens, such ignorance of and disinterest in language learning is yet another manifestation of the insularity and small-minded complacency that blight English culture and society. Just as unwillingness to speak anything other than English suggests a closed mind, willingness to learn another language suggests openness to another culture, a readiness to engage with "foreign" ideas.

In the extract from *Nicholas Nickleby*, 1838–39, Dickens pokes fun at English insularity by giving the ludicrously self-important water-rate collector Mr Lillyvik an opportunity to express his views on the French language, which Nicholas has been engaged to teach to the children of the lowly but socially aspiring Kenwigses. In *Our Mutual Friend*, 1864–65, the satire has a sharper edge. Podsnap, an embodiment of many of the characteristics that Dickens most despised – among them bigotry, pomposity, small-minded nationalism, conservative respectability, and philistinism – gives a dinner party, to which he has invited a Frenchman. This "unfortunately-born foreigner," patronized and confused by his host and fellow guests, becomes a foil for the ignorance and prejudice that lie at the heart of Podsnap's value system.

Long before he introduced Podsnappery to the world, Dickens had been struck by the culturally blinkered tendency of the English to disregard their own incompetence in languages while readily asserting their sense of superiority over foreigners doing their best to communicate in English. In a letter of 1846, written from Geneva, he tells of the behavior of an Englishman towards his French travelling companion:

> The Englishman can't speak a word of French, but the Frenchman can speak a very little English, with which he helps the Englishman out of abysses and ravines of difficulty. The Englishman instead of being obliged by this, condescends, good humouredly, to correct the Frenchman's pronunciation – patronizes him – would pat him on the head, if he could reach so high – and screeches at his mistakes...(*Pilgrim*, 4, p 639).

Dickens himself had no truck with such attitudes and took language learning seriously. In "His Boots" he insists that a reading knowledge is not enough – learning a language means learning to use it:

> Mr The Englishman was not particularly strong in the French language as a means of oral communication, though he read it very well. It is with languages as with people – when you only know them by sight, you are apt to mistake them; you must be on speaking terms before you can be said to have established an acquaintance.

He appears over the years to have developed his French to a high standard. He certainly wrote it fluently – there are many letters in elegant French among the pages of his correspondence. He also came to understand spoken French with ease. In a letter of 16 February 1855 to Georgina Hogarth he notes with evident pleasure the moment he attained this level (a significant stage for any language learner):

> My ear has gradually become so accustomed to French, that I understand the people at the theatres (for the first time) with perfect ease and satisfaction. (*Pilgrim*, 7, p 541.)

We can never know how well Dickens actually spoke French, but it is unlikely that he would have reached the listening level he records above without a concurrent development of his conversational skills. According to Forster, although he "practised himself into writing it with remarkable ease and fluency," he "never spoke that language very well, his accent being somewhat defective" (*Life*, 5, Chapter 7). However, a strong English accent does not preclude conversational fluency. In the February 1855 letter to Georgina Hogarth, he says that he has "received many compliments on my angelic manner of speaking the celestial language" – the "angelic manner" perhaps a French comment on his accent – and in February 1856 he wrote jokingly to Forster about his embarrassed pleasure when the editor and translator Amédée Pichot complimented him on his French during a dinner in Paris:

> He informed the company at dinner that he had rarely met a foreigner who spoke French so easily as your inimitable correspondent, whereat your correspondent blushed modestly, and almost immediately afterwards so nearly choked himself with the bone of a fowl (which is still in his throat), that he sat in torture for ten minutes… (*Life*, 7, Chapter 5).

Whatever the case, Dickens knew that learning the language of a country was a vital part of understanding its culture. His determination to develop his French language skills is at once indicative of his desire to engage with the country and its culture and a refutation of the narrow-minded bigotry he satirizes so effectively in the characters of Lillyvick and Podsnap.

Nicholas gives his first French lesson (illustration by Phiz)

EXTRACT FROM NICHOLAS NICKLEBY

(NICHOLAS TEACHES FRENCH)

Narrative context: Nicholas, accompanied by Smike, has returned to London from the Yorkshire school where he has defied and thrashed the tyrannical schoolmaster Squeers. Preparing to confront his uncle, Ralph Nickleby, who placed him with Squeers, he is staying in the small garret apartment of Newman Noggs. The morning after his arrival in London, Nicholas has been out looking for employment, but without success. The extract is from Chapter 16.

Smike had scraped a meal together from the remnant of last night's supper, and was anxiously awaiting his return. The occurrences of the morning had not improved Nicholas's appetite, and by him the dinner remained untasted. He was sitting in a thoughtful attitude, with the plate which the poor fellow had assiduously filled with the choicest morsels untouched, by his side, when Newman Noggs looked into the room.

"Come back?" asked Newman.

"Yes," replied Nicholas, "tired to death; and what is worse, might have remained at home for all the good I have done."

"Couldn't expect to do much in one morning," said Newman.

"May be so, but I am sanguine, and did expect," said Nicholas, "and am proportionately disappointed." Saying which, he gave Newman an account of his proceedings.

"If I could do anything," said Nicholas, "anything however slight, until Ralph Nickleby returns, and I have eased my mind by confronting him, I should feel happier. I should think it no disgrace to work, Heaven knows. Lying indolently here like a half-tamed sullen beast distracts me."

"I don't know," said Newman; "small things offer – they would pay the rent, and more – but you wouldn't like them; no, you could hardly be expected to undergo it – no, no."

"What could I hardly be expected to undergo?" asked Nicholas, raising his eyes. "Show me, in this wide waste of London, any honest means by which I could even defray the weekly hire of this poor room, and see if I shrink from resorting to them. Undergo! I have undergone too much, my friend, to feel pride or squeamishness now. Except –" added Nicholas hastily, after a short silence, "except such squeamishness as is common honesty, and so much pride as constitutes self-respect. I see little to choose, between the assistant to a brutal pedagogue, and the toad-eater of a mean and ignorant upstart, be he member or no member."[1]

"I hardly know whether I should tell you what I heard this morning or not," said Newman.

"Has it reference to what you said just now?" asked Nicholas.

"It has."

"Then in Heaven's name, my good friend, tell it me," said Nicholas. "For God's sake consider my deplorable condition; and while I promise to take no step without taking counsel with you, give me, at least, a vote in my own behalf."

Moved by this entreaty, Newman stammered forth a variety of most unaccountable and entangled sentences, the upshot of which was, that Mrs Kenwigs[2] had examined him at great length that morning touching the origin of his acquaintance with, and the whole life, adventures, and pedigree of Nicholas; that Newman had parried these questions as long as he could, but being at length hard pressed and driven into a corner, had gone so far as to admit, that Nicholas was a tutor of great accomplishments, involved in some misfortunes which he was not at liberty to explain, and bearing the name of Johnson. That Mrs Kenwigs, impelled by gratitude, or ambition, or maternal pride, or maternal love, or all four powerful motives conjointly, had taken secret confidence with Mr Kenwigs, and finally returned to propose that Mr Johnson should instruct the four Miss Kenwigses in the French language as spoken by natives, at the weekly stipend of five shillings current coin of the realm, being at the rate of one shilling per week per each Miss Kenwigs, and one shilling over, until such time as the baby might be able to take it out in grammar.

"Which, unless I am very much mistaken," observed Mrs Kenwigs in making the proposition, "will not be very long; for such clever children, Mr Noggs, never were born into this world I do believe."

"There," said Newman, "that's all. It's beneath you, I know; but I thought that perhaps you might—"

"Might!" said Nicholas, with great alacrity; "of course I shall. I accept the offer at once. Tell the worthy mother so without delay, my dear fellow; and that I am ready to begin whenever she pleases."

Newman hastened with joyful steps to inform Mrs Kenwigs of his friend's acquiescence, and soon returning, brought back word that they would be happy to see him in the first floor as soon as convenient; that Mrs Kenwigs had upon the instant sent out to secure a second-hand French grammar and dialogues, which had long been fluttering in the sixpenny box at the book-stall round the corner; and that the family, highly excited at the prospect of this addition to their gentility, wished the initiatory lesson to come off immediately.

And here it may be observed, that Nicholas was not, in the ordinary sense of the word, a young man of high spirit. He would resent an affront to himself, or interpose to redress a wrong offered to another, as boldly and freely as any knight that ever set lance in rest; but he lacked that peculiar excess of coolness and great-minded selfishness, which invariably distinguish gentlemen of high spirit. In truth, for our own part, we are rather disposed to look upon such gentlemen as being rather incumbrances than otherwise in rising families, happening to be acquainted with several whose spirit prevents their settling down to any grovelling occupation, and only displays itself in a tendency to cultivate mustachios, and look fierce; and although mustachios and ferocity are both very pretty things in their way, and very much to be commended, we confess to a desire to see them bred at the owner's proper cost, rather than at the expense of low-spirited people.

Nicholas, therefore, not being a high-spirited young man according to common parlance, and deeming it a greater degradation to borrow, for the supply of his necessities, from Newman Noggs, than to teach French to the little Kenwigses for five shillings a week, accepted the offer with the alacrity already described, and betook himself to the first floor with all convenient speed.

Here he was received by Mrs Kenwigs with a genteel air, kindly intended to assure him of her protection and support; and here too he found Mr Lillyvick and Miss Petowker:[3] the four Miss Kenwigses on their form of audience, and the baby in a dwarf porter's chair[4] with a deal tray before it, amusing himself with a toy horse without a head; the said horse being composed of a small wooden cylinder, not unlike an Italian iron,[5] supported on four crooked pegs, and painted in ingenious resemblance of red wafers set in blacking.

"How do you do, Mr Johnson?" said Mrs Kenwigs. "Uncle – Mr Johnson."

"How do you do, sir?" said Mr Lillyvick – rather sharply; for he had not known what Nicholas was, on the previous night, and it was rather an aggravating circumstance if a tax collector had been too polite to a teacher.

"Mr Johnson is engaged as private master to the children, uncle," said Mrs Kenwigs.

"So you said just now, my dear," replied Mr Lillyvick.

"But I hope," said Mrs Kenwigs, drawing herself up, "that that will not make them proud; but that they will bless their own good fortune, which has born them superior to common people's children. Do you hear, Morleena?"

"Yes, ma," replied Miss Kenwigs.

"And when you go out in the streets, or elsewhere, I desire that you don't boast of it to the other children," said Mrs Kenwigs; "and that if you must say anything about it, you don't say no more than 'We've got a private master comes to teach us at home, but we ain't proud, because ma says it's sinful.' Do you hear, Morleena?"

"Yes, ma," replied Miss Kenwigs again.

"Then mind you recollect, and do as I tell you," said Mrs Kenwigs. "Shall Mr Johnson begin, uncle?"

"I am ready to hear, if Mr Johnson is ready to commence, my dear," said the collector, assuming the air of a profound critic. "What sort of language do you consider French, sir?"

"How do you mean?" asked Nicholas.

"Do you consider it a good language, sir?" said the collector; "a pretty language, a sensible language?"

"A pretty language, certainly," replied Nicholas; "and as it has a name for everything, and admits of elegant conversation about everything, I presume it is a sensible one."

"I don't know," said Mr Lillyvick, doubtfully. "Do you call it cheerful language, now?"

"Yes," replied Nicholas, "I should say it was, certainly."

"It's very much changed since my time, then," said the collector, "very much."

"Was it a dismal one in your time?" asked Nicholas, scarcely able to repress a smile.

"Very," replied Mr Lillyvick, with some vehemence of manner.

"It's the war time that I speak of; the last war.[6] It may be a cheerful language. I should be sorry to contradict anybody; but I can only say that I've heard the French prisoners, who were natives, and ought to know how to speak it, talking in such a dismal manner, that it made one miserable to hear them. Ay, that I have, fifty times, sir – fifty times!"

Mr Lillyvick was waxing so cross, that Mrs Kenwigs thought it expedient to motion to Nicholas not to say anything; and it was not until Miss Petowker had practised several blandishments, to soften the excellent old gentleman, that he deigned to break silence, by asking,

"What's the water in French, sir?"

"*L'Eau*," replied Nicholas.

"Ah!" said Mr Lillyvick, shaking his head mournfully, "I thought as much. Lo, eh? I don't think anything of that language – nothing at all."

"I suppose the children may begin, uncle?" said Mrs Kenwigs.

"Oh yes; they may begin, my dear," replied the collector, discontentedly. "*I* have no wish to prevent them."

This permission being conceded, the four Miss Kenwigses sat in a row, with their tails all one way, and Morleena at the top, while Nicholas, taking the book, began his preliminary explanations. Miss Petowker and Mrs Kenwigs looked on, in silent admiration, broken only by the whispered assurances of the latter, that Morleena would have it all by heart in no time; and Mr Lillyvick regarded the group with frowning and attentive eyes, lying in wait for something upon which he could open a fresh discussion on the language.

EXTRACT FROM OUR MUTUAL FRIEND

(PODSNAP'S DINNER PARTY)

Narrative context: Although Podsnap has already made an appearance in the novel, it is at this point that he is fully introduced to the reader. The extract, from Book 1 Chapter 11 ("Podsnappery"), is Dickens's definitive analysis of the character of Podsnap and the values he represents.

Mr Podsnap was well to do, and stood very high in Mr Podsnap's opinion. Beginning with a good inheritance, he had married a good inheritance, and had thriven exceedingly in the Marine Insurance way, and was quite satisfied. He never could make out why everybody was not quite satisfied, and he was conscious that he set a brilliant social example in being particularly well satisfied with most things, and, above all other things, with himself.

Thus happily acquainted with his own merit and importance, Mr Podsnap settled that whatever he put behind him he put out of existence. There was a dignified conclusiveness – not to add a grand convenience – in this way of getting rid of disagreeables which had done much towards establishing Mr Podsnap in his lofty place in Mr Podsnap's satisfaction. "I don't want to know about it; I don't choose to discuss it; I don't admit it!" Mr Podsnap had even acquired a peculiar flourish of his right arm in often clearing the world of its most difficult problems, by sweeping them behind him (and consequently sheer away) with those words and a flushed face. For they affronted him.

Mr Podsnap's world was not a very large world, morally; no, nor even geographically: seeing that although his business was sustained upon commerce with other countries, he considered other countries, with that important reservation, a mistake, and of their manners and customs would conclusively observe, "Not English!" when, PRESTO! with a flourish of the arm, and a flourish of the face, they were swept away. Elsewise, the world got up at eight, shaved close at a quarter-past, breakfasted at nine, went to the City at ten, came home at half-past five, and dined at seven. Mr Podsnap's notions of the Arts in their integrity might have been stated thus. Literature; large print, respectfully descriptive of getting up at eight, shaving close at a quarter-past, breakfasting at nine, going to the City at ten, coming home at half-past five, and dining at seven. Painting and Sculpture; models and portraits representing Professors of getting up at eight, shaving close at a quarter-past, breakfasting at nine, going to the City at ten, coming home at half-past five, and dining at seven. Music; a respectable performance (without variations) on stringed and wind instruments, sedately expressive of getting up at eight, shaving close at a quarter-past, breakfasting at nine, going to the City at ten, coming home at half-past five, and dining at seven.[1] Nothing else to be permitted to those same vagrants the Arts, on pain of excommunication. Nothing else To Be – anywhere!

As a so eminently respectable man, Mr Podsnap was sensible of its being required of him to take Providence under his protection. Consequently he always knew exactly what Providence meant. Inferior and less respectable men might fall short of that mark, but Mr Podsnap always came up to it. And it was very remarkable (and must have been very comfortable) that what Providence meant, was invariably what Mr Podsnap meant.

These may be said to have been the articles of a faith and school which the present chapter takes the liberty of calling, after its representative man, Podsnappery. They were confined within close bounds, as Mr Podsnap's own head was confined by his shirt-collar;

and they were enunciated with a sounding pomp that smacked of the creaking of Mr Podsnap's own boots.

There was Miss Podsnap. And this young rocking-horse was being trained in her mother's art of prancing in a stately manner without ever getting on. But the high parental action was not yet imparted to her, and in truth she was but an undersized damsel, with high shoulders, low spirits, chilled elbows, and a rasped surface of nose, who seemed to take occasional frosty peeps out of childhood into womanhood, and to shrink back again, overcome by her mother's head-dress and her father from head to foot – crushed by the mere dead-weight of Podsnappery.

A certain institution in Mr Podsnap's mind which he called "the young person" may be considered to have been embodied in Miss Podsnap, his daughter. It was an inconvenient and exacting institution, as requiring everything in the universe to be filed down and fitted to it. The question about everything was, would it bring a blush into the cheek of the young person? And the inconvenience of the young person was, that, according to Mr Podsnap, she seemed always liable to burst into blushes when there was no need at all. There appeared to be no line of demarcation between the young person's excessive innocence, and another person's guiltiest knowledge. Take Mr Podsnap's word for it, and the soberest tints of drab, white, lilac, and grey, were all flaming red to this troublesome Bull of a young person.

The Podsnaps lived in a shady angle adjoining Portman Square.[2] They were a kind of people certain to dwell in the shade, wherever they dwelt. Miss Podsnap's life had been, from her first appearance on this planet, altogether of a shady order; for, Mr Podsnap's young person was likely to get little good out of association with other young persons, and had therefore been restricted to companionship with not very congenial older persons, and with massive furniture. Miss

Podsnap's early views of life being principally derived from the reflections of it in her father's boots, and in the walnut and rosewood tables of the dim drawing-rooms, and in their swarthy giants of looking-glasses, were of a sombre cast; and it was not wonderful that now, when she was on most days solemnly tooled through the Park by the side of her mother in a great tall custard-coloured phaeton,[3] she showed above the apron of that vehicle like a dejected young person sitting up in bed to take a startled look at things in general, and very strongly desiring to get her head under the counterpane again.

Said Mr Podsnap to Mrs Podsnap, "Georgiana is almost eighteen."

Said Mrs Podsnap to Mr Podsnap, assenting, "Almost eighteen."

Said Mr Podsnap then to Mrs Podsnap, "Really I think we should have some people on Georgiana's birthday."

Said Mrs Podsnap then to Mr Podsnap, "Which will enable us to clear off all those people who are due."

So it came to pass that Mr and Mrs Podsnap requested the honour of the company of seventeen friends of their souls at dinner; and that they substituted other friends of their souls for such of the seventeen original friends of their souls as deeply regretted that a prior engagement prevented their having the honour of dining with Mr and Mrs Podsnap, in pursuance of their kind invitation; and that Mrs Podsnap said of all these inconsolable personages, as she checked them off with a pencil in her list, "Asked, at any rate, and got rid of;" and that they successfully disposed of a good many friends of their souls in this way, and felt their consciences much lightened.

There were still other friends of their souls who were not entitled to be asked to dinner, but had a claim to be invited to come and take a haunch of mutton vapour-bath at half-past nine. For the clearing off of these worthies, Mrs Podsnap added a small and early evening to the dinner, and looked in at the music-shop to bespeak a well-conducted automaton to come and play quadrilles for a carpet dance.

Mr and Mrs Veneering, and Mr and Mrs Veneering's bran-new bride and bridegroom,[4] were of the dinner company; but the Podsnap establishment had nothing else in common with the Veneerings. Mr Podsnap could tolerate taste in a mushroom man[5] who stood in need of that sort of thing, but was far above it himself. Hideous solidity was the characteristic of the Podsnap plate. Everything was made to look as heavy as it could, and to take up as much room as possible. Everything said boastfully, "Here you have as much of me in my ugliness as if I were only lead; but I am so many ounces of precious metal worth so much an ounce; – wouldn't you like to melt me down?" A corpulent straddling epergne,[6] blotched all over as if it had broken out in an eruption rather than been ornamented, delivered this address from an unsightly silver platform in the centre of the table. Four silver wine-coolers, each furnished with four staring heads, each head obtrusively carrying a big silver ring in each of its ears, conveyed the sentiment up and down the table, and handed it on to the pot-bellied silver salt-cellars. All the big silver spoons and forks widened the mouths of the company expressly for the purpose of thrusting the sentiment down their throats with every morsel they ate.

The majority of the guests were like the plate, and included several heavy articles weighing ever so much. But there was a foreign gentleman among them: whom Mr Podsnap had invited after much debate within himself – believing the whole European continent to be in mortal alliance against the young person – and there was a droll disposition, not only on the part of Mr Podsnap but of everybody else, to treat him as if he were a child who was hard of hearing.

As a delicate concession to this unfortunately-born foreigner, Mr Podsnap, in receiving him, had presented his wife as "Madame Podsnap;" also his daughter as "Mademoiselle Podsnap," with some inclination to add "ma fille," in which bold venture, however, he checked himself. The Veneerings being at that time the only other arrivals, he had added (in a condescendingly explanatory manner), "Monsieur Vey-nair-reeng," and had then subsided into English.

"How Do You Like London?" Mr Podsnap now inquired from his station of host, as if he were administering something in the nature of a powder or potion to the deaf child; "London, Londres, London?"

The foreign gentleman admired it.

"You find it Very Large?" said Mr Podsnap, spaciously.

The foreign gentleman found it very large.

"And Very Rich?"

The foreign gentleman found it, without doubt, enormément riche.

"Enormously Rich, We say," returned Mr Podsnap, in a condescending manner. "Our English adverbs do Not terminate in Mong, and We Pronounce the 'ch' as if there were a 't' before it. We say Ritch."

"Reetch," remarked the foreign gentleman.

"And Do You Find, Sir," pursued Mr Podsnap, with dignity, "Many Evidences that Strike You, of our British Constitution in the Streets Of The World's Metropolis, London, Londres, London?"

The foreign gentleman begged to be pardoned, but did not altogether understand.

"The Constitution Britannique," Mr Podsnap explained, as if he were teaching in an infant school. "We Say British, But You Say Britannique, You Know" (forgivingly, as if that were not his fault). "The Constitution, Sir."

The foreign gentleman said, "Mais, yees; I know eem."

A youngish sallowish gentleman in spectacles, with a lumpy forehead, seated in a supplementary chair at a corner of the table, here caused a profound sensation by saying, in a raised voice, "ESKER," and then stopping dead.

"Mais oui," said the foreign gentleman, turning towards him. "Est-ce que? Quoi donc?"

But the gentleman with the lumpy forehead having for the time delivered himself of all that he found behind his lumps, spake for the time no more.

"I Was Inquiring," said Mr Podsnap, resuming the thread of his discourse, "Whether You Have Observed in our Streets as We should say, Upon our Pavvy as You would say, any Tokens—"

The foreign gentleman, with patient courtesy entreated pardon; "But what was tokenz?"

"Marks," said Mr Podsnap; "Signs, you know, Appearances – Traces."

"Ah! Of a Orse?"[7] inquired the foreign gentleman.

"We call it Horse," said Mr Podsnap, with forbearance. "In England, Angleterre, England, We Aspirate the 'H,' and We Say 'Horse.' Only our Lower Classes Say 'Orse!'"

"Pardon," said the foreign gentleman; "I am alwiz wrong!"

"Our Language," said Mr Podsnap, with a gracious consciousness of being always right, "is Difficult. Ours is a Copious Language, and Trying to Strangers. I will not Pursue my Question."

But the lumpy gentleman, unwilling to give it up, again madly said, "ESKER," and again spake no more.

"It merely referred," Mr Podsnap explained, with a sense of meritorious proprietorship, "to Our Constitution, Sir. We Englishmen are Very Proud of our Constitution, Sir. It Was Bestowed Upon Us By Providence. No Other Country is so Favoured as This Country."

"And ozer countries?—" the foreign gentleman was beginning, when Mr Podsnap put him right again.

"We do not say Ozer; we say Other: the letters are 'T' and 'H;'

You say Tay and Aish, You Know; (still with clemency). The sound is 'th' – 'th!' "

"And *ot*her countries," said the foreign gentleman. "They do how?"

"They do, Sir," returned Mr Podsnap, gravely shaking his head; "they do – I am sorry to be obliged to say it – *as* they do."

"It was a little particular of Providence," said the foreign gentleman, laughing; "for the frontier is not large."

"Undoubtedly," assented Mr Podsnap; "But So it is. It was the Charter of the Land. This Island was Blest,[8] Sir, to the Direct Exclusion of such Other Countries as – as there may happen to be. And if we were all Englishmen present, I would say," added Mr Podsnap, looking round upon his compatriots, and sounding solemnly with his theme, "that there is in the Englishman a combination of qualities, a modesty, an independence, a responsibility, a repose, combined with an absence of everything calculated to call a blush into the cheek of a young person, which one would seek in vain among the Nations of the Earth."

Having delivered this little summary, Mr Podsnap's face flushed, as he thought of the remote possibility of its being at all qualified by any prejudiced citizen of any other country; and with his favourite right-arm flourish, he put the rest of Europe and the whole of Asia, Africa, and America nowhere.

NOTES

"A Flight," pp 5–16

1. The Chaff-wax, or Chafe-wax, was an officer of the Lord Chancellor whose task it was to prepare the wax for sealing documents. The post was abolished in 1852. Dickens had hit out at bureaucrats in an earlier article about patent applications, "A Poor Man's Tale of a Patent" (*Household Words*, 19 October 1850), in which the narrator-inventor says, "I went through thirty-five stages. I began with the Queen upon the Throne. I ended with the Deputy Chaff-wax." The article foreshadows the thorough satirical beating given to the administrative bureaucracy in *Little Dorrit*, 1855–57, with its Circumlocution Office and the trials of the inventor Daniel Doyce.

2. London Bridge Station had been rebuilt in 1849 and divided into two parts. The South Eastern Railway Company operated from one side and the London, Brighton and South Coast Railway from the other.

3. The French travellers have no doubt been to Covent Garden market to buy their pineapples. The market was a major tourist attraction: Peter Cunningham, in his *Hand-Book of London*, 1850, listed it as one of the "places which a stranger in London must see." It was internationally renowned for the variety and quality of its fruit and vegetables, and the pineapples were among the most admired of its produce. According to John Timbs, writing in *Curiosities of London*, 1855, "There is more certainty of being able to purchase a pine-apple here, every day in the year, than in Jamaica and Calcutta, where pines are indigenous." The young David Copperfield wandered down to the market and "stared at the pineapples" (*David Copperfield*, 1849–50, Chapter 11), and Tom and Ruth Pinch wonder at "the magnificence of the pine-apples and melons" (*Martin Chuzzlewit*, 1843–44, Chapter 40).

4. The reference is to the bookseller and theatrical impresario John Mitchell (1806–74), who put on seasons of French plays at the St James's Theatre in King Street, London SW1 between 1842 and 1854. The theater was demolished in the 1950s.

5. From or characteristic of Algiers or Algeria.

6. Abd-el-Kader (1807–83), born in Mascara, was an Algerian nationalist who led a long struggle against the French after their conquest of Algiers. He surrendered in 1847.

7. Neat, pointed beard after the style typically depicted in portraits by Sir Anthony Van Dyck (1599–1641).

8. A demonic character in the opera *Der Freischütz* by Carl Maria von Weber (1786–1826).

9. "City" refers to the area known as the City of London (the site of the

Roman city of Londinium), where many of the major financial institutions are located (including the Stock Exchange). Dickens is using the word, as it used today, to evoke the world of banking and finance.

10. The district of Bermondsey, on the bank of the Thames east of London Bridge, was a center of the leather industry – the industry has now gone from the area but its spirit lingers in street names like Tanner Street, Morocco Street, and Leathermarket Street.

11. Under the provisions of the Railways Act of 1844, the railway companies had to provide covered third-class accommodation on at least one train per day in both directions on every line. The third-class ticket price was not to exceed a penny per mile and the trains were to travel at a minimum speed of 12 miles per hour. The aim of these "Parliamentary Trains" was to make rail travel available to the working classes.

12. Dickens had developed this point in some detail in his 1848 article, "Judicial Special Pleading" (included in this volume). The Reign of Terror ran from September 1793 to July 1794.

13. Versions of this curse "in the Persian manner" appear several times in Dickens's correspondence. In a letter to Forster of 15 April 1842 he writes "My face, like Haji Baba's, turns upside down, and my liver is changed to water..." (*Pilgrim*, 3, p 196). On 8 September 1842 he asks Thomas Beard, "When is that jolly old Baronet (may Jackasses sit upon his Grandfather's grave!) coming home?" (*Pilgrim*, 3, p 321). Apologizing to Marion Ely on 19 April 1846 for an inadvertent discourtesy, he writes, "At the apparent rudeness of my reply, my face, as Hadji Baba says, was turned upside down and fifty donkeys sat upon my father's grave..." (*Pilgrim*, 4, p 536). And in a letter to T.J. Thompson of 10 June 1847 he exclaims, "For which, may jackasses browze upon his father's grave!" (*Pilgrim*, 5, p 85). The *Pilgrim* editors identify the source as the *Hajji Baba* books of James J. Morier (?1780–1849). Morier's *The Adventures of Hajji Baba of Ispahan* was published in 1824 to popular acclaim. The sequel, *The Adventures of Hajji Baba in England*, appeared in 1828.

14. "Trains arrive direct from London in two hours and a half, with passengers for the Continent, who alight at the station on the harbour, close to the steam packet," writes J. S. Mackie (*A Descriptive and Historical Account of Folkestone and Its Neighbourhood*, 1856). Mackie describes the Royal George as one of several "very good hotels of the usual class [where] very respectable accommodation will be found."

15. The first of the "namesakes" is the British naval vessel The Royal George, which sank on 29 August 1782 during repair work at Spithead (the eastern part of the strait between Portsmouth and the Isle of Wight). About 800 people were drowned – William Cowper commemorated the tragedy in his poem "On the Loss of the Royal George." The monarch at the time of the incident was George III, who is "under earth at Windsor"

– he is buried at Windsor Castle, as is his successor George IV.

16. New arrivals from Britain were greeted by a throng of hotel touts clamoring for business (see also "Our French Watering-Place," with its reference to a "howling wilderness" of touts). Boulogne was by no means unique in this respect: Dickens describes the touts of Calais in "The Calais Night Mail" and in chapter 20 of *Little Dorrit* – see note 3 under "Clennam in Calais," p 337.

17. In the reign of Louis XIV, the celebrated military engineer Sébastien Le Prestre Vauban (1633–1707) designed and supervised the building of fortresses around the coasts and borders of France. In all, he built 33 forts and fortified towns and restored and strengthened 300 others. There were many examples of his work in northern France (and some remain). Dickens paints a detailed picture of life in a fortified town in his short story "His Boots" (included in this volume).

18. A public stage-coach. According to *Galignani's New Paris Guide* of 1852, *diligences* "carry generally 15 to 18 passengers, and contain four kinds of places – the *coupé*, which holds three; *intérieur*, six; *rotonde*, six; and *banquette*, three."

19. The Gare du Nord (opened in 1846).

20. Cabs were readily available for hire in Paris and were well regulated: "Every morning the overseer of the stand inspects them, to ascertain whether they are in a fit state for service. The amount of fare is printed on parchment, and stuck inside for the information of the public. Imposition on the part of the driver is severely punished." (*Galignani's New Paris Guide*, 1852.) At the Gare du Nord, cabriolets and omnibuses awaited the arrival of the trains.

21. The Bains Chinois, on the boulevard des Italiens, was a core attraction of what was then one of the liveliest streets in the city, lined with famous cafés, restaurants, and theaters. It was a restaurant and café as well as a bathing establishment and was renowned as much for its fantastic pagoda-style architecture as for what was inside it. Opened in 1792, it was replaced in 1853 by the Café du Helder.

There were many public baths of all kinds in Paris. Félix and Louis Lazare note that there were 136 *établissements de bains de santé* as at 31 December 1853 (*Dictionnaire administratif et historique des rues et des monuments de Paris*, 1855). *Galignani's New Paris Guide* of 1852 records 125 establishments "which afford every kind of accommodation at a low charge, and furnish on average 2,116,300 baths per annum to the public. They are formed of ranges of small rooms, furnished with every necessary appendage." Oriental associations were common in the more up-market ones, such as the Bains Deligny on the Seine (reconstructed with oriental décor in the 1840s) and the four bathing establishments of M. Vigier, also on the Seine. "*Au bain*," writes Eugène Briffault of the Bains Vigier in

Paris dans l'eau, 1844, "*le bourgeois de Paris rêve l'Orient, ses délices, ses voluptés, ses parfums et ses odalisques, l'opium et ses extases...*" (See also note 16 under "Travelling Abroad," p 339.)

22. The statue of Napoléon on top of the Colonne Vendôme. The statue that stood on the column in 1851, when "A Flight" was published, is now in the Cour d'Honneur of the Hôtel des Invalides. It was unveiled in 1833 and surmounted the column until 1863, when it was replaced with the one that is there today – a replica of the original statue, torn down by Royalists in 1814 (the replica itself survived the destruction of the column by Communards in 1871).

23. Dickens is referring to the statues of the Duke of Wellington at Hyde Park Corner and the Royal Exchange.

24. The *barrières* were the city gates of Paris. By order of the *fermiers généraux* (tax collectors under the *ancien régime*), a wall had been built around the city in the eighteenth century denoting its administrative boundaries, in order to collect duty, or *octroi*, on goods brought into Paris. There were originally 54 *barrières*, but eight of those were closed between 1818 and 1855, while a further nine were opened between 1820 and 1854. The *Barrière de l'Étoile*, also know as the *Barrière de Neuilly*, was located at the end of the avenue des Champs-Élysées between the current rues de Presbourg and de Tilsitt, which circle what is now the place de Charles de Gaulle (still commonly known as the place de l'Étoile). The *Barrière de l'Étoile* comprised two imposing neo-classical toll-houses, one on either side of the avenue, connected by a long railing. *Galignani's New Paris Guide* of 1852 recommends it to visitors, explaining that it "consists of two pavilions and a handsome iron railing, beyond which rises the triumphal arch de l'Etoile." The toll-houses were demolished in 1860.

25. A nymph of the Muslim Paradise, used allusively to describe a beautiful woman.

"The Calais Night Mail," pp 23–32

1. Cap Gris-Nez, a headland on the French coast and the nearest point to Dover.

2. "A bank of sand silt, etc, across the mouth of a river, which obstructs navigation" (*Oxford English Dictionary*). Dickens anticipates the rolling and heaving of the ship when it encounters the turbulent waters of the bar. Thus Tennyson, in his allegorical 1889 poem "Crossing the Bar," wishes for a full tide and a peaceful passage: "And may there be no moaning of the bar,/When I put out to sea,/But such a tide as moving seems asleep,/Too full for sound and foam..."

3. Before the devastating bombs of the Second World War, Calais was a medieval walled town, the defenses of which had been considerably

strengthened in the 1840s. *A Handbook for Visitors to Paris*, 1864, describes it as "surrounded by strong fortifications" and *A Handbook for Travellers in France*, 1864, mentions "a large and strong citadel and several forts."

4. The Lord Warden Hotel (taking its name from the Lord Warden of the Cinque Ports), was built close to the pier by the South Eastern Railway Company. Murray's *Handbook for Travellers in Kent and Sussex*, 1863, describes it as "good and not extravagant." Dickens stayed at the hotel on various occasions and Mr and Mrs Birmingham were long-standing acquaintances. John Birmingham, the proprietor of the Lord Warden, had previously been the host of the Ship, another well-known Dover hotel, which Dickens had patronized in earlier days.

5. Trains carrying the mail from London to Dover ran at fixed times in the morning and evening. The South Eastern Railway Company's train that Dickens describes here would have come from London Bridge station – the South Eastern also ran mail trains from Charing Cross to Dover, but that line did not open until 1864 (this article was published in 1863).

6. That is, the military drumming from the barracks on the Western Heights.

7. An allusion to the opening soliloquy of Shakespeare's *Richard III* ("…Deform'd, unfinish'd, sent before my time/Into this breathing world scarce half made up,/And that so lamely and unfashionable/That dogs bark at me as I halt by them …").

8. The railway lines ran down to the end of the pier, so that trains connecting with the cross-Channel steamers could carry passengers as close as possible to their ship.

9. An allusion to the "Uncommercial Traveller" persona – see page 17.

10. This recalls the text of "At the Burial of their Dead at Sea" from "Forms of Prayer to be Used at Sea," *The Book of Common Prayer*, 1662: "We therefore commit his body to the deep, to be turned into corruption, looking for the resurrection of the body (when the sea shall give up her dead)…"

11. The two lighthouses at South Foreland, a headland near Dover and the nearest point to the French coast. The lighthouses, one higher than the other, date from 1843. They still exist, but neither is in use. The upper and main light continued to operate until 1988.

12. "Rich and Rare Were the Gems She Wore," the ballad that preoccupies Dickens and gets tangled up with his other thoughts and perceptions as he tries to ignore the miseries of the crossing, is from *Irish Melodies* by Thomas Moore (1779–1852), published in ten "Numbers" between 1807 and 1834. Dickens knew Moore's work well and found his verses eminently quotable: the *Pilgrim* editors note that there are "over 30 allusions to Moore's poems and songs, mostly parodies, in CD's novels and sketches" (*Pilgrim*, 5, p 496, note 2). "Rich and Rare…" was included

in the First Number and reads as follows:

> Rich and rare were the gems she wore,
> And a bright gold ring on her wand she bore;
> But oh! her beauty was far beyond
> Her sparkling gems, or snow-white wand.

> "Lady! dost thou not fear to stray,
> So lone and lovely, through this bleak way?
> Are ERIN's sons so good or so cold,
> As not to be tempted by woman or gold?"

> "Sir Knight! I feel not the least alarm,
> No son of ERIN will offer me harm: –
> For though they love woman and golden store,
> Sir Knight! they love honour and virtue more!"

> On she went, and her maiden smile
> In safety lighted her round the green isle;
> And blest for ever is she who relied
> Upon ERIN's honour and ERIN's pride!

13. The Exeter Telegraph was a fast stage-coach that ran from London to Exeter. Dickens mentions it in a letter to his wife Catherine of 5 March 1839, written while he was staying at Exeter and suggesting that his mother might "come down ... by the Telegraph on Thursday Morning." "The fare inside is *Three Pounds* ... It goes from the Black Bear Piccadilly, just beyond the Burlington Arcade." (*Pilgrim*, 1, p 518.) The coach-lamps are "for ever extinguished" because the railway system had rendered the stage-coach obsolescent.

14. Dickens describes this experience in chapter 12 of *American Notes for General Circulation*, 1842.

15. Franconi's famous equestrian circus had been a main attraction in Paris since the early 19th century, when Antonio Franconi and his sons established their Cirque Olympique. In Dickens's time, the Franconi troupe gave performances during the summer at the Cirque des Champs-Élysées (carré Marigny), later renamed Cirque de l'Impératrice, and in winter at the Cirque Olympique, boulevard du Temple. The latter was transformed into a theater in 1847 and demolished in 1862. Meanwhile, however, the Cirque Napoléon, later (and still) known as the Cirque d'Hiver, had opened at the junction of the boulevards du Temple and des Filles-du-Calvaire in 1852 (Victor Franconi, grandson of Antonio, took over the running of the Cirque d'Hiver from Louis Dejean in 1870).

16. Recounted in chapter 1 of Daniel Defoe's *Robinson Crusoe*, 1719.
17. A lantern (so called because of the bull's-eye, the hemispherical or plano-convex glass, inserted in the side of the lantern).
18. The story of the Burghers of Calais is told by the historian Jean Froissart in his *Chroniques* (*c*1360–*c*1400). According to Froissart, after Calais had been under siege by the English for almost a year the citizens sought terms with the English King, Edward III. Edward agreed to pardon the inhabitants of the town provided that six of its principal citizens were sent out to him with bare heads and feet, ropes around their necks and the keys of the town and castle in their hands – their fate would be at his disposal. Six wealthy merchants of Calais volunteered and surrendered themselves to the English and probable execution. In the event, they were saved from death by the pleading of Edward's wife, Philippa of Hainault. The heroism of the six burghers is famously commemorated in Rodin's sculpture "Monument des Bourgeois de Calais," which depicts the men as they leave the town expecting to die – it currently stands outside the Hôtel de Ville in Calais.
19. "At high-water the steamer lands its passengers close to the Rly. Stat., which adjoins Calais Pier. When the tide is low the steamer is obliged to stop near the end of the pier ... and it becomes advisable to engage porters, or to hire a carriage to convey ladies and baggage to the Rly." (*A Handbook for Travellers on the Continent*, 1871.)
20. The Hôtel Dessin had been widely known as the best inn in Calais since the 18th century – Laurence Sterne cemented its fame when he featured it in *A Sentimental Journey through France and Italy*, 1768 (the room he slept in was subsequently marked "Sterne's Room"). With regard to the list of shouted hotel names that follows, the Hôtel Meurice in Calais had nothing to do with its famous namesake in Paris. On hotel touts, see note 3 under "Clennam in Calais," p 337.
21. A reference to the words of Queen Mary I spoken, as recorded in Holinshed's *Chronicles*, during her last illness to a lady-in-waiting: "... when I am dead and opened you shall find Calis lieng in my hart" (1808 edition, 4, p 137). Calais was lost to the French in 1558 after over two hundred years of English possession.
22. The official responsible for collecting *octroi* – the duty levied on various goods when entering a town.
23. From Trinculo's speech on stumbling upon Caliban in Shakespeare's *The Tempest* (2, 2): "... a very ancient and fish-like smell ..."
24. Dickens describes a journey through this region in "In the French-Flemish Country" (included in this volume).
25. In this context, humble taverns.
26. See note 17 under "A Flight," p 331.
27. A reference to Corporal Théophile and the child Bebelle in Dickens's

story "His Boots" (included in this volume).

28. Cf Dickens's recollections here with his description of such a fair in "In the French-Flemish Country": "Or, being French-Flemish man or woman, boy or girl, I might have circled all night on my hobby-horse, in a stately cavalcade of hobby-horses four abreast, interspersed with triumphal cars, going round and round and round and round, we the goodly company singing a ceaseless chorus to the music of the barrel-organ, drum, and cymbals." See also note 29 below.

29. Dickens is using the term "Richardson's" generically to describe the type of portable theater popularized by the itinerant showman John Richardson (1767?–1837). He provides an eye-witness account of Richardson's theater in his article "Greenwich Fair," 1835 (included in *Sketches by Boz*, 1836): "This immense booth, with the large stage in front, so brightly illuminated with variegated lamps, and pots of burning fat, is 'Richardson's', where you have a melodrama (with three murders and a ghost), a pantomime, a comic song, an overture, and some incidental music, all done in five and twenty minutes." Portable theaters, which varied from small and basic to large and luxurious, were popular throughout the 19th century.

With regard to the "Religious Richardson's" in "The Calais Night Mail," Slater and Drew (2000) draw attention to a letter to John Forster written from Arras on 7 February 1863 (Dickens's birthday). In the course of the letter, Dickens writes "Here too I found, in a by-country place just near, a Fair going on, with a Religious Richardson's in it – THÉÂTRE RELIGIEUX – 'donnant six fois par jour, l'histoire de la Croix en tableaux vivants, depuis la naissance de notre Seigneur jusqu'à son sépulture. Aussi l'immolation d'Isaac, par son père Abraham.' It was just before nightfall when I came upon it; and one of the three wise men was up to his eyes in lamp oil, hanging the moderators. A woman in blue and fleshings (whether an angel or Joseph's wife I don't know) was addressing the crowd through an enormous speaking-trumpet; and a very small boy with a property lamb (I leave you to judge who *he* was) was standing on his head on a barrel-organ." (*Life*, 8, Chapter 6.)

30. Short for moderator-lamp – "a lamp in which, by a mechanical contrivance, the passage of the oil from the reservoir to the burner is regulated or moderated to a uniform flow" (*Oxford English Dictionary*).

31. The journey continues in "Some Recollections of Mortality" (included in this volume).

Extract from *Little Dorrit* (Clennam in Calais), pp 33–36

1. See note 2 under "The Calais Night Mail," p 332.
2. See note 19 under "The Calais Night Mail," p 335. Clennam is less

fortunate than Dickens in "The Calais Night Mail" – this time the steamer enters Calais at low tide and the passengers have to walk the length of the pier – "nearly 3/4 m. long" according to *A Handbook for Travellers in France*, 1854 (the length of the "hand-to-hand scuffle" to which Clennam and his fellow travellers are subjected).

3. *A Handbook for Travellers on the Continent*, 1850, warns, "When the steamboat reaches its destined port, the shore is usually beset by a crowd of clamorous agents from the different hotels, each vociferating the name and praises of that for which he is employed, stunning the distracted stranger with their cries, and nearly scratching his face with their proffered cards." See also note 16 under "A Flight," p 331.

4. Calais was a popular refuge for English people who had run foul of the law (hence the earlier reference to "English outlaws") or were in financial difficulties of one kind or another. "The *walls* round the town, and the *pier* jutting out nearly 3/4 m. from the shore, are admirable promenades, and command a distinct view of the white cliffs of England, – a tantalizing sight to the English exiles, fugitives from creditors, or *compelled* from other causes to leave their homes – a numerous class both here and in Boulogne. There are many of our countrymen besides, who reside merely for the purpose of economising; so that the place is half Anglicised, and our language generally spoken." (*A Handbook for Travellers in France*, 1854.)

5. The debtors prison in the London borough of Southwark which features prominently in *Little Dorrit* and where Dickens's own father was imprisoned in 1824. The Marshalsea was closed in 1842.

"Travelling Abroad," pp 40–54

1. This carriage "of German make" seems to be modelled on the "English travelling-carriage of considerable proportions fresh from the shady halls of the Pantechnicon" that features in *Pictures from Italy*, 1846. Forster describes Dickens's acquisition of the carriage in 1844 in preparation for the family journey to Italy in July of that year: "... it occurred to him that he might perhaps get for little money 'some good old shabby devil of a coach – one of those vast phantoms that hide themselves in a corner of the Pantechnicon'; and exactly such a one he found there; sitting himself inside it, a perfect Sentimental Traveller, while the managing man told him its history." Dickens described the carriage to Forster as "... about the size of your library; with night-lamps and day-lamps and pockets and imperials and leathern cellars, and the most extraordinary contrivances." (*Life*, 4, Chapter 3.) On the Pantechnicon, see note 30 below.

2. Reflecting the Uncommercial Traveller persona and possibly also a deliberate echo of Sterne's comic categorization of travellers as

"Sentimental Traveller," "Inquisitive Traveller," "Vain Traveller," etc (*A Sentimental Journey through France and Italy*, 1768, "Preface in the Desobligeant").

3. Trunks or cases for luggage adapted for or fitted on carriage roofs.

4. The famous scene in Shakespeare's *King Henry IV, Part 1* (2, 2), in which Falstaff and his companions rob some travellers at Gad's Hill and then in turn are robbed by Prince Hal and Poins in disguise.

5. The very queer small boy's story is Dickens's own. The house in question is Gad's Hill Place, which Dickens purchased in 1856 and which remained his home until his death in 1870. Writing to W.H. Wills in February 1855 that he has seen that the house is for sale, he comments "... the spot and the very house are literally 'a dream of my childhood'..." (*Pilgrim*, 7, p 531). In a later account, to W.W.F. de Cerjat in January 1857, he writes "And my poor father used to bring me to look at it, and used to say that if ever I grew up to be clever man, perhaps I might own that house, or such another house" (*Pilgrim*, 8, p 266). As Slater and Drew (2000, p 84) note, the fact that Dickens saw fit to include a version of the anecdote in this essay suggests that it was sufficiently well known for a fair number of his readers to get the point. The very queer small boy's story itself, of course, gave it greater circulation. It was certainly no secret in the 1860s: Murray's *Handbook for Travellers in Kent and Sussex*, 1863, for example, explains that "A house of red brick, on the l. side of the hill, near the Falstaff Inn, and marked by some dark spreading cedars, is the country residence of Charles Dickens, Esq ... who is said, at a very early period of his career, to have fixed on this very house as his future home." Gad's Hill Place still stands (it is now a school).

6. The Old Dover Road, following the course of the Roman Watling Street and for centuries the London–Dover highway.

7. Song in *As You Like It* (2, 7).

8. An allusion to Shakespeare's portrayal of complaining carriers in an inn yard at Rochester in *King Henry IV, Part 1*(2, 1).

9. Cap Gris-Nez, a headland on the French coast and the nearest point to Dover.

10. See note 2 under "The Calais Night Mail," p 332.

11. Louis Roche, the courier who accompanied the Dickens family to Italy in 1844 and to Switzerland in 1846. Dickens thought very highly of him and often referred to him as "the brave courier." In a letter of July 1845 he describes Roche as "one of the most honest and excellent servants in the World" (*Pilgrim*, 4, p 326) and in *Pictures from Italy* he introduces him as the "best of servants and most beaming of men." Roche was taken ill in 1848 and died in 1849 – of heart disease according to Forster (*Life*, 5, Chapter 3). On the duties of couriers, see under "*Pictures from Italy* (Sens)," note 3, p 369.

12. Sterne's "poor Maria," an Ophelia-like character who has lost her senses along with her lover, is first discovered in a French village by Tristram Shandy (*The Life and Opinions of Tristram Shandy*, 1759–67, 9, Chapter 24) and reappears in *A Sentimental Journey through France and Italy*, 1768, when the narrator takes a detour to visit her. Unlike the "old French lunatic" here, Maria is beautiful and an object of sorrow and compassion.

13. Given that he is recalling a journey to Paris by coach, Dickens probably has in mind either the Hôtel Meurice, where he and his family stayed in July 1844 on their way to Italy (his first visit to Paris), or the Hôtel Brighton, where they stayed in November 1846 before moving into the house at 48 rue de Courcelles. Later, in the 1850s, he also stayed at the Wagram and Windsor hotels on the rue de Rivoli (and again at the Meurice).

14. The "old grey man" whom Dickens remembers here is probably the one he mentioned to Forster when describing a visit to the Morgue on 31 December 1846. "On the day that closed the old year," writes Forster, "he had gone into the Morgue and seen an old man with grey head lying there." In his letter to Forster Dickens wrote, "It seemed the strangest thing in the world that it should have been necessary to take any trouble to stop such a feeble, spent, exhausted morsel of life. It was just dusk when I went in; the place was empty; and he lay there, all alone, like an impersonation of the wintry eighteen hundred and forty-six..." (*Life*, 5, Chapter 7). That experience may also have informed the description of the "poor spare white-haired old man" in "Some Recollections of Mortality" (included in this volume).

The description of the "flaxen-haired boy" recalls both the corpse "with a bullet through the temple" and the "handsome youth" mentioned in "Railway Dreaming" (included in this volume).

In his account of the "large dark man," whose appearance so disturbs him, Dickens may be describing what it was that shocked him on one of his visits to the Morgue in 1846. According to Forster, "He went at first rather frequently to the Morgue, until shocked by something so repulsive that he had not courage for a long time to go back..." (*Life*, 5, chapter 7).

For more information on the Morgue, see the introduction to the chapter "A Flâneur in Paris," p 126.

15. A quack who performed tricks, juggling, etc, to attract his audience. Dickens describes other performers he has seen outside the Morgue in "Railway Dreaming."

16. When "Travelling Abroad" was written (and at the earlier time Dickens is writing about) the Morgue was on the quai du Marché-Neuf (Île de la Cité). Although there were other up-market river-bathing establishments in the vicinity, "the great floating bath" is probably the huge and luxurious Bains Deligny (an *école de natation* as well as a bathing

establishment) which was located close to the Pont de la Concorde by the quai d'Orsay. The Bains Deligny, originally built at the beginning of the 19th century, was reconstructed and redesigned with no expense spared in the 1840s. It rose in a new incarnation from the ashes of a fire in 1954 and survived until 1993 when a leak in one of the supporting barges ended its long history on the Seine.

In *Paris dans l'eau*, 1844, Eugène Briffault describes the then newly reconstructed Bains Deligny. A great floating rectangle, it was 105 metres long and 26 metres wide, enclosing a swimming area which was 89 metres long and 26 metres wide and divided into two sections by a diving bridge. The long galleries, on two floors, included among other things 340 individual changing rooms, six special rooms that were let by the year, seven large communal rooms, and a royal suite. The proprietors also provided a hairdressing salon, a pedicure salon, and various other amenities for the man about town. The café and socializing area, where the customers would relax, drink coffee, and smoke, as in the picture Dickens paints for us here, was in a large rotunda at one end of the baths. Briffault describes the décor of the Bains Deligny as combining "*avec beaucoup de goût le luxe, la légèreté et la fantaisie élégante, les teintes vives, les nuances variées et les découpures de l'architecture orientale.*" (See also note 21 under "A Flight," p 331.)

17. Dickens uses this spelling to convey the French appropriation of "box" in a letter to Forster of June 1846, in which he describes an argument at a roadside inn. He elaborates facetiously on the use of the word: "After various defiances on both sides, the landlord said 'Scélérat! Mécréant! Je vous boaxerai!' to which the voiturier replied, 'Aha! Comment dites-vous? Voulez-vous boaxer? Eh? Voulez-vous? Ah! Boaxez-moi donc! Boaxez-moi!' – at the same time accompanying these retorts with gestures of violent significance which explained that this new verb-active was founded on the well-known English verb to boax, or box. If they used it once, they used it at least a hundred times, and goaded each other to madness with it always." (*Life*, 5, Chapter 2.)

18. The shops in the arcades of the Palais Royal were ideal for window-shoppers. According to *Galignani's New Paris Guide* of 1844, "The shops, all on the ground floor, are among the most elegant in Paris, arranged with the greatest taste and neatness, and, being chiefly devoted to the sale of articles of luxury, produce a most brilliant effect. ... The best time for seeing this brilliant bazaar is in the evening, when the garden and arcades are brilliantly illuminated and full of people..." Murray's *Handbook for Visitors to Paris*, 1864, comments "How so many jewellers and watchmakers can find a living is a problem which may puzzle a stranger."

19. Strasbourg was famous for its *pâtés de foie gras*.

20. Soldiers were always plentiful in Strasbourg, a strongly fortified frontier

city. A large garrison was maintained there even in peacetime.

21. A cylindrical peaked military cap, topped with a plume or tuft.

22. Versions of the traditional nursery rhyme vary, notably in their characterization of the lady as either "fine" or "old." Dickens's description of her as "venerable" suggests that he has in mind the version in James Orchard Halliwell's 1842 collection, or something like it: "Ride a cock-horse to Banbury Cross,/To see an old lady upon a white horse,/Rings on her fingers, and bells on her toes,/And so she makes music wherever she goes." (*The Nursery Rhymes of England*, 1842).

23. Forster quotes Dickens's description of one of these contests at a country fête near Lausanne, which he attended, according to Forster, "in the third week after his arrival" in Switzerland in the summer of 1846: "Farther down the hill, other peasants were rifle-shooting for prizes, at targets set on the other side of a deep ravine, from two to three hundred yards off. It was quite fearful to see the astonishing accuracy of their aim, and how, every time a rifle awakened the ten thousand echoes of the green glen, some men crouching behind a little wall immediately in front of the targets, sprung up with large numbers in their hands, denoting where the ball had struck the bull's eye..." (*Life*, 5, Chapter 3).

24. An allusion to the legend of William Tell, said to have been a peasant in the canton of Uri in the early fourteenth century who resisted Austrian oppression and was taken prisoner. The tyrannical Austrian governor, Gessler (the double "s" is the usual spelling), promised Tell his liberty if he could hit an apple on the head of his son with his bow and arrow. Tell ultimately took his revenge on Gessler by shooting him through the heart in an ambush.

25. Dickens wrote to Forster in August 1846 about "...a Lord Vernon, who is well-informed, a great Italian scholar deep in Dante, and a very good-humoured gentleman, but who has fallen into the strange infatuation of attending every rifle-match that takes place in Switzerland, accompanied by two men who load rifles for him, one after another, which he has been frequently known to fire off, two a minute, for fourteen hours at a stretch, without once changing his position or leaving the ground. He wins all kinds of prizes; gold watches, flags, teaspoons, teaboards, and so forth; and is constantly travelling about with them, from place to place, in an extraordinary carriage..." (*Life*, 5, Chapter 4). This was George John Warren Vernon (1803–66), the fifth Baron Vernon, who lived for much of his life in Florence and studied Italian language and history. He published a scholarly three-volume edition of Dante's *Inferno* in 1858 for private circulation. He was also an "expert rifle shot" (*Dictionary of National Biography*).

26. An itinerant hawker – typically announcing arbitrary prices for his goods and then gradually reducing them.

27. "A trunk covered with skin retaining the hair" (*Oxford English Dictionary*).
28. The adventure on the wooden horse is described in Part 2, Chapter 41 of Miguel de Cervantes Saavedra's *Don Quixote*.
29. Flogged with a 'knout,' a scourge that was used in Russia, often with fatal effect.
30. Described by Peter Cunningham as "a large bazaar and carriage and furniture repository" (*Hand-Book of London*, 1850), the Pantechnicon was in Motcomb Street, near Belgrave Square in London. Built in 1830, it comprised around two acres of warehouses, carriage houses, stables, and wine vaults (Weinreb and Hibbert, 1993). "The building is well ventilated, and considered fire-proof;" writes Cunningham, "but the risk (if any) of accidents by fire, civil commotion, or otherwise, will attach to the owners of the property sent to the Pantechnicon to be warehoused." Wise precautionary words – the building and its contents were destroyed by fire in 1874.

"Our French Watering-Place," (pp 60–76)

1. Broadstairs in Kent, where Dickens and his family spent many summer holidays between 1837 and 1851. He bid, in Forster's words "a pleasant adieu" (*Life*, 6, Chapter 6) to Broadstairs in the essay "Our Watering Place" published in *Household Words* on 2 August 1851 (entitled "Our English Watering-Place" in *Reprinted Pieces*).
2. The abattoir, built in 1838, was in the rue du Faubourg de Brequerecque on the outskirts of the town (Brunet, 1862). It was situated in the section of the road that is now known as the avenue John Kennedy, which runs into the rue de Brequerecque (Service des Archives Municipales de la Mairie de Boulogne-sur-Mer, personal communication, 2003). The rest of the "long road" comprised the rue Royale (now rue Nationale) and the rue de l'Écu (now rue Victor Hugo).
3. See note 18 under "A Flight," p 331. The *coupé* was the front section of the *diligence*. *A Handbook for Travellers in France*, 1854, describes it as "shaped like a chariot or post-chaise, holding 3 persons, quite distinct from the rest of the passengers, so that the ladies may resort to it without inconvenience, and, by securing all 3 places to themselves, travel nearly as comfortably as in a private carriage. The fare is more expensive than in other parts of the vehicle."
4. See note 2 under "The Calais Night Mail," p 332.
5. See note 16 under "A Flight," p 331.
6. Slater (1998) identifies an allusion to Coleridge's "Kubla Khan," 1816: "And all should cry, Beware! Beware!/His flashing eyes, his floating hair!"
7. La Ville Haute, the old town of Boulogne, is enclosed by ramparts that

date from the 13th century (the fortifications were strengthened in the 16th and 17th centuries).

8. The belfry, behind the Hôtel de Ville, dates from the 13th century.

9. "Bilkins" is a fictitious name, used here to denote the pompous and opinionated kind of travel writer who sets himself up as an arbiter of taste and presents his subjective enthusiasms and preferences as authoritative judgements.

10. "The *Remparts* form an airy and agreeable walk, running uninterruptedly round the town, and commanding views in all directions, over the sea and port, and over the high ground to the E. ... and along the roads to Calais and Paris." (*A Handbook for Travellers in France*, 1854.)

11. Presumably the red ribbon accompanying the badge of the Légion d'honneur, the non-hereditary order instituted by Napoléon to recognize military and civilian merit. Boulogne has a particular association with the honour: the first distribution ceremony was held in July 1804 in Paris and the second in August in Boulogne, where Napoléon kept a large army encampment as part of his preparations to invade England. The occasion is commemorated by the Stèle de la Légion d'honneur, reputedly on the site of the throne used by Napoléon for the ceremony, in the vallon de Terlincthun.

12. The main square of the Haute Ville (now place Godefroy de Bouillon). Dickens's account of the various markets in this paragraph is consistent with that of Brunet, who mentions, for example, the "corn market in the Upper Town" and the "rag and second-hand clothes market at the top of the Grande Rue" (*New Guide to Boulogne-sur-Mer and its Environs*, 1862).

13. St-Nicolas in place Dalton, at the lower end of the Grande Rue, where there is still a market twice a week.

14. The old man is a *marchand de coco. Coco*, a licorice-based drink, was sold by street vendors in France throughout the nineteenth century. An example of the temple-like piece of equipment that the *marchands de coco* used to carry and dispense their drink is on display at the Carnavalet museum in Paris.

15. As is evident from the vivid description that follows, Dickens was much taken with the fishing people of Boulogne and their *quartier*. He praises them several times in his correspondence, commenting, for example, in a letter to Forster of 13 June 1853, "As to the fishing people (whose dress can have changed neither in colour nor in form for many many years), and their quarter of the town cobweb-hung with great brown nets across the narrow up-hill streets, they are as good as Naples, every bit." (*Life*, 7, Chapter 4.)

According to *A Handbook for Travellers in France*, 1854, "Almost all the 1300 vessels belonging to Boulogne are engaged in fishery, and the arrival and departure of the boats collects a crowd of fishermen and fisherwives in their singular and picturesque costume. ... These people occupy a distinct quarter of the town on the N. side of the harbour, the streets of which are draped with nets hung out from the fronts of the houses to dry, and in dress and manner they are distinct from the rest of the inhabitants, speaking a peculiar patois, and rarely intermarrying with the other townsfolk."

The *quartier* of Saint Pierre, where the fishing people lived, was destroyed by the bombardments of the Second World War.

16. In Roman mythology, the wife and sister of Jupiter and queen of the gods.

17. Street dwellers or vagabonds – they were so common in Naples in the nineteenth century that the city became associated with them.

18. Dickens was in Naples in November 1853. He had earlier expressed his feelings about the city in the "A Rapid Diorama" chapter of *Pictures from Italy*, pointing up the contrast between the romance and beauty of Naples and its squalor, poverty, and corruption, the latter set of characteristics often ignored by tourists and writers of the Bilkins persuasion: "But, lovers and hunters of the picturesque, let us not keep too studiously out of view the miserable depravity, degradation, and wretchedness, with which this gay Neapolitan life is inseparably associated! It is not well to find St Giles's so repulsive, and the Porta Capuana so attractive."

The favourable comparison of the picturesque qualities of under-praised Boulogne with those of over-praised Naples clearly struck Dickens forcibly. He wrote to Forster about it in June 1853 (see note 15 above). A month earlier he had mentioned it to W. J. Clement, writing that "odd bits" of Boulogne "are as picturesque as Naples – and it is thriving and industrious, and not like that horribly degraded place otherwise" (*Pilgrim*, 7, p 89). And he told Hablot Knight Browne in a letter of 29 June 1853 that Boulogne was "a very capital place, with quite as much that is quaint and picturesque among the fishing-people and their quarter of the Town, as is to be found (if you'll believe me in a whisper) at Naples" (*Pilgrim*, 7, p 107).

19. Based on Ferdinand Beaucourt-Mutuel (1805–81) – see introduction, p 58. Dickens makes it plain in several letters that the description of Loyal is a true-to-life picture of Beaucourt: for example, "I wish you would read, in next week's No. of Household Words, an article called Our French Watering Place (with a portrait of my Boulogne landlord)..." (to Miss Burdett Coutts, 26 October 1854, *Pilgrim*, 7, p 444). See the introduction for other relevant quotations.

20. Le Château des Moulineaux, rue de Beaurepaire, described by Forster as "a house on the high ground near the Calais Road; an odd French place with the strangest little rooms and halls, but standing in the midst of a large garden, with wood and waterfall, a conservatory opening on a great bank of roses, and paths and gates on one side to the ramparts, on the

other to the sea" (*Life*, 7, Chapter 4). Dickens describes it in detail in a letter to Forster of 26 June 1853. "This house," he writes, "is on a great hill-side, backed up by woods of young trees. It faces the Haute Ville with the ramparts and the unfinished cathedral – which capital object is exactly opposite the windows. On the slope in front, going steep down to the right, all Boulogne is piled and jumbled about in a very picturesque manner. The view is charming – closed in at last by the tops of swelling hills; and the door is within ten minutes of the post office and within quarter of an hour of the sea." (*Life*, 7, Chapter 4.) See note 27 below for details of the second of Monsieur Beaucourt's/Loyal's holiday villas.

21. In one of his greatest victories, Napoléon defeated the combined Russian and Austrian armies at the Battle of Austerlitz, 2 December 1805.

22. The veteran regiments of Napoléon's famous Imperial Guard. Fiercely loyal, the Imperial Guard resisted to the end at Waterloo.

23. The Garde Nationale was originally formed in 1789 as a volunteer citizens' militia tasked with keeping order (it temporarily became a compulsory armed force in 1793). It was revived periodically in the 19th century until 1871, when it ceased to exist. Beaucourt served for a time as a Captain in the Fourth Company, Second Battalion of the Garde Nationale de Boulogne. When the workers' insurrection of June 1848 broke out in Paris (the "*journées de juin*"), he volunteered for a detachment that left Boulogne on 25 June to help the forces of General Cavaignac crush the uprising. The detachment arrived in the city too late to see action, but it took part in a military review held by Cavaignac on the Champs-Élysées and in the place de la Concorde. (Watrin, 1992; Lottin, 1983.) Beaucourt obviously told his tenant about the experience, which Dickens relates to Forster in a letter of 3 July 1853: "He was a captain in the National Guard, and Cavaignac his general. Brave Capitaine Beaucourt! said Cavaignac, you must receive a decoration. My General, said Beaucourt, No! It is enough for me that I have done my duty. I go to lay the first stone of a house upon a Property I have – that house shall be my decoration." (*Life*, 7, Chapter 4.)

24. The French equivalent of a "castle in the air" is a "château en Espagne."

25. Dickens tells Forster in a letter of 26 June 1853 that Beaucourt was "a linen draper in the town, where he still has a shop, but is supposed to have mortgaged his business and to be in difficulties – all along of this place..." (*Life*, 7, Chapter 4).

26. Fulham, now a built-up area of south-west London, was at the time of Monsieur Beaucourt's/Loyal's visit, a village famous for its market gardens and nurseries. Dickens tells the story of Beaucourt's English adventure much as he tells it here in a letter to Forster of 3 July 1853 (*Life*, 7, Chapter 4).

27. That is, the summer of 1854, during which the Dickens family stayed at

the second residence for visitors on Monsieur Beaucourt's "property," the Villa du Camp de Droite. This was at the top of the hill (see note 19 above), with a private path that led out to the Colonne de la Grande Armée (commemorating the assembly of Napoléon's forces at Boulogne for the intended invasion of England). Forster describes the house as "a really pretty place, rooms larger than in the other house, a noble sea view, and plenty of sloping turf" (*Life*, 7, Chapter 4).

This was the time of the Crimean War, with France and Britain joining forces against Russia. The formation of the Camp du Nord just outside Boulogne began in June 1854, as Napoléon III assembled his expeditionary forces and reserves for the Baltic campaign – hence the billeting of soldiers. In a letter to Wilkie Collins of 12 July 1854, Dickens writes, "About 150 soldiers have been at various times billeted on Beaucourt since we have been here – and he has clinked glasses with them every one..." (*Pilgrim*, 7, p 367).

28. Beaucourt was a Conseiller Municipal in Boulogne from 1849 to 1860 (Watrin, 1992, p 19).

29. "Half and half," a mixture of two different malt liquors in equal quantities – such as ale and porter.

30. Ratcliff (usually spelled without the 'e') is on the north bank of the Thames in the East End of London. In the nineteenth century it was a poor and heavily populated area with a bad reputation. It would have been anything but a comfortable part of town for a stranger at night. Ratcliff also had macabre associations because of the notorious Ratcliff Highway murders of December 1811, which claimed seven victims.

31. A horse-drawn changing room on wheels, which took the bather into the sea.

32. "On one side of the harbour, on the margin of a fine sandy beach, is the *Etablissement des Bains*, a showy building, fronted with colonnades, containing subscription, ball, and reading rooms. In front is drawn up in long array a number of genuine bathing machines (voitures baignoires), to be found in very few places in France." (*A Handbook for Travellers in France*, 1854.)

33. A play on the name of the real-life Monsieur Sauvage, proprietor of a private bathing-machine business and a brave *sauveteur* (Watrin, 1992, p 113).

34. The theater in the rue Monsigny was destroyed by a fire in 1854 (it was later rebuilt). Dickens was in a nearby street when the fire broke out and saw the whole thing. He gives his eye-witness account of the conflagration and the failed attempts to extinguish it in a letter to Wilkie Collins of 26 September 1854 (*Pilgrim*, 7, p 424). He describes a visit to the "beautiful little theatre, with a very good company" in letters to Forster and Macready of 24 July 1853 (*Pilgrim*, 7, pp 118, 119).

35. In this context, a light stage play interspersed with songs.
36. "The Société de Bienfaisance give, at least once a fortnight, either in the square of the Tintelleries, which has been laid out into charming gardens, or in the avenue of the same name, fêtes in the day for children, and in the evening, balls for the public with splendid illuminations and brilliant fireworks." (*Boulogne-sur-Mer, Bathing Town and Ville de Plaisance*, 1857.) "Almost every Sunday we have a fête," Dickens wrote to Forster in 1853, "where there is dancing in the open air, and where immense men with prodigious beards revolve on little wooden horses like Italian irons, in what we islanders call a round-about, by the hour together. But really the good humour and cheerfulness are very delightful." (*Life*, 7, Chapter 4.) According to Brunet (1862), the Société de Bienfaisance was founded in 1850 "to procure employment to poor workmen."
37. This alludes to the fact that the fêtes were held on Sunday (as noted by Dickens in a letter to Forster, 24 July 1853, *Pilgrim*, 7, p 118, and by Brunet in his *New Guide to Boulogne-sur-Mer and Its Environs*, 1862: "The village festivals ... take place periodically every year, but always on Sundays and continue on Mondays."). The aside is tongue-in-cheek – Dickens was a vigorous opponent of Sabbatarianism (see note 14 under "In the French-Flemish Country," p 349).
38. A *ducasse*, in the regional dialect of Northern France and Belgium, is the word for a fête, usually a *fête patronale*.
39. Sir Richard Owen (1804–92), the celebrated English naturalist and anatomist.
40. According to *A Handbook for Travellers in France*, 1854, at least 7,000 of the 29,145 inhabitants of Boulogne were permanent English residents. Describing Boulogne as "one of the chief British colonies abroad," the *Handbook* notes, "The town is enriched by English money; warmed, lighted, and smoked by English coal; English signs and advertisements decorate every other shop-door, inn, tavern, and lodging-house; and almost every third person you meet is either a countryman or speaking our language..." Dickens was often critical of the English abroad and showed no inclination to mingle with them. Aside from the "bores" whose picture he paints here, in a letter to Forster of 1856 he describes how, visiting the pier in the evening, he felt ashamed of the vulgarity of the English people he saw there: "But I never did behold such specimens of the youth of my country, male and female, as pervade that place. They are really, in their vulgarity and insolence, quite disheartening. One is so fearfully ashamed of them, and they contrast so very unfavourably with the natives." (*Life*, 7, Chapter 4.)
41. Probably Merridew, on the rue de l'Écu (now rue Victor Hugo), where there was an English reading-room and circulating library.
42. Dickens mentions the use of "mingle" for "mangle" in a letter to Mark

Lemon of 15 June 1856, noting "I observe more Mingles in the laundresses' shops, and one inscription, which looks like the name of a duet or chorus in a playbill, 'Here they mingle.'" (*Pilgrim*, 8, p 136). "Nokemdon" is a corruption of "knock-'em-down," in which the targets to be knocked down are coconuts or suchlike mounted on sticks.

"In the French-Flemish Country," pp 81–93

1. The *départements* of France are subdivided into administrative districts or *arrondissements*. At the time Dickens was writing, there were seven *arrondissements* in the Département du Nord, each named after its principal town. The *préfecture*, or seat of the departmental administration, was (and is) Lille. The other six *arrondissements* were Avesnes, Cambrai, Douai, Dunkerque, Hazebrouck, and Valenciennes. The present-day Département du Nord has six *arrondissements* in total – all the above with the exception of Hazebrouck.
2. In this context, a light stage play interspersed with songs.
3. An allusion to the American Civil War (1861–65), which was in progress when this article was written. The word "irrepressible" had become inextricably linked with the war thanks to a speech in 1858 by Senator William Henry Seward, a committed opponent of slavery. Seward referred to an "irrepressible conflict" between the opposing systems of free labor and slavery, and the term became a catchphrase of the anti-slavery movement. Undoubtedly deriving from this, the phrase "irrepressible negro" or "irrepressible nigger" was frequently used during the war years.
4. That is, checking tickets. "Check" could refer to the leaving of cloaks and bags, etc, at a cloakroom, or to the ticket or token issued as verification of payment and for readmission to the performance – both senses were current in the nineteenth century – but here it is almost certainly the latter.
5. A fairground version of the medieval military exercise of tilting at a target, often with a sandbag attached which would swing round and strike the inaccurate tilter.
6. In "The Calais Night Mail" Dickens recalls a visit to a fair at Hazebrouck "where the oldest inhabitants were circling round and round a barrel-organ on hobby-horses, with the greatest gravity." As Slater and Drew (2002, p 297) point out, this puts Hazebrouck on the list of possible candidates for the unnamed town in "In the French-Flemish Country." Provincial fairs, however, were far from rare, hobby-horses were a standard attraction, and there is no other similarity in the descriptions, so Hazebrouck remains simply one of several possibilities.
7. The Ring, a two-way enclosed carriage drive around Hyde Park, was the most fashionable promenade in London from the 1660s until the 1730s,

when it gave place to Rotten Row (Imwood, 1998, p 316). London's wealthiest families would display their splendid equipages by driving them round and round the enclosure, making it the place to see and be seen. The Ring was partially destroyed in the reign of George II when the Serpentine was formed by order of Queen Caroline and in subsequent periods the carriage drives and walks were considerably extended. Hyde Park remained the parade ground of choice for followers of fashion all through the nineteenth century, although the most favored area of the park changed frequently. According to *Dickens's Dictionary of London*, 1888, "For two or three hours every afternoon in the season, except Sunday, the particular section of the drive which happens that year to be 'the fashion' is densely thronged with carriages moving round and round at little more than a walking pace, and every now and then coming to a dead-lock."

8. The imperial eagle was the emblem of France under the First (1804–14) and Second (1852–70) Empires.

9. "A lamp in which, by a mechanical contrivance, the passage of the oil from the reservoir to the burner is regulated or moderated to a uniform flow." (*Oxford English Dictionary.*)

10. Faubourg St Germain (the sixth and seventh *arrondissements* of Paris) was home to the old aristocracy.

11. War-disabled or retired soldiers accommodated at the Hôtel des Invalides in Paris.

12. Napoléon Bonaparte.

13. France was at war with Mexico, ostensibly because of non-repayment of debt, from late 1861 until 1864, when Napoléon installed Archduke Maximilian of Austria as emperor. Maximilian ruled under French protection until 1867, when Napoléon withdrew his forces and the Mexican adventure thus ended ignominiously (Maximilian was executed in 1867). The Crimean War, which Dickens also mentions here, ended in 1855.

14. This is a tongue-in-cheek remark, indicating that the ball took place on a Sunday. Dickens makes a similar comment in "Our French Watering-Place" (see note 37 for that article, p 347). Throughout his career he was an outspoken opponent of Sabbatarianism and of the various attempts by its supporters, typically middle-class evangelical Anglicans, to enact legislation prohibiting most activities on a Sunday, including public entertainment. There were strong feelings on either side of the debate and, always heated, it was fuelled in the 1850s by the introduction of various bills to increase the already considerable restrictions on Sunday activities. Although many of the proposals did not pass into law, the Sabbatarians scored some successes (including the ending of Sunday postal deliveries – a measure that was rapidly revised following the

inconvenience it caused – and further restrictions on Sunday opening hours for public houses). In 1855 there were mass demonstrations in Hyde Park against a bill to prohibit most Sunday trading in London – the bill failed but the controversy continued.

Dickens's central objection to Sabbatarianism concerned its impact on the working class. In a speech of 27 June 1855, with the Sunday Trading Bill in mind, he referred to "bills which cramp and worry the people, and restrict their scant enjoyments" (Fielding, 1988, p 202). He was outraged by the notion that hard-working people should be restricted from enjoying themselves as they pleased on the one day in the week when they were able to relax – something that he clearly delights in witnessing in "In the French-Flemish Country" and "Our French Watering-Place." His writings on the subject include the early and outspoken essay *Sunday Under Three Heads*, 1836, and Book 1, Chapter 3 of *Little Dorrit* ("Home"), a masterly description of the miseries of Sunday under the constraints of Sabbatarianism.

15. Presumably because the observance of Sunday was especially strict in Scotland, with its powerful Presbyterian tradition.

16. Whitechapel, a traditionally poor quarter in the East End of London, lent its name to a variety of ironic expressions that played on the area's lowly reputation. For example, a "Whitechapel fortune" was "a clean gown and pair of pattens" (*A Dictionary of Slang, Jargon & Cant*, 1897) and a "Whitechapel brougham" was a costermonger's barrow (*The Slang Dictionary*, 1869). Thus the idea behind a "Whitechapel shave" is that it substitutes for the expense of getting a proper shave at the barbershop.

17. In this context, a humble tavern.

18. A traditional character in French Pantomime, Pierrot was a clown dressed in loose white clothes and with a whitened face.

19. The conscripts were presumably on their way to the Camp de Châlons, established by Napoléon III at Châlons-sur-Marne (now called Châlons-en-Champagne). This huge training camp was opened in August 1857 and was famous until the end of the Second Empire, receiving frequent and widely reported visits from the Emperor. It accommodated some 20,000 men in its opening year (*The Times*, 16 September 1857) and was linked by rail to the Paris–Strasbourg line (*The Times*, 18 September 1857, records the opening of the branch line). Apart from its function as a training ground, the Châlons camp was also a showcase for the imperial forces and attracted large numbers of civilian visitors.

After a period of abandonment at the end of the Second Empire the camp was put back into use – in its current incarnation it is known as the Camp de Mourmelon.

20. A cylindrical peaked military cap, topped with a plume or tuft.

"His Boots," pp 99–120

1. Recalling, and presumably based on, Ferdinand Beaucourt-Mutuel, Dickens's landlord in Boulogne in the 1850s (portrayed as Monsieur Loyal-Devasseur in "Our French Watering-Place") and in nearby Condette in the 1860s – see p 58. For readers interested in such matters, in his article "Bebelle and 'His Boots': Dickens, Ellen Ternan and the *Christmas Stories*," John Bowen (2000) speculates that the inclusion of Beaucourt-Mutuel in "His Boots" may offer clues as to what was going on in Dickens's private life in the early 1860s. Whether or not that is the case it is clear, from the descriptions of him in "Our French Watering-Place" and in the correspondence, that Beaucourt-Mutuel would readily have occurred to Dickens as a natural embodiment of the values celebrated in the story, and this would seem to be the obvious and primary explanation for his appearance in it.
2. The red ribbon, also worn by one of the three old men described in "Our French Watering-Place," is presumably the red ribbon accompanying the badge of the Légion d'honneur – see note 11 under "Our French Watering-Place," p 343.
3. An allusion to the popular song "The Snug Little Island" by Thomas John Dibdin (1771–1841), son of Charles Dibdin. The song, first performed at Sadler's Wells in 1797 (*Dictionary of National Biography*), includes the lines "O, it's a snug little Island!/A right little, tight little Island!" and "We'd show 'em some play for the Island./We'd fight for our right to the Island" (*The Book of English Songs*, 1851).
4. A stiff, close-fitting neckcloth. The Victorian soldier's stock was made of leather, which must have been especially uncomfortable.
5. This comparison of the organization, training, and versatility of the French and British armies to the considerable disadvantage of the latter reflects a view expressed by Dickens in a letter to Mrs Brown of 24 October 1862. Writing of his travels in France that year he tells her, "Of the daily lives and exercises of the soldiers I have seen a great deal, in the out-of-the-way fortified towns where such things are the only business. In all respects of sensible training and an admirable adaptation of the men to the purposes and the purposes to the men, I believe this army, as compared with ours, advances 50 years in every year we live." (*Pilgrim*, 10, p 149.)
6. The military engineer Sébastien Le Prestre Vauban (1633–1707). See note 17 under "A Flight," p 331.
7. Loose trousers gathered closely at their lowest point, in this case around the center of the calf.
8. In this context, a charlatan.
9. Salvers, small trays.

10. That is, *octroi* – the duty levied on various articles when entering a town.
11. From John, 9:4: "I must work the works of him that sent me, while it is day: the night cometh, when no man can work."

Extract from *Pictures from Italy* (Paris on Sunday Morning), p 130

1. From 1804 to 1864 the Morgue was on the quai du Marché-Neuf, on the Île de la Cité.
2. We are told in the opening paragraph of the "Going through France" chapter of *Pictures from Italy* that Dickens and family had started out from the Hôtel Meurice, rue de Rivoli. Their carriage has therefore crossed the Pont Neuf from the Right to the Left Bank, so "across the River" here refers to the Right Bank. This visit (1844) was well before the *Haussmannisation* of Paris (see note 5 under "Some Recollections of Mortality," p 358), during which most of these "funnel-like streets" disappeared.

"Railway Dreaming," pp 131–139

1. Dickens lived in Paris during the winter of 1855–56. From October 1855 until the end of April 1856 he and his family stayed at 49 avenue des Champs-Élysées (although he mentions a beautiful May morning in Paris, he in fact left the city on 29 April).
2. Beer brewed in the winter using malts and hops from the last harvest.
3. Presumably the Mooninian name for the Café de Paris, one of the famous cafés on the boulevard des Italiens (it closed in October 1856).
4. An allusion to Herod's slaying of the innocents, the babies in and around Bethlehem, recounted in Matthew, 2:16.
5. A halo.
6. The pursuit of wealth and pleasure was especially intense during the Second Empire, fuelled by industrial and commercial progress and by the resplendent example of its glamorous high society. As Dickens describes in this paragraph, Paris was in the grip of speculation fever, with fortunes routinely made and lost and people living the high life while they could, on less than solid financial foundations.

   At a dinner given by the wealthy journalist and press entrepreneur Émile de Girardin (1806–81), Dickens met a product of this get-rich-quick culture. "A little man who dined," he wrote to Forster, "was blacking shoes 8 years ago, and is now enormously rich – the richest man in Paris – having ascended with rapidity up the usual ladder of the Bourse. By merely observing that perhaps he might come down again, I clouded so many faces as to render it very clear to me that *everybody present* was at the same game for some stake or other!" (*Life*, 7, Chapter 5.)

The description of speculation fever in "Railway Dreaming" resembles that in another letter to Forster of April 1856: "If you were to see the steps of the Bourse at about 4 in the afternoon, and the crowd of blouses and patches among the spectators there assembled, all howling and haggard with speculation, you would stand aghast at the consideration of what must be going on. Concierges and people like that perpetually blow their brains out, or fly into the Seine, 'à cause des pertes sur la Bourse.' I hardly ever take up a French paper without lighting on such a paragraph. On the other hand, thoroughbred horses without end, and red velvet carriages with white kid harness on jet black horses, go by here all day long; and the pedestrians who turn to look at them, laugh, and say 'C'est la Bourse!'" (*Life*, 7, Chapter 5.)

7. The avenue des Champs-Élysées. The Champs-Élysées came into its own during the Second Empire (1852–70) as one of the wealthiest and most fashionable parts of Paris.

8. That is, the carriages of the Emperor and Empress and their entourage – Dickens is struck by the lack of public acknowledgement of them as they pass by. The official residence of Napoléon III was the Palais des Tuileries and his carriage would have been a common enough sight on the nearby Champs-Élysées. In his description of Dickens's apartment, Forster notes that "... all Paris, including Emperor and Empress coming from and returning to [the Palais de] St Cloud, thronged past the windows in open carriages or on horseback, all day long." (*Life*, 7, Chapter 5.)

9. The virtuous farmer or rustic was a familiar character in English comedies of the late 18th and early 19th centuries – examples include Farmer Harrowby in *The Poor Gentleman* (1801) and Zekiel Homespun in *The Heir at Law* (1797), both by George Colman (the younger), and Farmer Ashfield in Thomas Morton's *Speed the Plough* (1798). Dickens's quotation bears similarities in sentiment and to a lesser extent in style to a speech in Act 3, Scene 3 of *Speed the Plough*, in which Ashfield refuses to be bribed into a wrongful action by Sir Philip Blandford ("... I'll never hit thic hand against here, but when I be zure that zomeit at inzide will jump against it with pleasure. I do hope you'll repent of all your zins – I do indeed, Zur..."). Dickens may have this scene in mind, or may be quoting directly from another example of the genre that the editor has been unable to identify.

10. The Strand was, and is, a busy thoroughfare in London lined with shops, theaters, and restaurants. About three-quarters of a mile long, it runs from Charing Cross to Fleet Street and so links the West End with the City. Somerset House is located towards the City end of the street and was in Dickens's time largely given over to government offices (it is now best known as the home of the Courtauld Institute of Art).

11. A *marchand de coco* (see note 14, "Our French Watering-Place," p 343).

12. Presumably the Cirque Napoléon, which was open from 1 November to 30 April (see note 15 under "The Calais Night Mail," p 334). Dickens mentions it in a letter of 16 February 1855 to Georgina Hogarth: "There is a winter Franconi's now, high up on the Boulevards, just like the round theatre on the Champs Elysées, and as bright and beautiful." (*Pilgrim*, 7, p 541.)

13. Dickens was understandably less than impressed by the custom of holding coroners' inquests in public houses, as convenient places to gather together juries and witnesses. He describes such an inquest in detail in chapter 11 of *Bleak House*, 1852–53. ("The Coroner frequents more public-houses than any man alive. The smell of sawdust, beer, tobacco-smoke, and spirits, is inseparable in his vocation from death in its most awful shapes.")

14. See introduction, p 126.

15. The German artist Hans Holbein the Younger (1497/8–1543). Dickens refers here to Holbein's famous series of woodcuts illustrating *The Dance of Death*, dating from the 1520s and published in Lyon in 1538.

16. A major shopping street in the West End of London, Regent Street was a center of fashion in the nineteenth century. It was characterized by large stores with enough space for expansive window displays.

17. Forster, writing of Dickens's visit to Paris in 1846, reports that "... he had noticed the keeper smoking a short pipe at his little window, and 'giving a bit of fresh turf to a linnet in a cage'" (*Life*, 5, Chapter 7).

18. From 1804 to 1864 the Morgue was on the quai du Marché-Neuf, a short distance from Notre-Dame.

19. Quacks who performed tricks, juggling, etc, to attract an audience.

20. Clown or juggler, traditionally dressed in a costume of blue and white check.

21. See note 14 under "Travelling Abroad," p 339.

22. Émile Zola identifies a similar variety of visitors to the Morgue in chapter 13 of Thérèse Raquin, 1867: "Des ouvriers entraient, en allant à leur ouvrage, avec un pain et des outils sous le bras [...] Puis venaient des petits rentiers, des vieillards maigres et sec, des flâneurs qui entraient par désoeuvrement [...] Les femmes étaient en grand nombre; il y avait de jeunes ouvrières toutes roses, le linge blanc, les jupes propres, qui allaient d'un bout à l'autre du vitrage, lestement, en ouvrant de grands yeux attentifs, comme devant l'étalage d'un magasin de nouveautés; il y avait encore des femmes du peuple, hébétées, prenant des airs lamentables, et des dames bien mises, traînant nonchalamment leur robe de soie [...] Par moments, arrivaient des bandes de gamins, des enfants de douze à quinze ans, qui couraient le long du vitrage, ne s'arrêtant que devant les cadavres de femmes." ("Workmen came in on their way to work, with their bread and tools under their arms [...] Then there were shabby genteel types,

wasted and dry old people and flâneurs who wandered in for want of something better to do and who looked at the corpses with the foolish, weak eyes of mild and sensitive men. Women were there in great numbers; there were young, rosy-cheeked working women in white linen and clean skirts, who walked nimbly from one end of the window to the other, their sharp eyes wide open as if they were walking past the window display of a fashionable clothes shop; then again there were poor women, looking stupefied and pathetic, and elegant ladies whose silk dresses trailed casually along the ground [...] Every now and then gangs of young boys would turn up, kids of twelve to fifteen, and they would run the length of the widow, pausing only in front of the corpses of women.")

23. See the description from *A Handbook for Visitors to Paris* quoted in the introduction, p 126.

24. See, for example, note 20 under "A Flight," p 331. In the "Paris upon Wheels" chapter of his *Imperial Paris*, 1855, W. Blanchard Jerrold goes into entertaining detail on the apprenticeship and management of cab drivers in Paris. He stresses the exacting street knowledge requirements, the strict policing, and the rigorously enforced cleanliness and comfort of the cabs. Contrasting the leisurely pace of Parisian cabs with the uncomfortable hurry of their London counterparts, he concludes, "The Englishman is always eager to arrive at his destination, and would travel in a coal-box to save five minutes; whereas the Frenchman, provided the cushions are soft, and the cigar a tolerable one, is not particular as to the hour at which he may reach his journey's end."

25. A response that Dickens was later to put into the mouth of Mr Podsnap, his withering portrayal of the bourgeois and narrow-minded Little Englander in *Our Mutual Friend*, 1864–65. When a mild-mannered dinner guest suggests that something must be wrong somewhere because so many people are dying of starvation in the streets, Podsnap thunders, "Easy to say somewhere; not so easy to say where! But I see what you are driving at. I knew it from the first. Centralization. No. Never with my consent. Not English." (*Our Mutual Friend*, Book 1, Chapter 11.)

26. Dickens famously associated this word with the inefficiencies of the British administrative system in his satirical creation of the Circumlocution Office in *Little Dorrit*, 1855–57.

"New Year's Day," pp 141–145

1. That is, the line of the Grands Boulevards, from the boulevard de la Madeleine to the boulevard du Temple. See also note 2 below.

2. The French tradition of New Year's Day gifts (*étrennes*) struck Dickens forcibly during his stay in Paris in the winter of 1855–56. Forster writes, "It was the festival time of the New Year, and Dickens was fairly lost in a

mystery of amazement at where the money could come from that everybody was spending on the étrennes they were giving to everybody else. All the famous shops on the Boulevards had been blocked for more than a week." Dickens also wrote to Forster of the huge festive "fair" he describes here: "There is now a line of wooden stalls, three miles long, on each side of that immense thoroughfare; and wherever a retiring house or two admits of a double line, there it is. All sorts of objects from shoes and sabots, through porcelain and crystal, up to live fowls and rabbits which are played for at a sort of dwarf skittles ... are on sale in this great Fair." (*Life*, 7, Chapter 5.)

The play on 'Universe' (*univers*) may include an allusion to the Exposition Universelle, which was held in Paris in 1855.

3. A play on *restaurateurs*.

4. The Théâtre des Variétés (boulevard Montmartre), the Théâtre du Vaudeville (place de la Bourse) and the Théâtre du Palais Royal (north-western corner of the Palais Royal) all specialized in vaudevilles and farces. The Théâtres des Variétés and du Palais Royal exist today. The Théâtre du Vaudeville was demolished as part of Haussmann's redevelopment program and relocated to the boulevard des Capucines, where it was later converted into a cinema.

5. The Théâtre de l'Ambigu-Comique (boulevard St Martin), the Théâtre de la Porte St Martin (boulevard St Martin), and the Théâtre de la Gaîté (boulevard du Temple) staged melodramas and vaudevilles. The Théâtre de la Gaîté was one of a cluster of theaters on a section of the boulevard du Temple which earned it the nickname "boulevard du Crime" because of their reputation for especially dark and heart-rending melodramas. Most of these theaters, including the Gaîté, were demolished for the enlargement of the place du Château d'Eau (now place de la République) in 1862. The Théâtre de l'Ambigu-Comique survived, undergoing various transformations, until the 1960s, but the site is now occupied by an office block. The Théâtre de la Porte St Martin still exists: it was burned down during the Commune, but rebuilt in 1873.

6. Long lines for the theaters were common even on ordinary days of the year and, like the cinema lines in present-day Paris, they were orderly and well regulated. According to *Galignani's New Paris Guide* of 1854, "The visitors who await the opening of the doors are arranged in files of two or three abreast; and although the crowd probably consists of several hundreds, but little pressure or inconvenience is felt, and every person is admitted in his turn. Such, indeed, is the ardour for theatrical amusements exhibited by the population of Paris, that a crowd ... may always be found at the door of any popular theatre for several hours before the time of admission." Dickens mentions the Parisian passion for theater in a letter of 13 February 1855: "All the French Theatres are at

work as usual, and everybody seems to go to all of them, though the Snow lies thick and the cold is severe. What a model people!" (*Pilgrim*, 7, p 536.)

7. The *barrières*, the city gates of Paris. For more detail see note 24 under "A Flight," p 332.

8. A reference to Aladdin's adventure in the magical garden, where the trees bear glittering jewels instead of fruit, in the *Arabian Nights* story of Aladdin and the wonderful lamp ("The Story of Alla ad Deen; or, The Wonderful Lamp," in Vol 4 of Jonathan Scott's 1811 translation).

9. Illegal ticket touting was common. It was the practice of touts to "purchase tickets wholesale from the directors of the theatres, or else, on a new piece anxiously expected coming out, to forestall the public by buying up at the door nearly all the tickets for the best places on sale, and then to sell them outside to the public; in the former case, at lower prices than are paid at the doors; in the latter, at any price they choose to ask" (*Galignani's New Paris Guide*, 1854).

10. The restaurants Dickens lists here were among the most famous and fashionable of Second Empire Paris. The Trois Frères Provençaux (a favourite with Dickens), Véfour (where he "assisted at a little course of dissection of pig's feet (and Truffles)" – *Pilgrim*, 7, p 752), and Véry were all in the Palais Royal (the Véfour is still there today). The Café de Paris and La Maison Dorée were on the boulevard des Italiens.

11. The Café Champeaux was a well known business-class restaurant in the place de la Bourse, on the corner of the rue Vivienne and the rue des Filles-Saint-Thomas.

12. Abd-el-Kader (1807–83), born in Mascara, was an Algerian nationalist who led a long struggle against the French after their conquest of Algiers. He surrendered in 1847.

13. The subject of the comic song, "Le Sire de Franc-Boisy" ("Franc-Boisy" was corrupted into "Framboisie" or "Framboisy"). Written in 1855 by Ernest Bourget and Laurent de Rillé, the song tells of Le Sire de Franc-Boisy's unwise marriage to a beautiful young woman and its unfortunate consequences. It rapidly gained huge popularity and provided a source for many Vaudeville pieces and review sketches.

14. See note 5 above.

15. This name does not seem to have any obvious French counterpart. Slater (1998), keeping in mind the type of entertainment being staged and the location, suggests the Théâtre des Funambules as a possible candidate. Like the Gaîté, which Dickens has just left, the Funambules ("tight-rope walkers") was on the boulevard du Temple. It specialized in circus-type shows, featuring rope-dancers, clowns, etc. Another possibility is Le Petit Lazzari (also spelt "Lazari" or "Lazary"). This too was on the boulevard du Temple and offered "a species of spectacle for the lower classes and

children" (*Galignani's New Paris Guide*, 1854) – formerly a puppet theater, it specialized in vaudeville in the 1850s (*Guide dans les théâtres*, 1855). "Lazzari" may have suggested *lazzaroni* to Dickens and thus by association "scavengers."

16. Act 3 Scene 2 of *Black-Eyed Susan*, 1829, by Douglas Jerrold (1803–57). In a naval court martial the hero William is found guilty of attempting to kill a superior officer and is sentenced to death.

17. A reference to the fact that many French plays of the time were collaborative efforts.

"Some Recollections of Mortality," pp 146–158

1. This refers to the end of "The Calais Night Mail" (p 32), published in *All the Year Round* two weeks earlier (2 May 1863). "Some Recollections" picks up the journey where the previous article left off.

2. Broad-brimmed hats, turned up at the sides and projecting shovel-like at the front and back – as worn by priests.

3. An allusion to the "Uncommercial Traveller" persona – see page 17.

4. The brother of Ali in the *Arabian Nights* story of Ali Baba and the forty thieves. After killing Cassim Baba, the robbers cut his body into quarters. ("Story of Ali Baba and the Forty Robbers destroyed by a Slave," in Vol 5 of Jonathan Scott's 1811 translation.)

5. A result of the *Haussmannisation* of Paris – the extensive program of urban improvement and transformation that took place under the direction of Baron Georges Haussmann (1809–91), Préfet de la Seine from 1853 to 1870 – see the introduction to this chapter, p 123. Dickens here witnesses *Haussmannisation* in progress on the Île de la Cité, which had been a warren of narrow and twisting medieval streets packed with ancient and decaying houses three or four stories high. Most of these buildings were demolished – only a few houses in the rue Chanoinesse and part of the place Dauphine escaped destruction (Fierro, 1996; Hillairet, 1970). The space in front of Notre-Dame was cleared for the construction of the huge square that is the current Parvis de Notre-Dame – some six times as large as the medieval *parvis* that preceded it (Hillairet, 1970).

6. From 1804 to 1864 the Morgue was on the quai du Marché-Neuf. In 1864, because the building that housed it was scheduled for demolition, it was moved to a new home on the quai de l'Archevêché behind Notre-Dame, where it remained until 1914.

7. The Hôtel-Dieu. In Dickens's time it occupied the south side of what is now the Parvis de Notre-Dame, from the Petit Pont to the Pont au Double. That building was completely demolished in 1878, when the construction of the current Hôtel-Dieu, on the north side of the Parvis de Notre-Dame, had been completed (Hillairet, 1970).

8. British name for the colorful opera *La Muette de Portici* by Daniel Auber (1782–1871), first performed in Paris in 1828. It was a great success in the 19th century and was famous for its spectacular scenery and stage effects. Set in 17th century Naples, it tells the story of a rebellion led by a Neapolitan fisherman against Spanish oppressors.

9. See the description from *A Handbook for Visitors to Paris* quoted in the introduction, p 126.

10. Dickens has crossed from the Île de la Cité to the Right Bank. The square de la Tour de Saint-Jacques-la-Boucherie, or simply square Saint-Jacques, is next to the place du Châtelet, just across the river from the Île. The 16th-century tower is all that remains of the Église Saint-Jacques-la-Boucherie, founded in the 11th century and demolished in the 18th. The tower was extensively renovated in 1852 and the square and its garden were created in 1858. This whole area, previously crammed with narrow streets and alleyways, changed dramatically with the transformation and expansion of the place du Châtelet, also completed in 1858. Of the Tour Saint-Jacques, *Galignani's New Paris Guide* of 1860 comments, "This interesting structure now occupies the centre of an elegant square laid out as a garden, once intersected by the filthiest streets of the metropolis, haunted by vendors of rags and other commodities of a similar nature."

11. Gloucester Gate comprises a group of terraced and detached houses on the edge of Regent's Park in Northwest London, designed by John Nash and dating from 1827. In the winter of 1861, which was indeed a "hard" one (Dickens wrote vividly about it to W.W.F. de Cerjat on 1 February 1861, *Pilgrim*, 9, pp 380–381), the Dickens family rented a furnished house in Hanover Terrace, across the park from Gloucester Gate (their main home was then at Gad's Hill in Kent).

12. Regent's Canal, opened in 1820, runs from Paddington in West London to Limehouse in the East. It later formed part of the Grand Union Canal. The canal runs through Regent's Park on its route eastwards towards Camden Town. The "iron-bound road" was a bridge in front of Gloucester Gate over a branch of the canal that ran south alongside the park to Cumberland Market (forming the Cumberland Basin). It was replaced by the current Gloucester Gate Bridge in 1878. The Cumberland Branch of Regent's Canal was filled in in 1942.

13. Chalk Farm is an area of Northwest London close to Camden Town. Judging from Dickens's description, the cab stopped at the Water Meeting Bridge on Prince Albert Road (then simply Albert Road). The name of the bridge derives from its location at the junction of the main canal and the Cumberland Branch. It was rebuilt in 1961.

14. A phrase from the "At the Burial of the Dead" section of the *Book of Common Prayer*, 1662: "For as much as it hath pleased Almighty God of his great mercy to take unto himself the soul of our dear brother here

departed; we therefore commit his body to the ground, earth to earth, ashes to ashes..."

15. After his stroll in front of the Hôtel de Ville, Dickens is walking up the boulevard de Sébastopol (one of the huge new arterial streets created by Haussmann – see note 5 above) towards the northern boulevards, or Grands Boulevards, which were then the focus of Parisian high-life. According to *Galignani's New Paris Guide* of 1860, "The northern boulevards are now the pride and glory of Paris ... Their great extent, the dazzling beauty, the luxury of the shops, the restaurants, the cafés ... the crowds of well-dressed persons who frequent them; the glancing of lights among the trees; the sounds of music; the incessant roll of carriages, all this forms a medley of sights and sounds anything but unpleasing to the visitor ..." As for the boulevard de Sébastopol, Murray's *A Handbook for Visitors to Paris*, 1864, describes it as "a magnificent street, of great width, planted with trees on each side ... The greater part of this street has been cut through the thickest mass of houses; it was opened between 1855 and 1860." It originally ran from the Gare de l'Est down to the place du Châtelet, across the Île de la Cité and then on down the Left Bank to the boulevard du Montparnasse – it now ends at the place du Châtelet.

16. The parish of Marylebone. Dickens and his family moved into 1 Devonshire Terrace, near the York Gate entrance to Regent's Park, in December 1839, and lived there until 1851. Writing to Forster when the negotiations for the lease were still in progress he described it as "a house of great promise (and great premium), 'undeniable' situation and excessive splendour" (*Life*, 2, Chapter 5). Devonshire Terrace, now demolished, was almost opposite York Gate on the Marylebone Road (known as the New Road until 1857). No 1 was on the corner of Marylebone Road and Marylebone High Street, where Ferguson House, 15 and 17 Marylebone Road, now stands (a plaque marks the spot).

17. An inferior parish officer, appointed to keep order, act as parish messenger, perform administrative duties, etc. Beadles were not, as evidenced by his withering portrait of Mr Bumble in *Oliver Twist*, among Dickens's favorite people. See also his early article on beadles and other parish officials ("The Beadle – The Parish Engine – The Schoolmaster," first published in 1835 and included in the "Our Parish" section of *Sketches by Boz*).

18. An allusion to "The Epitaph" section of "Elegy Written in a Country Churchyard" by Thomas Gray (1716–71): "Here rests his head upon the lap of Earth/A Youth to Fortune and to Fame unknown./Fair Science frowned not on his humble birth,/And Melancholy marked him for her own."

19. The inquest that is the subject of the remainder of this article has been identified as that concerning the body of the new-born baby of Eliza

Burgess, a young housemaid, held on 14 January 1840 at the Marylebone Workhouse (Carlton, 1956). Forster, without naming the parties, refers to Dickens's participation: "... he was summoned, and obliged to sit, as juryman at an inquest on the body of a little child alleged to have been murdered by its mother..." (*Life*, 2, Chapter 8). The inquest is reported in some detail in *The Times*, 15 January 1840, p 7. In summary, Eliza Burgess, aged 24, was in the service of a Mrs Simmonds, the wife of a wealthy merchant, who lived at 65 Edgware Road. Suspecting that the housemaid had given birth to a child in secret, Mrs Simmonds challenged her about it. "The servant at first denied it," reports *The Times*, "but being threatened with medical examination, she confessed the fact, and said she had hid it in a pot or species of kettle under the dresser, where it was found." The housemaid said that she had been in labor in the kitchen when the doorbell had sounded and had given birth to the child just as she had risen to let the people in – when she returned to the kitchen she found it dead. The issue for the inquest was thus whether the child had been killed or whether it had been stillborn.

Thanks to Dickens's interventions and the Coroner's support, the jury agreed a verdict of "found dead" and the housemaid was sent to trial for the much lesser charge of unlawfully concealing the birth of a child. Dickens arranged for the barrister Richard Doane to be retained for her defense and the trial took place on 9 March 1840 at the Old Bailey. It was reported in *The Times* on 10 March 1840 (p 7). In his address to the jury Doane said "... he was sure that the jury would take a merciful view of the case when he informed them that the unfortunate young woman at the bar was of weak intellect, and had been imposed upon by some heartless fellow, who took advantage of the state of the law to effect her ruin, knowing that the consequences would not be visited on himself." Eliza also received valuable support from a previous employer, a Mr Clarkson, who said that he was in the process of procuring a place for her at the Magdalen Asylum and would take her back into his service in the mean time. The jury found her guilty of the concealment but strongly recommended her to mercy. The judge concluded that "under these circumstances, he would respite the judgement on the prisoner until the next session, and in the mean time she might be liberated."

20. A reference to *Douglas*, a tragedy by John Home (1722–1808), first performed in 1756 and included in Elizabeth Inchbald's *The British Theatre* (1824 edition, Volume 2). In Act 2 Scene 1, Norval describes how "...the shepherds fled for safety and for succour" from a band of attacking barbarians. Dickens refers to the shepherds as "Northern" because the action takes place in Scotland.

21. The South American region of Patagonia is home to one of the tallest races in the world (the Tehuelches). Slater and Drew (2000) suggest an

allusion to Letter 114 of *The Citizen of the World*, 1762, by Oliver Goldsmith (1728–74), in which there is a reference to "the giant fair ones of Patagonia." If it is present, the allusion is a tenuous one but Dickens was certainly familiar with Goldsmith's characterization of Patagonians, which he mentions in a letter to Frederick Dickens of 10 August 1842 (*Pilgrim*, 3, p 308), and it is conceivable that he had it in mind here.

22. From Prospero's words to Miranda in Shakespeare's *The Tempest* (1, 2): "Thy mother was a piece of virtue…"

23. Thomas Wakley (1795–1862), surgeon, founder of *The Lancet*, and Member of Parliament. Wakley was an ardent reformer and a radical politician. He was elected Coroner for West Middlesex on 25 February 1839 and became known for his efforts "to raise the status of coroner's juries and establish a decorous mode of procedure at inquests" (*Dictionary of National Biography*). As Dickens records here, he combined professional expertise with compassion and sensitivity in conducting his inquests. Wakley strongly believed that a coroner's duties required a medical rather than legal education: Dickens provides an illustration of why that should be so in his report, towards the end of this article, of a private conversation with Wakley about the cause of the baby's death. (Wakley's contention that coroners should have a medical background is, incidentally, the subject of debate at a dinner party in chapter 16 of George Eliot's *Middlemarch*, 1871–72.) Dickens had previously praised Wakley's thoroughness and fairness as Coroner in an article published in *The Examiner* in 1849 ("The Paradise at Tooting," included in Slater, 1996, p 147).

24. Forster records that Dickens wrote to him the day after the inquest: "How much he felt the little incident, at the actual time of its occurrence, may be judged from the few lines written next morning." Dickens referred in that letter to his sleepless night: "Whether it was the poor baby, or its poor mother, or the coffin, or my fellow-jurymen, or what not, I can't say, but last night I had a most violent attack of sickness and indigestion which not only prevented me from sleeping, but even from lying down. Accordingly Kate and I sat up through the dreary watches." (*Life*, 2, Chapter 8.)

25. See above, note 19.

26. An essential component of the Beadle's incongruously elaborate uniform: "A field-marshal has his uniform; a bishop his silk apron; a counsellor his silk gown; a beadle his cocked hat." (*Oliver Twist*, Chapter 37.)

Extract from *Pictures from Italy* (Lyon, the Rhône, Avignon), pp 162–172

1. The Saône and the Rhône.

2. An allusion to Mark, 5:9. Christ, having forced the "unclean spirit" out of a man, asks, "What is thy name? And he answered, saying, My name is

Legion: for we are many."

3. A vessel emptied of air.

4. Not cleaned.

5. Dickens wrote of his detestation of Lyon to the Count d'Orsay in a letter of 7 August 1844: "Were you ever at Lyons? *That's* the place. It's a great Nightmare – a bad conscience – a fit of indigestion – the recollection of having done a murder. An awful place!" (*Pilgrim*, 4, p 170.) He was not alone in his aversion: while noting the stately appearance of Lyon and the attractions of its location, Murray's *Hand-Book for Travellers in France*, 1843, describes the inner city as "one stack of lofty houses, penetrated by lanes so excessively narrow and nasty as not to be traversed without disgust."

6. Madame Marie Tussaud (1760–1850) established her Waxworks exhibition in London's Baker Street in 1835, where it rapidly became the major attraction it still is today (it moved to its current site on the Marylebone Road in 1884).

7. Wax effigies from the funeral services of sovereigns and other notables were traditionally displayed in Westminster Abbey – the wax-work exhibition, which included additional figures specially manufactured by the Abbey for the purpose, was irreverently known as "The Play of the Dead Volks" (Cunningham, 1850). It was discontinued in 1839. The funeral effigies are now exhibited in the Abbey's Undercroft Museum.

8. One of the highly successful series of travel guides, or *Handbooks*, published by the family firm of John Murray (several of the guides were written by John Murray III himself). Dickens is presumably referring here to *A Hand-Book for Travellers in France*, 1843.

9. The astronomical clock, built by the Basle craftsman Nicolas Lippius in 1598, is still on display in the cathedral. When Dickens saw it, it was in disrepair and visitors had to pay the sacristan to put it into action (*A Hand-Book for Travellers in France*, 1843). Dickens relates this incident in similar detail (although with a more horrified sacristan at the end of the story) in a letter to the Count d'Orsay of 7 August 1844 (*Pilgrim*, 4, p 170).

10. From Canto 3, 71, of Byron's *Childe Harold's Pilgrimage*, 1812–18: "By the blue rushing of the arrowy Rhone."

11. The lowest order of the Légion d'honneur (the medal is attached to a red ribbon) – see note 11 under "Our French Watering-Place," p 343.

12. *Tom Noddy's Secret* by Thomas Haynes Bayly (1797–1839). The play was first performed in 1838 and is included in Webster's *The Acting National Drama*, Vol 5, 1838. Tom Noddy is forever tying knots in his handkerchief and forgetting why he tied them.

13. This great stone bridge across the Rhône was completed in 1309. Of its 25 arches, 19 date back to the original construction. When Dickens saw it in 1844 it had 26 arches, 21 of them original and five dating from the 18th

century. Two more of the 14th century arches were replaced in 1860 by a single metal arch (and subsequently by a suspension bridge after war damage).

14. Napoléon, then Lieutenant Bonaparte, was stationed at Valence (and studied at its École d'Artillerie) from October 1785 to August 1786 and again from May to October 1791.

15. The famous Pont d'Avignon or Pont St-Bénézet, dating from the twelfth century (reconstructed in the thirteenth) and largely destroyed – now, as when Dickens saw it, only four arches remain (the original bridge had 22). It suffered frequent flood damage and was extremely expensive to repair: the last, abandoned attempt to repair it was made in the seventeenth century, after which it was left to its fate.

16. An allusion to the *Arabian Nights* tale of the porter and the ladies of Baghdad. The "delicious purchases" are made by a woman at the beginning of the story who hires the porter and fills his basket with luxurious food, drink, perfumes, etc, and then leads him to the house where she lives with her two sisters. The "three one-eyed Calendars" are mendicant monks, each blind in one eye, who call at the house. A condition of the ladies' hospitality is that their guests should not ask questions about matters that do not concern them, but the porter persists in doing so. ("Story of the Three Calendars, Sons of Sultans; and of the Five Ladies of Bagdad" in Vol 1 of Jonathan Scott's 1811 translation.)

17. To go sightseeing.

18. Part of the restoration work that was done in the cathedral (Notre-Dame-des-Doms) in the 1840s. Dickens recalls this fresco painting by the French artist and his pupil in a letter to Daniel Maclise of 22 July 1844, commenting that it "was as bright and airy as anything can be; nothing dull or dead about it" (*Pilgrim*, 4, p 161). The artist in question was presumably Eugène Devéria (1805–65), who decorated one of the chapels.

19. The family of Dr Primrose, the vicar in *The Vicar of Wakefield*, 1766, by Oliver Goldsmith (1728–74). The "painter" is probably Daniel Maclise (1806–70), who depicted a scene from chapter 11 of the novel in his picture *Hunt the Slipper at Neighbour Flamborough's – Unexpected Visit of the Fine Ladies* (exhibited at the Royal Academy in 1841). Dickens wrote to Maclise about the painting in a letter of 12 July 1841 (*Pilgrim*, 2, p 330).

20. The enormous fortress-like Palais des Papes was built in the 14th century to accommodate the Papal Court following its temporary transfer from Rome to Avignon. Construction began under Benoît XII (1334–42) and was largely completed under Clément VI (1342–52), with subsequent additions and embellishments under Innocent VI (1352–62) and Urbain V (1362–70). After the Papal Court had returned to Rome, the palace was occupied by papal legates and vice-legates until 1791. It survived the

Revolution thanks to its conversion into a prison and barracks, but the interior was greatly changed and damaged. The army departed in 1906 and extensive restoration work began in 1920.

21. The Inquisition was a judicial institution established by the Roman Catholic Church in the 13th century to identify, try, and sentence people suspected of heresy or other offenses against the Church. Inquisitors could imprison people they suspected of lying and the use of torture was officially sanctioned in 1252 by Pope Innocent IV.

22. Tavern.

23. An "oubliette" is a secret dungeon, accessible only by a trapdoor.

24. The Roman patriot and popular leader, Cola di Rienzi (?1313–54). From humble origins, Rienzi set himself up in opposition to Rome's aristocratic rulers and assumed power in May 1347 with widespread support, styling himself "Tribune." Pope Clement VI, offended by his policies, incited the barons to defeat him and his short rule ended in December 1347, when he fled from Rome. He was jailed by Clement at the Palais des Papes in 1352, but was subsequently released by Clement's successor, Innocent VI. He returned to Rome and to power in 1354, only to be killed in a riot shortly afterwards. His life and adventures inspired Edward Bulwer-Lytton's popular novel *Rienzi, the Last of the Roman Tribunes*, 1835, Wagner's opera *Rienzi*, 1840 (first performed 1842), and Holman Hunt's painting *Rienzi*, 1849.

25. Dungeons.

26. That is, the Holy Office of the Inquisition, the tribunal.

27. At the time Dickens visited, this room was thought to have been a torture chamber, but it has since been identified as a medieval kitchen and is exhibited as such today. In his *A Little Tour in France*, 1884, Henry James refers to it as "the funnel-shaped torture-chamber (which, after exciting the shudder of generations, has been ascertained now, I believe, to have been a mediaeval bakehouse)..."

28. The atrocity that Dickens describes took place in the Tour de la Glacière.

29. Louis Roche – see note 11 under "Travelling Abroad," p 338.

30. This is the end of the chapter entitled "Lyons, the Rhone, and the Goblin of Avignon." The next paragraph opens the "Avignon to Genoa" chapter.

31. The Dutch painter Adriaen van Ostade (1610–85), known for his depictions of peasant life, typically interiors featuring old women or drunken tavern scenes.

Extract from *Pictures from Italy* (Travelling through France), pp 179–181

1. "Astley's" was the famous equestrian circus founded by Philip Astley (1742–1814) in 1769. It was enormously popular in the nineteenth century. Its London base, Astley's Amphitheatre, later known as Astley's

Royal Amphitheatre, was in Westminster Bridge Road. Rebuilt several times after catastrophic fires, it was finally demolished in 1893. Among the main attractions of Astley's were its "hippodramas" – plays performed on horseback and featuring spectacular trick riding. In Dickens's time, the rider Andrew Ducrow (1793–1842) was its internationally renowned star (and its proprietor from 1830 to 1842). His performance as "The Courier of Saint Petersburg" was among his best known acts. Ducrow entered the ring astride two horses and, in the course of the drama, three to seven horses galloped between the first two – as they passed beneath him Ducrow grabbed the reins and managed all the horses simultaneously (Saxon, 1968).

Dickens wrote an article on Astley's in 1835 for the *Evening Chronicle*, subsequently included in *Sketches by Boz*, and there are descriptions of performances at the Amphitheatre in *The Old Curiosity Shop*, chapter 39 and *Bleak House*, chapter 21.

For details of "Franconi's," the famous Paris-based circus, see note 15 under "The Calais Night Mail," p 334.

2. Chalon-sur-Saône.

3. That is, with cone-shaped roofs, looking like candle extinguishers.

4. A play on the proverb "Good wine needs no bush." The ivy bush, because of its association with Bacchus, was the traditional sign of taverns and ale and wine sellers.

5. A play on the expression "green old age," used in reference to people who remain fit and youthful in spirit in their old age.

6. A public stage-coach. According to *Galignani's New Paris Guide* of 1844, *diligences* 'carry generally 15 to 18 passengers, and contain four kinds of places – the *coupé*, which holds three; *intérieur*, six; *rotonde*, six; and *banquette*, three.' The outside seats on the *banquette* were the cheapest. See also note 3, under "Our French Watering-Place," p 342.

7. The cabriolet-style hood for the *banquette* (see above), which was on the roof of the *coupé*, the front division of the *diligence*.

8. *Les Jeunes-France*, the name given to a group of young second-generation Romantic writers and artists who defended their strong views aggressively and frequently offended conventional attitudes – and who often dressed eccentrically, as described here. Théophile Gautier (1811–72) was one of the more prominent figures associated with the group – he poked fun at it in a series of sketches entitled *Les Jeunes-France, romans goguenards*, 1833.

9. The French equivalent of the English mail coach. *Malles Postes* were allowed to carry two or three passengers.

Extract from _Dombey and Son_ (Carker's Flight from Dijon), pp 181–191

1. A premonition of his death – shortly after his return to England, Carker is run over by a train.
2. A light, open four-wheeled carriage.
3. The inn where the post-horses were kept ('post'-horses being hired and changed from stage to stage). Carker has to hire his horses separately and settle for an old carriage because "The furnishing of post-horses does not, as in England, include a _post chaise_, and those who mean to post in France must have a carriage of their own. It is true the French postmasters are obliged to keep a cabriolet or small calèche for hire, but it is usually a rickety vehicle holding only 2 persons, with no room for baggage beyond a sac de nuit, and is therefore seldom˜ resorted to." (_A Hand-Book for Travellers in France_, 1847.)
4. The marriage of Mr Dombey to Edith Granger.
5. Mr Dombey's son and daughter.
6. That is, the tips of the cone-shaped roofs that look like candle extinguishers.
7. A _barrière_, or city gate – see note 24 under "A Flight," p 332.

Extract from _Pictures from Italy_ (Marseille), pp 191–194

1. That is, posting stages – inns where the post horses (hired from stage to stage) were changed. 'Stage' was also used to mean the distance between two posting stages.
2. These were the _bastides_ of the middle-class citizens of Marseille, built on the surrounding hillsides to provide them some relief from the heat and bustle of the busy narrow streets of the town. Murray's _Hand-Book for Travellers in France_, 1843, describes them as "little country boxes, which entirely dot the slopes around the town, prolonging it apparently to the tops of the surrounding hills. Some of them are handsome, and surrounded by gardens, but the greater part stand in mere bare enclosures, between 4 walls, destitute of shade and water, their only recommendation being that they are out of town. Every merchant, citizen, or shopkeeper must have one, and their number is said to exceed 6,000."
3. He was in Marseille again briefly on 7 September 1844, in fair weather, to meet his brother Frederick who was coming to stay with the family at Genoa for a brief holiday. Dickens wrote to his wife Catherine from the Hôtel du Paradis (_Pilgrim_, 4, p 192), the hotel mentioned later in this extract, and also refers to the visit in the "Genoa and its Neighbourhood" section of _Pictures from Italy_ (p 75, 1846 edition). He was back in Marseille, in foul weather, on 17–19 December 1844, on his way home to

Genoa after a trip to England. Describing his delay at the port, he explains that "there was detention at Marseilles from stress of weather; and steamers were advertised to go, which did not go ..." (*Pictures from Italy*, p 142). In a self-mocking letter of 10 March 1845 to Mrs Macready, he recollects this experience as "three days of waking nightmare" (*Pilgrim*, 4, p 277). In addition to the frustrations caused by the weather, he had passport problems and was forced to write to the British Consul in Genoa from on board the steamer to explain that he had failed to obtain the appropriate visa because his passport had "fallen into the hands of a rival boat at Marseilles, which promised to sail and didn't, and still wanted to keep it and me, waiting at that delightful town until Heaven knows when ..." (letter of 20 December 1844, *Pilgrim*, 4, p 240).

4. The most spectacular view of Marseille itself and out over the Mediterranean was and is to be had from the top of the hill of Nôtre-Dame de la Garde, "so-called from the curious chapel situated within a small fort on its summit" (*A Hand-Book for Travellers in France*, 1843). That chapel was replaced by the present one, completed in 1864.

5. *A Hand-Book for Travellers in France*, 1843, warned travellers about this olfactory hazard, describing the harbor as "the sewer of the city – the receptacle of all its filth, stagnating in a tideless sea and under a burning sun, until a SE wind produces that circulation in its waters which the tide would do on other seas. The stench emanating from it at times is consequently intolerable, except for natives ..."

6. Listed in *A Hand-Book for Travellers in France*, 1843, and used by Dickens again on his next visit to the city (see above, note 3).

7. Another little portrait of the hairdresser and his window display is the only information that Dickens offers us in *Pictures* about his second visit to Marseille (see above, note 3): "The corpulent hairdresser was still sitting in his slippers outside his shop-door there, but the twirling ladies in the window, with the natural inconstancy of their sex, had ceased to twirl, and were languishing, stock still, with their beautiful faces addressed to blind corners of the establishment, where it was impossible for admirers to penetrate." (*Pictures from Italy*, p 75, 1846 edition).

8. Described by Peter Cunningham as "a large bazaar and carriage and furniture repository" (*Hand-Book of London*, 1850), the Pantechnicon was in Motcomb Street, near Belgrave Square in London. For more details see under "Travelling Abroad," note 30, p 342. On Dickens's acquisition of the carriage, see under "Travelling Abroad," note 1, p 337.

Extract from *Little Dorrit* (Marseille), pp 194–196

1. The oppressive summer heat of Marseille, which Dickens uses to such great effect in this passage, was something he had personally experienced

(see previous extract). Murray's *Handbook* warned travellers against it: "The climate of Marseilles for a large portion of the year is delightful, but in summer and autumn the heat is at times intense – the streets like an oven, so that it is scarcely possible to move abroad during the daytime, and all rest during the night is likely to be destroyed by the mosquitoes." (*A Handbook for Travellers in France*, 1856.)

2. *A Handbook for Travellers in France*, 1856, describes a view of the city as "an arid prospect of dazzling white, interspersed, but unrelieved, by dark streaks of dusky green."

3. See under "*Pictures from Italy* (Marseille)," note 5, p 368.

4. The building of the city and tower of Babel is the subject of Genesis, 11. "Therefore is the name of it called Babel; because the Lord did there confound the language of all the earth: and from thence did the Lord scatter them [the people] abroad upon the face of all the earth." (Genesis, 11:9.)

5. Italian for cicada.

Extract from *Pictures from Italy* (Sens), pp 196–201

1. See under "*Pictures from Italy* (Marseille)," note 1, p 367.

2. The Hôtel de l'Écu in Sens, recommended as "fairly good" in *A Hand-Book for Travellers in France*, 1843 (upgraded to "very good" in the 1847 edition).

3. Louis Roche – see under "Travelling Abroad," note 11, p 338. Couriers were responsible for the safety and efficiency of the journey and for ensuring good accommodation en route and negotiating the arrangements and the bill with innkeepers. They were especially valuable for travellers in foreign countries in the days of carriage travel, when frequent negotiations at inns and post-houses were inevitable. *A Hand-Book for Travellers on the Continent*, 1843, spells out their most important duties and sheds light on Roche's various activities in this extract: "A courier, however, though an expensive luxury, is one which conduces much to the ease and pleasure of travelling, and few who can afford one will forego the advantage of his services. He relieves his master from much fatigue of body and perplexity of mind, in unravelling the difficulties of long bills and foreign moneys, sparing his temper the trials it is likely to endure from disputes with innkeepers, postmasters and the like. ... He must make arrangements for his employer's reception at inns where he intends to pass the night; must secure comfortable rooms, clean and well-aired beds, and order meals to be prepared, fires to be lighted, taking care that his master is called in proper time, and that the post horses are ordered at the right hour. He ought to have a thorough knowledge of everything that relates to the care of a carriage; he should examine it at the end of each

day's journey, to ascertain whether it requires any repairs, which should be executed before setting out; and it is his fault if any accident occur *en route*, from neglect of such precautions. He should superintend the packing and unpacking of the luggage, should know the number of parcels, &c., and be on his guard against leaving any thing behind. It falls to the courier to pay innkeepers, postmasters, and postboys, and he ought to take care that his master is not overcharged. Besides this, he performs all the services of waiting and attendance, cleaning and brushing clothes, &c. He ought to write as well as speak the language of the countries he is about to visit, so as to be able to communicate by letter to innkeepers, when it is necessary to bespeak accommodation beforehand, and he is not perfectly accomplished unless he have a smattering of the art of cookery."

4. Catherine Dickens (born Catherine Hogarth). The other family members mentioned in this paragraph are as follows: the "sister of the family" is Georgina Hogarth; the two little boys are Charles (known as Charley, born 1837) and Walter (born 1841); the two little girls are Mary (Mamie, born 1838) and Katherine (Katey, born 1839); and the baby is Francis (born in January 1844).

5. Presumably the taller of the two towers of Sens Cathedral, the south tower (La Tour de Pierre), topped by the campanile that so fascinates Mrs Lirriper (see the extract from *Mrs Lirriper's Legacy*).

6. The inn where the post-horses were kept ('post'-horses being hired and changed from stage to stage).

7. A device (usually an iron shoe) used to slow the wheels of the carriage when descending a hill.

8. The open market outside Sens Cathedral that Dickens describes here was replaced by the current *marché couvert* in 1882.

Extract from *Mrs Lirriper's Legacy*, pp 201–221

1. Members of the Plymouth Brethren, an evangelical religious sect. The Brethren, led by the ex-Anglican clergyman John Nelson Darby (1800–82), originated in Ireland in the 1820s and acquired its name *c*1830 when Darby moved to Plymouth and he and his colleagues established a chapel there.

2. Government securities consolidated into a single interest-bearing stock (derived from "consolidated annuities").

3. The *mairie* or town hall.

4. That is, *département* or administrative district.

5. The Strand was, and is, a busy thoroughfare lined with shops, theaters, and restaurants. About three-quarters of a mile long, it runs from Charing Cross to Fleet Street (ending at Temple Bar in Dickens's time) and so links the West End with the City. Norfolk Street no longer exists – it ran

from the Strand to the Thames and was situated between Arundel Street and Surrey Street.

6. The imperial eagle was the emblem of France under the First (1804–14) and Second (1852–70) Empires.

7. First appearing in 1700 as *Vox Stellarum, an Almanac for 1701 with Astrological Observations* by the physician and astrologer Francis Moore (1657–1714), *Old Moore's Almanac* was extremely popular throughout the nineteenth century with its combination of practical information and astrological forecasts. It is still published today.

8. Street musicians (organ-grinders). This refers to a description in *Mrs Lirriper's Lodgings* of the Major's efforts to chase them away so that the noise would not disturb the ailing and pregnant "Mrs Edson" (little Jemmy's mother): "... I could not have believed it was in any gentleman to have such a power of bursting out with fire-irons walking-sticks water-jugs coals potatoes off his table the very hat off his head, and at the same time so furious in foreign languages ..."

9. Orson in the French romance *Valentine and Orson*, in which infant twin brothers are abandoned in the woods. Valentine is rescued and brought up to be a courtier while Orson is carried off and raised by a bear and becomes a wild man of the woods. The tale was very well known in 19th century England. It was popular as a story for children: in "The Child's Story" (*Household Words*, 18 December 1852) Dickens refers to "astonishing picture books: all about ... blue-beards and bean-stalks and riches and caverns and forests and Valentines and Orsons..."; and Valentine "and his wild brother" are among the heroes conjured up from Scrooge's childhood reading by the Ghost of Christmas Past (*A Christmas Carol*, Stave Two). It was also popular in the theater: there were various adaptations during the century and Valentine and Orson made frequent appearances in burlesques and pantomimes. Among the best known dramatizations of the story were the melodrama by Thomas John Dibdin (1771–1841), first performed 1804, the burlesque principally by Tom Taylor (1817–80), 1844, and, post-dating Mrs Lirriper, the pantomime by Charles Kenney (1821–81), 1867 (all entitled *Valentine and Orson*). The great Joseph Grimaldi, whose memoirs Dickens edited, was among the many interpreters of the role of Orson (Findlater, 1955).

10. Fortunatus is the hero of a medieval romance that became a popular children's story. He meets the goddess of Fortune who offers him a choice of gift – health, wisdom, strength, beauty, long life, or riches. He chooses riches and is given a magic purse that constantly replenishes the money he takes from it.

11. That is, the train carrying the mail.

12. The home-made model railway of Jemmy and the Major that Mrs Lirriper describes earlier in the story.

13. The confusions caused by "Gallic-English" (and "Anglican-French") are the subject of Blanchard Jerrold's essay "English Spoken" (*Imperial Paris*, 1855). "Gallic-English," he writes, "is to be heard in every corner of Paris; it is talked by the student of the Ecole du Droit, who asks you whether 'you speak an Englishmans?...'" Among the many other examples he notes are an advertisement for "comfortable pastry" and one for a dinner comprising "a potage; three dishes; two legumes, and a dessert."

14. This practice clearly struck Dickens as odd – he mentions it also in "New Year's Day," in which he describes the "women money-takers" at the theaters "shut up in strong iron-cages" (see p 142).

15. Mrs Lirriper is describing the slender campanile that surmounts the imposing south tower of Sens Cathedral (La Tour de Pierre).

16. The Hôtel de l'Écu, also described in *Pictures from Italy*. John Ruskin stayed at the inn and endorsed Mrs Lirriper's account of it, referring in *Proserpina*, 1875–86 (2, Part 4), to "the old inn at Sens, which Dickens has described in his wholly matchless way." He also mentions it in his autobiography *Praeterita*, 1885–89 (2, Chapter 11), in which he tells his readers that "the inn is fully and exquisitely described by Dickens in *Mrs Lirriper's Lodgings*" (meaning *Mrs Lirriper's Legacy*). (*The Works of John Ruskin*, Vols 25 and 36.)

17. Mrs Lirriper seems to be describing the towers as Dickens would have seen them in 1844. The north tower, La Tour de Plomb, was then surmounted by a lead-covered timbered belfry and would, like the south tower, have cast an imposing shadow. The belfry, however, was destroyed in 1848, leaving the north tower too short to cast a distinct shadow.

18. See under "*Pictures from Italy* (Sens)," note 8, p 370.

19. Some of these stories were told in *Mrs Lirriper's Lodgings* and more are told in *Mrs Lirriper's Legacy*. The linking device for the tales in these 1863 and 1864 Christmas Numbers of *All the Year Round* was that they had all been written by the Major and were based on the reminiscences of former lodgers.

20. Recalling "... ye have sinned against the Lord: and be sure your sin will find you out" (Numbers, 32:23).

21. In *Mrs Lirriper's Lodgings*, Mrs Lirriper tells how she promised the dying woman that she would look after her child and then, "I don't know how to tell it right, but I saw her soul brighten and leap up, and get free and fly away in the grateful look."

22. Mrs Lirriper's words here recall parts of the "The Order for Morning and Evening Prayer Dayly" section of the *Book of Common Prayer*, 1662: from the opening "Sentences from the Scriptures," "Rend your hearts, and not your garments, and turn unto the Lord your God..." (quoted from Joel, 2:13); and, from the prayer for the "Absolution or Remission of Sins," "He pardoneth and absolveth all them that truly repent..."

23. In the context of horse-drawn vehicles, a 'head' was a cover or hood.
24. Weak, low-quality wine.
25. See note 19 above.
26. At this point in *Mrs Lirriper's Legacy* there follow various tales by the other contributors. Mrs Lirriper then continues her narrative in the chapter reproduced here and so concludes both her story and the 1864 Christmas Number of *All the Year Round*.
27. Large copper vessels for boiling, used for cooking or laundry.
28. A reference back to a schoolboy rhyme that Jemmy recited in *Mrs Lirriper's Lodgings*: "Once upon a time, When pigs drank wine, And Monkeys chewed tobaccer, 'Twas neither in your time nor mine, But that's no macker—" The rhyme also makes an appearance in *Sketches of Young Gentlemen*, an early collection of short satirical essays by Dickens that was published anonymously in 1838. The essay on "The Political Young Gentleman" begins "Once upon a time – NOT in the days when pigs drank wine, but in a more recent period of our history ..."
29. The church of St Clement Danes is on the Strand, very near to the site of Norfolk Street (see note 5 above). Mrs Lirriper talks about her association with it in *Mrs Lirriper's Lodgings*: "It is forty years ago since me and my poor Lirriper got married at St Clement's Danes where I now have a sitting in a very pleasant pew with genteel company and my own hassock and being partial to evening service not too crowded."

Extract from *Little Dorrit* (Rigaud at Chalon-sur-Saône), pp 221–224

1. An allusion to the fate of Cain after he has slain Abel (see Genesis, 4:11–15) – "... and I shall be a fugitive and a vagabond in the earth ..."
2. Street gutters.
3. A public stage-coach (see under "A Flight," note 18, p 331, for further details).
4. In this context, a lowly tavern.

"Judicial Special Pleading," pp 230–235

1. Chartism was a working-class pro-democracy movement that began in the late 1830s. The aim of the movement, which became a focus for working-class discontent, was to establish a parliamentary democracy as a means towards the end of social and economic reform. It took its name from the "People's Charter," published in 1838 and presented to the House of Commons in 1839 as a public petition with over 1,200,000 signatures. Its six principles were: votes for all adult men; vote by ballot; equal electoral districts; annual elections; abolition of the property qualification for MPs; and payment for MPs. The petition was overwhelmingly rejected by

Parliament, as it was when it was presented again in 1842 and 1848.

The "physical force" Chartists, as opposed to the peaceful "moral force" strand of the movement, advocated violence where necessary and engaged in riots and targeted vandalism, encouraged by firebrand leaders. The government stamped down hard on law-breaking demonstrators and activists and many were arrested and convicted.

In spring 1848, fears and anxieties about the revolutionary potential of the movement were at their height, fuelled by various violent incidents, the connection of the Chartists with Irish nationalism, exaggerated press coverage, and the overthrowing of conservative governments on the Continent (Louis-Philippe abdicated in February). The planned gathering and march in London on 10 April to present the third Chartist petition prompted massive government security measures: over 7,000 military personnel were in readiness to intervene if the 4,000 police and some 85,000 special constables were unable to handle the situation (Saville, 1987, p 109). In the event, a mass meeting took place on Kennington Common but the planned march was abandoned – signalling in effect a defeat for the Chartists and marking the beginning of the end of the movement. Demonstrations and meetings continued over the next few months, especially in London and the industrial north, but in the summer of 1848 there were large-scale arrests and the Chartist flame was all but extinguished by September. The political trials that followed, at the Central Criminal Court in London and at the Assizes in the provinces, were mainly presided over by eight judges, of whom Alderson, Dickens's target in this article, was typical – they were middle-class conservatives who felt that their values had been seriously threatened by the Chartist movement. Their speeches and directions to the juries were loaded with prejudice and political bias. As Saville (1987, p 174) puts it, "The English political trials of 1848 were exercises in the miscarriage of justice; the obliteration of reason by prejudice and the subversion of legal principles by partisanship of a virulent order."

2. The use of police spies and informers was widespread during the summer of 1848 and their reports greatly increased fears of illegal conspiracy and violent revolution. Although there were serious incidents (including the killing of a policeman in the northern town of Ashton in August) and credible indications of planned violent uprisings, Dickens was skeptical about the real extent of the danger. In a letter of 17 June 1848 to D.M. Moir he commented, "There is nothing new in London. Chartist fears and rumours shake us, now and then, but I suspect the Government make the most of such things for their own purpose, and know better than anybody else how little vitality there is in them." (*Pilgrim*, 5, p 342.)

3. Sir Edward Hall Alderson (1787–1857). He became a "Baron" (judge) of the Court of the Exchequer in 1834. The *Dictionary of National Biography*

describes him as a conservative who never entered parliament and who "took little part in politics," adding that he was a man of "much religious feeling, a humane judge, with a desire to restrict capital punishment." (The title of Baron became obsolete in 1875 when the Court of the Exchequer was merged into the High Court of Judicature.)

4. Special Assizes were held in December 1848 at Chester and Liverpool for the trials of Chartist prisoners.

5. A phrase that commonly occurred in accounts of boxing matches. Dickens uses it comically in *Dombey and Son* in his portrayal of the Game Chicken, the pugilist whose opinion is that you should always "go in and win" (Chapter 22) and who is "gone into and finished" in his fight with the Larkey Boy (Chapter 44).

6. Alderson's opening address to the jury of 6 December was extensively reported in *The Times* on 8 December 1848, p 7. It makes extraordinary reading, given its judicial context, with its massive political bias, its clear prejudicial intent and its patronizing and ignorant approach to the issues of poverty and deprivation. Alderson first appealed to the fears of the jurymen with references to the overthrowing of "ancient dynasties" in Europe. He then argued against the notion that political or systemic change was a means to alleviate the suffering of the poor, attributing such reasoning to the "mischievous designs" of "evil men." In support of his point that "the possession of political rights was no indication of a guarantee for the possession of physical comforts," he referred in some detail to "certain documents" that, he claimed, showed that the people of Paris were worse off after the Revolution than before it – this is the section of the speech that Dickens chooses as the prime target for his attack. In the latter part of his address, Alderson suggested that the real answer to the problems of the poor lay in "education rightly directed." Essentially, he argued that the people needed to be taught to trust in God and their neighbors and should be instructed "much in the same way as a good father would teach his children." In this way, he said, people would be brought to understand that the "accumulation of capital in the manufacturing districts" and the possession of large estates were factors that would work to their advantage through the provision of employment, schools, etc. He concluded by recommending to the jury that they should take every opportunity of helping the poor – "for affording an opportunity of exercising virtue in this manner might be one reason why Providence permitted so much suffering."

7. Isaac Bickerstaff, originally a fictional astrologer created by Swift, was developed by Sir Richard Steele into the fictional editor-author of *The Tatler*. Many of Bickerstaff's articles are written from his apartment in Sheer Lane (not Shoe Lane) near Temple Bar (the street no longer exists). He describes his "Ecclesiastical Thermometer" in issue No 220

of *The Tatler* (5 September 1710).

8. This resembles Adolphe Thiers's description of the crowds who flocked to the capital during the disastrous winter of 1788–89: "A great number of vagabonds, without profession and without resources, thronged from all parts of France, and paraded their indigence and their nakedness from Versailles to Paris." (*The History of the French Revolution*, translated by F. Shoberl, 1838, 1, p 21.)

9. Louis-Philippe-Joseph d'Orléans (1747–93), Duc d'Orléans, was the younger brother of the king. He courted favor with the people with various magnanimous gestures, the best known of which was his order in the winter of 1788–89 that public tables be spread for the poor in the streets of Paris. During the Revolution he became known as "Égalité" (the name was officially bestowed on him in September 1792). Like many others, he fell foul of Robespierre and went to the guillotine in November 1793.

10. Adolphe Thiers (1797–1877) was a political journalist, historian, and statesman. His *Histoire de la Révolution française* was published in 1823–27. Dickens quotes here from the 1838 English translation, *The History of the French Revolution*, 1, p 20.

11. The three orders of the *ancien régime*: (a) the nobility, (b) the clergy, and (c) the "Third Estate" (Le Tiers État), which included all who were excluded from the other two orders, ranging from wealthy financiers and professionals to the peasant laborer. The newly elected deputies (national elections were held in early 1789) were in Paris in May for the États Généraux – see note 14 below. Dickens borrows directly from Thiers when he refers to the "extraordinary magnificence" of the court and "all the great dignatories of the state" – see the quoted passage in note 13 below.

12. The nobility had been determined to resist any change in its élite status, characterized by extensive feudal privileges and tax exemptions – a primary cause of peasant discontent. In August 1789, in an attempt to quell the increasingly violent protests, the aristocratic representatives offered to renounce certain of their feudal privileges. The king, however, withheld his consent. After the forced return of the royal family to Paris from Versailles in October, writes Thiers, "the aristocracy, separated from Louis XVI and incapable of executing any enterprise by his side, dispersed itself abroad and in the provinces" (*The History of the French Revolution*, 1, p 112).

13. The grand procession to open the 1789 États Généraux (see note 14 below) took place on 4 May. It started at the Church of Saint Louis in Versailles and ended at Notre-Dame. It is described by Carlyle ("The Procession," *The French Revolution*, Part 1, 4, Chapter 4) and by Thiers, who highlights the pomp and ceremony: "The King, the three orders, all

the great dignatories of the state, repaired to the church of Notre-Dame. The court had displayed extraordinary magnificence. The two higher orders were splendidly dressed. Princes, dukes and peers, gentlemen, prelates, were clad in purple, and wore hats with plumes of feathers..." (*The History of the French Revolution*, 1, p 24).

14. The "States-General," or États Généraux, was an assembly of the elected representatives of the three orders, or "estates" (see note 11 above). The assemblies, which typically went on for several weeks, were called by the king at times of national crisis, usually to discuss and give consent to fiscal reforms and subsidies. The 1789 États Généraux, the first since 1614, began in Paris on 5 May.

15. This wording is taken directly from Thiers (*The History of the French Revolution*, 1, p 35). Faced with the insistence of the two higher orders that the respective assemblies should be kept separate from one another, thus reducing the potential influence of Le Tiers État, the assembly of the Tiers proclaimed itself the Assemblée Nationale on 17 June 1789.

16. Following the elections of representatives and the subsequent establishment of the Assemblée Nationale, the electors refused to disperse. Thiers writes: "Paris then exhibited a new and extraordinary spectacle. The electors, assembled in [Dickens corrects "in" to "from"] sixty districts, refused to separate after the elections, and they remained assembled either to give instructions to their deputies, or from that fondness for agitation which is always to be found in the human heart, and which bursts forth with the greater violence the longer it has been repressed." (*The History of the French Revolution*, 1, pp 50–51.)

17. Follows Thiers. "This magnificent garden, surrounded by the richest shops in Europe, and forming an appurtenance to the palace of the Duke of Orleans, was the rendezvous of foreigners, of debauchees, of loungers, and, above all, of the most vehement agitators." (*The History of the French Revolution*, 1, p 51.)

18. Follows Thiers. "Ever since the cruel winter which had succeeded the disasters of Louis XIV, and immortalized the charity of Fenelon, so severe a season had not been known as that of 1788–89." (*The History of the French Revolution*, 1, p 21.) Fénelon (1651–1715) was a churchman, mystic, and prolific writer. He was appointed Archbishop of Cambrai in northern France in 1695, where, after falling out of favor with Louis XIV, he spent the last 15 years of his life. He became renowned and respected for his humane and philanthropic actions, typified by his hospitality to the armies fighting in Flanders.

19. Honoré-Gabriel Riqueti, Comte de Mirabeau (1749–91) became one of the most influential figures in the early stages of the Revolution, thanks to his charisma, political skills, and aggressively articulate oratory. He was a representative in the États Généraux (Député du Tiers État for Aix-en-

Provence) and played a key role in the establishment of the Assemblée
Nationale, in which he was a prominent actor. Mirabeau referred to
"famished Paris" on 15 July 1789, the day after the storming of the
Bastille, in his address to a deputation of representatives preparing to set
out from the Assemblée to try to obtain concessions from the king. Thiers
quotes part of the speech, in which Mirabeau calls on the deputies to tell
Louis that "his ferocious counsellors are turning back the flour that
commerce is sending to faithful and famished Paris" (*The History of the
French Revolution*, 1, p 63).

20. This incident, according to Thiers, occurred on 5 October 1789 (*The
History of the French Revolution*, 1, p 97). In response to a shortage of bread
in the bakers' shops, a large crowd of furious women made for the Hôtel
de Ville. A riot broke out, during which some of the demonstrators
occupied the bell tower and sounded the bell, sending a revolutionary call
to arms to the faubourgs. Following the incident, a deputation of women
demanding bread was received by the king at Versailles. The women
were accompanied by a mob of armed and hungry demonstrators and the
situation became increasingly dangerous as more and more people arrived
from Paris. The upshot was the royal family's forced return to Paris on 6
October.

Extract from *A Tale of Two Cities* (Quartier Saint Antoine), pp 235–239

1. See note 6 below on the poor state of Parisian streets in the 18th century.
2. Street cleaner.
3. A very common occupation in 18th century Paris: wood, rather than coal,
   was the heating fuel of the city. Its use diminished during the 19th
   century as coal was increasingly adopted in industrial and commercial
   settings, and for heating public buildings, but wood continued to be the
   fuel for domestic heating until gas, electricity, and oil replaced it (Fierro,
   1996). "*On le brûle à Paris comme on y dissipe la vie, sans y faire trop
   d'attention*," comments Louis-Sébastien Mercier (1740–1814) in his
   Tableau de Paris, 1782–88 (7, Chapter 567, "Bois à brûler").
4. The suburb of Saint Antoine centered around the rue du Faubourg Saint
   Antoine, which runs between what are now the place de la Bastille and the
   place de la Nation (along the border of the 11th and 12th *arrondissements*).
   Then a poor working-class district, it was here that the demonstrations and
   rioting of April 1789 broke out – presaging the storming of the Bastille on
   14 July. Dickens follows Carlyle (*The French Revolution*, 1837) in using the
   quartier Saint Antoine to portray the discontent and growing revolutionary
   fervor of the Parisian poor in general.
5. The "fabulous mill" is also mentioned in *The Mystery of Edwin Drood*,
   1870, Chapter 21: " 'It is not, Miss,' said the Billickin, with a sarcastic

smile, 'that I possess the mill I have heard of, in which old single ladies could be ground up young...,' " and in an article that Dickens wrote in collaboration with Mark Lemon: "It is like the Mill of the child's story, that ground old people young." ("A Paper-Mill," *Household Words*, 31 August 1850, included in Stone, 1969). Scholars have suggested various sources for this now obscure allusion and the present editor has been unable to find any new alternatives. Professor Andrew Sanders provides the most lucid and probable explanation: "This mill seems to have been a popular folk-device related to the wonder-working fountain of youth. Representations of a miller grinding old men and women into boys and girls appear with some regularity on eighteenth-century transfer-printed Staffordshire ware. ..." (Sanders, 2002, p 44).

6. Dickens's description of the street here is historically accurate. Murray's *A Handbook for Visitors to Paris*, 1864, for example, notes that until the 1840s "Foot pavement was unknown, except in two or three of the widest streets; everywhere else it consisted of large uneven stones, sloping from the houses down to the middle of the road, along which ran a copious gutter; and carriages were obliged to run with one wheel high up near the houses, the other low down in the gutter, splashing the foot-passengers." Arthur Young notes in his journal entry for 25 October 1787, "The streets are very narrow, and many of them crouded, nine tenths dirty, and all without foot-pavements." (*Travels in France during the Years 1787, 1788, 1789*, 1792.) And Mercier bemoans the lack of pedestrian pavements in *Tableau de Paris* (5, Chapter 438, "Trotoirs").

7. This street lighting system was introduced in the seventeenth century during the reign of Louis XIV. By the period covered in *A Tale of Two Cities*, lamps had replaced the original lanterns, but otherwise the system remained the same: the lamps were suspended from an iron bar by a rope and were lowered and raised by means of a simple pulley. *Galignani's New Paris Guide* of 1854 comments that formerly the city was "lighted by lamps suspended from ropes hung across the street, which, though aided by reflectors, and kept well cleaned, served for little else than to make the darkness visible. Gas has, however, long superseded these old contrivances." The old contrivances, as Dickens notes in the next paragraph, were to be put to macabre use during the Revolution (see, for example, the references to hangings from lamp-irons in Carlyle's *The French Revolution*, Part 1, 5, Chapters 7 and 9). Mercier comments on the inadequacy of Parisian street lighting in *Tableau de Paris* (9, Chapter 708, "Réverbères").

Extract from *A Tale of Two Cities* (The Aristocracy), pp 239–249

1. Dickens follows his principal sources in his use of this title. Mercier adopts the representative appellation "Monseigneur" in his portrayals of

the upper echelons of the aristocracy (see, for example, *Tableau de Paris*, 5, Chapter 371, "Audiences"), as does Carlyle (see, for example, *The French Revolution*, Part 1, 2, Chapter 6).

2. The *sanctum sanctorum* or Holy of Holies was the innermost apartment in the Jewish tabernacle, forbidden territory to everyone except the high priest. (The Ark of the Covenant was kept in the *sanctum sanctorum* of the Temple of Jerusalem.) The satirical analogy (and other details in the description) may derive from the chapter on "Audiences" in *Tableau de Paris* (5, Chapter 371). Mercier describes a similar reception – one of the regular social events that provided toadying guests with an opportunity to seek favors and patronage from the powerful host (*"puissant par le crédit du moment"*). In Mercier's account, the visitors crowd together *"dans les anti-chambres qui précedent le sanctuaire où monseigneur repose et prend son chocolat."*

3. A detail taken from the chapter on "Domestiques. Laquais" (2, Chapter 172) of *Tableau de Paris*: *"...un laquais du dernier ton porte deux montres comme son maître..."* Mercier comments facetiously on the tendency of servants to ape the manners and style of their masters – the more senior and style-conscious the servant, the more precise the imitation becomes. He also provides an acid commentary on the contemporary vogue of retaining large numbers of servants for no other purpose than to demonstrate wealth and influence (*"cette armée de domestiques inutiles, et faits uniquement pour la parade"*) – no doubt a source of inspiration for Dickens's description of Monseigneur's attendants in this paragraph.

4. That is, Monseigneur had been enjoying the company of ladies of the theater.

5. Charles II, known as the "Merry Monarch" because of his liking for the good life, was, like Monseigneur, preoccupied with the attractions of actresses and ladies of fashion. "... I find that there is nothing almost but bawdry at Court from top to bottom..." comments Pepys in his diary entry of 1 January 1663. Dickens writes that Charles "sold" England because he signed the secret Treaty of Dover with France in 1670 which committed him to finding a pretext for a war with Holland so that England could join France in attacking it – in return he received a substantial financial reward from Louis XIV. When he heard early rumors of a possible deal with France, Pepys noted, "But this is a thing that will make the Parliament and the Kingdom mad, and will turn to our ruine – for with this money the King shall wanton away his time in pleasures, and think nothing of the main till it be too late." (Diary entry of 28 April 1669.)

6. "The earth is the Lord's and the fulness thereof ..." (Psalms, 24:1); "For the earth is the Lord's, and the fulness thereof." (1 Corinthians, 10:26).

7. The *fermiers généraux* were tax collectors under the *ancien régime* working

under contract for the government, to which they paid set fees in advance in return for the right to collect various taxes – the more tax revenue they collected, the more money they made. They were generally wealthy and thus constituted useful connections by marriage for hard-up aristocrats with extravagant lifestyles. See also under "A Flight," note 24, p 332.

8. There are various stories involving golden apples in Greek and Roman mythology and fairy tales. Given that the Farmer-General's golden apple, clearly symbolizing his wealth, is associated with his winning the "prize" of Monseigneur's sister, the most likely allusion is to "The White Snake," a tale by the Brothers Grimm. A young servant performs seemingly impossible tasks in an attempt to win the hand of the king's daughter, but she continues to refuse him because of his lowly station until he succeeds in the ultimate task and brings her home a golden apple from the tree of life. The story is included M.L. Davis's 1850s translation of the Grimms' tales, published as *Home Stories*, 1855. Other possible candidates include the golden apples of Milanion who used them to beat Atalanta in a race and so win her hand; the "apple of discord" of Eris, inscribed "for the fairest" and thrown into a gathering of fellow gods and goddesses; and the golden apples guarded by the Hesperides and given to Hera as a marriage gift.

9. This account of the respective motivations and attitudes behind the alliance by marriage of Monseigneur's sister with the Farmer-General derives from a passage in the chapter on "Domestiques. Laquais" (2, Chapter 172) of *Tableau de Paris*, which it closely reflects. Mercier witheringly describes the willingness of nobles to marry for money and of ambitious commoners to marry for name. "*Il est assez plaisant,*" he writes, "*de voir un comte ou un vicomte, qui n'a qu'un beau nom, rechercher la fille opulente d'un financier; et le financier qui regorge de richesses, aller demander la fille de qualité, nue, mais qui tient à une illustre famille.*" He goes on to satirize the symbiotic vanities of commoner husband and aristocratic wife that Dickens touches upon in this paragraph. The reference to the convent as the alternative fate for Monseigneur's sister echoes Mercier's "*fille de condition ... menacée de passer dans un couvent le reste de sa vie.*"

10. These numbers are taken directly from Mercier's account of a typical farmer-general's stables and household in *Tableau de Paris*, 2, Chapter 172 ("Domestiques. Laquais").

11. The poor *quartier* of Saint Antoine (see previous extract) on the eastern side of Paris and the rich *quartier* of the Faubourg Saint Honoré on the western. The rue du Faubourg Saint Honoré, in what is now the eighth *arrondissement*, became a center of wealth and fashion in the 18th century. By the time of which Dickens is writing, it was lined with splendid mansions, like that of Monseigneur, and was rivalling the Faubourg Saint Germain as the principal aristocratic *quartier* of Paris.

12. This description and the details that follow of a society in which the senior military, religious, and professional positions are occupied by incompetent charlatans seem to derive largely from *Tableau de Paris*. For example, in his essay entitled "Officiers" (2, Chapter 106), Mercier comments that the large majority of military officers "*n'ont jamais vu le feu*" and that in general they are "*fort désoeuvrés et très-peu instruits.*" In "Du ton militaire" (8, Chapter 640), he writes of the lack of military training and discipline, suggesting that the officer "*ne craint point le péril, mais la fatigue, et surtout l'absence du luxe.*" Senior ecclesiastics are also a recurrent target of ridicule in the *Tableau*: Mercier criticizes their idleness and love of luxury in, for example, "Abbés" (1, Chapter 90), "Évêques" (1, Chapter 91) and "Le clergé" (4, Chapter 345). The arrogance and ignorance of "civil officers" are highlighted in "Bureaucratie" (9, Chapter 695).

13. The medical profession is another of Mercier's favorite targets. He criticizes the ignorant conservatism and the hypocrisy of doctors in, for example, "Médecins" (2, Chapter 135) and "Conseil de Santé" (2, chapter 204), noting in the latter that "... *les médecins ne songent pas à conserver la santé de l'homme; ils attendent le profit de la maladie.*"

14. A rendering of Mercier's "Faiseurs de projets," the title and subject of Volume 1, Chapter 73 of *Tableau de Paris*. These were the numerous well-meaning but inept and blinkered theorists who wasted their time developing impractical and unrealistic schemes for solving political, economic, and social problems on a grand scale, usually ignoring essential details. Mercier returns to them in his essay on "Rêves politiques" (6, Chapter 497), likening their plans to that of the architect who, in his design of a magnificent and beautifully proportioned mansion, forgets to include a staircase.

15. In Volume 7, Chapter 580 of *Tableau de Paris* ("Philosophie"), Mercier writes of the degradation of philosophical thought in the various pronouncements of foolish, ignorant, or self-seeking authors. Dickens's reference to Babel reflects Mercier's contention that "*il en résulte une confusion et une discordance qui ne produisent que de bruit.*" Carlyle, too, writes of the decadence and appropriation by fashionable society of the *philosophe*: "Philosophism sits joyful in her glittering saloons, the dinner-guest of Opulence grown ingenuous, the very Nobles proud to sit by her..." (*The French Revolution*, Part 1, 2, Chapter 1).

The adjective "Unbelieving" refers to the spread of atheism among sections of the privileged classes, which Mercier associates with arrogance, fashionable *insouciance*, and uncaring hedonism (7, Chapter 595, "Athéisme").

The "Unbelieving Chemists" are no doubt representative of Mercier's "*charlatans ... dans l'empire des sciences et de la littérature*" whose claims and projects he satirizes in his chapter on "Charlatans" (3, Chapter 220) – *"L'un vous promet la découverte démontrée et la définition exacte d'un agent universel, qui a la propriété de modifier la matière en tout sens, et d'opérer toutes les merveilles de la nature."* The "transmutation of metals," or the search for the Philosopher's Stone which would turn baser metals into gold, was one of the principal goals of alchemists, whose proliferation Mercier notes in "Chercheurs de la Pierre philosophale" (9, Chapter 685).

16. Dickens follows *Tableau de Paris* in suggesting that the use of spies was widespread in pre-Revolutionary Paris. Mercier describes them as *"l'instrument universel dont on se sert à Paris pour pomper les secrets,"* and suggests that their reports were more influential in determining the actions of government ministers than reasoned argument or policy (1, Chapter 59, "Espions").

17. Elderly ladies who behave as if they are very young ladies come in for hard treatment in Dickens's work – see, for example, the portrayals of Mrs Skewton in *Dombey and Son* and Lady Tippins in *Our Mutual Friend*. In the context of Pre-Revolutionary Paris, Sanders (2002, p 84) identifies a close approximation of this sentence in *Tableau de Paris*: *"Il n'y a qu'à Paris où les femmes de soixante ans se parent encore comme à vingt ..."* (2, Chapter 177, "Remarques"). Regarding the reference to mothers who have little to do with their children, Sanders points to a comment in the same chapter: *"Avec des nourrices, des gouvernantes, des précepteurs, des colleges et des couvens, certaines femmes ne s'apperçoivent presque pas qu'elles sont mères."*

18. Les Convulsionnaires – the name derives from the exhibitionist antics of the crowds who gathered around the tomb of the strict Jansenist François de Pâris at the Saint-Médard cemetery in Paris in the late 1720s and early 1730s. There were claims of miracle cures and increasing numbers of people indulged in demonstrations of mass hysteria, speaking in tongues, prophesies, contortions and convulsions, and various other physical and psychic disorders. The theatricality of the practices brought the sect widespread notice and, while it did no good to the reputation of Jansenism, it gained some fashionable popularity during the eighteenth century. Mercier mentions the Convulsionists in the *Tableau* in "Les j'ai vu, et les je n'ai point vu" (2, Chapter 190) and "Amour du merveilleux" (2, Chapter 191), noting in the latter the dramatic effectiveness of some Convulsionist performances. In "Prédicateurs" (7, Chapter 582), however, he describes a Jansenist fanatic who is clearly a member of the sect, and derides *"des contorsions et du style de l'énergumène"* as he addresses his audience.

19. A name given to various mendicant orders connected with the Muslim faith. Dickens presumably has in mind the "Whirling Dervishes," who express their religious fervor in energetic dances.

20. Mercier describes this sect in Volume 2, Chapter 191 of the *Tableau*

("Amour du merveilleux"), including the details that Dickens gives here.

21. The Palais des Tuileries, the royal palace built in 1564 and destroyed by the Communards in 1871. Louis XVI lived there following his arrest in October 1789.

22. Reflecting Mercier's words in Volume 3, Chapter 279 ("Le bourreau") of *Tableau de Paris*: "*Il est frisé, poudré, galonné, en bas de soie blancs, en escarpins pour monter au fatal poteau ...*"

23. Again, these details are from Volume 3, Chapter 279 of the *Tableau*: "*Entr'eux*," writes Mercier of France's public executioners, "*ils s'appellent (à l'instar des évêques) Monsieur de Paris, Monsieur de Chartres, Monsieur d'Orléans, etc.*"

24. This description of the fawning and servile attitudes of the guests draws on Mercier's account of such a reception in Volume 5, Chapter 371 ("Audiences") of the *Tableau*, as does the next paragraph, with its description of Monseigneur's behavior towards his hopeful visitors.

25. Sanders (2002) notes an allusion to Matthew 10:14: "And whosoever shall not receive you, nor hear your words, when ye depart out of that house or city, shake off the dust of your feet."

26. Mercier makes many references in *Tableau de Paris* to the dangers of being a pedestrian in eighteenth century Paris, attributable, as Dickens describes here, both to the lack of foot pavements and to the reckless speed with which carriages were driven through the streets. See in particular "Gare! Gare!" (1, Chapter 39), in which Mercier writes at length on the frequency of accidents and the heedlessness of carriage owners and drivers to the damage they may do or have done. "*Les roues menaçantes qui portent orgueilleusement le riche, n'en volent pas moins rapidement sur un pavé teint du sang des malheureuses victimes qui expirent dans d'effroyables tortures...*," he comments, bringing to mind the carriage of Dickens's Monsieur le Marquis. Arthur Young, too, was struck by this criminal carelessness during his stay in Paris in October 1787, and writes of "... an infinity of one-horse cabriolets, which are driven by young men of fashion and their imitators, alike fools, with such rapidity as to be real nuisances, and render the streets exceedingly dangerous, without an incessant caution" (*Travels in France during the Years 1787, 1788, 1789*, 1792).

27. The extent to which Dickens was inspired by a particular source for this important incident in the novel is open to speculation. The causes of the accident – reckless driving and the lack of protection for pedestrians – clearly derive from Mercier and probably also from Young (see note 26 above). The choice of a child victim is characteristic: in Dickens's work the victimized or suffering child is often symbolic of an uncaring and dysfunctional system (Oliver Twist, Little Nell, young David Copperfield, Florence Dombey, etc). This too, however, may have been inspired by one or more of his sources. In his journal entry for 25 October

1787, following the above-quoted comments about the dangerous streets of Paris, Arthur Young notes, "I saw a poor child run over and probably killed..." (*Travels in France*). Furthermore, Sanders (2002, p 88) suggests that the source may be the German Prince von Pueckler-Muskau's account of an incident in which his own reckless driving caused his carriage to run over a little boy (an English translation of Pueckler-Muskau's letters was published in 1832). This did not take place in Paris, the child was not killed, and the Prince's attitude is very different from that of the Marquis, but there is some similarity in the detail of the two descriptions.

28. Madame Defarge, the sinister and pitilessly vengeful wife of Ernest Defarge. Her "knitting" identifies her as a future *Tricoteuse*, one of the ardent Revolutionary *citoyennes* who took their knitting with them to meetings of the Convention Nationale and of its Tribunal Révolutionnaire and, most notoriously, to public executions. Carlyle describes them as "famed *Tricoteuses*, Patriot Knitters" who "shriek or knit as the case needs" (*The French Revolution*, Part 3, 2, Chapter 5).

Extract from *A Tale of Two Cities* (The Storming of the Bastille), pp 250–257

1. See the extract on "Quartier Saint Antoine" (pp 235–239) and note 4 to that piece (p 378).
2. Dickens bases his narrative of the preparations for the assault on the Bastille, the assault itself and the immediate aftermath on Carlyle's historical account in *The French Revolution*, Part 1, 5, Chapters 5 ("Give us Arms," on the preparations), 6 ("Storm and Victory," again on the preparations and then the sacking of the Bastille) and 7 ("Not a Revolt," on the release of the prisoners and the killings that followed). Examples of specific parallels are given in the notes below.
3. In *A Tale of Two Cities* Defarge and his fellow revolutionaries use the name Jacques as an instrument of anonymity and to identify each other as followers of the cause. "Jacques" is a name traditionally associated with the French peasantry, condescendingly referred to as "Jacques Bonhomme" in the 14th century – hence *jacquerie*, originally the name given to a peasant uprising of the 1350s in the Île de France and subsequently adopted as a term for any peasant revolt.
4. Dickens's vision of the mob as a "living sea," which he sustains throughout this narrative, seems to derive from Carlyle, who refers, for example, to the "swelling tide of men" and to a "living deluge."
5. These details are consistent with Carlyle's description of the building (*The French Revolution*, Part 1, 5, Chapter 6). There is a detailed description of the exterior and interior of the Bastille in Berville and Barrière's edition of the memoirs of Linguet and Dusaulx, which was one

of Carlyle's sources (Berville and Barrière, 1821, pp 237–249).

6. Carlyle mentions a wine-seller among the most prominent combatants: "Cholat the wine-merchant has become an impromptu cannoneer" (*The French Revolution*, Part 1, 5, Chapter 6). According to Dusaulx's account of the siege, Cholat, like Defarge, was also prominent in the capture of the governor of the Bastille (*De l'Insurrection parisienne et de la prise de la Bastille*, 1790, p 340).

7. Sanders (2002, p 118) suggests that this image of the South Seas may derive from a passage in Oliver Goldsmith's *History of the Earth and Animated Nature* (1774), which was in Dickens's library. The passage, quoted at length by Sanders, describes the "great weight and irregularity" of the surf in various parts of the world, especially "upon the coasts of the East Indies."

8. Dusaulx records the pillaging of the archives of the Bastille and, with regard to the two cries that follow, the exploration of the dungeons and the search for instruments of torture (*De l'Insurrection parisienne et de la prise de la Bastille*, 1790, p 346).

9. This relates to the fictional narrative of *A Tale of Two Cities*. The North Tower was the location of the cell in which Dr Alexandre Manette was imprisoned. Defarge looked after Manette following his release and is now in search of any revealing documents that may be hidden his cell. The search for incriminating letters, evidence of past injustice and cruelty, has its basis in fact. Carlyle writes, "Likewise ashlar stones of the Bastille continue thundering through the dusk; its paper archives shall fly white. Old secrets come to view; and long-buried Despair finds a voice." (*The French Revolution*, Part 1, 5, Chapter 7.) And Dusaulx refers to "*les papiers! ces formidables témoins*" (*De l'Insurrection parisienne et de la prise de la Bastille*, 1790, p 346).

As regards the "North Tower," this does not correspond to any of the names by which the eight towers of the Bastille were officially known (see Berville and Barrière, 1821, pp 237–249) and may simply be an invention. However, Maxwell (2003, p 455) intriguingly cites a passage from *The Marchioness of Brinvilliers*, 1846, a novel by Albert Smith (1816–60), in which Smith claims that the Tour de la Liberté of the Bastille was also known as the Tour du Nord. This seems improbable, although there is a glimmer of logic in it. The Bastille was rectangular, with two towers on the shorter north and south sides – there was, therefore no one northern tower. In addition, the Tour de la Liberté was on the western side of the building, while the northern towers were the Tours du Puits and du Coin. But, according to Smith, the name dates from an early period of the building's history before those two towers existed (the Bastille was built between 1370 and 1382, although some accounts hold that the Tours du Puits and du Coin were added in the 16th century). The Tour de la Liberté did predate the Tours du Puits and du Coin and before their construction would have been, with the Tour de la Chapelle, one of the northern towers. Further, plans of the building show that the Tours de la Liberté and de la Chapelle were not exactly opposite each other and that the former was more to the north than the latter. There is, therefore, some thread of logic in Smith's explanation, but it is a very slender one and no history of the Bastille that this editor has read refers to an alternative name for the Tour de la Liberté (Maxwell also was unable to identify Smith's source). Nevertheless, whatever the historical accuracy of Smith's account, it does seem possible that Dickens had it in mind when he chose the name North Tower.

10. When asked his name in an early chapter of the novel, the traumatized Dr Manette responds, "One Hundred and Five, North Tower." This is consistent with the actual practice in the Bastille, where prisoners were known by their cell number and the tower in which it was located: "... *les prisonniers étaient appelés du nom de la tour où ils étaient renfermés, joint au numéro de leur chambre*" (Berville and Barrière, 1821, p 246).

11. The physical details of the cell seem to be historically accurate. Linguet, for example, refers to the small window ("*un seul soupirail*") with three iron grills, one on the inside, one in the middle and the other on the outside of the prison wall (*Mémoires sur la Bastille*, p 62). Another account refers to the narrow chimneys that were "*fermées dans le bas, au haut, et quelquefois de distance en distance, par des barres de fer*" (Berville and Barrière, 1821, p 246). As to furniture, the same account lists a straw bed, "*une ou deux tables*," and "*deux ou trois chaises*" as the standard items. Linguet writes bitterly of his two worm-ridden mattresses, folding table, and one worn out cane chair (*Mémoires sur la Bastille*, p 65).

12. It was a common habit, apparently, of prisoners of the Bastille to write their names and messages on the walls of their cells: "*Les murs étaient nus et seulement variés çà et là par des noms de prisonniers, des dessins au charbon ou à l'ocre, des vers, des sentences et autres expressions du long ennui des habitants de ces tristes lieux*" (Berville and Barrière, 1821, p 247).

13. The governor of the Bastille was the Marquis de Launay (1740–89). Unlike Carlyle, Dickens does not name him, but in other respects the details of his arrest and subsequent fate are consistent with those in *The French Revolution* (Part 1, 5, Chapter 7). Both narratives describe him as "old," but, as can be seen from his dates above, this is something of an exaggeration.

14. cf Carlyle, "in grey frock with poppy-coloured riband." The decoration was the Croix de Saint-Louis which, according to Linguet, de Launay had and which, he says, was given to senior officers of the Bastille as a matter of course "*afin de leur donner apparemment un extérieur plus imposant*" (*Mémoires sur la Bastille*, p 135).

15. This account of the killing of de Launay is historically accurate (see *The French Revolution*, Part 1, 5, Chapter 7) except of course for the involvement of the fictional Madame Defarge. In reality, the person who cut off the dead governor's head was an unemployed cook called Desnot.

16. See note 7 to the extract on Saint Antoine, p 379.

17. At the time of the assault on the Bastille, there were only seven prisoners to be released. Of these, two were insane (an Irishman who had been arrested for spying and a man called Tavernier, suspected of complicity in an assassination attempt on Louis XV and imprisoned since 1759); four were forgers; and one was an aristocrat who had been imprisoned at the request of his family (sources vary on the reason).

18. An allusion to the Day of Judgement, with the prisoners like souls brought up from hell: "And the sea gave up the dead which were in it; and death and hell delivered up the dead which were in them: and they were judged every man according to their works." (Revelations, 20:13.)

19. cf Carlyle: "Along the streets of Paris circulate Seven Bastille Prisoners, borne shoulder-high; seven Heads on pikes; the Keys of the Bastille; and much else." (*The French Revolution*, Part 1, 5, Chapter 7.)

20. This reverts to the fictional narrative. Lucie is the daughter of Dr Manette and the wife of Charles Darnay, now living in London. Her "fancy" is her increasing sense of foreboding, described earlier in the chapter and developed through the metaphor of "echoing footsteps."

21. The incident described in the extract on Saint Antoine, p 235.

Extract from *A Tale of Two Cities* (The Terror), pp 258–259

1. The "new era" of the Republic was heralded by the introduction of an entirely new calendar. It was formally adopted in October 1793, and backdated to the day on which the Republic was inaugurated, 22 September 1792, which then became 1 Vendémiaire, An I. In *The French Revolution* Carlyle explains the new system and provides a table of months and days (Part 3, 4, Chapter 4).

2. Louis XVI was executed on 21 January 1793.

3. A slogan quoted in *The French Revolution*. According to Carlyle, it appeared in "huge tricolor print" on the wall of the Palais Royal (then renamed Palais Égalité): "REPUBLIC ONE AND INDIVISIBLE; LIBERTY, EQUALITY, FRATERNITY OR DEATH: *National Property*" (Part 3, 5, Chapter 2).

4. The "tyrants of the earth" were the European monarchies gathering against Republican France, outraged by the execution of Louis XVI and worried by the expansionist rhetoric of Revolutionary leaders. In his chapter "Fatherland in Danger," covering March 1793, Carlyle describes the massive recruiting drive that took place in France in the face of

advancing Prussian and Austrian forces and indications of aggression from other European powers, including Britain, "that tyrannous Island" (*The French Revolution*, Part 3, 3, Chapter 4). The "recruitment of Three-hundred Thousand men, which was the decreed force for this year, is like to have work enough laid to its hand," he writes. With regard to Dickens's reference to a black flag on Notre Dame, in the same chapter Carlyle comments, "And so there is Flag of *Fatherland in Danger* waving from the Townhall, Black Flag from the top of Notre-Dame Cathedral..."

5. To "sow dragon's teeth" is to foment strife or war. The expression derives from the myth of Cadmus, the founder of Thebes, who slew a dragon and, following the advice of Athene, sowed its teeth, from which fully armed warriors instantly sprang up. They fought each other until only five survived (these five helped Cadmus to build Thebes and became its noble ancestors).

6. See note 1 above. The first year of the new calendar (1 Vendémiaire–30 Fructidor, An I) ran from 22 September 1792 to 21 September 1793.

7. An allusion to the story of the flood, in which "the windows of heaven were opened" to let the rain fall for forty days and nights (Genesis, 7:11 and 12).

8. An allusion to the biblical story of the creation: "And God called the light Day, and the darkness he called Night. And the evening and the morning were the first day" (Genesis, 1:5).

9. See note 2 above. Carlyle describes the execution and holding up of the head in Part 3, 2, Chapter 8 of *The French Revolution*.

10. In the last months of her life, Marie Antoinette was imprisoned in the Conciergerie, the famous prison attached to the Palais de Justice on the Île de la Cité. She was executed on 16 October 1793. Carlyle describes her trial and execution, referring to her as "a worn discrowned Widow of Thirty-eight; grey before her time ..." (*The French Revolution*, Part 3, 4, Chapter 7).

11. The Tribunal Révolutionnaire was set up by the Convention Nationale in March 1793 to try people accused of counter-revolutionary activities or activities that threatened public safety. The Convention nominated the judges, juries, and the public accuser (Fouquier-Tinville), who became one of the most feared men during The Terror. The "revolutionary committees" were the Comités de Surveillance that were set up, also in March 1793, in every commune of France. These committees comprised twelve elected members and were charged with arresting and examining anyone suspected of anti-Republic activities. According to Carlyle, there were "some Forty-four Thousand of them awake and alive all over France" (*The French Revolution*, Part 3, 3, Chapter 5).

12. The "Loi des Suspects" was passed by the Convention Nationale on 17 September 1793 and marked the beginning of The Terror. People could

be arrested simply for the expression of counter-revolutionary sentiments or if they had not been formally approved as "good citizens" by their Comité de Surveillance (a process inevitably polluted by personal prejudice and corruption). On 10 June 1794 (22 Prairial, An II), the Loi du 22 Prairial considerably broadened the basis on which people could be arrested as "suspects" and made the trial of anyone thus accused no more than a nominal process, at the end of which execution was more or less guaranteed. Carlyle refers to the "Law of the Suspect" in Part 3, 4, Chapter 6 of *The French Revolution* and to the "Law of Prairial" in Part 3, 6, Chapter 4.

13. The use of a beheading machine as the method of execution in France was proposed by a doctor named Joseph Ignace Guillotin (1738–1814), from whom it derived its name – "which product popular gratitude or levity christens by a feminine derivative name, as if it were his daughter: *La Guillotine!*" (*The French Revolution*, Part 1, 4, Chapter 4). The machine that resulted from Guillotin's proposal was formally adopted and first put to work in the spring of 1792.

14. There were many facetious terms and phrases for the Guillotine and its sinister function. Among the ones Dickens lists here, cf Carlyle's "their 'national razor,' their *rasoir national,*" (*The French Revolution*, Part 3, 5, Chapter 3) and "They too must 'look through the little window;' they too must 'sneeze into the sack,' *éternuer dans le sac ...*" (Part 3, 6, Chapter 1).

15. There was widespread ransacking of churches and destruction of Christian monuments and relics, and anti-Christian celebrations substituted symbols of the Revolution for objects of Christian worship. "This, O National Convention wonder of the universe, is our New Divinity; *Goddess of Reason*, worthy, and alone worthy of revering," writes Carlyle, describing a Revolutionary festival held in Notre-Dame (*The French Revolution*, Part 3, 5, Chapter 4).

16. These were leading representatives of the Girondins, the moderate party in the Convention Nationale. The Girondins were overthrown in May–June 1793, when 22 of their leaders were arrested and imprisoned. In October, they were tried and sentenced to death. One of the group stabbed and killed himself in court, but his body was taken to the guillotine nevertheless and beheaded with the rest. See *The French Revolution*, Part 3, 4, Chapter 8 ("The Twenty-Two") for Carlyle's account of the trial and executions.

17. The Chief Executioner at this stage of the Revolution was Henri Sanson (Samson) (1767–1840), who had taken over from his father, Charles-Henri Sanson (1740–1806) after the execution of Louis XVI. Dickens plays on the name to evoke the biblical story of Samson who, renowned for his great strength, tore away the gates of Gaza (Judges, 16:3) and was later blinded by the Philistines (Judges, 16:21). "God's own temple" is the

body: "Know ye not that your body is the temple of the Holy Ghost which is in you, which ye have of God, and ye are not your own?" (1 Corinthians, 6:19).

Extract from *A Tale of Two Cities* (The Guillotine), pp 260–265

1. Tumbrils, or open carts, were used during the Revolution to convey people from prison to the Guillotine. Carlyle mentions them frequently in *The French Revolution* and names a chapter after them (Part 3, 6, Chapter 3).
2. See note 13 to the previous extract, p 390.
3. An allusion to Jesus's words as he casts out the traders and moneylenders from the temple at Jerusalem: "Is it not written, My house shall be called of all nations the house of prayer? but ye have made it a den of thieves." (Mark, 11:17.)
4. From the Second Calendar's tale in the *Arabian Nights* story of the porter and the ladies of Baghdad. These words are spoken by a Princess to a man who has been transformed into an ape. On hearing them he returns to his true form.
5. Dickens's metaphor derives from the tumbrils' peaceful agricultural origins. The contrast between the sinister use to which the carts were put during the Revolution and their normal function provides a powerful symbol of the transforming nature of violence.
6. Sanders (2002, p 163) notes that this description of the victims' behavior is consistent with Carlyle's account in Part 3, 5, Chapter 7 of *The French Revolution*: "Men have adjusted themselves: complaint issues not from that Death-tumbril. Weak women and *ci-devants*, their plumage and finery all tarnished, sit there; with a silent gaze, as if looking into the Infinite Black. The once light lip wears a curl of irony, uttering no word; and the Tumbril fares along." Carlyle also mentions the increasing familiarity of the sight of the tumbrils, which Dickens describes in the preceding paragraph: "And daily, we say, like a black Spectre, silently through that Life-tumult, passes the Revolution Cart ... A Spectre with which one has grown familiar."
7. The tumbrils are on their way from the Conciergerie, the prison attached to the Palais de Justice on the Île de la Cité, to the place de la Révolution (place de la Concorde). At the time of the Revolution, the rue de Rivoli did not exist (its construction began early in the next century) and so the tumbrils took what was then the main route, the rue St Honoré, which they joined at the end of the rue du Roule.
8. This is the fictional character John Barsad (the adopted name of Solomon Pross), whom Carton has compelled to help in the plot to save Darnay. Barsad is a prison spy, or *mouton* (hence Dickens's "prison-sheep").

Carlyle writes that the public accuser Fouquier-Tinville had "... his *moutons*, detestable traitor jackals, who report and bear witness; that they themselves may be allowed to live ..." (*The French Revolution*, Part 3, 6, Chapter 5).

9. The family name by which Charles Darnay is known in France.

10. The tumbrils are turning off the rue St Honoré into the rue Royale (then rue de la Révolution) to enter the place de la Concorde (then place de la Révolution).

11. *Tricoteuses* – see note 28, p 385. The enthusiastic female spectators at public executions were also known as the *furies de guillotine*. Mercier describes them in chapter 55 of *Le Nouveau Paris*, 1799: "*elles environnaient les échafauds; elles vociféraient dans les groupes ...*".

12. A minor character in the novel, a friend and follower of Madame Defarge. Her adoption of an abstract Revolutionary concept as a name is historically sound – the practice was not unknown and reflected the Revolutionary obsession with obliterating all connections with the past (as illustrated, for example, by the new calendar and the changing of the names of streets and buildings that had any monarchical associations).

13. Madame Defarge, unbeknown to The Vengeance, has just been killed.

14. One of the many ironic names by which the Guillotine was known (see also note 14, p 390). "Sainte Guillotine" is mentioned by Carlyle in Part 3, 4, Chapter 1 of *The French Revolution*.

15. This is an exact quotation from the "Burial of the Dead" section of the *Book of Common Prayer* (it derives from John, 11:25 and 26 – "Jesus said unto her, I am the resurrection and the life: he that believeth in me, though he were dead, yet shall he live: And whosoever liveth and believeth in me shall never die."). In an earlier chapter, the words come repeatedly into Sydney Carton's mind as he wanders around the streets of Paris, contemplating his planned sacrifice and reflecting on his past life.

"A Monument of French Folly," pp 275–289

1. The Court of the Common Council of the Corporation of London (the governing body of the City of London), responsible for the administration and management of the Corporation's affairs.

2. The meeting in question was held on 11 July 1850 and was reported at length in *The Times* (12 July 1850, p 8). The subject of the debate was the negative reaction of the Royal Commission on Smithfield Market and the Meat Supply of London to the recommendations of the Council's Markets Improvement Committee and the Committee's rebuttal of the Commission's comments. Essentially, the report of the Royal Commission had recommended removing the livestock market from the "thickly-inhabited parts of the metropolis" to the suburbs (its conclusions

were published in *The Times* on 3 June 1850). In an effort to resist the change, the Markets Improvement Committee had devised a (very expensive) plan for the enlargement and improvement of the existing site.

At the meeting of 11 July the Committee Chairman, H.L. Taylor, delivered a speech full of die-hard rhetoric that attempted to discredit members of the Royal Commission and the press and espoused a bigoted nationalism in its rejection of the idea that England might follow the example of the Continent, specifically France, in the arrangement of livestock markets and abattoirs. In a leader of 17 July 1850 (p 4), *The Times*, which had campaigned for the removal of the market (for example, in its leader comment of 3 June 1850, p 4) and was one of Taylor's prime targets, referred to the bombast and incoherence of the Committee's reaction and described it as the "final growl of a threatened interest."

The day Dickens read the report of Taylor's speech, he wrote to W.H. Wills (Sub Editor of *Household Words*): "I observe a report in the Times this morning of a most intolerably asinine speech about Smithfield, made in the Common Council by one Taylor. ... If you will look to the other papers, and send me the best report, or a collation of the greatest absurdities enunciated by this wiseacre, I will try to make something of it ..." (*Pilgrim*, 6, p 129). The result was the acutely satirical article "Lively Turtle" (*Household Words*, 26 October 1850), in which Dickens mimics the tone and reactionary opinions of Taylor and his fellow Common Councillors to great effect.

The reference to "frog-eating" was in fact an interjection from another Councillor during the chairman's speech. H.L. Taylor, rejecting the notion that London should adopt the continental system of abattoirs, insisted that "He would prefer remaining English. (Cheers.) He did not want to go to France to learn how to live. (Continued cheering.) ... It was notorious that the people of France lived on soups made of very poor beef. (Mr G. Taylor – 'Frogs, too.')" (*The Times*, 12 July 1850, p 8). There is no reference to "wooden shoes" in *The Times* report, but this was probably one of the gems that Wills produced from another source, as it is included in Dickens's brief description of the meeting in "Lively Turtle": "A good deal of it was what I call a sound, old English discussion. One eloquent speaker objected to the French as wearing wooden shoes; and a friend of his reminded him of another objection to that foreign people, namely, that they eat frogs."

3. This is in the style of Doctor Caius in Shakespeare's *The Merry Wives of Windsor* (performed by Dickens's amateur theatrical company in 1848).

4. Strictly, a blue neckerchief with white spots and a dark blue spot in the center (named after the pugilist Jim Belcher), but also used more generally to mean a parti-colored handkerchief.

5. Smithfield, in the City of London, has been the site of a meat market
since the Middle Ages. The City of London Corporation formally
established a cattle market there under Royal Charter in 1638. As the
market grew in size and the city grew around it, it became more and more
a matter for public concern, not only because of the huge numbers of live
cattle and sheep that were herded through the streets and treated with
considerable cruelty, but also because of what Timbs describes as its
"attendant nuisances of knackers' yards, tainted-sausage makers,
slaughter-houses, tripe-dressers, cat's-meat boilers, catgut-spinners,
bone-houses, and other noxious trades, in the very heart of London"
(*Curiosities of London*, 1855). The livestock market was condemned by law
in 1852 and closed in June 1855, when it was transferred to the
Metropolitan Cattle Market in Islington. A new market was built on the
Smithfield site and opened in 1868 as the London Central Meat Market
(dealing in dead meat only). It is still in business, but has been
extensively refurbished.

6. A play on the expression "he that runs may read," derived from the Bible
(Habbakuk, 2:2 – "And the Lord answered me, and said, Write the vision,
and make it plain upon tables, that he may run that readeth it."). Dickens
probably has in mind John Keble's version of it in his popular book of
sacred verse *The Christian Year*, 1827: "There is a book, who runs may
read,/Which heavenly truth imparts,/And all the lore its scholars
need,/Pure eyes and Christian hearts."

7. An area in East London. In the 19th century, it was poor and densely
populated.

8. Newgate Market, a meat market, was between Paternoster Row and
Newgate Street in the City. Whitechapel, in East London not far from
Spitalfields, was one of the poorest and most disreputable quarters of the
Victorian capital. Newport Market, a meat market, was in Soho.
Leadenhall Market, in Gracechurch Street in the City, was a general
market with large sections dedicated to meat (it had formerly been
renowned for its meat but by the 1850s was better known for poultry and
game). Clare Market, between Lincoln's Inn Fields and the Strand, was
a meat, fish, and vegetable market. All these markets have long since
disappeared except for Leadenhall, which was rebuilt in 1881 and
continues to trade.

9. The small sunken court at the front of a house, shut off from the
pavement by railings and reached by the basement stairs.

10. Sir Richard Owen (1804–92), the celebrated naturalist and anatomist.
Owen was appointed in 1847 to a government commission charged with
inquiring into the health of the metropolis and in 1849 to the Royal
Commission on Smithfield (see above, note 2). He was strongly opposed
to on-site slaughterhouses and the driving of cattle and sheep through

the crowded streets of London.

11. Streets in the immediate neighborhood of Smithfield. Snow Hill is described in chapter 4 of *Nicholas Nickleby* – the famous old inn the Saracen's Head (favored in the novel by Mr Squeers on his London visits) was located there.

12. Echoing the chorus of the popular patriotic 18th century song "The Roast Beef of Old England," by Henry Fielding and Richard Leveridge: "Oh! the Roast Beef of Old England,/And oh! the old English Roast Beef." The song satirizes the weakness of contemporary England by comparison with its glorious past, blaming France for its decline: "But since we have learned from effeminate France/To eat their ragouts, as well as to dance,/We are fed up with nothing but vain complaisance,/Oh! the Roast Beef, &c" (*Book of English Songs*, 1851).

13. Mistress Quickly actually says that prawns, not prunes, are ill for a green wound (*Henry IV, Part Two*, 2, 1).

14. An allusion to "Rule Britannia," the famous patriotic song generally attributed to the poet James Thomson (1700–48). The chorus runs, "Rule Britannia, Britannia rules the waves;/Britons never will be slaves."

15. James Bruce (1730–94), the traveller and explorer who discovered the source of the Blue Nile. He spent almost two years in Abyssinia, which he describes in detail in his *Travels to Discover the Source of the Nile*, published in 1790.

16. According to the report in *The Times* (see note 2 above), Taylor had used the Royal Charter argument in his address to the Common Council, insisting that "The city should contend for its rights for a market which had been given to it by charter, confirmed by acts of Parliament, and which the Government ought not to take away from them unless it showed that they had neglected their duty and unless some well understood compensation was agreed upon." (See also note 5 above regarding the Royal Charter.)

17. These were the main cattle markets supplying Paris: the one at Poissy, to the west of the city, dated back to the 13th century and the Marché de Sceaux, to the south, was held at Bourg la Reine.

18. Until the beginning of the 19th century, the butchers of Paris did their own slaughtering and preparation. Thus the city had faced similar welfare and sanitary problems to those of London, with animals being driven through busy streets and slaughtered in the back yards of butchers' premises. By a decree of 1810, under Napoléon I, five abattoirs were to be built in what were then outer districts of the city. They were all ready for business in 1818 and private slaughtering henceforth became illegal. Three were in the north of Paris (the Abattoirs du Roule, de Montmartre, and de Popincourt) and the other two were in the south (Villejuif and Grenelle).

19. The Metropolitan Police Act of 1829 established the Metropolitan Police as the law-enforcement agency for London. A further act of 1839 absorbed the formerly independent Thames Police and Bow Street Runners into the Metropolitan Police and set up a special force for the City (which until then had continued to rely on Bow Street patrols and the antiquated system of night watchmen). The 1839 act, to which Dickens is presumably referring here, also considerably extended the powers of the police and the range of arrestable offenses.

20. See the introduction to this chapter.

21. Dickens visited Poissy on 13 February 1851, and wrote to his wife, "It continues to be delightful weather here – frosty, but very clear and fine. Leech and I had a charming country walk before breakfast this morning – at Poissy – and enjoyed it very much." (*Pilgrim*, 6, p 290.)

22. *Chiffonniers* (and *chiffonnières*) were in the rag-and-bone trade – the *chiffonnier* gathered his raw material by scouring the streets and searching through rubbish for rags, paper, old shoes, scrap metal, glass, etc, a lantern in one hand and an iron hook in the other, and a large basket on his back. It is not surprising that Dickens stumbles over one in the early hours of the morning – "Their great time," explains W. Blanchard Jerrold, "is from four in the morning until eight, at which hour the carts have cleared the streets." (*Imperial Paris*, 1855, p 180.) Jerrold devotes a chapter of *Imperial Paris* to the *chiffonniers*, and includes accounts of interviews and encounters with practitioners of the trade.

23. On this trip, Dickens was staying at the Hotel Wagram on the rue de Rivoli, opposite the Tuileries. During the French Revolution the Palais des Tuileries was home to Louis XVI following his arrest in October 1789. It was invaded by demonstrators in June 1792. In August of the same year there were horrible scenes of murder and brutality when an armed mob stormed the palace and massacred many members of the king's Swiss guards and palace servants. It was subsequently home to the Convention Nationale, the official residence of Napoléon I, the main residence of the royal family during the Restoration, home to Louis-Philippe during the July Monarchy and, at the time Dickens is writing, the official residence of Napoléon III. There were further attacks by rioters during the Parisian insurrection of 1830, which ended the reign of Charles X, and during the revolution of 1848, which led to the abdication of Louis-Philippe. Dickens knew it almost at the end of its long and turbulent history – it was destroyed by the Communards in 1871.

24. The Hôtel-Dieu on the Île de la Cité – see under "Some Recollections of Mortality," note 7, p 358.

25. The morgue was on the quai du Marché-Neuf on the Île de la Cité – see the introduction to "A Flâneur in Paris," p 126, for further details.

26. Street gutter.

27. Reminiscent of the "Break of Day" at Chalon-sur-Saône in *Little Dorrit,* with its "pictorial embellishment of billiard cue and ball" (see p 223).

28. The same kinds of insults that Dickens hears the drivers hurl at their horses in *Pictures from Italy* (see p 179) and that he puts into the mouth of Carker's driver in *Dombey and Son* (see p 187).

29. "Infants" is a literal rendering of *enfants,* used here in its colloquial sense of "lads" or "fellows." The literal translation, as well as conveying the French word that was actually used by the traders, allows Dickens to have some fun with the usage in the next paragraph.

30. The famous equestrian circus – see under "The Calais Night Mail," note 15, p 334.

31. A reference to the reforms instituted under Napoléon to regulate the handling and slaughtering of animals in and around Paris – see, for example, note 18 above. As Dickens describes here, livestock bought at Poissy and Sceaux had to follow fixed routes into the city.

32. As explained earlier in the article, pronging and tail-twisting were methods used to control cattle at Smithfield. They are among the many cruel practices described in "The Heart of Mid-London," an anti-Smithfield campaigning piece published in *Household Words* on 4 May 1850, co-written by Dickens and W.H. Wills: "To get the bullocks into their allotted stands, an incessant punishing and torturing of the miserable animals – a sticking of prongs into the tender part of their feet, and a twisting of their tails to make the whole spine teem with pain – was going on." (*Uncollected Writings*, p 104.)

33. The Caisse de Poissy, which had branches at the markets of Poissy, Sceaux, and the Halle aux Veaux, was "a fund paying ready money to graziers for the cattle sold at the market ... for the butchers of Paris, from whom it afterwards reimburses itself" (*Galignani's New Paris Guide*, 1852).

34. The duty levied on goods (in this case livestock) when entering the city.

35. See note 18 above.

36. The Abattoir Montmartre was situated on the avenue Trudaine, and occupied the space between the rue de Rochechouart, boulevard de Rochechouart, and rue Lallier (then a continuation of rue des Martyrs).

37. Surprisingly enough, the request was not an unusual one. The abattoirs were recommended in Paris guidebooks, both English and French. *Galignani's New Paris Guide* of 1852, for example, suggests that "Strangers should visit one of these establishments; they must apply for a guide at the porter's lodge, to whom a small fee is given."

38. An allusive swipe at the Common Council, echoing the opening words of Othello's address to the Duke and Senators of Venice: "Most potent, grave, and reverend signiors..." (*Othello*, 1, 3).

39. The Abattoir de Grenelle was next to the place de Breteuil, occupying the area between the rues Barthélémy and Pérignon.

40. Described at length in *Galignani's New Paris Guide*, 1852, which tells us that "The water rises 112 feet above the surface of the ground in a pipe supported by wooden scaffolding which is accessible by steps. At the mouth of the well it yields 2,500 litres, or 660 gallons, per minute; at an elevation of 112 feet it gives 1,200 litres."

"The Boy at Mugby," pp 289–300

1. See the introduction to this chapter for details of the incident on which the refreshment room and the character of the Boy are based.
2. By this time, the Smith's bookstall was a standard feature of English railway stations. The entrepreneurial William Henry Smith (1825–91), taking over the management of his father's newsagent business, negotiated with the various railway companies for the right to set up stalls on their stations. He opened the first bookstall at Euston in the late 1840s. By 1862 he had secured the exclusive right for W.H. Smith and Son to sell books and newspapers at the stations of all the main railways in England.
3. A mail train with only limited passenger accommodation.
4. Bandoline was a glutinous hair dressing for fixing the hair in place.
5. The telegraph was used to signal the arrival of a train.
6. Sir Charles Wheatstone (1802–75) and Sir William Fothergill Cooke (1806–79), inventors of the electric telegraph, for which they held various patents (the earliest was filed in 1837). In 1845, they produced a single-needle apparatus that made telegraphy affordable and very practical. It was rapidly adopted on railway lines throughout the country.
7. The Boy is cheekily adapting the words of the American national anthem, "The Star Spangled Banner" by Francis Scott Key (1779–1843), which refers to America as "the land of the free, and the home of the brave." There may also be a tongue-in-cheek allusion to a patriotic ballad (original authorship disputed) that was then popular on both sides of the Atlantic and of which there were both British and American versions. The British version, "Red, White, and Blue," begins "Britannia the pride of the ocean,/The home of the brave and the free," while the American version, "Columbia, the Gem of the Ocean," begins "O, Columbia! the gem of the ocean,/The home of the brave and the free."
8. A kind of hard toffee, of which the main ingredients are butter and sugar.
9. That is, London.
10. Eternal.
11. The name given to the South Eastern Railway trains that ran from London to Folkestone twice a day to connect with the steam packets leaving for Boulogne. Because of the shallow harbor at Folkestone, the packets could enter and leave only when the tide was at the right level.

The timing of the trains therefore varied from day to day to correspond to the tides and so they became known as the "Tidals."

12. The Boy's narrative is peppered with phrases and clichés from popular journalism and story-telling. "Ascended the fatal platform," for example, was often used in accounts of condemned prisoners mounting the scaffold for execution.

13. Echoing Macbeth's "Is this a dagger which I see before me..." (*Macbeth*, 2, 1).

14. Murray's *Handbook for Visitors to Paris*, 1864, confirms Our Missis's experience, bestowing high praise on the refreshment room at Boulogne (see chapter introduction).

15. Weak, everyday wine.

16. The radical MP John Bright (1811–89). He was one of Birmingham's two MPs (having started out as MP for Manchester) for over thirty years. Bright espoused causes that sought to improve the lives of working people and campaigned against the power and wealth of the privileged classes.

17. "Obelisk" is a malapropism: the Boy means basilisk. One species of this fabled animal, the "king of serpents," caused horror and death simply by looking at its victims (*Bulfinch's Mythology: The Age of Fable*, 1855).

"Insularities," pp 300–308

1. A nickname for the devil or evil one.

2. The cylindrical black silk men's hat colloquially known as the "chimney-pot" was fashionable throughout the latter half of the nineteenth century for all formal wear. As Dickens notes later in this paragraph, it was *de rigueur* in the City.

3. Traditionally London's main trading center for merchants and bankers, the Royal Exchange is in the heart of the City at the corner of Threadneedle Street and Cornhill. The current building dates from 1844, but it ceased to function as an exchange in 1939.

4. Colloquial name for a soft felt hat with a broad brim and low crown. "Said to have been punningly so-named as not having a 'nap'" (*Oxford English Dictionary*).

5. These were well-established banks. Smith, Payne and Smith was at 1 Lombard Street and Ransom & Co was at 1 Pall Mall East (*Webster's Royal Red Book*, January 1856). Both later amalgamated with other houses.

6. The Zouaves, a body of light infantry, were created in 1830 by General Clausel of the French army in Algeria. Famous during the Second Empire for their bravery and hard-living lifestyle, they were distinctive in both action and appearance. The Zouaves' uniform reflected their North African origins – a short embroidered jacket, baggy trousers, and a

tasselled cap (Holmes, 2001). In Paris on 29 December 1855, Dickens had watched the Zouaves of the Imperial Guard taking part with other regiments in a ceremonial march led by the Emperor from the place de la Bastille to the place Vendôme to mark their return from the Crimea. The ceremony was reported in *The Times*, 31 December 1855, which noted that the "Zouaves came in for a great share of the enthusiasm." Dickens wrote to Forster about them, noting, as he does in "Insularities," the practicality of their gaiters: "A remarkable body of men, ... wild, dangerous, and picturesque. Close-cropped head, red skull cap, Greek jacket, full red petticoat trousers trimmed with yellow, and high white gaiters – the most sensible things for the purpose I know, and coming into use in the line. A man with such things on his legs is always free there, and ready for a muddy march; and might flounder through roads two feet deep in mud, and, simply by changing his gaiters (he has another pair in his haversack), be clean and comfortable and wholesome again, directly." (*Life*, 7, Chapter 5.)

7. *The London Gazette*, an official newspaper of record which includes insolvency notices.

8. A Regency shopping arcade (built in 1819) between Piccadilly and Burlington Gardens.

9. Slater (1998, p 339) has identified this previous article as "Why Shave?" The article was written by Henry Morley and W.H. Wills (Lohrli, 1973) and published in the 13 August 1853 issue of *Household Words*. It too refers to the military exception: "In England the chin and, except in some regiments, the upper lip has to be shaved..."

10. The Exposition Universelle, held in Paris from May to November 1855, included a huge fine arts exhibition. Over 5,000 paintings and sculptures were displayed in a purpose-built Palais des Beaux-Arts on the avenue Montaigne. Comparing the French and English contributions, Dickens expressed views similar to those set out in this paragraph in a letter to John Forster of November 1855. According to Forster, Dickens "did not think that English art showed to advantage beside the French. It seemed to him small, shrunken, insignificant, 'niggling.' He thought the general absence of ideas horribly apparent..." "There is a horrid respectability about most of the best of them," he wrote of the English pictures, "a little, finite, systematic routine in them, strangely expressive to me of the state of England itself." By contrast, he admired the energy and innovation in the French paintings: "There are no end of bad pictures among the French, but, Lord! the goodness also! – the fearlessness of them; the bold drawing; the dashing conception; the passion and action in them!" (*Life*, 7, Chapter 5.)

11. A criticism to which Dickens referred and responded in his correspondence with Forster: "But the French themselves are a

demonstrative and gesticulating people, was Dickens's retort; and what thus is rendered by their artists is the truth through an immense part of the world." (*Life*, 7, Chapter 5.)

12. Maximilien Robespierre (1758–94), one of the leaders of the French Revolution, played a central role in the institution of The Terror.

13. In the 1850s Clapham, now a lively and socially diverse part of London, was a peaceful suburban town, popular with middle-class commuters. Richmond Hill in Surrey, on the outskirts of London and overlooking the Thames Valley, was traditionally favored by wealthy gentlemen with enough money to build fine houses in a picturesque riverside location. It retains the image of a well-heeled and "respectable" suburb.

14. Compare Dickens's words to Forster in his letter of November 1855: "I never saw anything so strange. They [the English] seem to me to have got a fixed idea that there is no natural manner but the English manner (in itself so exceptional that it is a thing apart, in all countries); and that unless a Frenchman – represented as going to the guillotine for example – is as calm as Clapham, or as respectable as Richmond Hill, he cannot be right." (*Life*, 7, Chapter 5.)

15. An allusion to Mrs Grundy, a character talked of but never seen in Thomas Morton's play *Speed the Plough*, 1798. She embodies strait-laced social convention and petty snobbery – Farmer Ashfield's wife is forever referring to her and asking "What would Mrs Grundy say?"

16. The Tory party was the more reactionary of the two great political parties (the Tories and the Whigs) that preceded the Conservative and Liberal parties – the term "Tory" is still used casually to refer to members of the British Conservative Party. "Old-school Tories" were staunch traditionalists and defenders of the status quo.

17. The politician and historian Thomas Babington Macaulay (1800–59). Dickens is referring to his *History of England*, the third and fourth volumes of which had been published the previous month (December 1855).

18. The quotation is from Volume 3, Chapter 13, p 302, of *The History of England*. Explaining why Oliver Goldsmith was less impressed by the Scottish Highlands than contemporary visitors (on the grounds that the area was less developed in Goldsmith's day), Macaulay writes, "Yet it is difficult to believe that the author of the Traveller and of the Deserted Village was naturally inferior in taste to the thousands of clerks and milliners who are now thrown into raptures by the sight of Loch Katrine and Loch Lomond." Loch Katrine (described in Scott's *Lady of the Lake*, 1810) and Loch Lomond (the largest loch in Scotland) are popular destinations for tourists in search of beautiful scenery.

19. The Early Closing Association was established in 1842 with the aim of shortening what were often appallingly long working hours for employees

in shops and warehouses. The Early Closing Movement was active for many years, and scored some successes (such as the introduction of Saturday afternoon closing by large stores), but it was not until the early twentieth century that the problem was addressed effectively through legislation.

20. Macaulay was a Whig MP (for Whig, see note 16 above).

21. Albert, Prince Consort of England (1819–61).

22. Frederick Waymouth Gibbs, a tutor to the Queen's son, Albert Edward, Prince of Wales (later Edward VII). He was mentioned frequently in court reports as accompanying the young princes on various outings.

23. Dickens is not exaggerating the mind-numbingly mundane and repetitive nature of the court reports, such as those in *The Times* (the daily "Court Circular" column) and the *Illustrated London News* (the weekly "The Court" column). The following examples are typical. "His Royal Highness the Prince went out hunting this morning." (*The Times*, 5 January 1855.) "The Queen, with the Princess Royal and Princess Alice, rode in the riding-house this morning."(*The Times*, 5 November 1855.) "On Saturday last, the Queen, with the Princess Alice, rode out on horseback, attended by the Hon. Flora Macdonald." (*Illustrated London News*, 24 November 1855.)

24. An allusion to Iago's words in *Othello*, 2, 1: "To suckle fools and chronicle small beer."

25. Lord Aberdeen – George Hamilton Gordon, Fourth Earl of Aberdeen (1784–1860) – was a Tory member of the House of Lords. He held various senior positions in government and became leader of the Peelites after Sir Robert Peel's death in 1850. He was Prime Minister from 1852 to 1855. Lord Palmerston – Henry John Temple (1784–1865) – was one of the most famous politicians of his day. He was Prime Minister from 1855 to 1858 (and therefore at the time Dickens is writing here) and again from 1859 to 1865. Lord Aldborough – Benjamin O'Neale Stratford, Sixth Earl of Aldborough (1808–75) – was an Irish peer. All were examples of what Dickens saw as the stultifying and alienating dominance of the aristocratic establishment in government: in April 1855 he wrote to the radical MP Austen Layard, "There is nothing in the present time at once so galling and so alarming to me as the alienation of the people from their own public affairs. I have no difficulty in understanding it. They have had so little to do with the Game through all these years of Parliamentary Reform, that they have sullenly laid down their cards and taken to looking on." (*Pilgrim*, 7, p 587.)

This last section of "Insularities" reflects Dickens's frustration with the separation of the people from the government, a separation sustained by the undue homage paid by the public to representatives of the aristocratic establishment and the consequent complacency of that establishment towards the public. This and other perceptions of administrative incompetence and corruption had already featured prominently in various fiercely satirical articles he had written for *Household Words* during 1855, contributions prompted by his disgust at the mismanagement of the Crimean War and his support for Layard and the Administrative Reform Movement (see note 26 below) – see, for example, "The Thousand and One Humbugs" (21 April 1855), "The Toady Tree" (26 May 1855), and "Cheap Patriotism" (9 June 1855).

26. Lord Palmerston had a reputation for making casually dismissive ripostes in debate: the *Dictionary of National Biography* refers to his "jaunty, confident, off-hand air in the house." Here, however, Dickens almost certainly has in mind a specific comment that Palmerston made about the first meeting of the Administrative Reform Association, formed to lobby for an end to patronage and favor in civil service and other administrative appointments. Its first official meeting was held on 13 June 1855 at the Drury Lane Theatre in London (reported in *The Times*, 14 June). On 15 June the Liberal MP Sir Austen Henry Layard (1817–94), a prominent voice of the Association, moved a resolution in Parliament "that this House views with increasing concern the state of the nation, and is of opinion that the manner in which merit and efficiency have been sacrificed, in public appointments, to party and family influences, and to a blind adherence to routine, has given rise to great misfortunes, and threatens to bring discredit upon the national character, and to involve the country in grave disasters." (*The Times*, 14 June 1855.) The resolution was defeated but attracted considerable media and public attention.

In the course of his Drury Lane speech, Layard had severely criticized Palmerston, accusing him of "jesting upon the sufferings of the people, and making light of their unfortunate condition." In the debate on Layard's Parliamentary resolution, Palmerston made a short intervention to deny the accusation, protesting that he felt "respect and admiration...for the people of this country" and concluding with characteristic dismissiveness, "I shall say no more about the Drury-lane theatricals" (*The Times*, 19 June 1855).

Dickens, who was a member of the Association and a keen supporter of its aims, was infuriated by what he called the "dandy insolence" of Palmerston (letter to W.C. Macready of 30 June 1855, *Pilgrim*, 7, p 664). Riled by the premier's jocular dismissal of a movement for fairer government, he got his own back in good measure. In a speech to a meeting of the Association at Drury Lane on 27 June he used the "private theatricals" joke to great effect against its originator, casting Palmerston in the role of the "comic old gentleman" and firing a volley of satirical theatrical metaphors at the Westminster establishment in general – referring among many other things to "the public theatricals which the noble Lord is so condescending as to manage." (The speech is included in Fielding, 1988, pp 197–208.)

27. The British Ambassador in Paris was Lord Cowley (Henry Richard Charles Wellesley, 1804–84). Dickens is referring here to his neglect of the British members of the International Jury for the Exposition Universelle of 1855 during their extended stay in Paris. There were 40 "ordinary jurors" and 10 "supplementary jurors," all of them prominent people in the arts, science, or commerce (their names and affiliations are detailed in *The Times*, 28 April 1855). A letter to *The Times* published on 25 July 1855 and signed by "A Member of the English Jury" complained bitterly about the lack of attention and hospitality the jurors had received from the Ambassador and noted the contrasting treatment that colleagues from other countries had received from their embassies. Significantly for Dickens's theme in "Insularities," the correspondent attributes the neglect to the lack of social rank of most of the jurors, commenting "I am not aware that any one, with the exception, no doubt, of one or two men of rank, have received the slightest notice from their ambassador," and expressing shame at belonging to "a nation in which rank alone is honoured by the representatives of the Government." A letter from "Another Member of the Jury" published in *The Times* on 31 July 1855 corroborates the statements of the first correspondent, praises the generous hospitality bestowed on the jurors by the French authorities and comments, "...we have experienced generally the greatest kindness and consideration from every quarter except the British Embassy." A suspiciously partisan letter published in *The Times* on 1 August 1855 and signed by "A Paris Resident" defends the Ambassador against the claims.

28. Dickens had previously written at length in *Household Words* on the unhealthily servile and adulatory attitude of the British towards their aristocracy ("The Toady Tree," 26 May 1855). And in a letter to Layard of 10 April 1855, he noted "Meanwhile, all our English Tufthunting, Toad Eating, and other manifestations of accursed Gentility ... are expressing themselves every day." (*Pilgrim*, 7, p 587.)

29. The wild man of the woods in the romance *Valentine and Orson*, in which infant twin brothers are abandoned in a forest. Valentine is rescued and brought up to be a courtier while Orson is carried off and raised by a bear.

30. An allusion to Thackeray's *Book of Snobs*, 1848. The King of Brentford features in the chapter on "The Snob Royal." A satirical portrait of George IV ("Gorgius IV"), the character is used to highlight the senselessness of fawning snobbery. Thackeray writes that the King "smiled with such irresistible fascination, that persons who were introduced into his august presence became his victims, body and soul, as a rabbit becomes the prey of a great big boa-constrictor." The King of

Brentford also appears in two of Thackeray's Ballads: "The King of Brentford's Testament," 1841, and "The King of Brentford," 1840.

31. An allusion to the story of the three tailors of Tooley Street, another instance of English pomposity. In his *Hand-Book of London*, 1850, Peter Cunningham explains: "Tooley-street will long continue to be famous from the well-known story related by Canning [George Canning, 1770–1827] of 'the three tailors of Tooley-street,' who formed a meeting for redress of popular grievances, and though no more than three in number, began their petition to the House of Commons with the universal opening of '*We* the people of England.'" The phrase "three tailors of Tooley Street" thus became a facetious description for any small coterie that styled itself as representative of the people or the nation.

Extract from *Nicholas Nickleby* (Nicholas Teaches French), pp 314–319

1. This refers to Mr Gregsbury, a cynical and self-regarding MP with whom Nicholas has just sought employment as a secretary. Gregsbury required so much and offered so little that Nicholas had to reject the position. The "brutal pedagogue" is, of course, Squeers.

2. The Kenwigses are the first-floor lodgers in the same seedy building. Comparatively well-off among the lodgers, they aspire to middle-class respectability.

3. Mr Lillyvick, the elderly and unmarried uncle of Mrs Kenwigs, is a water-rate collector who, in this humble society, is regarded as a man of wealth and standing. The Kenwigses expect to inherit his money. Miss Petowker, a friend of the family, is an actress at the Theatre Royal Drury Lane.

4. "A high-backed, partly enclosed chair, with a semi-circular hood..." (Gloag, 1952). Such chairs were designed for porters or pageboys so that they were protected from draughts as they sat on door duty in the entrance halls of large houses.

5. A cylindrical iron used for fluting or crimping lace, frills, etc. The iron itself was hollow so that the accompanying cylindrical heater could be inserted into it.

6. Mr Lillyvick is referring to the Napoleonic War (1805–15).

Extract from *Our Mutual Friend* (Podsnap's Dinner Party), pp 320–327

1. Compare Podsnap's "notions of the Arts" with Dickens's views on the British paintings on display at the Exposition Universelle of 1855: "There is a horrid respectability about most of the best of them – a little, finite, systematic routine in them, strangely expressive to me of the state of England itself." (*Life*, 7, Chapter 5.)

2. An elegant square in the West End of London, dating from the 18th century but largely rebuilt in the 20th. In the 19th century several of its stately houses were occupied by members of the aristocracy.

3. A four-wheeled open carriage.

4. The Veneerings are socially ambitious newcomers who clamber up the social ladder by making as many influential acquaintances as possible. Dickens introduces them in chapter 2 of the novel as "bran-new people in a bran-new house in a bran-new quarter of London. Everything about the Veneerings was spick and span new. All their furniture was new, all their friends were new, all their servants were new, their plate was new, their carriage was new, their harness was new, their horses were new, their pictures were new, they themselves were new, they were as newly married as was lawfully compatible with their having a bran-new baby…"

    The "bran-new bride and bridegroom" are the recently married Mr and Mrs Lammle, bound together by mutual deceit. Thanks to the encouragement of the Veneerings, each has married in the mistaken belief that the other has property.

5. That is, a social upstart.

6. A center-dish or ornament for the dinner table.

7. Poole (1997, p 812) suggests that the Frenchman thinks Podsnap is talking about the amount of horse manure on the streets of London. This is possible, but it may also be that he simply latches on to Podsnap's last word, "traces," and makes the connection with horses (traces being the side straps in a horse's harness that connect the collar to the crossbar, or swingletree).

8. Podsnap's authority for these remarks appears to be "Rule Britannia," the famous patriotic song generally attributed to the poet James Thomson (1700–48). The phrase "the charter of the land" occurs in the first verse and the final verse includes the line "Blest Isle! with matchless beauty crowned" (the second verse also refers to the nation as "blest").

407

SELECT BIBLIOGRAPHY

Note: General reference sources such as *Dictionnaire de biographie française, Dictionary of National Biography, Oxford English Dictionary, Grand dictionnaire universel du XIXe siècle, and Dictionnaire géographique et administratif de la France* (1890–1905) are not listed here, but are cited where appropriate in the text.

Forster's *The Life of Charles Dickens* is abbreviated throughout the text to *"Life"* and the Pilgrim edition of the *Letters* to *"Pilgrim."*

Editions of Dickens's works, correspondence, and speeches
See "Note on the texts" for the source editions used.

Bradbury, Nicola, ed (2003), *Bleak House*, Penguin, London.
Fielding, K.J., ed (1988), *The Speeches of Charles Dickens: A Complete Edition*, Harvester Wheatsheaf, Hemel Hempstead.
Flint, Kate, ed (1998), *Pictures from Italy*, Penguin, London.
Ford, Mark, ed (1999), *Nicholas Nickleby*, Penguin, London.
Glancy, Ruth, ed (1996), *The Christmas Stories*, J.M. Dent, London, and Charles E. Tuttle, Vermont.
House, Madeleine, Storey, Graham, and Tillotson, Kathleen, general eds (1965–2002), *The Letters of Charles Dickens*, British Academy Pilgrim Edition, 12 vols, edited by Madeline House and Graham Storey (Vols 1 and 2), Madeline House, Graham Storey and Kathleen Tillotson (Vol 3), Kathleen Tillotson (Vol 4), Graham Storey and K.J. Fielding (Vol 5), Graham Storey, Kathleen Tillotson and Nina Burgis (Vol 6), Graham Storey, Kathleen Tillotson and Angus Easson (Vol 7), Graham Storey and Kathleen Tillotson (Vol 8), and Graham Storey (Vols 9–12), Clarendon Press, Oxford.
Maxwell, Richard, ed (2003), *A Tale of Two Cities*, Penguin, London.
Mitchell, Charlotte, ed (2003), *Great Expectations*, Penguin, London.
Poole, Adrian, ed (1997), *Our Mutual Friend*, Penguin, London.
Sanders, Andrew, ed (1988), *A Tale of Two Cities*, Oxford University Press, Oxford.
Sanders, Andrew, ed (2002), *Dombey and Son*, Penguin, London.
Slater, Michael, ed (1994), *Dickens' Journalism, Volume 1: Sketches by Boz and Other Early Papers 1833–89*, J.M. Dent, London.
Slater, Michael, ed (1996), *Dickens' Journalism, Volume 2: "The Amusements of the People" and Other Papers: Reports, Essays and Reviews 1834–51*, J.M. Dent, London.
Slater, Michael, ed (1998), *Dickens' Journalism, Volume 3: "Gone Astray" and*

Other Papers from Household Words 1851–59, J.M. Dent, London.

Slater, Michael, and Drew, John, eds (2000), *Dickens' Journalism, Volume 4: "The Uncommercial Traveller" and Other Papers 1859–70*, J.M. Dent, London.

Slater, Michael, ed (1978) *Nicholas Nickleby*, Penguin, London.

Stone, Harry, ed (1969), *Charles Dickens' Uncollected Writings from Household Words, Volume 1, 1850–1859*, Indiana University Press, Bloomington, IL, and London.

Wall, Stephen, and Wall, Helen, eds (2003), *Little Dorrit*, Penguin, London.

Other works
19th century and earlier

– *The Arabian Nights Entertainments* (1811), translated by Jonathan Scott, Longman, Hurst, Rees, Orme and Brown, London.

Berville, Saint-Albin, and Barrière, Jean-François, eds (1821), *Mémoires de Linguet sur la Bastille et de Dusaulx sur le 14 Juillet*, Baudouin Frères, Paris.

– *Boulogne-sur-Mer, Bathing Town and Ville de Plaisance* (1857), published by the authority of the Committee of Organization and Publicity, Boulogne-sur-Mer.

Briffault, Eugène (1844), *Paris dans l'eau*, J. Hetzel, Paris.

Brunet, J. (1862), *New Guide to Boulogne-sur-Mer and its Environs*, 6th edition, C. Watel, Boulogne-sur-Mer.

Carlyle, Thomas (1837), *The French Revolution*, edition of 1989 (edited by Fielding, K.J., and Sorenson, D.), Oxford University Press, Oxford.

Cunningham, Peter (1850), *Hand-Book of London*, John Murray, London.

Dickens's Dictionary of London 1888 (1993), Old House Books, Moretonhampstead (facsimile edition).

Dolby, George (1885), *Charles Dickens as I Knew Him: The Story of the Reading Tours in Great Britain and America*, T. Fisher Unwin, London.

Dumersan, T.M. (1857), *Chansons nationales et populaires de la France*.

Dusaulx, Jean-Joseph (1790), *De l'Insurrection parisienne et de la prise de la Bastille*, Discours historique prononcé par extraits dans l'Assemblée nationale, in Berville, Saint-Albin, and Barrière, Jean-François, eds (1821), *Mémoires de Linguet sur la Bastille et de Dusaulx sur le 14 Juillet*, Baudouin Frères, Paris.

– *Galignani's New Paris Guide* (1844), Galignani, Paris.

– *Galignani's New Paris Guide* (1852), Galignani, Paris.

– *Galignani's New Paris Guide* (1854), Galignani, Paris.

– *Galignani's New Paris Guide* (1860), Galignani, Paris.

Forster, John (1876), *The Life of Charles Dickens*, revised edition, 2 vols, Chapman and Hall, London.

Gammage, R.G. (1894), *History of the Chartist Movement*, revised edition,

Browne and Browne, Newcastle-on-Tyne, and Truslove and Hanson, London.

Gaulle, Joséphine-Marie de (1852), *Itinéraire historique du chemin de fer du Nord*, L. Lefort, Lille.

Goncourt, Edmond de, Goncourt, Jules de, and Holff, Cornélius (1852), *Mystères des théâtres*, Librairie Nouvelle, Paris.

Greeley, Horace (1851), *Glances at Europe: in a series of letters from Great Britain, France, Italy, Switzerland &c during the summer of 1851*, Dewitt and Davenport, New York.

Grimm, Jacob Ludwig Carl, and Grimm, Wilhem Carl, "The White Snake", in *Home Stories, collected by the Brothers Grimm* (1855), translated by Matilda Louisa Davis, G. Routledge & Co, London.

– *Guide dans les théâtres* (1855), Paulin et Le Chevalier, Paris.

– *A Hand-Book for Travellers on the Continent* (1843), John Murray, London.

– *A Hand-Book for Travellers on the Continent* (1850), John Murray, London.

– *A Handbook for Travellers on the Continent* (1871), John Murray, London.

– *A Hand-Book for Travellers in France* (1843), John Murray, London.

– *A Hand-Book for Travellers in France* (1847), John Murray, London.

– *A Handbook for Travellers in France* (1854), John Murray, London.

– *A Handbook for Travellers in France* (1856), John Murray, London.

– *A Handbook for Travellers in France* (1864), John Murray, London.

– *A Handbook for Travellers in Kent* (1877), fourth edition, John Murray, London.

– *A Handbook for Travellers in Kent and Sussex* (1863), John Murray, London.

– *A Handbook for Visitors to Paris* (1864), John Murray, London.

Head, F.B. (1852), *A Faggot of French Sticks*, John Murray, London.

Inchbald, Elizabeth, ed (1824), *The British Theatre*, "new edition" in 20 volumes, Hurst, Robinson & Co, London.

Jerrold, W. Blanchard (1855), *Imperial Paris; including New Scenes for Old Visitors*, Bradbury and Evans, London.

Joanne, Adolphe (1859), *Atlas historique et statistique des chemins de fer français*, Librairie de L. Hachette et Cie, Paris.

Joanne, Adolphe (1863), *Le Guide parisien*, L. Hachette et Cie, Paris.

Lazare, Félix, and Lazare, Louis, *Dictionnaire administratif et historique des rues et des monuments de Paris* (1855), reprinted in 1994 by Maisonneuve et Larose, Paris.

Linguet, Simon-Nicolas-Henri (1782), *Mémoires sur la Bastille et sur la détention de l'auteur*, in Berville, Saint-Albin, and Barrière, Jean-François, eds (1821), *Mémoires de Linguet sur la Bastille et de Dusaulx sur le 14 Juillet*, Baudouin Frères, Paris.

Macaulay, Thomas Babington (1855), *The History of England from the Accession of James the Second*, Vol III, Longman, Brown, Green and Longmans, London.

Mackie, S.J. (1856), *A Descriptive and Historical Account of Folkestone and Its Neighbourhood*, J. English, Folkestone, and Simpkin & Marshall, London.

Mercier, Louis-Sébastien (1782–88), *Tableau de Paris*, new edition, 12 vols, Amsterdam.

Mercier, Louis-Sébastien (1799), *Le Nouveau Paris*, edition of 1994 (edited by Jean-Claude Bonnet), Mercure de France, Paris.

Moore, Thomas (1821), *Irish Melodies*, printed for J.Power and Longman, Hurst, Rees, Orme, and Brown, London.

ONIL (1851), *The Book of English Songs*, Office of the National Illustrated Library, London.

Owen, the Rev. Richard (1894), *The Life of Richard Owen*, John Murray, London.

Pendleton, John (1894), *Our Railways: Their Origin, Development, Incident and Romance*, Cassell and Company, London, Paris, Melbourne.

Priestly, J.O. (1831), *Historical Account of Navigable Rivers, Canals, and Railways of Great Britain*, Longman, Rees, Orme, Brown & Green, London.

Richard (1856), *Conducteur du voyageur en France*, 24th edition, Librairie de L. Maison, Paris.

Ruskin, John, in Cook, E.T., and Wedderburn, Alexander (1906), *The Works of John Ruskin*, Library Edition, Vols XXV and XXXV, George Allen, London.

Sterne, Laurence (1768), *A Sentimental Journey through France and Italy*, edition of 1967 (edited by A. Alvarez), Penguin, London.

Thiers, Adolphe (1838), *The History of the French Revolution*, translated by F. Shoberl, Richard Bentley, London [published in French 1823–27].

Timbs, John (1855), *Curiosities of London*, David Bogue, London.

Timbs, John (1867), *Curiosities of London*, enlarged and revised edition, John Camden Hotten, London.

Webster, Benjamin, ed (1838), *The Acting National Drama*, Vol 5, Chapman and Hall, London.

- – *Webster's Royal Red Book for January 1856* (1856), Webster and Co, London.

Young, Arthur (1792), *Travels in France during the Years 1787, 1788, 1789*, edition of 1889 (edited by Betham-Edwards, M.), George Bell and Sons, London.

Post-19th century

Ackroyd, Peter (1990), *Dickens*, Sinclair-Stevenson, London.

Ackroyd, Peter (2000), *London: The Biography*, Chatto & Windus, London.

Bagwell, Philip S. (1974), *The Transport Revolution from 1770*, Batsford, London.

Bowen, John (2000), "Bebelle and 'His Boots': Dickens, Ellen Ternan and the *Christmas Stories*", *The Dickensian*, Vol 96, Winter, pp 197–208.

Buck, Anne (1961), *Victorian Costume and Costume Accessories*, Herbert Jenkins, London.

Carlton, W.J. (1956), "Dickens in the Jury Box," *The Dickensian*, Vol 52, March, pp 69–86.

Carlton, W.J. (1966), "Dickens's Forgotten Retreat in France," *The Dickensian*, Vol 62, May, pp 65–69.

Clébert, Jean-Paul (1999), *La Littérature à Paris*, Larousse, Paris.

Clifford, Brendan (1984), *The Life and Poems of Thomas Moore*, Athol Books, London.

Collins, Philip (1981), *Dickens: Interviews and Recollections*, 2 vols, Macmillan, London.

Dickens, Sir Henry Fielding (1928), *Memories of My Father*, Victor Gollancz, London.

Donaldson, Frances, ed (1990), *Yours, Plum: The Letters of P.G. Wodehouse*, Hutchinson, London.

Drew, John M.L. (2003), *Dickens the Journalist*, Palgrave Macmillan, London.

Evans, James E., and Wall, John N. (1977), *A Guide to Prose Fiction in The Tatler and The Spectator*, Garland Publishing, New York and London.

Fierro, Alfred (1996), *Histoire et dictionnaire de Paris*, Robert Laffont, Paris.

Fierro, Alfred (1999), *Histoire et mémoire du nom des rues de Paris*, Parigramme, Paris.

Fierro, Alfred (2003), *Dictionnaire du Paris disparu*, Parigramme, Paris.

Findlater, R. (1955), *Grimaldi: King of Clowns*, MacGibbon and Kee, London.

France, Peter, ed (1995), *The New Oxford Companion to Literature in French*, Clarendon Press, Oxford.

Garrigues, Jean (2002), *La France de 1848 à 1870*, 2nd edition, Armand Colin, Paris.

Gloag, John (1952), *A Short Dictionary of Furniture*, George Allen & Unwin, London.

Godechot, Jacques (1965), *La Prise de la Bastille*, Gallimard, Paris.

Green, Julian (1991), *Paris*, bilingual edition, Marion Boyars, London and New York.

Harvey, Sir Paul, and Heseltine, J.E., eds (1959), *The Oxford Companion to French Literature*, Clarendon Press, Oxford.

Hawes, Donald (1998), *Who's Who in Dickens*, Routledge, London.

Hibbert, Christopher (1982), *The French Revolution*, Penguin, London.

Hillairet, Jacques (1970), *Dictionnaire des rues de Paris*, 4th edition, 2 vols, Éditions de Minuit, Paris.

Hillairet, Jacques (1993), *Connaissance du vieux Paris*, Payot & Rivages, Paris.

Holmes, Richard, ed (2001), *The Oxford Companion to Military History*, Oxford University Press, Oxford.

Horne, Alistair (2002), *Seven Ages of Paris: Portrait of a City*, Macmillan, London.

Inwood, Stephen (1998), *A History of London*, Macmillan, London.

Jones, John Bavington (1916), *Annals of Dover*, Dover.

Lancaster, Bill (1995), *The Department Store: A Social History*, Leicester University Press, London and New York.

Lohrli, Anne (1973), *Household Words: Conducted by Charles Dickens – table of contents, list of contributors and their contributions based on the Household Words office book in the Morris L. Parish Collection of Victorian Novelists*, University of Toronto Press, Toronto.

Lottin, Alain, ed (1983), *Histoire de Boulogne-sur-Mer*, Presses Universitaires de Lille.

McCormick, John (1993), *Popular Theatres of Nineteenth-Century France*, Routledge, London.

Monod, Sylvère (1979), *Charles Dickens et la France*, proceedings, Colloque International de Boulogne-sur-Mer, 3 June 1978, Presses Universitaires de Lille.

– *Northern France and the Paris Region*, Green Guide, Michelin, Clermont-Ferrand.

Peyrouton, N.C. (1964), "Dickens and the Chartists," *The Dickensian*, Vol 60, May, pp 78–88, and September, pp 152–161.

Philpotts, Trey (2003), *The Companion to Little Dorrit*, Helm Information, Mountfield.

Porter, Roy (1994), *London: A Social History*, Hamish Hamilton, London.

Ribaud, Jean-Claude (1993), *Restaurants de Paris*, Guides Gallimard, Paris.

Robertson, Ian (1994), *Blue Guide: France*, third edition, A&C Black, London.

Sadrin, Amy, ed (1999), *Dickens, Europe and the New Worlds*, Palgrave, Basingstoke.

Sanders, Andrew (2002), *The Companion to A Tale of Two Cities*, Helm Information, Mountfield.

Saville, John (1987), *1848: The British State and the Chartist Movement*, Cambridge University Press, Cambridge.

Saxon, A.H. (1968), *Enter Foot and Horse: A History of Hippodrama in England and France*, Yale University Press, New Haven and London.

Schlicke, Paul, ed (1999), *Oxford Reader's Companion to Dickens*, Oxford University Press, Oxford.

Stein, Gertrude (1936), "An American in France," in *What Are Masterpieces*, The Conference Press, Los Angeles, 1940.

Thomson, David (1957), *Europe Since Napoleon*, edition of 1990, Penguin, London.

Tomalin, Claire (1991), *The Invisible Woman: the Story of Nelly Ternan and Charles Dickens*, Penguin, London.

Trouilleux, Rodolphe (2003), *Paris secret et insolite*, Parigramme, Paris.

Watrin, Janine (1992), *De Boulogne à Condette: une histoire d'amitié – Charles Dickens, Ferdinand Beaucourt-Mutuel* (no publisher given).

Watts, Alan (1989), *Dickens at Gad's Hill*, Cedric Dickens and Elevendon Press, Reading.

Weinreb, Ben, and Hibbert, Christopher, eds (1993), *The London Encyclopaedia*, Macmillan, London (revised).

Woodford, Peter, ed (1995), *Primrose Hill to Euston Road*, Camden History Society, London.

INDEX

Streets, parks, monuments, theaters, etc are indexed under the city or town. All works by Dickens are indexed under his name. Bibliographical entries and citations are not included.

abattoirs 268–70, 275–89, 342, 393, 395–6, 397, 398; *see also* Paris
Abbeville 2, 13
Abd-el-Kader 5, 143, 329
Aberdeen, Lord 306, 402
Ackroyd, Peter 58, 59
Administrative Reform Movement 403
Aix-en-Provence xv, 175, 191–2
Albert, Prince Consort of England 306
Aldborough, Lord 306, 402
Alderson, Sir Edward Hall 225–6, 230, 231, 232–4, 374
All the Year Round: *see* Dickens, Charles, for article titles
American Civil War 27, 348
Amiens 2, 13, 30, 297
Arabian Nights (allusions to) 16, 165, 357, 358, 364, 391
Arras 30, 146, 297, 336
Auber, Daniel 359
Avallon 175
Avesnes 348
Avignon xv, 175, 191; cathedral 160, 165; Palais des Papes 160, 167–72, 364–5; Pont d'Avignon 164, 364; in *Pictures from Italy* 164–72

Bayly, Thomas Haynes 363
Beaucourt-Mutuel, Ferdinand xvi, 58, 344, 351; as "Loyal Devasseur" 58, 68–72; as "Monsieur Mutuel" 99–100, 114–6, 118, 120

Bible (allusions to) 352, 362–3, 369, 372, 380, 384, 388, 389, 390–1, 394
Book of Common Prayer (allusions to) 333, 359–60, 372, 392
Boulogne: CD's holiday villas 58, 68–9, 344; CD's liking for 56–7; CD's visits to vii, 55; compared to Naples 68, 344; English in 75, 347; fêtes 58, 74–5, 347; hotel touts 12, 331; lack of cleanliness xiii, 62; landing at 12, 60–1; market 58, 65–6; public amusements xii, 72–5; railway 2; refreshment room 12, 272, 399; sea-bathing 58, 72–3; Société de Bienfaisance 347
Buildings, monuments, etc: belfry 63, 343; Colonne de la Grande Armée 346; Custom House 61; Établissement des Bains 59, 73, 346; Ramparts 56, 58, 63–4, 343, 345; St-Nicolas 343; theater 73–4, 346
Streets, squares, etc: av. John Kennedy 342; fishing quarter 56, 58, 66–8, 343; Grande Rue 343; Haute Ville 56, 58, 63, 342, 343, 345; pl. d'Armes 65; pl. Dalton 343; pl. Godefroy de Bouillon 343; rue de Beaurepaire 344; rue de l'Écu/Victor Hugo 342, 347; rue du Faubourg de Brequerecque 342; rue Monsigny 346; rue Royale/Nationale 342; in "Our French Watering-Place"

55–76
see also Beaucourt-Mutuel
Bourg la Reine 395
Bourget, Ernest 357
Bowen, John 351
Briffault, Eugène 331–2, 340
Bright, John 298, 399
Broadstairs 55, 342
Browne, Hablot Knight (Phiz) 313
Bruce, James 278, 395
Brunet, J. 57, 343, 347
Burgess, Eliza (case of) 360–1
Byron, George Gordon 363

Calais xv, 19, 21, 22, 332–3; Custom
    House 29; English in 34–5, 337;
    Hôtel Dessin 29, 335; hotel
    touts 29, 34–5, 331; landing at
    29, 335, 337; pier and harbor 29,
    33–4, 335, 337; railway terminus
    30; in Little Dorrit 33–6; "The
    Calais Night Mail" 23–32
Calais, Burghers of 28, 335
Cambrai 348, 377
Canning, George 405
Cap Gris-Nez ("Cape Grinez") 23,
    28, 41, 332
Carlton, W.J. 58
Carlyle, Thomas, The French
    Revolution: CD's admiration of
    227; source for A Tale of Two
    Cities 227–8, 378–392;
    aristocracy 380; Bastille 385,
    386, 388; États Généraux 377;
    Girondins 390; Guillotine 390,
    392; "Law of the Prairial" 390;
    "Law of the Suspect" 390;
    Marie Antoinette 389; Marquis
    de Launay 387, 388; moutons
    391–2; "Philosophism" 382;
    ransacking churches 390;
    Revolutionary calendar 388;
    Revolutionary committees 389;

tricoteuses 385; tumbrils 391
Cavaignac, General 345
Châlons, Camp de 350
Châlons-sur-Marne 350
Chalon-sur-Saône xiv, 173, 174, 175,
    176–77, 397; in Little Dorrit
    221–4
Channel, crossing the 11, 17–21, 42;
    in "The Calais Night Mail"
    23–32; Little Dorrit 33–36; "Our
    French Watering-Place" 60–1;
    Mrs Lirriper's Legacy 205
Charles II, King ("Merry Stuart")
    240, 380
Charles X, King 396
Chartism and Chartists 225, 230,
    234, 373–4, 375
chiffonniers xvi, 280, 396
coaches and coach travel: CD's
    travelling/German chariot 37, 40,
    53, 337; diligences 14, 180–1, 223,
    331, 342, 366; obsolescence 14,
    27, 334; Malles Postes 181, 366;
    posting stages 367; travelling
    through France 42–3, 47–8, 159,
    174; in Dombey and Son 181–91;
    Pictures from Italy 179–81;
    "Travelling Abroad" 37–54
coco, marchand de 343
Coleridge, Samuel Taylor 342
Collins, Wilkie 58, 78, 95, 96, 125,
    346
Colman, George 353
Common Council, Corporation of
    London 269, 275, 278, 392–3,
    395, 397
Communards 332, 384, 396
Condette 58, 351
Convulsionnaires 383
Cooke, Sir William Fothergill 290,
    398
coroners 137, 354
couriers (duties of) 369–70

Cowley, Lord 404
Cowper, William 330
Creil 14
Crimean War 90, 349, 403
Cunningham, Peter, *Hand-Book of London*: Covent Garden 329; Smithfield 268; Pantechnicon 342; Tailors of Tooley Street 405

Daily News 159
Defoe, Daniel, *Robinson Crusoe* 27, 335
Département du Nord 77, 348; countryside 78, 81–3; peasant life 82–3; weaver's cottage 80, 83; in "In the French-Flemish Country" 81–93
Devéria, Eugène 364
Dibdin, Charles 351
Dibdin, Thomas John 351, 371
Dickens, Catherine 2, 56, 334, 367, 370
Dickens, Charles, *Characterizations of England and the English*: aristocratic establishment 306–8, 402–3; Court news 305–6; dislike things not English 268, 303, 355, 401; English travellers xiv; governmental incompetence 139, 403, 404; foreign languages 97, 109, 310–2; "horrid respectability" xiii, 62, 400, 405; insular 101, 272, 300, 310; lack self-respect 306–7; obsessed with aristocracy 273, 307–8, 404; Podsnap 310, 312, 320–7, 355; reserved 97, 101; resistant to change 273; sneer at popular pleasures 304, 305; snobbery and prejudice 273, 404; state of the nation 272, 400, 403, 405; "unreasonable" 272

Characterizations of France and the French: courtesy ix, xviii, 97; cruelty to calves xiii, 282, 283; cultural sophistication 125; demonstrative 401; gentleness xvii, 58, 97; good-humoured 76; make the most of life/simple pleasures xi, xii, 74–5, 79, 91, 227, 267, 304; openness 97, 272; spontaneity xv; suddenness and impressibility xv; tolerance viii–ix
Comparisons of France with England: 267–83; armies 101, 351; beards 302–3; cattle markets, abattoirs 269–70; courtesy 97, 270, 272; dress 300–2; fine arts xiii, 303–4, 400–1; railway catering 270–2; in "The Boy at Mugby" 289–300; "Insularities" 300–8; "A Monument of French Folly" 275–9
Feelings about France and the French: affinity vii; attraction to Paris viii, xii, 121–8
French language: literal translation xvii, 397; skills xviii, 310–2
Travelling: experience of xiv; sightseeing xiv; "traveller's trance" 38, 48
Works:
American Notes for the General Circulation 334
"The Beadle – The Parish Engine – The Schoolmaster" 360
Bleak House xv, xvii, 269, 354, 366
"The Boiled Beef of New England" xii
"The Boy at Mugby" 270–1, 289–300
"The Calais Night Mail" xiv, 17–21, **23–32**, 78, 128, 331, 358

"Cheap Patriotism" 403
"The Child's Story" 371
A Christmas Carol 371
David Copperfield xv, 126, 329
Dombey and Son xiv, xvii, 173–5,
    181–91, 375, 383, 397
"A Flight" xii, xiv, 1–3, 5–16, 174
Great Expectations xvi, 268
"Greenwich Fair" 336
"The Heart of Mid-London" 269,
    397
"His Boots" 58, 95–7, 98, 99–120,
    311, 331, 336
The Holly-Tree Inn xv
"In the French-Flemish Country"
    xi, xvii, 77–9, 81–93, 335, 336
"Insularities" 272–3, 300–8
"Judicial Special Pleading" 225–6,
    230–5, 330
Little Dorrit xv, 33–6, 173, 176–8,
    194–5, 221–4, 309–10, 329, 331,
    350, 355, 397
"Lively Turtle" 269, 393
Martin Chuzzlewit 329
"A Monument of French Folly"
    xiii, xviii, 268–70, 275–89
Mrs Lirriper's Legacy xi, xii, 173,
    175–6, 178, 201–21, 272
Mrs Lirriper's Lodgings 201, 371,
    372, 373
Mugby Junction 270
The Mystery of Edwin Drood, 378
"New Year's Day" 127, 141–5, 372
Nicholas Nickleby 310, 313, 314–9,
    395
The Old Curiosity Shop 127, 366
Oliver Twist 268, 362
"On Mr Fechter's Acting" xv
"Our French Watering-Place" xi,
    xiv, xvi, xvii, 55–59, 60–76, 97,
    267, 349, 350, 351
Our Mutual Friend xiii, xvi, 310,
    320–7, 355, 383

"Our Watering Place" 55, 342
"A Paper-Mill" 379
"The Paradise at Tooting" 362
Pictures from Italy 127, 130,
    159–60, 162–72, 173, 174, 175,
    179–81, 191–4, 196–201, 337,
    338, 344, 352, 397
"A Poor Man's Tale of a Patent"
    329
"Railway Dreaming" xiii, 127,
    131–9, 174, 267, 339
Reprinted Pieces 1, 55, 268, 342
Sketches by Boz 336, 360, 366
Sketches of Young Gentlemen 373
"Some Recollections of Mortality"
    xiv, 19, 127, 128, 146–58, 339
Somebody's Luggage 95, 309
"The Story of Richard
    Doubledick" xv
Sunday Under Three Heads 350
A Tale of Two Cities xi, xvi, xvii,
    226–8, 235–65
"The Thousand and One
    Humbugs" 403
"The Toady Tree" 403, 404
"Travelling Abroad" xiv, 37–8,
    40–54, 126, 127
"Travelling Letters" 159
The Uncommercial Traveller 17
"Why?" 271
"Why Shave?" 400
Dickens, Charles, Jnr (Charley) 370
Dickens, Francis 370
Dickens, Frederick 362, 367
Dickens, Katherine (Katey) 370
Dickens, Mary (Mamie) 370
Dickens, Sir Henry Fielding vii
Dickens, Walter 370
Dijon xiv, 173–4, 181
Dolby, George 271, 272
Don Quixote (allusions to) 52, 342
Douai 30, 348
Dover 41; Lord Warden Hotel 24,

333; in "The Calais Night Mail"
23–4
Drew, John 18, 78, 336, 338, 348,
362
Ducrow, Andrew 366
Dunkerque (Dunquerque) 78, 348
Dusaulx, Jean-Joseph 385, 386

Early Closing Movement 305,
401–2
Edward III, King 335
Edward VII, King 402
Eliot, George 362
Eugénie, Empress 123
Examiner, The 225, 362
Exposition Universelle, 1855 xiii, 400,
404, 405
Exposition Universelle, 1867 123

fairs, *fêtes* xvi–xvii, 32, 85–91, 336,
341, 347, 348
fairy tales (allusions to): Fortunatus
371; *Valentine and Orson* 371,
404; "The White Snake" 381
Fénelon 234, 377
fermiers généraux ("Farmers
General") 241, 332, 380–1
Fields, James T. viii
Folkestone 10, 271; *see also* Royal
George
Forster, John: on Boulogne 346;
Burgess case 361; CD and
Morgue 339, 354; CD's French
312; CD's carriage 337; *étrennes*
355–6; Louis Roche 338;
Uncommercial Traveller 18;
view from CD's apartment 353;
and *The Examiner* 225
CD writes to on: argument at inn
340; art 400; Beaucourt-Mutuel
58; Boulogne xvi, 56–7, 343,
344–5, 347; Broadstairs 342;
Burgess case 362; country fair

336; "demonstrative" French
401; Devonshire Terrace 360;
English in Boulogne 347;
affinity for France vii;
London–Paris express 2;
Morgue 339; New Year's Day,
Paris 355–6; speculation fever
352–3; speaking French 312; *A
Tale of Two Cities* 228; travels in
1846 341; Zouaves 400
Fouquier-Tinville, Antoine-
Quentin 389, 392
France, CD's visits to vii, 77
Franconi's: *see* Paris
French (language) xvii, 206, 309–12
French Revolution (causes and
history): aristocracy 227, 239–49,
380; *Assemblée Nationale* 233,
377, 378; Bastille 227, 235,
250–7, 378, 385–8; execution of
Louis XVI 258, 388, 390;
Girondins 390; Guillotine 259,
260–5; *Loi des Suspects* 389;
obliteration of past 392;
ransacking churches 390;
Revolutionary calendar 388;
Revolutionary committees 259,
389; Saint-Antoine 227, 235–9,
244, 250, 255, 256, 378; Terror 9,
227, 258–9, 260, 330, 389, 390,
401; *Tribunal Révolutionnaire*
259, 385, 389; *tricoteuses* 385,
392; Tuileries massacre 396; in
"Judicial Special Pleading"
225–6, 230–5; in *A Tale of Two
Cities*, 226–8, 235–65
Froissart, Jean 335

Gad's Hill Place 40–1, 338, 359
Galignani's New Paris Guide:
abattoirs 397; Artesian well 398;
Barrière de l'Étoile 332; baths
331; cabs 331; Caisse de Poissy

397; *diligences* 331; northern
boulevards 360; Palais Royal
340; street lighting 379; theater
queues 356; ticket touts 357;
Tour Saint-Jacques 359
Garde National (National Guard)
345
Gautier, Théophile 366
George III, King 330
George IV, King 404
Gibbs, Frederick Waymouth 306,
402
Girardin, Émile de 352
Goldsmith, Oliver, 362, 364, 386,
401
Gray, Thomas, 154, 360
Greeley, Horace 20
Green, Charles 98
Green, Julian 124
Grimaldi, Joseph 371
Grimm, Brothers 381
Guide Parisien 122
Guillotin, Joseph Ignace 390

Handbook for Travellers in France:
Boulogne 57, 343–4, 346, 347;
Calais 21, 333, 337; Channel
ferries 19–20; *diligences* 342;
hiring a *post chaise* 367; Lyon
363; Marseille 367, 368, 369;
Sens 369
*Handbook for Travellers in Kent and
Sussex*: Gad's Hill 338; Lord
Warden Hotel 333
*Handbook for Travellers on the
Continent*: Calais 335, 337;
couriers 369–70
Handbook for Visitors to Paris: 18th c.
streets 379; bd de Sébastopol
360; Boulogne 271–2, 399;
Calais 333; Champs-Élysées
122; Grands Boulevards 122;
Morgue 126; Palais Royal 340

Haussmann, Baron Georges xii,
123–4, 356, 358
Hazebrouck 30, 32, 78, 297, 348
Head, F.B. 126, 127
Hogarth, Georgina 56, 311, 312,
354, 370
Holbein, Hans 137, 354
Home, John 361
Household Words: see Dickens,
Charles, for article titles
Hunt, Holman 365

Illustrated London News 402

James, Henry 365
Jerrold, Douglas 358
Jerrold, W. Blanchard 355, 372, 396
Jeunes-France, Les ("Young
France") 180, 366

Keble, John 394
Kenney, Charles 371
Key, Francis Scott 398

Launay, Marquis de 229, 387
Layard, Sir Austen Henry 402, 403,
404
Lille 30
Linguet, Simon-Nicolas-Henri 385,
387
London, *Areas of*: Bermondsey 7,
330; Blackheath 40; Chalk Farm
152, 359; City 6, 16, 268, 321,
329, 399; Clapham 303, 401;
Fulham 70, 345; Marylebone
360; Ratcliff, 346; Richmond
Hill 303, 401; Soho 394;
Spitalfields 276, 394;
Whitechapel 276, 277, 350, 394
Buildings, monuments, parks, etc:
Gloucester Gate Bridge 359;
Hyde Park 86, 348–9, 350;
Kennington Common 374;

Lincoln's Inn Fields 394;
London Bridge Station 5, 329,
333; Marshalsea 35; Old Bailey
157, 361; Pantechnicon 53, 194,
337, 342; Regent's Canal 359;
Regent's Park 152, 359, 360;
Royal Exchange 301, 332, 399;
Somerset House 135, 353; St
Clement Danes 219, 373;
Temple Bar 370, 375; Water
Meeting Bridge 359;
Westminster Abbey 163, 363;
Windsor Castle 331
Markets: Clare 276, 394; Covent
Garden 329; Leadenhall 276,
394; Newgate 276, 394;
Newport 276, 394; Smithfield
268–70, 275–9, 392–3, 394, 397
Streets, squares, etc: Arundel Street
371; Baker Street 363; Bleeding
Heart Yard 309; Burlington
Arcade 302, 334; Burlington
Gardens 400; Cornhill 399;
Devonshire Terrace 360; Fleet
Street 353, 370; Gloucester Gate
152, 359; Gracechurch Street
394; Hanover Terrace 359; Hyde
Park Corner 16, 332; Lombard
Street 399; Marylebone High
Street 360; Marylebone Road
360, 363; Motcomb Street 342;
Newgate Street 394; Norfolk
Street 203, 215, 219, 371, 373;
Old Kent Road 40; Pall Mall
399; Paternoster Row 394;
Piccadilly 334, 400; Portman
Square 322; Prince Albert Road
359; Ratcliff Highway 72, 346;
Regent Street 137, 354; Sheer
Lane 375; Shooter's Hill 40;
Snow Hill 277, 395; Strand 134,
135, 203, 353, 370, 373, 394;
Surrey Street 371;

Threadneedle Street 399;
Warwick Lane 277; Westminster
Bridge Road 366
Theaters, circuses: Astley's 179,
365–6; Drury Lane 403, 405; St
James's 5, 329
Louis XIV, King 234, 331, 377, 379,
380
Louis XV, King 388
Louis XVI, King 384, 388, 390, 396
Louis-Philippe, King 122, 374, 396
Lyon xiii, 160, 161, 174, 363; in
    Pictures from Italy 162–3
Lytton, Edward Bulwer- 228, 365

Macaulay, Thomas Babington 305,
401, 402
Maclise, Daniel 364
Macready, W.C. 58, 78, 125, 403
Marie Antoinette 389
Marseille xiii, xv, 159, 173, 175, 221,
281, 292, 367–8; CD delayed in
368; hairdresser 193, 368; harbor
193–4; heat xv, 175, 368–9;
Hôtel du Paradis 193, 367; in
Little Dorrit 194–5; *Pictures from
Italy* 191–4
Mary I, Queen 335
Maximilian, Archduke of Austria
349
Maxwell, Richard 228, 386
Mercier, Louis-Sébastien, *Le
Nouveau Paris: furies de guillotine*
392; *Tableau de Paris*: source for
A Tale of Two Cities 228, 379–85;
aristocracy 380; atheism 382–3;
charlatans 382–3; Convulsionists
383; doctors 382; ecclesiastics
382; elderly women 383;
executioner (*bourreau*) 384;
farmer-generals 381; commoners
marrying aristocrats 381; military
382; pavements 379;

professional classes 382;
servants 380; speeding carriages
384; spies 383; street lighting
379; philosophers 382; wood-
burning 378
Mirabeau, Comte de 234, 377–8
Mitchell, John ("Meat-chell") 5,
329
Moore, Thomas 26, 333–4
Morier, James J. 330
Morley, Henry 400
Morton, Thomas 353, 401
myths and legends (allusions to)
"apple of discord" 381; basilisk
399; Cadmus 389; Hesperides
381; Milanion 381; William Tell
51, 341

Naples 68, 344, 359
Napoléon I (Napoléon Bonaparte)
16, 69, 164, 209, 284, 295, 332,
343, 345, 364, 395, 396, 397
Napoléon III (Louis-Napoléon
Bonaparte) vii, 123, 346, 349,
350, 353, 396

Old Moore's Almanac 204, 371
Orléans, Duc d' (Égalité Orléans)
231, 376
Ostade, Adriaen van 172, 365
Owen, Sir Richard 74, 277, 278, 394

Palmerston, Lord 306, 402, 403–4
Paris: 18th c. streets 379;
abattoirs/livestock markets
269–70; bathing establishments
45, 331–2; cabs 331, 355; café
culture x–xi, 127, 135–6; CD's
affection for 125; CD's first
impressions xii, 121, 125, 127;
CD's readings viii, 122; CD's
residence in, 1855–56 vii, 127,
352; CD's visits vii, 121–2;

dining 133–4; fictional
characters' responses to xvii;
gaslight 136; Haussmannisation
123–4, 352, 358; heating fuel
378; speculation fever 352–3;
secret character of 124–5;
theater box offices 142, 208;
ticket touts 142, 357;
wickedness of 125–6
Buildings, monuments, gardens, etc:
Abattoirs de Grenelle 288, 395,
397, Montmartre 285–8, 395,
397, Popincourt 395, Villejuif
395; Abattoir du Roule 395;
Bains Deligny 331, 339–40;
Bains Vigier 331; Barrière de
l'Étoile 16, 332; Bastille 171,
229, 250–57, 378, 385–8; Bois de
Boulogne 142; Bourse 133, 143;
Colonne Vendôme 332;
Conciergerie 389, 391; Gare de
l'Est 360; Gare du Nord 331;
Hôtel de Ville 152, 234, 256,
360, 378; Hôtel des Invalides
332, 349; Hôtel-Dieu 280, 358,
396; Morgue xiii, 38, 39, 44–7,
126–7, 128, 130, 137–9, 146–52,
280, 339, 352, 354–5, 358;
Notre-Dame 45, 124, 146, 233,
242, 258, 280, 287, 358, 389,
390; Palais des Beaux-Arts 400;
Palais de Justice 389; Palais
Royal xii, 16, 46, 141, 233, 340,
356, 357, 388; Petit Pont 358;
Pont au Double 358; Pont de la
Concorde 287, 340; Pont Neuf
130, 352; Tour Saint-Jacques
152, 359; Tuileries (gardens) 43,
122, 396; Tuileries (palace) 244,
353, 384, 396
Cafés, restaurants: Bains Chinois
("Chinese Baths") 15, 331; Café
Champeaux 143, 357; Café de

Paris ("Café de la Lune") 132, 143, 352, 357; Café du Helder 331; Maison Dorée 143, 357; Trois Frères Provençeaux 143, 357; Véfour 143, 357; Véry 143, 357
Hotels where CD stayed: Brighton 339; Meurice 122, 339, 352; Wagram 339, 396; Windsor 339
Streets, quartiers, etc: av. des Champs-Élysées 121, 122, 131, 142, 332, 345, 352, 353; av. Montaigne 400; av. Trudaine 397; bd de la Madeleine 355; bd de Rochechouart 397; bd de Sébastopol 153, 360; bd des Capucines 356; bd des Filles-du-Calvaire 334; bd des Italiens 122, 331, 352, 357; bd du Montparnasse 360; bd du Temple 124, 128, 334, 355, 356, 357; bd Montmartre 356; bd St Martin 356; Faubourg St Germain 89, 349, 381; Faubourg St Honoré 381, 382; Grands Boulevards 122, 128, 141, 355, 360; Grenelle 270; Île de la Cité 126, 128, 339, 358, 359, 360, 389, 396; Montmartre 270; parvis de Notre-Dame 358; pl. Charles de Gaulle 332; pl. Dauphine 358; pl. de Breteuil 397; pl. de la Bastille 378, 400; pl. de la Bourse 356, 357; pl. de la Concorde 345, 391; pl. de la Nation 378; pl. de l'Étoile 123; pl. du Château d'Eau/ République 356; pl. du Châtelet 359, 360; pl. Vendôme 4, 16, 400; quai d'Orsay 340; quai de l'Archevêché 358; quai du Marché-Neuf 339, 354; quartier Saint Antoine 227, 235–9, 244, 250, 255, 256, 378, 381; rue Barthélémy 397; rue Chanoinesse 358; rue de Courcelles 121, 339; rue de Presbourg 332; rue de Rivoli xii, 16, 43, 122, 129, 339, 352, 391; rue de Rochechouart 397; rue de Tilsitt 332; rue des Filles-Saint-Thomas 357; rue des Martyrs 397; rue du Faubourg St Honoré 122, 381; rue du Helder 122; rue du Roule 391; rue Lallier 397; rue Pérignon 397; rue Royale 392; rue St Honoré 45, 262, 391; rue Vivienne 357; sq. St Jacques 359
Theaters, circuses: Cirque des Champs-Élysées (Impératrice) 334, Napoléon (d'Hiver) 334, 354, Olympique 334; Franconi's 27, 145, 179, 283, 334, 354; Théâtre de l'Ambigu Comique 141, 356, de la Gaîté 141, 143, 356, de la Porte St Martin 141, 356, des Funambules 357, des Variétés 141, 356, du Palais Royal 141, 356, du Vaudeville 141, 356, Le Petit Lazzari 357
in *Bleak House* xv, xvi; *Dombey and Son*, 190; "A Flight" 15–16; *Little Dorrit* xv; "New Year's Day" 141–5; *Mrs Lirriper's Legacy* 206–8; *Our Mutual Friend* xvi; *Pictures from Italy* 130; "Railway Dreaming" 131–9; "Some Recollections of Mortality" 146–58; "Travelling Abroad" 43–7
Peel, Sir Robert 402
Pendleton, John 19
Pepys, Samuel 380
Pichot, Amédée 312
Pinwell, G.J. 39

Poissy 396; market 270, 279, 282–5, 395, 397; town 280–2
Pont d'Esprit 164
Poole, Adrian 406
Pueckler-Muskau, Prince von 385

railways and rail travel: Dover–Calais night mail 2, 24–5; electric telegraph 398; expansion 2; journey times 1–2; London–Paris express 1–3; Parliamentary Train 8, 330; Smith's bookstalls 398; tidal trains 1–2, 399; in "A Flight" 1–16; "The Calais Night Mail" 31–2
railway catering 270–2
Rhône 160, 163–4, 363
Richardson, John 32, 336
Rienzi, Cola di 168, 365
Rillé, Laurent de 357
Robespierre, Maximilien 303, 376, 401
Roche, Louis ("brave courier") 37, 42, 43, 171, 197, 198, 199–200, 338, 369
Royal Commission on Smithfield 269, 392–3, 394
Royal George Hotel, Folkestone 10, 330
Rugby ("Mugby") 271
Ruskin, John 372

Sabbatarianism 347, 349–50
Sanders, Andrew 228, 379, 383, 384, 385, 386, 391
Sanson, Charles-Henri 390
Sanson, Henri 390
Saône 222
Sceaux 279, 395, 397
Scott, Sir Walter 401
Second Empire vii, 122, 123, 350, 352, 353, 399
Seine 331, 353

Sens 175–6; cathedral 176, 178, 199, 200, 208, 209, 370, 372; Hôtel de l'Écu 175, 176, 200, 208, 369; market 175, 176, 200–1, 208, 370; in *Mrs Lirriper's Legacy* 202, 204, 208–20; *Pictures from Italy* 196–201
Shakespeare (allusions to) 41, 333, 335, 338, 362, 393, 395, 397, 399, 402
Slater, Michael 18, 78, 225, 336, 338, 342, 348, 357, 362, 400
Smith, Albert 386
Smith, William Henry 290, 398
Songs (allusions to): "Columbia, the Gem of the Ocean" 398; *Irish Melodies* 333–4; "Red, White, and Blue" 398; "The Roast Beef of Old England" 395; "Rule Britannia" 395, 406; "Le Sire de Franc-Boisy" 357; "The Snug Little Island 351; "The Star Spangled Banner" 398
South Eastern Railway Company 1, 3, 5, 7, 14, 16, 329, 333, 398
Steele, Sir Richard 375
Stein, Gertrude ix
Sterne, Lawrence 18, 38, 267, 335, 337–8, 339
Strasbourg 37, 38, 48–50, 281, 340
Switzerland 37, 38, 51–3, 302, 338
Tatler, The 375
Taylor, H.L. 269–70, 393, 395
Taylor, Tom 371
Tennyson, Alfred Lord 332
Ternan, Ellen 58–9, 77, 78
Thackeray, William Makepeace 404–5
Theatrical performances 74, 84–5, 143–4
Thiers, Adolphe, *History of the French Revolution*: source for

"Judicial Special Pleading" 226, 376, 376–8; on *Assemblée Nationale* 377; *États Généraux* 376, 377; flight of aristocracy 376; Mirabeau 378; winter of 1788–89 376

Thomson, James 395, 406

Timbs, John, *Curiosities of London*: Covent Garden 329; Smithfield 268, 394

Times, The: Administrative Reform Association, 403; Alderson's speech 225, 375; British Embassy in Paris 404; Burgess case 361; Camp de Châlons 350; Court Circular 402; express trains 1; Smithfield 269, 392–3; Zouaves 400

Tomalin, Claire 59

Tooley Street, Three Tailors of 405

Tussaud, Marie 163, 363

Uncommercial Traveller (persona) 17–8

Valence 164, 364

Valenciennes 348

Vauban, Sébastien Le Prestre 32, 102, 119, 331

Vernon, Lord 341

Versailles 376, 378

Wagner, Richard 365

Wakley, Thomas 156, 362

Watrin, Janine 58

Weber, Carl Maria von 329

Wheatstone, Sir Charles 290, 398

Wills, W.H. 3, 55, 78, 96, 124, 125, 269, 271, 338, 393, 397, 400

Wodehouse, P.G. ix

Wordsworth, William 128

Young, Arthur 379, 384, 385

Zola, Émile 127, 354–5

Zouaves 301, 399–400

✳ ✳ ✳